Agile Model-Based Systems Engineering Cookbook

Improve system development by applying proven recipes for effective agile systems engineering

Dr. Bruce Powel Douglass, Ph.D.

BIRMINGHAM—MUMBAI

Agile Model-Based Systems Engineering Cookbook

Group Product Manager: Aaron Lazar

Associate Publishing Product Manager: Alok Dhuri

Senior Editor: Rohit Singh

Content Development Editor: Tiksha Lad

Technical Editor: Pradeep Sahu

Copy Editor: Safis Editing

Project Coordinator: Deeksha Thakkar

Proofreader: Safis Editing

Indexer: Pratik Shirodkar

Production Designer: Vijay Kamble

First published: March 2021

Production reference: 1260321

Published by Packt Publishing Ltd.

Livery Place

35 Livery Street

Birmingham

B3 2PB, UK.

ISBN 978-1-83898-583-7

www.packt.com

To Sarah, the best waifu ever

– Dr. Bruce Powel Douglass, Ph.D.

Contributors

About the author

Dr. Bruce Powel Douglass was raised by wolves in the Oregon wilderness. He taught himself to read at age 3 and calculus before age 12. He dropped out of school when he was 14 and traveled around the US for a few years before entering the University of Oregon as a mathematics major. He eventually received his MS in exercise physiology from the University of Oregon and his Ph.D. in neurocybernetics from the USD Medical School.

Bruce has worked as a software developer and systems engineer in safety-critical real-time embedded systems for almost 40 years and is a well-known speaker, author, and consultant in the area of real-time embedded systems, UML, and SysML. He is a coauthor of the UML and SysML standards. He develops and teaches courses as well as consulting in real-time systems and software design and project management and has done so for many years. He has authored articles for many journals and periodicals, especially in the real-time domain. He worked at I-Logix, Telelogic, and IBM on the Rhapsody modeling tool. He is currently a senior principal agile systems engineer at MITRE, and the principal at A-Priori Systems (www.bruce-douglass.com).

He is the author of several other books on systems and software development, including *Doing Hard Time: Developing Real-Time Systems with UML,*

Objects, Frameworks and Patterns (Addison-Wesley, 1999), Real-Time Design Patterns:

Robust Scalable Architecture for Real-Time Systems (Addison-Wesley, 2002), Real-Time

UML 3rd Edition: Advances in the UML for Real-Time Systems (Addison-Wesley, 2004),

Real-Time Agility (Addison-Wesley, 2009), Design Patterns for Embedded Systems in C

(Elsevier, 2011), Real-Time UML Workshop for Embedded Systems (Elsevier, 2014), Agile

Systems Engineering (Elsevier, 2016), and several others, including a short textbook on table tennis.

Bruce is an active Ironman triathlete and competitive ultra-marathon cyclist.

About the reviewer

Saulius Pavalkis spent 18 years at Dassault Systems (No Magic) in model-based solutions and the core R&D team. Currently, he is working as an MBSE transformation leader. He is an expert in systems modeling, simulation, the MBSE ecosystem, interfaces and integrations, traceability, and queries.

He has won the INCOSE CSEP, OMG OCSMP, and No Magic lifetime modeling and simulation excellence awards and is a community author for the largest SysML simulation channel (`youtube.com/c/MBSEExecution`) and an MBSE success cases blog, (`blog.nomagic.com`).

He is also the author of multiple papers on MBSE at INCOSE and NDIA. In 2020, he acquired a $20 million budget for the implementation of the V&V paper. He is also a representative at INCOSE CAB and supports MBSE adoption in A&D, T&M, and other domains. His major clients are P&W, Boeing, NASA, BAE Systems, Raytheon Technologies, NGC, and Ford.

Table of Contents

2

System Specification

3
Developing System Architectures

4

Handoff to Downstream Engineering

5

Demonstration of Meeting Needs: Verification and Validation

Appendix A – The Pegasus Bike Trainer

Other Books You May Enjoy

Index

Preface

Welcome to *Agile Model-Based Systems Engineering Cookbook*! There is a plethora of published material available in relation to agile methods, provided that you want to create software and it is also the case that the system is small, the team is co-located, and it needn't be certified, or safety-critical, or have high reliability.

Model-Based Systems Engineering (**MBSE**) is, of course, none of these things. The output of MBSE isn't software implementation but system specification. It is usually applied to more complex and larger-scale systems. The teams are diverse and often spread out across departments and companies. Much of the time, the systems produced must be certified under various standards, including safety standards. So how do you apply agile methods to such an endeavor?

Most of the work in MBSE can be managed through a set of workflows that produce a set of interrelated work products. Each of these workflows can be described with relatively simple recipes for creating the work products for MBSE, including system requirements, system architecture, system interfaces, and deployment architecture. That's what this book brings to the table and what sets it apart.

Who this book is for

The book is intended, first and foremost, for systems engineers who need to produce work products for the specification of systems that include combinations of engineering disciplines, such as software, electronics, and mechanical engineering. More specifically, this book is about MBSE using the **Systems Modeling Language** (**SysML**) to capture, render, and organize the engineering data. Furthermore, this book is especially concerned with how to do all that in a way that achieves the benefits of agile methods – verifiably correct, adaptable, and maintainable systems. We assume a basic understanding of SysML and at least some experience as a systems engineer.

What this book covers

Chapter 1, Basics of Agile Systems Modeling, discusses come fundamental agile concepts, expressed as recipes, including managing your backlog, using metrics effectively, managing project risk, agile planning, work effort estimation and prioritization, starting up projects, creating an initial systems architecture, and organizing your systems engineering models. The recipes all adopt a systems engineering slant and focus on the work products commonly developed in a systems engineering effort.

Chapter 2, System Specification, is concerned with agile model-based systems requirements – capturing, managing, and analyzing system specifications. One of the powerful tools that MBSE brings to the table is its ability to analyze requirements by developing computable and executable models. This chapter provides recipes for several different ways of doing that, as well as recipes for model-based safety and cyber-physical security analysis, and the specification of details held within the system.

Chapter 3, Developing System Architecture, covers recipes focused on the development of systems architecture. It begins with a way of conducting model-based trade studies (sometimes known as an "analysis of alternatives"). The chapter goes on to provide recipes for integrating use case analyses into a systems architecture, applying architectural patterns, allocating requirements to a systems architecture, and creating subsystem-level interfaces.

Chapter 4, Handoff to Downstream Engineering, answers one of the most common questions asked in relation to MBSE: how to hand the information developed in the models off to implementation engineers specializing in software, electronics, or mechanical engineering. This chapter provides detailed recipes for getting ready to do the handoff, creating a federation of models to support the collaborative engineering effort to follow, converting the logical systems engineering interfaces to physical interface schemas, and actually performing allocation to the engineering disciplines involved.

Chapter 5, Demonstration of Meeting Needs – Verification and Validation, deals with a key concept in agile methods, that you should never be more than minutes away from being able to demonstrate that, while the system may be incomplete, what's there is correct. This chapter has recipes for model simulation, model-based testing, computable constraint modeling, adding traceability, how to run effective walk-throughs and reviews, and, my favorite, test-driven modeling.

Appendix A, The Pegasus Bike Trainer, details a case study that will serve as the basis for most of the examples in the book. This is a "smart" stationary bike trainer that interacts with net-based athletic training systems to allow athletes to train in a variety of flexible ways. It contains aspects that will be implemented in mechanical, electronic, and software disciplines in an ideal exemplar for the recipes in the book.

To get the most out of this book

To get the most out of this book, you will need a solid, but basic, understanding of SysML. In addition, in order to create the models, you will require a modeling tool. The concepts here are expressed in SysML, so any standards-compliant SysML modeling tool can be used.

All the example models in this book are developed using the IBM Rhapsody modeling tool (Designer for Systems edition). To execute models and run simulations, you will need the Cygwin C++ compiler (available at https://www.cygwin.com), although other C++ compilers could be used instead, such as Visual C++. The computable parametrics models use the Rhapsody **Parametric Constraint Evaluator** (**PCE**) profile that ships with Rhapsody and the Maxima mathematical tool (available at http://maxima.sourceforge.net) for evaluation.

Remember, the Rhapsody tool is not required in order to create these models. Other tools, such as Cameo Systems Modeler (https://www.nomagic.com/products/cameo-systems-modeler) can be used instead. If you use Cameo Systems Modeler, you will want to use Cameo Simulation Toolkit for simulation and computation support.

Software/hardware covered in the book	OS requirements
Rhapsody Designer for Systems, or Rhapsody Developer	Windows
Cygwin C++	Windows
Maxima	Windows

You can access Cygwin C++ from https://www.cygwin.com and Maxima from http://maxima.sourceforge.net.

Download the example models

You can download the example models for this book from GitHub at https://github.com/PacktPublishing/Agile-Model-Based-Systems-Engineering-Cookbook. In case there's an update to the model, it will be updated on the existing GitHub repository. Note that these models are all in Rhapsody-specific format and, in general, won't be readable by other modeling tools.

We also have other code bundles from our rich catalog of books and videos available at https://github.com/PacktPublishing/. Check them out!

Where to go from here

Visit the author's website, www.bruce-douglass.com, for papers, presentations, models, engineering forums, and more.

Download the color images

We also provide a PDF file that has color images of the screenshots/diagrams used in this book. You can download it here:

```
https://static.packt-cdn.com/downloads/9781838985837_
ColorImages.pdf
```

Conventions used

There are a number of text conventions used throughout this book.

Italics are used for new concepts and for tool features. **Bold** text indicates the name of a model element or feature of interest.

`Code in text`: Indicates code words in text, database table names, folder names, filenames, file extensions, pathnames, dummy URLs, user input, and Twitter handles. Here is an example: "I normally name the new package something like `WBScenarios`."

Bold: Indicates a new term, an important word, or words that you see on screen. For example, words in menus or dialog boxes appear in the text like this. Here is an example: "Rhapsody hint: Right-click on white space in the diagram and select **Auto Realize All Elements** to add event receptions and operations to match the diagram."

> **Tips or important notes**
> Appear like this.

Sections

In this book, you will find several headings that appear frequently (*Getting ready, How to do it..., How it works..., There's more...,* and *See also*).

To give clear instructions on how to complete a recipe, use these sections as follows:

Getting ready

This section tells you what to expect in the recipe and describes how to set up any software or any preliminary settings required for the recipe.

How to do it...

This section contains the steps required to follow the recipe.

Example

This section usually consists of a detailed explanation of what happened in the previous section.

Get in touch

Feedback from our readers is always welcome.

General feedback: If you have questions about any aspect of this book, mention the book title in the subject of your message and email us at customercare@packtpub.com.

Errata: Although we have taken every care to ensure the accuracy of our content, mistakes do happen. If you have found a mistake in this book, we would be grateful if you would report this to us. Please visit www.packtpub.com/support/errata, selecting your book, clicking on the Errata Submission Form link, and entering the details.

Piracy: If you come across any illegal copies of our works in any form on the internet, we would be grateful if you would provide us with the location address or website name. Please contact us at copyright@packt.com with a link to the material.

If you are interested in becoming an author: If there is a topic that you have expertise in, and you are interested in either writing or contributing to a book, please visit authors. packtpub.com.

Reviews

Please leave a review. Once you have read and used this book, why not leave a review on the site that you purchased it from? Potential readers can then see and use your unbiased opinion to make purchase decisions, we at Packt can understand what you think about our products, and our authors can see your feedback on their book. Thank you!

For more information about Packt, please visit packt.com.

1
The Basics of Agile Systems Modeling

For the most part, this book is about systems modeling with SysML, but doing it in an Agile way. Before we get into the detailed practices of systems modeling with that focus, however, we're going to spend some time discussing important project-related Agile practices that will serve as a backdrop of the modeling work.

Almost all of the Agile literature focuses on the "3 people in a garage developing a simple application" scope. The basic assumptions of such projects include the following:

- The end result is software that runs on a general-purpose computing platform (in other words, it is not embedded software).

- Software is the only truly important work product. Others may be developed but they are of secondary concern. *Working software is the measure of success.*

- The software isn't performance-, safety-, reliability-, or security-critical.

- It isn't necessary to meet regulatory standards.

- The development team is small and co-located.

- The development involves time and effort, not a fixed-price cost.

- The development is fundamentally code-based and not model-or design-based.

- Any developer can do any task (no specialized skills are necessary).

- Formalized requirements are not necessary.

Yes, of course, there is much made about extensions to Agile practices to account for projects that don't exactly meet these criteria. For example, some authors will talk about a "scrum of scrums" as a way of scaling up to larger teams. That works to a point, but it fails when you get to much larger development teams and projects. I want to be clear – I'm not saying that Agile methods cannot be applied to projects that don't fall within these basic guidelines – only that the literature doesn't address how it will do so in a coherent, consistent fashion. The further away your project strays from these assumptions, the less you will find in the literature for Agile ways to address your needs.

In this book, we'll address a domain that differs significantly from the prototypical Agile project. We will concern ourselves with the following:

- Projects that are systems-oriented, and that may contain software but will typically also contain electronic and mechanical aspects. *It's about the system and not the software.*

- Projects that employ a **Model-Based Systems Engineering (MBSE)** approach using the SysML language.

- Projects that may range from small to very large scale.

- Projects that have to develop a number of different work products. These include, but are not limited to, the following:

  a. Requirements specifications

  b. Analysis of requirements, whether this is done with use cases or user stories

  c. System architectural specifications

  d. System interface specifications

  e. Trace relations between the elements of the different work products

  f. Safety, reliability, and security (and resulting requirements) analyses

  g. Architectural design trade studies

- Projects that are handed off to downstream engineering, which includes interdisciplinary subsystem teams containing team members who specialize in software, electronics, mechanical, and other design aspects.

At its core, however, the fundamental difference between this book and other Agile books is that *the outcome of systems engineering isn't software, it's specification*. Downstream engineering will ultimately do the low-level design and implementation of those specifications. Systems engineering provides the roadmap that enables different engineers with different skill sets working in different engineering disciplines to collaborate together to create an integrated system combining all their work into a cohesive whole.

This book will not provide a big overarching process that ties all the workflows and work products together, although it is certainly based on one. That process, should you be interested in exploring it, is detailed in the author's *Agile Systems Engineering* book. A detailed example is provided with his *Harmony aMBSE Deskbook*, available at `www.bruce-douglass.com`.

The outcome of software development is implementation.

The outcome of systems engineering is specification.

> **Note**
>
> Please refer to **Agile Systems Engineering** by Bruce Powel Douglass for more information: `https://www.amazon.com/Agile-Systems-Engineering-Bruce-Douglass/dp/0128021209/ref=sr_1_3?dchild=1&keywords=agile+systems+engineering&qid=1603658530&sr=8-3`.

What's Agile all about?

Agile methods are, first and foremost, a means of improving the quality of your engineering work products. This is achieved through the application of a number of practices meant to continuously identify quality issues and immediately address them. Secondly, Agile is about improving engineering efficiency and reducing rework. Let's talk about some basic concepts of agility.

Incremental development

This is a key aspect of Agile development. Take a big problem and develop it as a series of small increments, each of which is verified to be correct (even if incomplete).

Continuous verification

The best way to have high-quality work products is to continuously develop and verify their quality. In other books, such as *Real-Time Agility* or the aforementioned *Agile Systems Engineering* books, and here, I talk about verification taking place in three timeframes:

- **Nanocycle**: 30 minutes to 1 day
- **Microcycle**: 1–4 weeks
- **Macrocycle**: Project length

Furthermore, this verification is best done via execution and the testing of computable models. We will see in later chapters how this can be accomplished.

Continuous integration

Few complex systems are created by a single person. Integration is the task of putting together work products from different engineers into a coherent whole and demonstrating that, as a unit, it achieves its desired purpose. This integration is often done daily, but some teams increment this truly continuously, absorbing work as engineers complete it and instantly verifying that it works in tandem with the other bits.

Avoiding big design up front

The concept of incremental development means that one thing that we *don't* do is develop big work products over long periods of time and only then try to demonstrate their correctness. Instead, we develop and verify the design work we need right now, and defer design work that we won't need until later. This simplifies the verification work and also means much less rework later in the project.

Working with stakeholders

A key focus of the Agilista is the needs of the stakeholders. The Agilista understands that there is an "air gap" between what the requirements say and what the stakeholder actually needs. By working with the stakeholder, and frequently offering them versions of the running system to try, the systems are more likely to actually meet their needs. Additionally, user stories are a way to work with the stakeholder to understand what they actually need.

Model-based systems engineering (MBSE)

Systems engineering is an independent engineering discipline that focuses on system properties, including functionality, structure, performance, safety, reliability, and security. Systems engineering is largely independent of the engineering disciplines used to implement these properties. Systems engineering is an interdisciplinary activity that focuses more on this integrated set of system properties than on the contributions of the individual engineering disciplines. It is an approach to developing complex and technologically diverse systems.

Systems engineering is normally thought of in a V-style process approach (see *Figure 1.1*), in which the "*left side of the V*" emphasizes the specification of the system properties (requirements, architecture, interfaces, and overall dependability), the "lower part of the V" has to do with the discipline-specific engineering and design work, and the "right side of the V" has to do with the verification of the system against the specifications developed on the left side:

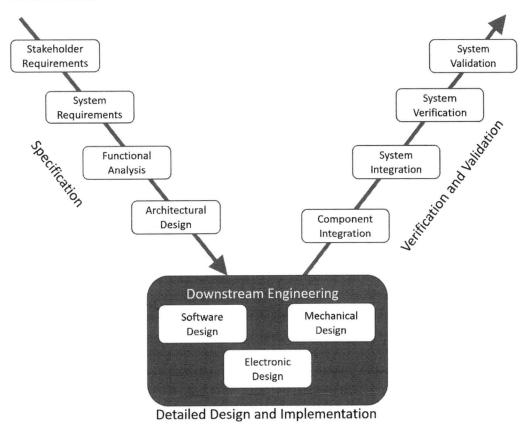

Figure 1.1 – Standard V model life cycle

Of course, we'll be doing things in a more Agile way (*Figure 1.2*). Mostly, we'll focus on incrementally creating the specification work products and handing them off to downstream engineering in an Agile way:

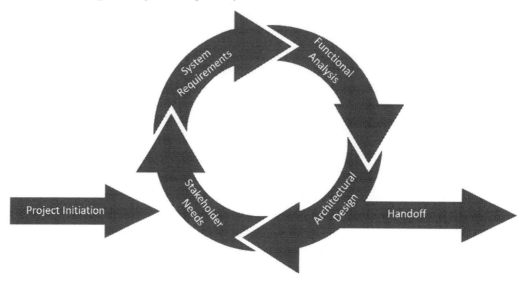

Figure 1.2 – Basic Agile systems engineering workflow

The basis of most of the work products developed in MBSE is, naturally enough, *the model*. For the most part, we mean the set of engineering data relevant to the system captured in a SysML model. The main model is likely to be supplemented with models in other languages, such as performance, safety, and reliability (although you can use SysML for that too; we'll discuss that in *Chapter 2, System Specification*). The other primary work product will be *textual requirements*. While they are imprecise, vague, ambiguous, and hard to verify, they have the advantage of being easy to communicate. Our models will cluster these requirements into usage chunks – epics, use cases, and user stories – but we'll still need requirements. These are generally managed either as text or in text-based requirement management tools, such as IBM DOORS™, although they can be completely managed in models, if desired.

Our models will consist of formal representations of our engineering data as *model elements*. These elements may appear in one or more views, including diagrams, tables, or matrices. The model is a coherent collection of model elements that represent the important engineering data around our system of interest.

In this book, we assume you are already familiar with SysML. If you aren't, there are many books available for that. This book is a collection of short, high-focused workflows that create one or a small set of engineering work products that contain relevant model elements.

Now, let's talk about some basic Agile recipes and how they can be done in a model-centric environment.

We will cover the following recipes in this chapter:

- Managing your backlog
- Measuring your success
- Managing risk
- Product roadmap
- Release plan
- Iteration plan
- Estimating effort
- Work item prioritization
- Iteration 0
- Architecture 0
- Organizing your models

Managing your backlog

The *backlog* is a prioritized set of *work items* that identify work to be done. There are generally two such backlogs. The *project backlog* is a prioritized list of all work to be done in the current project. A subset of these is selected for the current increment, forming the *iteration backlog*. Since engineers usually work on the tasks relevant to the current iteration, that is where they will go to get their tasks. *Figure 1.3* shows the basic idea of backlogs:

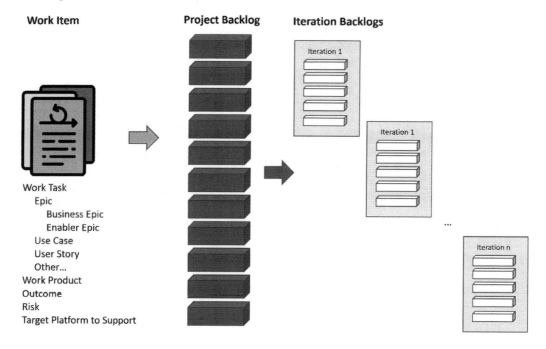

Figure 1.3 – Backlogs

Work to be done, nominally referred to as *work items*, is identified. Work items detail the work to be done, including the following:

- Analyzing or implementing an epic, use case, or user story to ensure a solid understanding of the need and the adequacy of its requirements

- Creating or modifying a work product, such as a requirements specification or a safety analysis

- Arranging for an outcome, such as certification approval

- Addressing a risk, such as determining the adequacy of the bus bandwidth

- Supporting a target platform, such as an increment with hand-built mechanical parts, lab-constructed wire wrap boards, and partial software

The work items go through an acceptance process and, if approved, are put into the project backlog. Once there, they can be allocated to an iteration backlog.

Purpose

The purpose of managing your backlog is to provide clear direction for the engineering activities, so as to push the project forward in a coherent, collaborative way.

Inputs and preconditions

The inputs are the work items. The functionality-based work items originate with one or more stakeholders, but other work items might come from discovery, planning, or analysis.

Outputs and post conditions

The primary outputs are the managed project and iteration backlogs. Each backlog consists of a set of work items around a common purpose, or *mission*. The mission of an iteration is the set of work products and outcomes desired at the end of the iteration. An iteration mission is defined as shown in *Figure 1.4*:

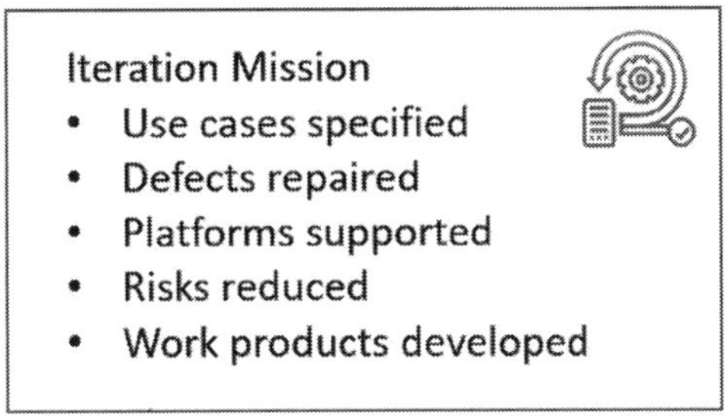

Iteration Mission
- Use cases specified
- Defects repaired
- Platforms supported
- Risks reduced
- Work products developed

Figure 1.4 – Iteration mission

In a modeling tool, this information can be captured as metadata associated with tags.

How to do it...

There are two workflows to this recipe. The first, shown in *Figure 1.5*, adds a work item to the backlog:

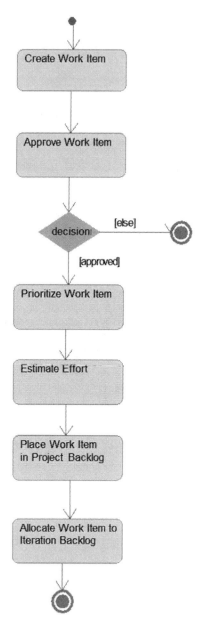

Figure 1.5 – Adding a work item

The following workflow in *Figure 1.6* removes it:

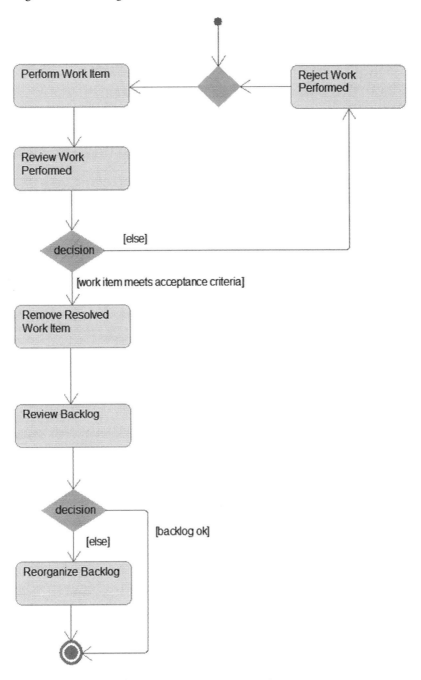

Figure 1.6 – Removing a work item

Creating a work item

From the work to be done, a work item is created to put into the backlog. The work item should include the properties shown in *Figure 1.7*:

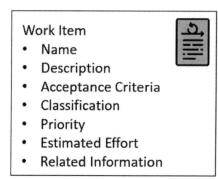

Figure 1.7 – Work item

Here are its properties:

- The name of the work item.

- A description of the work to be done, the work product to be created, or the risk to be addressed.

- The acceptance criteria – how the adequacy of the work performed, the work product created, or the outcome produced will be determined.

- The work item's classification identifies the kind of work item it is, as shown on the left side of *Figure 1.3*.

- The work item's priority is an indication of how soon this work item should be addressed. This is discussed in the *Prioritizing a work item* step of this recipe.

- The estimated effort is how much effort it will take to perform the task. This can be stated in absolute terms (such as hours) or relative terms (such as user story points). This topic is addressed in the *Estimating effort* recipe later in this chapter.

- Links to important related information, such as standards that must be met, or sources of information that will be helpful for performance of the work.

Approving a work item

Before a work item can be added, it should be approved by the team or the project leader, whoever is granted that responsibility.

Prioritizing a work item

The priority of a work item determines in what iteration the work will be performed. Priority is determined by a number of factors, including the work item criticality (how important it is), its urgency (when it is needed), the availability of specialized resources needed to perform it, the usefulness to the mission of the iteration, and risk. The general rule is that high-priority tasks are performed before lower-priority tasks. This topic is covered in the *Work item prioritization* recipe later in this chapter.

Estimating effort

An initial estimate of the cost of addressing the work item is important because as work items are allocated to iterations, the overall effort budget must be balanced. If the effort for addressing a work item is too high, it may not be possible to complete in the iteration with all of its other work items. The Agile practice of work item estimation is covered in the *Estimating effort* recipe later in this chapter.

Placing a work item in the project backlog

Once approved and characterized, the work item can then be put into the project backlog. The backlog is priority-ordered so that higher-priority work items are "on top" and lower priority work items are "below."

Allocating a work item to the iteration backlog

Initial planning includes the definition of a planned set of iterations, each of which has a mission, as defined above. Consistent with that mission, work items are then allocated to the planned iterations. Of course, this plan is volatile and later work or information can cause replanning and a reallocation of work items to iterations. Iteration planning is the topic of the *Iteration plan* recipe later in this chapter.

In the second workflow of this recipe, the work is actually being done. Of relevance here is how the completion of the work affects the backlog (*Figure 1.6*).

Performing a work item

This action is where the team member actually performs the work to address the work item, whether it is to analyze a use case, create a bit of architecture, or perform a safety analysis.

Reviewing work performed

The output and/or outcome of the work item is evaluated with respect to its acceptance criteria and is accepted or rejected on that basis.

Rejecting work performed

If the output and/or outcome does not meet the acceptance criteria, the work is rejected and the work item remains in the backlog.

Removing a resolved work item

If the output and/or outcome does meet the acceptance criteria, the work is accepted and the work item is removed from the project and iteration to-do backlog. This usually means that it is moved to a "done" backlog so that there is a history of the work performed.

Reviewing the backlog

It is important that as work progresses, the backlog is maintained. Often, valuable information is discovered that affects work item effort, priority, or value during project work. When this occurs, other affected work items must be reassessed and their location within the backlogs may be adjusted.

Reorganizing the backlog

Based on the review of the work items in the backlog, the set of work items, and their prioritized positions within those backlogs, may require adjustment.

Example

Consider a couple of use cases for the sample problem, the Pegasus Bike Trainer summarized in *Appendix A* (see *Figure 1.8*):

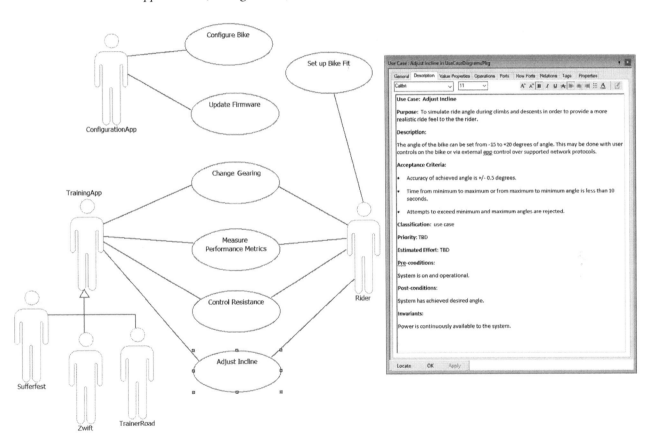

Figure 1.8 – Example use case work items in the backlog

You can also show at least high-level backlog allocation to an iteration in a use case diagram, as shown in *Figure 1.9*. You may, of course, manage backlogs in generic Agile tools such as Rational Team Concert, Jira, or even with post-it notes:

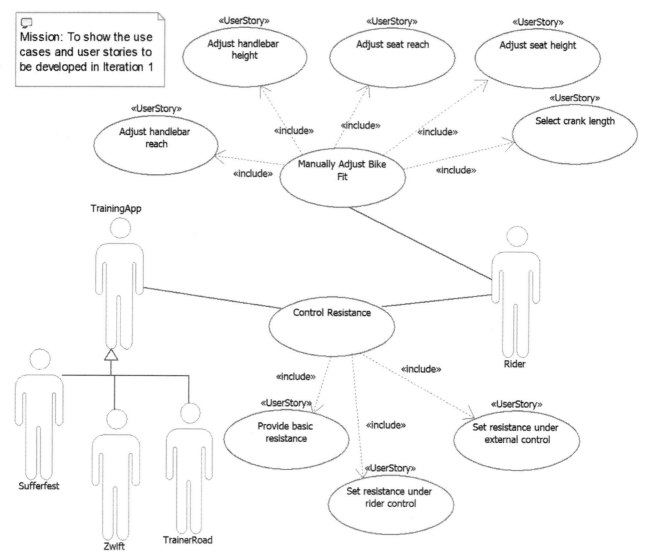

Figure 1.9 – Use case diagram for the iteration backlog

Let's now apply the workflow shown in *Figure 1.5* to add the use cases and user stories from *Figure 1.8* and *Figure 1.9*.

Creating a work item

In *Figure 1.8* and *Figure 1.9*, we see a total of seven use cases and eight user stories. For our purposes, we will just represent the use case data in tabular form and will concentrate only on the two use cases and their contained user stories from *Figure 1.9*. The description of the user stories is provided in canonical form for a user story (see *Chapter 2, System Specification,* for more details):

Name	OK	Description	Acceptance	Classification	Priority	Effort	Iteration	Related
Manually adjust bike fit		Enable rider to adjust bike fit prior to ride.	Standard riders* can replicate their road bike fit on the Pegasus.	Use case				*Standard riders include 5 riders of height 60, 65, 70, 75, and 76 inches.
Adjust handlebar reach		As a rider, I want to replicate the handlebar reach on my fitted road bike.	Standard riders* can replicate their handlebar reach from their fitted road bikes.	User story				
Adjust handlebar height		As a rider, I want to replicate the handlebar height on my fitted road bike.	Standard riders* can replicate their handlebar height from their fitted road bikes.	User story				
Adjust seat reach		As a rider, I want to replicate the seat reach on my fitted road bike.	Standard riders* can replicate their seat reach from their fitted road bikes.	User story				
Adjust seat height		As a rider, I want to replicate the seat height on my fitted road bike.	Standard riders* can replicate their seat height from their fitted road bikes.	User story				
Select crank length		As a rider, I want to replicate the crank arm length on my road bike.	Support crank lengths of 165, 167.5, 170, 172.5, and 175 mm.	User story				

Name	OK	Description	Acceptance	Classification	Priority	Effort	Iteration	Related
Control resistance		Control the resistance to pedaling in a steady and well-controlled fashion within the limits of normal terrain road riding.	Replicate pedal resistance to within 1% of measured pedal torque under the standard ride set*.	Use case				*Standard ride set includes rides of all combinations of rider weights (50, 75, 100 kg), inclines (-10, 0, 5, 10, 20%), and cadences (50, 70, 80, 90, 110).
Provide basic resistance		As a rider, I want basic resistance provided to the pedals so I can get a workout with an on-road feel in resistance mode.	Control resistance by setting the pedal resistance to 0-2000 W in 50 watt increments for standard ride set*.	User story				
Set resistance under user control		As a rider, I want to set the resistance level provided to the pedals to increase or decrease the effort for a given gearing, cadence, and incline.	Control resistance via user inputs by manually setting the incline, gearing, and cadence for a standard ride set*.	User story				
Set resistance under external control		As a rider, I want the external training app to set the resistance to follow the app's workout protocol to get the desired workout.	Control resistance via app control by manually setting the incline and gearing and allow the user to supply the cadence for a standard ride set*.	User story				

Table 1.1 – Initial work item list

Approving a work item

Working with the team and the stakeholders, we get approval for the work items in *Table 1.1*. As we get approval, we mark the *OK* column in the table.

Prioritizing a work item

Using the techniques from the *Work item prioritization* recipe later in this chapter, we add the priorities to the work items.

Estimating effort

Using the techniques from the *Estimating effort recipe* later in this chapter, we add the estimated effort to the work items.

Our final set of work items from this effort is shown in *Table 1.2*:

Name	OK	Description	Acceptance	Classification	Priority	Effort	Iteration	Related
Manually adjust bike fit		Enable rider to adjust bike fit prior to ride.	Standard riders* can replicate their road bike fit on the Pegasus.	Use case	4.38	13		*Standard riders include 5 riders of height 60, 65, 70, 75, and 76 inches.
Adjust handlebar reach		As a rider, I want to replicate the handlebar reach on my fitted road bike.	Standard riders* can replicate their handlebar reach from their fitted road bikes.	User story	3.33	3		
Adjust handlebar height		As a rider, I want to replicate the handlebar height on my fitted road bike.	Standard riders* can replicate their handlebar height from their fitted road bikes.	User story	4.33	3		
Adjust seat reach		As a rider, I want to replicate the seat reach on my fitted road bike.	Standard riders* can replicate their seat reach from their fitted road bikes.	User story	11.67	3		
Adjust seat height		As a rider, I want to replicate the seat height on my fitted road bike.	Standard riders* can replicate their seat height from their fitted road bikes.	User story	13.33	3		

Name	OK	Description	Acceptance	Classification	Priority	Effort	Iteration	Related
Select crank length		As a rider, I want to replicate the crank arm length on my road bike.	Support crank lengths of 165, 167.5, 170, 172.5, and 175 mm.	User story	1.2	1		
Control resistance		Control the resistance to pedaling in a steady and well-controlled fashion within the limits of normal terrain road riding.	Replicate pedal resistance to within 1% of measured pedal torque under the standard ride set*.	Use case	2	115		*Standard ride set includes rides of all combinations of rider weights (50, 75, 100 kg), inclines (-10, 0, 5, 10, 20%), and cadences (50, 70, 80, 90, 110).
Provide basic resistance		As a rider, I want basic resistance provided to the pedals so I can get a workout with an on-road feel in resistance mode.	Control resistance by setting the pedal resistance to 0 -2000 W in 50 watt increments for standard ride set*.	User story	1.42	55		
Set resistance under user control		As a rider, I want to set the resistance level provided to the pedals to increase or decrease the effort for a given gearing, cadence, and incline.	Control resistance via user inputs by manually setting the incline, gearing, and cadence for a standard ride set*.	User story	1.00	21		
Set resistance under external control		As a rider, I want the external training app to set the resistance to follow the app's workout protocol to get the desired workout.	Control resistance via app control by manually setting the incline and gearing, and allow the user to supply the cadence for a standard ride set*.	User story	0.30	39		

Table 1.2 – Final work item list

Placing **work items** in the project backlog

As we complete the effort, we put all the approved work items into the project backlog, along with other previously identified use cases, user stories, technical work items, and spikes.

Allocating work items to the iteration backlog

Using the technique from the *Iteration plan* recipe later in this chapter, we put relevant work items from the project backlog into the backlog for the upcoming iteration. In *Table 1.2*, this would be done by filling in the **Iteration** column with the number of the iteration in which the work item is performed.

With regard to the second flow from *Figure 1.6*, we can illustrate how the workflow might unfold as we perform the work in the current iteration.

Performing a work item

As we work in the iterations, we detail the requirements, and create and implement the technical design. For example, we might perform the mechanical design of the handlebar reach adjust or the delivery of basic resistance to the pedals through the use of an electric motor.

Reviewing work performed

As the work on the use case and user stories completes, we apply the acceptance criteria via *verification testing and validation*. In the example we are considering, for the set of riders of heights 60, 65, 70, 75, and 76 inches, we would measure the handlebar height from their fitted road bikes and ensure that all these conditions can be replicated on the bike. For the **Provide basic resistance** user story, we would verify that we can create a pedal resistance of [0, 50, 100, 150, … 2000] watts of resistance at pedal cadences of 50, 70, 80, 90, and 110 rpm ± 1%.

Measuring your success

One of the core concepts of effective Agile methods is to continuously improve how you perform your work. This can be done to improve quality or to get something done more quickly. In order to improve how you work, you need to know how well you're doing *now*. That means applying metrics to identify opportunities for improvement and then changing what you do or how you do it. Metrics are a general measurement of success in either achieving business goals or complying with a standard or process. A related concept, a **Key Performance Indicator** (**KPI**), is a quantifiable measurement of accomplishment against a crucial goal or objective. The best KPIs measure achievement of goals rather than compliance to a plan. The problem with metrics is that they generally measure something that you believe correlates to your objective, but not the objective itself. Examples of this from software development include the following:

Objective	Metric	Issues
Software size	Lines of code	Lines of code for simple, linear software aren't really the same as lines of code for complex algorithms.
Productivity	Shipping velocity	Ignores the complexity of the shipped features, penalizing systems that address complex problems.
Accurate planning	Compliance with schedule	This metric rewards people who comply with even a bad plan.
Efficiency	Cost per defect	Penalizes quality and makes buggy software look cheap.
Quality	Defect density	Treats all defects the same, whether they are using the wrong sized font or something that brings an aircraft down.

Consider a common metric for high-quality design, cyclomatic complexity. It has been observed that highly complex designs contain more defects than designs of low complexity. Cyclomatic complexity is a software metric that computes complexity by counting the number of linearly independent paths through some unit of software. Some companies have gone so far as to require that all software should not exceed some arbitrary, cyclomatic complexity value in order to be considered acceptable. This approach disregards the fact that some problems are harder than others and any design addressing such problems must be more complex.

A better application of cyclomatic complexity is to use it as a *guide*. It can identify those portions of a design that are more complex and should be subjected to additional testing. Ultimately, the problem with this metric is that complexity correlates only loosely to quality. A better metric for the goal of improving quality might be the ability to successfully pass tests that traverse all possible paths of the software.

Good metrics are easy to measure, and, ideally, easy to automate. Creating test cases for all possible paths can be tedious, but it is possible to automate with appropriate tools. Metrics that require additional work by engineering staff will be resented and achieving compliance in terms of use of the metric may be difficult.

While coming up with good metrics may be difficult, the fact remains that **you can't improve what you don't measure**. Without measurements, you're guessing where problems lie, and your solutions are likely to be ineffective or solve the wrong problem. By measuring how you're doing against your goals, you can improve your team's effectiveness and your product quality. However, it is important that metrics are used as indicators rather than as performance standards because, ultimately, the world is more complex than a single, easily computed measure.

Metrics should be used for guidance, not as goals for strict compliance.

> **Note**
>
> Refer to *The Mess of Metrics by Capers Jones (2017)* for more information:
>
> ```
> https://www.ppi-int.com/wp-content/
> uploads/2018/02/The-Mess-of-Software-Metrics_
> Jones-C_2017.pdf
> ```

Purpose

The purpose of metrics is to measure, rather than guess, how your work is proceeding with respect to important qualities so that you can improve.

Inputs and preconditions

The only preconditions for this workflow are the desire, ability, and authority to improve.

Outputs and post conditions

The primary output of this recipe is an objective measurement of how well your work is proceeding or the quality of one or more work products. The primary outcome is the identification of some aspect of your project work to improve.

How to do it...

Metrics can be applied to any work activity for which there is an important output or outcome (which should really be all work activities). The workflow is fairly straightforward, as shown in *Figure 1.10*:

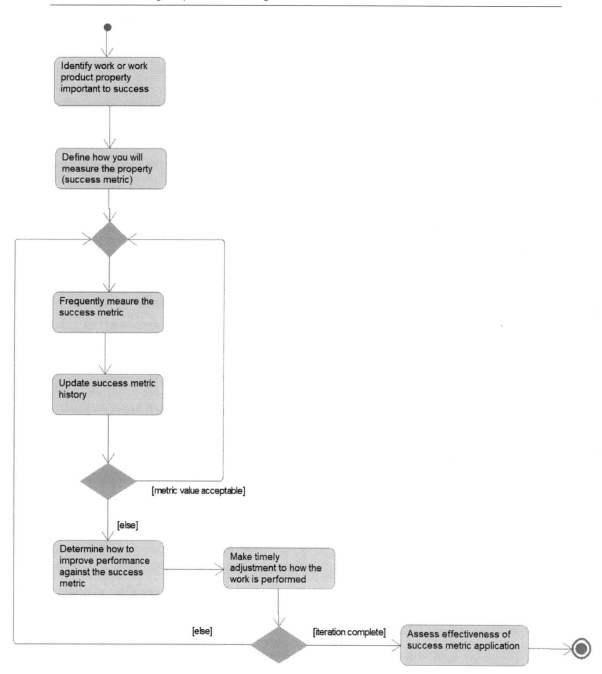

Figure 1.10 – Measuring success

Identifying work or a work product property that is important to success

One way to identify a property of interest is to look where your projects have problems or where the output work products fail. For engineering projects, work efficiency being too low is a common problem. For work products, the most common problem is the presence of defects.

Defining how you will measure the property (success metric)

Just as important to identifying what you want to measure is coming up with a quantifiable measurement that is simultaneously easy to apply, easy to measure, easy to automate, and accurately captures the property of interest. It's one thing to say "the system should be fast," but quite another to define a way to measure the speed in a fashion that can be compared to other work items and iterations.

Frequently measuring the success metric

It is common to gather metrics for a review at the end of a project. This review is commonly called a *project post-mortem*. I prefer to do frequent retrospectives, at least one per iteration, which I refer to as a *celebration of ongoing success*. To be applied in a timely way, you must measure frequently. This means that the measurements must require low effort and be quick to compute. In the best case, the environment or tool can automate the gathering and analysis of the information without any ongoing effort by the engineering staff. For example, time spent on work items can be captured automatically by tools that check out and check in work products.

Updating the success metric's history

For long-term organizational success, a recorded performance history is crucial. I've seen far too many organizations miss their project schedules by 100% or more, only to do the very same thing on the next project, and for exactly the same reasons. A metric history allows longer-term trends and improvements to be identified. That enables the reinforcement of positive aspects and the discarding of approaches that fail.

Determining how to improve performance against the success metric

If the metric result is unacceptable, then you must perform root cause analysis to uncover what can be done to improve it. If you discover that you have too many defects in your requirements, for example, you may consider changing how requirements are identified, captured, represented, analyzed, or assessed.

Making timely adjustments to how the activity is performed

Just as important to measuring how you're doing against your project and organizational goals is acting on that information. This may involve changing a project schedule to be more accurate, performing more testing, creating some process automation, or even getting training on some technology.

Assessing the effectiveness of the application of the success metric

Every so often, it is important to look at whether applying a metric is generating project value. A common place to do this is the *project retrospective* held at the end of each iteration. Metrics that are adding insufficient value may be dropped or replaced with other metrics that will add more value.

Some commonly applied metrics are shown in *Figure 1.11*:

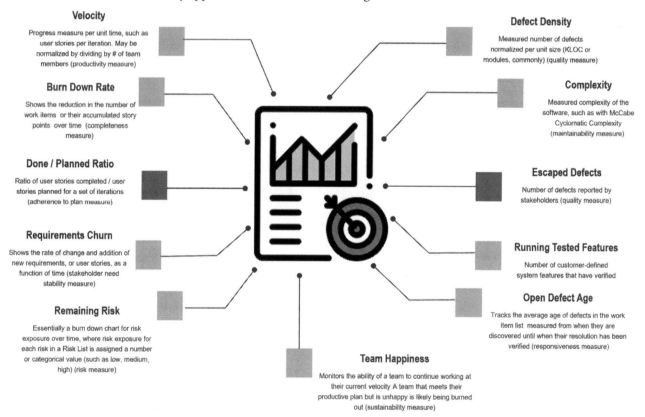

Velocity

Progress measure per unit time, such as user stories per iteration. May be normalized by dividing by # of team members (productivity measure)

Defect Density

Measured number of defects normalized per unit size (KLOC or modules, commonly) (quality measure)

Burn Down Rate

Shows the reduction in the number of work items or their accumulated story points over time (completeness measure)

Complexity

Measured complexity of the software, such as with McCabe Cyclomatic Complexity (maintainability measure)

Done / Planned Ratio

Ratio of user stories completed / user stories planned for a set of iterations (adherence to plan measure)

Escaped Defects

Number of defects reported by stakeholders (quality measure)

Requirements Churn

Shows the rate of change and addition of new requirements, or user stories, as a function of time (stakeholder need stability measure)

Running Tested Features

Number of customer-defined system features that have verified

Remaining Risk

Essentially a burn down chart for risk exposure over time, where risk exposure for each risk in a Risk List is assigned a number or categorical value (such as low, medium, high) (risk measure)

Open Defect Age

Tracks the average age of defects in the work item list measured from when they are discovered until when their resolution has been verified (responsiveness measure)

Team Happiness

Monitors the ability of a team to continue working at their current velocity A team that meets their productive plan but is unhappy is likely being burned out (sustainability measure)

Figure 1.11 – Some common success metrics

It all comes back to **you can't improve what you don't measure**. First, you must understand how well you are achieving your goals now. Then you must decide how you can improve and make the adjustment. Repeat. It's a simple idea.

Visualizing velocity is often done as a velocity or burn down chart. The former shows the planned velocity in work items per unit of time, and such use cases or user stories per iteration. The latter shows the rate of progress of handling the work items over time. It is common to show both planned values in addition to actual values. A typical velocity chart is shown in *Figure 1.12*:

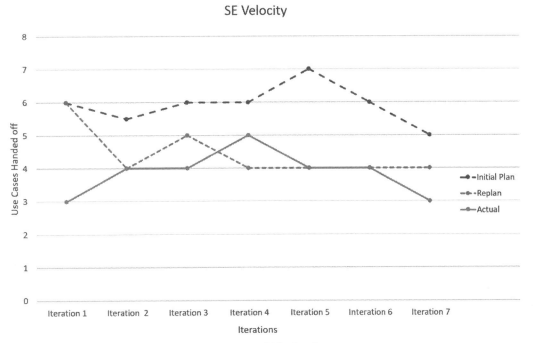

Figure 1.12 – Velocity chart

Example

Let's look at an example of the use of metrics in our project.

Identifying work or a work product property that is important to success

Let's consider a common metric used in Agile software development and apply it to systems engineering: *velocity*. Velocity underpins all schedules because it represents how much functionality that is delivered per unit of time. Velocity is generally measured as the number of completed user stories delivered per iteration. In our scope, we are not delivering implemented functionality, but we are incrementally delivering a handoff to downstream engineering. Let's call this **System Engineering (SE) velocity**, which is "specified use cases per iteration" and includes the requirements and all related SE work products.

This might not provide the granularity we desire, so let's also define a second metric, **SE fine-grained velocity**, which is the number of story points specified in the iteration.

Defining how you will measure the property (success metric)

We will measure the number of use cases delivered, but have to have a "definition of done" to ensure consistency of measurement. SE velocity will include the following:

- A use case with the following:

    a. A full description identifying the purpose, pre-conditions, post-conditions, and invariants

    b. A normative use case state machine in which all requirements traced to and from the use case are represented

    c. A "minimal spanning set" of scenarios in which all paths in the normative use case state machine are represented at least once

- Trace links to all related functional requirements and quality of service (performance, safety, reliability, security, and so on) requirements

- Architecture into which the implementation of the use cases and user stories will be placed

- System interfaces with a physical data schema to support the necessary interactions of the use cases and user stories

- Logical test cases to verify the use cases and user stories

- Logical validation cases to ensure that implementation of the use cases and user stories satisfies stakeholder requirements

SE velocity will simply be the number of such use cases delivered per iteration. SE fine-grained velocity will be the estimated effort (as measured in story points; refer to the *Estimating effort* recipe).

Frequently measuring the success metric

We will measure this each iteration. If our project has 35 use cases, our project heartbeat is 4 weeks, and the project is expected to take 1 year, then our SE velocity should be about 3. If the average use case is 37 story points, then our SE detailed velocity should be about 108 story points per iteration.

Updating the success metric's history

As we run the project, we will measure SE velocity and SE fine-grained velocity. We can plot those values over time to get velocity charts:

SE Velocity Charts

Iteration	Use Cases	Cum UC	Story Points	Cum SP
1	2	2	70	70
2	2	4	85	155
3	2	6	78	233
4	3	9	92	325

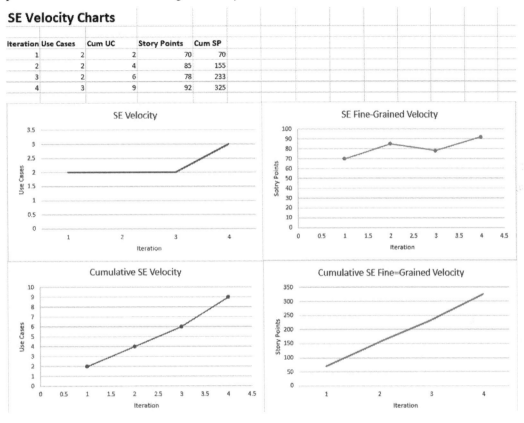

Figure 1.13 – SE velocity charts

Determining how to improve performance against the success metric

Our plan calls for 3 use cases and 108 story points per iteration, so we can see from *Figure 1.13* that we are underperforming. This could either be because 1) we over-estimated the planned velocity, or 2) we need to improve our work efficiency in some way. We can therefore simultaneously attack the problem on both fronts.

To start, we should replan based on our measured velocity, which is averaging 2.25 use cases and 81 story points per iteration, as compared to the planned 3 use cases and 108 story points. This will result in a longer, but hopefully more realistic, project plan and extend the planned project by an iteration or so.

In addition, we can analyze why the specification effort is taking too long and perhaps implement changes in process or tooling to improve.

Making timely adjustments to how the activity is performed

As we discover variance between our plan and our reality, we must adjust either the plan or how we work, or both. This should happen at least every iteration, as the metrics are gathered and analyzed. The iteration retrospective that takes place at the end of the iteration performs this service.

Assessing the effectiveness of the application of the success metric

Lastly, are the metrics helping the project? It might be reasonable to conclude that the fine-grained metric provides more value than the more general SE velocity metric, and so the latter is abandoned.

Some considerations

I have seen metrics fail in a number of organizations that are trying to improve. Broadly speaking, the reasons for failure are one of the following.

Measuring the wrong thing

Many qualities of interest are hard to identify precisely (think of *code smell*) or difficult to measure directly. Metrics are usually project qualities that are easy to measure, but only measure imprecisely what you actually want. The classic measure of software progress – lines of code per day – turns out to be a horrible measure, because it doesn't measure the quality of the code, so it cannot take into account the rework required when fast code production results in low code quality, nor is refactoring code "negative work" because it results in fewer lines of code. A better measure would be velocity, which is a measure of tested and verified features released per unit of time.

Another often abused measure is *hours worked*. I have seen companies require detailed reporting on hours spent per project, only to also levy the requirement that any hours worked over 40 hours per week should not be reported. This constrained metric does not actually measure the effort expended on project tasks.

> **Note**
>
> You can read more about code smell here: `https://en.wikipedia.org/wiki/Code_smell`.

Ignoring the metrics

I have seen many companies spend time and resources gathering metric data (and yes, it does require some effort and does cost some time, even when mostly automated), only to make the very same mistake time after time. This is because while they are capturing the data, they never actually use the data to improve.

No authority to initiate change

Gathering and analyzing metrics is often seen as less value than "real work" and so personnel tasked with these activities have little or no authority.

A lack of willingness to follow through

I have seen companies pay for detailed, quantified project performance data only to ignore it because there was little willingness to follow through with necessary changes. This lack of willingness can come from management being unwilling to pay for organizational improvement, or from technical staff afraid of trying something different.

Metrics should always be attempting to measure an objective rather than a means. Rather than "lines of code per day", it is better to measure "delivered functionality per day."

Managing risk

In my experience, most projects fail because they don't properly deal with project risk. Project risk refers to the issue that a team will fail to meet some or all of a project's objectives. Risk is defined to be the product of an event's likelihood of occurrence times its severity. Risk is always about the unknown. There are many different kinds of project risk, for example:

- Resource risk
- Technical risk
- Schedule risk
- Business risk

Risks are always about the *unknown,* and risk mitigation activities, known as *spikes* in Agile literature, are work undertaken to uncover information to reduce risk. For example, a technical risk might be that the selected bus architecture might not have sufficient bandwidth to meet the system performance requirements. A spike to address the risk might measure the bus under stress similar to what is expected for the product. Another technical risk might be the introduction of a new development technology, such as SysML, to a project. A resulting spike might be to bring in an outsider trainer and mentor for the project.

The most important thing you want to avoid is *ignoring risk.* It is common, for example, for a project to have "aggressive schedules" and for project leaders and members to ignore obvious signs of impending doom. It is far better to address the schedule risk by identifying and addressing likely causes of schedule slippage and replan the schedule.

Purpose

The purpose of the *Managing risk* recipe is to improve the likelihood of project success.

Inputs and preconditions

Project risk management begins early and should be an ongoing activity throughout the project. Initially, a project vision or preliminary plan or roadmap serves as the starting point for risk management.

Outputs and post conditions

Intermediate outputs include a *risk management plan* (sometimes called a *risk list*) and work time resulting from it, allocated to the release and iteration plans. The risk management plan provides not only the name of the risk, but also important information about it. Longer-term results include a (more) successful project outcome than one that did not include risk management.

How to do it...

Figure 1.14 shows how risks are identified, put into the risk management plan, and then result in spikes:

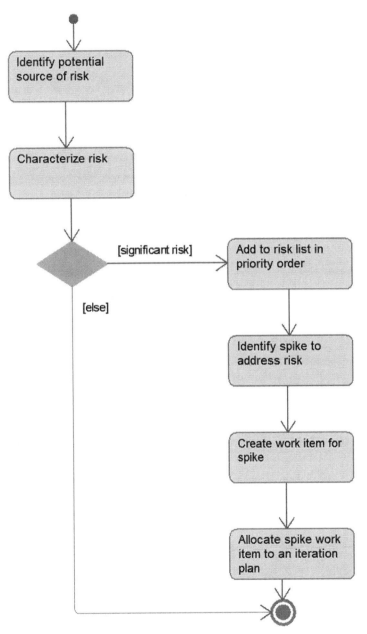

Figure 1.14 – Managing risk

Figure 1.15 shows how, as spikes are performed in the iterations, the risk management plan is updated:

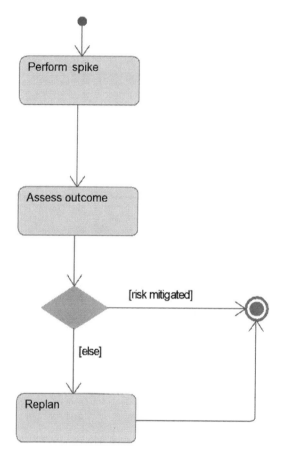

Figure 1.15 – Reducing risk

Identifying potential sources of risk

Risk identification shouldn't just be done at the outset of the project. At least once per iteration, typically during the project's retrospective activity, the team should look for new risks that have arisen as the project has progressed. Thus, the workflow in *Figure 1.14* isn't performed just once, but many times during execution of the project. In addition, it sometimes happens that risks disappear if their underlying causes are removed, so you might end up removing risk items, or at least marking them as avoided, during these risk reassessments.

Characterizing risk

The name of the risk isn't enough. We certainly need a description of how the risk might manifest itself and what it means. We also need to know how likely the negative outcome is to manifest (*likelihood*) and how bad things will be should that occur (*severity*). Some outcomes have a minor impact, while others may be show stoppers.

Adding to the risk list in priority order

The risk management plan maintains the list in order sorted by risk magnitude. If you have quantified both the risk's likelihood and severity, then risk magnitude is the product of those two values. The idea is that the higher-priority risks should have more attention and be addressed earlier than the lower-priority risks.

Identifying a spike to address risk

A spike is work that is done to reduce either the likelihood or the severity of the risk outcome, generally the former. We can address knowledge gaps with training; we can address bus performance problems with a faster bus; we can solve schedule risks with feature-cide. Whatever the approach, a spike seeks to reduce risk.

Creating a work item for a spike

Work items come in many flavors. Usually, we think of use cases or user stories (functionality) as the work items. However, work items can refer to any work activity, as we discussed in the earlier recipe for backlog management. Specifically, in this case, spikes are important work items to be put into the product backlog.

Allocating a spike work item to an iteration plan

As previously discussed, work items must be allocated to iterations to result in a release plan.

Performing a spike

This action means to perform the identified experiment or activity. If the activity is to get training, then complete the training session. If it is to perform a lab-based throughput test for a piece of hardware, then do that.

Assessing the outcome

Following the spike, it is important to assess the outcome. Was the risk reduced? Is a change in plan, approach, or technology warranted?

Updating the risk management plan

The risk management plan must be updated with the outcome of the spike.

> **Note**
> Featurecide is the removal of features of low or questionable stakeholder value or work items that you just don't have the bandwidth to address. Featurecide is one means to address schedule risk.

Replanning

If appropriate, adjust the plan in accordance with the outcome of the spike. For example, if a proposed technology cannot meet the project's needs, then a new technology or approach must be selected and the plan must be updated to reflect that.

Example

Here is an example risk management plan, captured as a spreadsheet of information. Rather than show the increasing level of detail in the table step by step, we'll just show the end state (*Table 1.3*) to illustrate a typical outcome from the workflow shown in *Figure 1.14*.

It can be sorted by the **State** and **Risk Magnitude** columns to simplify its use:

Risk Management Plan (Risk List)													
Risk ID	Headline	Description	Type	Impact	Probability	Risk Magnitude	State	Precision	Raised on	Iteration #	Impacted Stakeholder	Owner	Mitigation Strategy (Spike)
1	Robustness of main motor	The system must be able to maintain 2000 W for up to 5 minutes and sustain 1000 W for 4 hours, with an MTBF of 20,000 hours. The current motor is unsuitable.	Technical	80%	90%	72%	Open	High	1/5/2020	1	Maintainer, user	Sam	Meet with motor vendors to see whether 1) they have an existing motor that meets our needs or 2) they can design a motor within budget to meet requirements.
2	Agile MBSE impact	The team is using both Agile and MBSE for the first time. The concern is that this may lead to bad technical choices.	Technical	80%	80%	64%	Open	Medium	1/4/2020	0	User, buyer, product owner	Jill	Bring in consultant from A Priori Systems for training and mentoring.

Risk ID	Headline	Description	Type	Impact	Probability	Risk Magnitude	State	Precision	Raised on	Iteration #	Impacted Stakeholder	Owner	Mitigation Strategy (Spike)
3	Robustness of USB connection	Users will be inserting and removing the USB while under movement stress, so it is likely to break.	Technical	40%	80%	32%	Open	Medium	2/16/2020	3	User, manufacturing	Joe	Standard USB connectors are too weak. We need to mock up a more robust physical design.
4	Aggressive Schedule	Customer schedule is optimistic. We need to address this either by changing the expectations or figuring out how to satisfy the schedule.	Schedule	40%	100%	40%	Mitigated	Low	12/5/2019	0	Buyer	Susan	Iteration 0, work with the customer to see whether the project can be delivered in phases, or if ambitious features can be cut.
5	Motor response lag time	To simulate short high-intensity efforts, the change in resistance must be fast enough to simulate the riding experience.	Technical	20%	20%	4%	Open	High	12/19/2019	6	User	Sam	Do response time study with professional riders to evaluate the viability of the current solution.
6	Team availability	Key team members have yet to come off the aerobike project and are delayed an estimated 6 months.	Resource	60%	75%	45%	Obsolete	Low	3/1/2020	0	Product owner, buyer		See whether the existing project can be speed up. If not, draw up a contingency plan to either hire more or delay the project's start.

Table 1.3 – Example risk list

For an example of the risk mitigation workflow in *Figure 1.15*, let's consider the first two risks in *Table 1.3*.

Performing a spike

For Risk 2, "Agile MBSE Impact", the identified spike is "Bring in consultant from *A Priori Systems* for training and mentoring." We hire a consultant from *A Priori Systems*. He then trains the team on Agile MBSE, gives them each of a copy of his book, *Agile Systems Engineering*, and mentors the team through the first three iterations. This spike is initiated in iteration 0, and the mentoring lasts through iteration 3.

For Risk 1, "Robustness of the main motor", the identified spike is "Meet with motor vendors to see whether 1) they have an existing motor that meets our needs or 2) they can design a motor within our budget to satisfy requirements." Working with our team, the application engineer from the vendor assesses the horsepower, torque, and reliability needs and then finds a version of the motor that is available within our cost envelope. The problem is resolved.

Assessing the outcome

The assessment of the outcome of the spike for Risk 2 is evaluated in four steps. First, the engineers attending the AgileMBSE workshop provide an evaluation of the effectiveness of the workshop. While not giving universally high marks, the team was very satisfied overall with their understanding of the approach and how to perform the work. The iteration retrospectives for the next three iterations all look at expected versus actual outcomes and find that the team is performing well. The assessment of the risk is that it has been successfully mitigated.

For Risk 1, the assessment of the outcome is done by the lead electronics engineer. He obtains five instances of the suggested motor variant and stress tests them in the lab. He is satisfied that the risk has been successfully mitigated and that the engineering can proceed.

Updating the risk management plan

The risk management plan is updated to reflect the outcomes as they occur. In this, example, *Table 1.4* shows the updated **State** column in which the two risk states are updated to **Mitigated**:

Risk Management Plan (Risk List)

Risk ID	Headline	Description	Type	Impact	Probability	Risk Magnitude	State	Precision	Raised on	Iteration #	Impacted Stakeholder	Owner	Mitigation Strategy (Spike)
1	Robustness of main motor	The system must be able to maintain 2000 W for up to 5 minutes and sustain 1000 W for 4 hours, with an MTBF of 20,000 hours. The current motor is unsuitable.	Technical	80%	90%	72%	Mitigated, updated motor selection to appropriate variant.	High	1/5/2020	1	Maintainer, user	Sam	Meet with motor vendors to see whether 1) they have an existing motor that meets our needs or 2) they can design a motor without our OEM costing to meet requirements.
2	Agile MBSE impact	The team is using both Agile and MBSE for the first time. The concern is that this may lead to back technical choices.	Technical	80%	80%	64%	Mitigated, updated modeling tool to Rhapsody, and MBSE workflows updated.	Medium	1/4/2020	0	User, buyer, product owner	Jill	Bring in consultant from A Priori Systems for training and mentoring.

Table 1.4 – Updated risk plan (partial)

Replanning

In this example, the risks are successfully mitigated, and the changes noted in the **State** column. For Risk 1, a more appropriate motor is selected with help from the motor vendor. For Risk 2, the tooling was updated to better reflect the modeling requirements of the project and minor tweaks were made to the detailed MBSE workflows.

Product roadmap

A *product roadmap* is a plan of action for how a product will be introduced and evolved over time. It is developed by the *product owner*, an Agile role responsible for managing the product backlog and feature set. The product roadmap is a high-level strategic view of the series of delivered systems mapped to capabilities and customer needs. The product roadmap takes into account the market trajectories, value propositions, and engineering constraints. It is ultimately expressed as a set of initiatives and capabilities delivered over time.

Purpose

The purpose of the product roadmap is to plan and to provide visibility to the release of capabilities to customers over time. The roadmap is initially developed in iteration 0, but as in all things Agile, the roadmap is updated over time. A typical roadmap has a 12-24 month planning horizon, but for long-lived systems, the horizon may be much longer.

Inputs and preconditions

A product vision has been established that includes the business aspects (such as market and broad customer needs) and technical aspects (the broad technical approach and its feasibility).

Outputs and post conditions

This is a product roadmap, with a time-based view of capability releases of the system.

How to do it...

The product roadmap is organized around larger-scale activities (epics) for the most part, but can contain more detail if desired. An *epic* is a capability that spans multiple iterations. Business epics provide visible value to stakeholders, while technical epics (also known as enabler epics) provide behind-the-scenes infrastructure improvement, such as architecture implementation or the reduction of technical debt.

In an MBSE approach, epics can be modeled as stereotypes of use cases and are decomposed to use cases, which are, in turn, decomposed into user stories and scenarios. While epics are implemented across multiple iterations, a use case is implemented in a single iteration. A user story or scenario takes only a portion of an iteration to complete. User stories and scenarios are comparable in scope and intent. This taxonomy is shown in *Figure 1.16*, along with where they typically appear in planning:

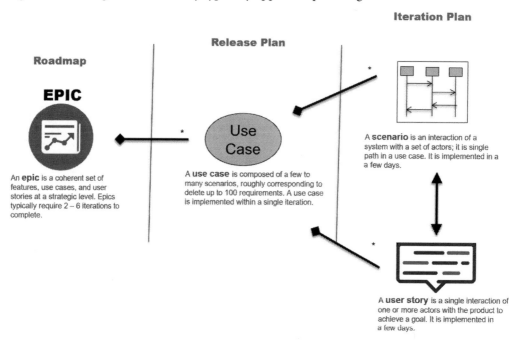

Figure 1.16 – Epics, use cases, and user stories

The product roadmap is a simple planning mechanism relating delivered capability to time, iterations, and releases. Like all Agile planning, the roadmap is adjusted as additional information is discovered, improving its accuracy over time. The roadmap updates usually occur at the end of each iteration during the iteration retrospective, as the actual iteration outcomes are compared with the planned outcomes.

The roadmap also highlights milestones of interest and technical evolutions paths. Milestones may include customer reviews or important releases, such as alpha, beta, **Initial Operating Condition (IOC)**, or **Final Operating Condition (FOC)**:

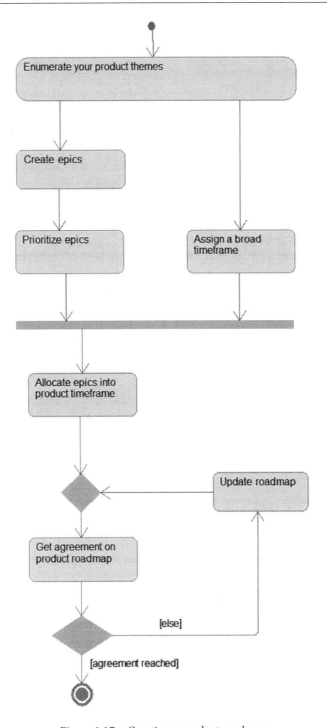

Figure 1.17 – Creating a product roadmap

Enumerating your product themes

The product themes are the strategic objectives, values, and goals to be realized by the product. The epics must ultimately refer back to how they aid in the achievement of these themes. This step lists the product themes to drive the identification of the epics and work items going forward. In some Agile methods, the themes correlate to *value streams*.

Creating epics

Epics describe the strategic capabilities of the system to realize the product themes. They can be either *business epics*, which bring direct value to the stakeholders, or *technical* (aka *enabler*) *epics*, which provide technological infrastructure to support the business epics. Epics may be thought of as large use cases that generally span several iterations. This step identifies the key epics to be put into the product roadmap.

Prioritizing epics

Prioritization identifies the order in which epics are to be developed. Prioritization can be driven by urgency (timeliness of the need), criticality (importance of meeting the need), the usefulness of the capability, the availability of the required resource, the reduction in project risk, natural sequencing, or meeting opportunities, or any combination of the above. The details of how to perform prioritization are the subject of its own recipe (refer to the *Work item prioritization* recipe in this chapter), but this is one place where prioritization can be used effectively.

Assigning a broad timeframe

The product roadmap ultimately defines a range of time in which capabilities are to be delivered. This differs from traditional planning, which attempts to nail down to the second when a product will be delivered in spite of the lack of adequate information to do so. The product roadmap usually defines a large period of time, say, a month, season, or even a year, in which a capability is planned to be delivered, but with the expectation that this timeframe can be made more precise as the project proceeds.

Allocating epics to the product timeframe

Epics fit into the product timeframe to allow project planning at a strategic level.

Getting agreement on a product roadmap

Various stakeholders must agree on the timeframe. Users, purchasers, and marketeers must agree that the timeframe meets business needs and the epics provide the appropriate value proposition. Engineering staff must agree that the capabilities can be reasonably expected to be delivered with an appropriate level of quality within the timeframe. Manufacturing staff must agree that the system can be produced in the plant. Regulatory authorities must agree that the regulatory objectives will be achieved.

Updating the roadmap

If stakeholders are not all satisfied, then the plan should be reworked until an acceptable roadmap is created. This requires the modification and re-evaluation of an updated roadmap.

Example

Let's create a product roadmap for the Pegasus system by following the steps outlined here.

Enumerating your product themes

Product themes include the following:

- Providing a bike fit as close as possible to a serious cyclist's fit on their road bike
- Providing a virtual ride experience that closely resembles outside riding, including:

  a. Providing resistance to pedals for a number of conditions, including flats, climbing, sprinting, and coasting for a wide range of power outputs from casual to professional riders

  b. Simulating gearing that closely resembles the most popular gearing for road bicycles

  c. Incline control to physically incline or decline the bike

- Permitting programmatic control of resistance to simulate changing road conditions in a realistic fashion
- Interfacing with cycling training apps, including Zwift, Trainer Road, and The Sufferfest
- Gathering information regarding the ride, performance, and biometrics for analysis by third-party apps
- Providing seamless **Over-The-Air (OTA)** updates of product firmware to simplify maintenance

Creating epics

Epics describe the strategic capabilities of the system to realize the product themes. This step identifies the key epics to be put into the product roadmap. Epics include the following:

Business epics:

- Physical bike setup
- Ride configuration
- Firmware updates
- Control resistance
- Monitoring road metrics
- Communicating with apps
- Emulating gearing
- Incline control

Enabler epics:

- Mechanical frame development
- Motor electronics development
- Digital electronics development

Prioritizing epics

These epics are not run fully sequentially, as some can be done in parallel. Nevertheless, the basic prioritized list is as follows:

Prioritized epics:

- Mechanical frame development
- Motor electronics development
- Digital physical bike setup
- Monitoring road metrics
- Ride configuration
- Control resistance
- Emulating gearing

- Communicating with apps
- Firmware updates
- Incline control
- Electronics development

Assigning a broad timeframe

For this project, the total timeframe is about 18 months, beginning in early Spring 2021 and ending at the end of 2022, with milestones for Fall 2021 (demo at the September Eurobike tradeshow), Spring 2022 (alpha release), Summer 2022 (beta), and its official release (October 2022).

Allocating epics to the product's timeframe

Figure 1.18 shows a simple product roadmap for the Pegasus system. Along the top we see the planned iterations and their planned completion dates. Below that, important milestones are shown. The middle part depicts the evolution plan for the three primary hardware aspects (mechanical frame, motor electronics, and digital electronics). Finally, the bottom part shows the high-level system capabilities as epics over time, using color coding to indicate priority:

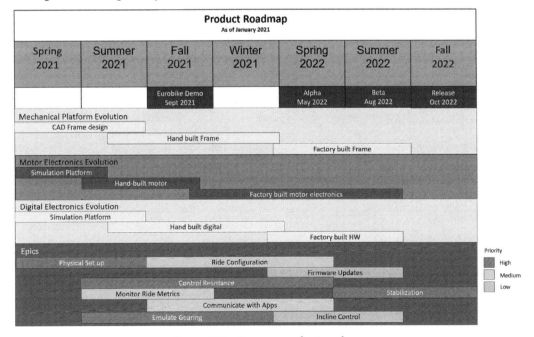

Figure 1.18 – Pegasus product roadmap

Getting agreement on a product roadmap

We discuss the roadmap with stakeholders from marketing, engineering, manufacturing, and our customer focus group to agree on the product themes, epics, and timeframes.

Updating the roadmap

The focus group identifies that there is another tradeshow in June 2022 that we should try to have an updated demo for. This is then added to the product roadmap.

Release plan

While the product roadmap is strategic in nature, the *release plan* is more tactical. The product roadmap shows the timing of release goals, high-level product capabilities, and epics that span multiple iterations, but the release plan provides more detail on a per-iteration basis. The product roadmap has a longer planning horizon of 12-24 months, while a release plan is more near term, generally 3-9 months out. This recipe relies on the *Managing your backlog* recipe, which appears earlier in this chapter.

Purpose

The purpose of the release plan is to show how the product backlog is allocated to the upcoming set of iterations and releases over the next 3-9 months.

Inputs and preconditions

The product vision and roadmap are sketched out and a reasonably complete product backlog has been established with work items that can fit within a single iteration.

Outputs and post conditions

The release plan provides a plan of the mapping of work items to the upcoming set of iterations and releases. Of course, the plan is updated frequently – at least once per iteration – as work is completed and the depth of understanding of the product development increases.

How to do it...

Epics and high-level goals need to be decomposed into work items that can be completed within a single iteration. Each of these work items is then prioritized and its effort is estimated. The release plan identifies the specific planned iterations, each with a mission (as shown in *Figure 1.4*). There is some interplay between the missions of the iterations and the priority of the work items. The priority of a work item might be changed so that it is completed in the same iteration as a set of related work items.

Once that has been done, the mapping of the work items to the iterations can be made. The mapping must be evaluated for reasonableness and adjusted until the plan looks both good and achievable. This workflow is shown in *Figure 1.19*:

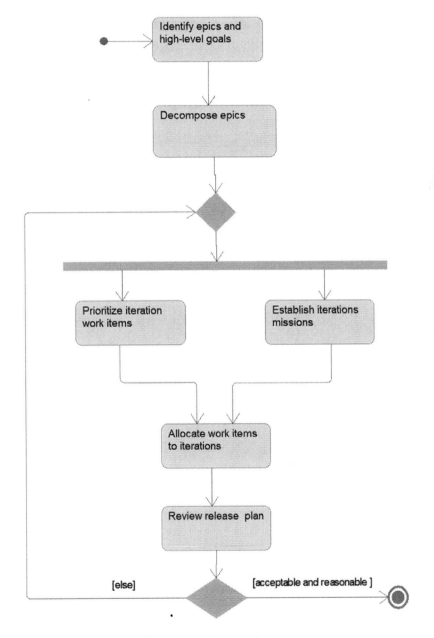

Figure 1.19 – Release planning

Identifying epics high-level goals

If you're done with the product roadmap (see the *Product roadmap* recipe), then you are likely to have already established the epics and high-level goals (themes) for the product. If not, refer to that recipe for how to do that.

Decomposing epics

Epics are generally too large to be completed in a single iteration, so they must be decomposed into smaller pieces – use cases and technical work items – that can be completed within a single iteration. These will be the work elements allocated to the iterations.

Establishing iteration missions

Each iteration should have a mission, including purpose, scope, and themes. This was discussed in the *Managing your backlog* recipe earlier in this chapter. This mission includes the following:

- Use cases to be implemented
- Defects to be repaired
- Platforms to be supported
- Risks to be reduced
- Work products to be developed

Prioritizing iteration work items

A work item's priority specifies the order in which it should be developed. Prioritization is a subject of its own recipe, *Work item prioritization*. Here it is enough to say that higher-priority work items will be performed in earlier iterations than lower-priority work items.

Allocating work items to iterations

This step provides a detailed set of work items to be performed within the iteration (known as the *iteration backlog*). Ultimately, all work items are either allocated to an iteration, decomposed into smaller work items that are allocated, or are removed from the product backlog.

Reviewing the release plan

Once the allocations are done, the iteration plan must be reviewed to ensure that it satisfies the following objectives:

- It is consistent with the product roadmap.

- It has iteration allocations that can be reasonably expected to be achievable.

- It has work item allocations that are consistent with the mission of their owner iterations.

Example

While the product roadmap example we did in the previous recipe focused on a somewhat vague strategic plan, release planning is more tactical and detailed. Specific work items are allocated to specific iterations and reviewed and *rebalanced* if the release plan has discernible flaws. For this example, we'll look at a planning horizon of 6 iterations (plus iteration 0) and focus on the allocations of functionality, technical work items, platforms to be supported, and spikes for the reduction of specific risks.

Identifying high-level goals

The high-level goals are identified in the project plan from the previous recipe, as exemplified in the business and enabler epics.

Decomposing epics

The epics to be implemented in the iterations in this planning horizon must be decomposed into use cases and technical work items achievable within the allocated iteration. *Figure 1.20* shows the decomposition of the epics into use cases and user stories. Note that epics (and, for that matter, user stories) are modeled as stereotypes of use cases, and the diagram is a use case diagram with the purpose of visualizing that decomposition:

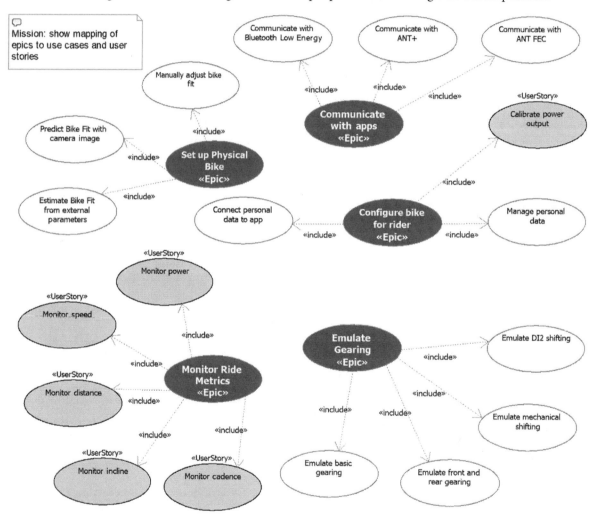

Figure 1.20 – Mapping epics to use cases

Establishing iteration missions

To establish the mission for each iteration, a spreadsheet is created (*Table 1.5*) with the iterations as the columns and the primary aspects of the mission as rows.

Prioritizing iteration work items

Work items are prioritized to fit to help us understand the sequencing of the work in different iterations. As much as possible, elements with similar priorities are put within the same iteration. As discussed in the *Work item prioritization* recipe, during review, we may increase or decrease a work item's priority to ensure congruence with other work items implemented in a specific iteration.

Allocating work items to iterations

Based on the prioritization and the work capacity within an iteration, the work items are then allocated (*Table 1.5*).

Table 1.5 shows an example in which allocations are made based on priority (see the *Work item prioritization* recipe), estimated effort (see the *Estimating effort* recipe), and the congruency of the functionality to the mission of the use case:

Release Plan	Iteration 0	Iteration 1	Iteration 2	Iteration 3	Iteration 4	Iteration 5	Iteration 6
Functionality		Initial frame mockup, basic motor electronics, basic rider controls, basic resistance	Set up bike fit (seat), basic digital electronics, calibrate power output, basic gearing	Set up bike fit (handlebars), manually adjust bike fit, monitor power	Set up bike fit (cranks), monitor speed, monitor distance, Bluetooth, monitor cadence, data to app	Bike fit with external parameters, motorized incline, monitor incline, ANT+, ANT FEC	Manage personal data, predict bike fit with camera image, external resistance control, ERG mode
Target Platforms		Hand-built mechanicals, hand-built analog electronics, simulated digital electronics	Basic hand-built mechanicals, hand-built electronics	Prototype mechanicals for manufacturing	First run factory electronics	First run mechanicals	Second run factory electronics, second run factory mechanicals
Technical Work Items		Analyze frame stability and strength, refine SW/EE deployment architecture	Design cable runs, analyze electrical power needs, add in SW concurrency architecture	Add in SW distribution framework	Finalize flywheel mass	EMI conformance testing	
Spikes	Team availability, aggressive schedule, agile MBSE impact	Motor response time	Robustness of main motor	USB robustness			

Table 1.5 – Release plan

Reviewing the release plan

We then look at the release plan and see whether we think it is achievable, whether the missions of the iterations are reasonable, and whether the allocation of work items makes sense for the project.

Iteration plan

The iteration plan plans out a specific iteration in more detail, so that the planning horizon is a single iteration. This is typically 1-4 weeks in duration. This is the last chance to adjust the expectations of the iteration before work begins.

Purpose

The purpose of the iteration plan is to ensure that the work allocated to the iteration is achievable, decompose the larger-scale work items (for example, use cases and technical work items) into smaller work items, and plan for completion of the iteration.

Inputs and preconditions

Preconditions include the release plan and the initial iteration backlog.

Outputs and post conditions

Post conditions include the complete work items, generated engineering work products, identified defects, and technical work items (pushed into the product backlog), and uncompleted work items (also pushed back onto the product backlog).

How to do it...

Use cases in the iteration backlog, which may take an entire iteration to fully realize, are decomposed into user stories or scenarios, each of which takes a few hours to a few days to realize. The iteration plan is created *just-in-time* before the start of the iteration, but is based on the release plan. This flow is shown in *Figure 1.21*:

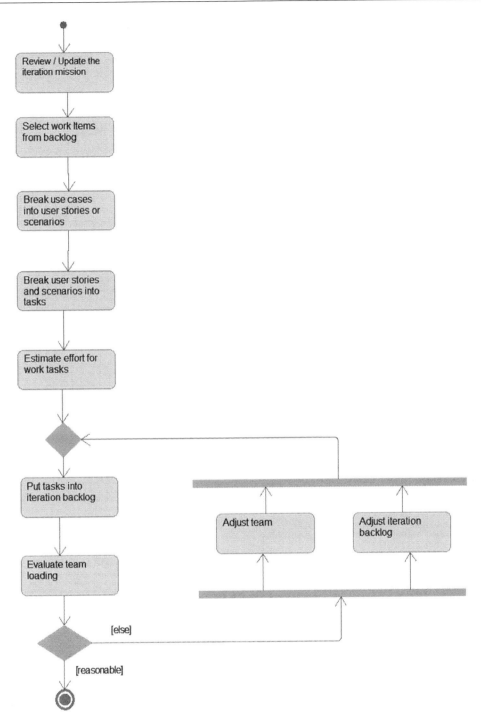

Figure 1.21 – Iteration planning

Reviewing/updating the iteration mission

The iteration should already have a mission from the release plan. This will include the following:

- The functionality to be achieved (in use cases, user stories, and/or scenarios)
- The target platforms to be supported
- Architectural and other technical work items to support the functionality and technical epics
- Defects identified in previous iterations
- Spikes to reduce risks

There is a decent chance that this mission will require updating, based on lessons learned in preceding iterations, so this is a place to do that if it has not already been done. Any changes made here may impact the allocation of work items to the iteration backlog.

Selecting work items from the backlog

Based on the iteration mission, the list of work items allocated is reviewed. Some may be removed or new ones added, as necessary and appropriate.

Breaking down use cases into user scenarios or user stories

Use cases themselves are generally rather large and it is useful to have smaller work items in the backlog. These work items might be estimated to take anywhere from a few hours to a few days. Note that the estimation of epics and use cases is often done using relative measures (for example, use case points), but once you get down a few hours in duration, estimates often transition to hour-based, as determined by the team's velocity.

Breaking down user stories into tasks

If the user stories are small, then this step can be slipped. If they are still rather large, say a week or two, then they might be decomposed further into smaller tasks. This step is optional.

Estimating the effort for work tasks

If you've decomposed the original iteration backlog work items, then those elements should be estimated. This can be done either using relative measures, such as user stories, or absolute measures, such as the number of hours to complete.

Putting tasks into the iteration backlog

Any modified or newly created work item tasks must be added to the backlog for the iteration.

Evaluating team loading

Once we have a detailed vision of the expected work to do in the upcoming iteration and a pretty good idea of the effort, we can re-evaluate whether the scope of work is reasonable.

Adjusting the team

The size or makeup of the team may be adjusted to better fit the more detailed understanding of the scope of work to be undertaken.

Adjusting the backlog

If the scope looks too demanding for the team, items can be removed from the iteration backlog and pushed back to the product backlog. This will spin off an effort later to rebalance the release plan. Note that this is also done at the end of the iteration, when the team can see what planned work was not achieved.

Iteration planning is pretty simple as long as you keep some guidelines in place. The larger-scale work items allocated to the iteration are sized to fit into a single iteration. However, they are decomposed into somewhat smaller pieces, each taking from a few hours to a few days to complete. For use cases, this will be either user stories or scenarios; this decomposition and analysis will be detailed in the recipes of the next chapter. The work items should all fit within the mission statement for the iteration, as discussed in the first *Managing your backlog* recipe.

The work items should all contribute to the mission of the iteration. If not, they should either be pushed back to the product backlog or the iteration mission should be expanded to include them. It is also helpful to have the larger-scale work items broken down into relatively small pieces; you should be less concerned about whether they are called use cases, user stories, scenarios, or tasks, and more concerned that they 1) contribute to the desired functionality and 2) are in the right effort scope (a few hours to a few days). Work items that are too large are difficult to estimate accurately and may not contribute to understanding the work to be done. Work items that are too small waste planning time and effort.

Example

For our example, let's plan iteration 4.

Reviewing/updating the iteration mission

The mission for a hypothetical iteration is shown in *Table 1.6*:

Release Plan	Iteration Use Cases	Iteration User Stories	Effort (hours)
Functionality	Predict Bike Fit with Camera		
	Estimate Bike Fit from External Parameters		
		Monitor Distance	
		Calibrate Power Output	
		Provide Basic Resistance	
		Set Resistance under User Control	
Target Platforms	First Run Factory Electronics Hand-Built Mechanical Frame		
Technical Work Items	Finalize Flywheel Mass		
Spikes	\<none>		

Table 1.6 – Iteration mission

Selecting work items from the backlog

These work items are selected from the product backlog and placed in the iteration backlog.

Breaking down use cases into user scenarios or user stories

Figure 1.22 shows the planned functionality for our hypothetical iteration of the Pegasus bike trainer. The ovals without stereotypes are use cases that are decomposed with the «include» relation into user stories. Each of these is then estimated to get an idea of the scope of the work for the iteration:

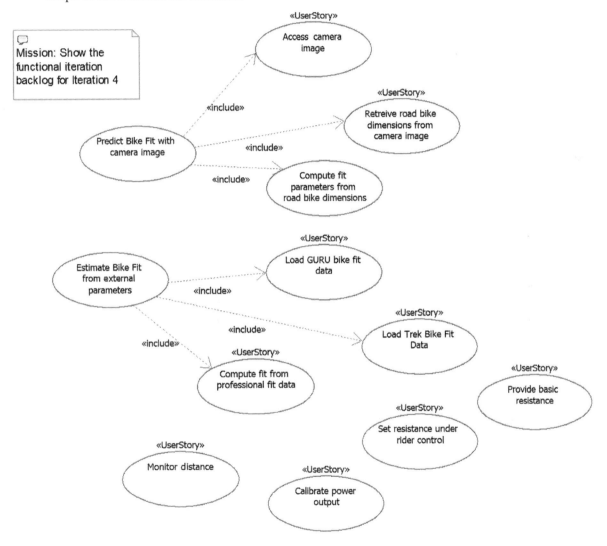

Figure 1.22 – Iteration planning example

Breaking down user stories into tasks

These user stories are all pretty small, so this optional step is skipped.

Estimating the effort for work tasks

We then estimate the hours required to complete these small work items for the task. This results in the updated table in *Table 1.7*:

Release Plan	Iteration Use Cases	Iteration User Stories/Work Items	Effort (Hours)
Functionality	Predict Bike Fit with Camera	Access Camera Image	2
		Retrieve Road Bike Dimensions from Camera Image	16
		Compute Fit Parameters from Road Bike Dimensions	4
	Estimate Bike Fit from External Parameters	Load GURU Bike Fit Data	4
		Load Trek Bike Fit Data	4
		Compute Fit from Professional Fit Data	2
		Monitor Distance	6
		Calibrate Power Output	12
		Provide Basic Resistance	20
		Set Resistance under User Control	4
Target Platforms	First Run Factory Electronics Hand-Built Mechanical Frame		
Technical Work Items		Finalize Flywheel Mass	4
Spikes	<none>		
Totals			78

Table 1.7 – Iteration 4 mission with estimates

Putting tasks into the iteration backlog

The work items from the **Iteration User Stories/Work Items** column are added to the backlog for the iteration.

Evaluating team loading

The 6-person team executing the iteration should be able to complete the estimated 78 hours of work in the 2-week iteration timeframe.

Adjusting the team

No adjustment to the team is necessary.

Adjusting the backlog

No adjustment to the backlog is necessary.

Estimating effort

Traditionally, absolute duration measures, such as person-hours, are used to estimate tasks. Agile approaches generally apply relative measures, especially for large work items such as epics, use cases, and larger user stories. When estimating smaller work items of a duration of a few hours, it is still common to use person hours. The reasoning is that it is difficult to accurately estimate weeks- or months-duration work items, but there is better accuracy in estimating small work items of 1-4 hours.

There are a number of means by which effort can be estimated, but the one we will discuss in this recipe is called *planning poker*. This is a cooperative game-like approach to converge on a relative duration measure for a set of work items.

Purpose

The purpose of effort estimation is to understand the amount of effort required to complete a work item. This may be expressed in absolute or relative terms, with relative terms preferred for larger work items.

Inputs and preconditions

This has a backlog of work items for estimation.

Outputs and post conditions

For each work item being considered, the output of this recipe is either an estimate of the effort required to complete it or a note that more information is necessary to provide such an estimate.

How to do it...

Work durations come in different sizes. For the most part, *epics* are capabilities that require at least two iterations to perform. Epics are typically broken down into *use cases* that are expected to be completed within a single iteration. *User stories* and *scenarios* are singular threads within a use case that require a few hours to a few days to complete. To be comparable, the epics work estimates must be, in some sense, the sum of the work efforts for all its contained use cases, and use case work estimates are the sum of the effort of all of its contained user stories and scenarios.

Of course, the real world is slightly more complex than that. The last sentence of the preceding paragraph is true only when the user stories and scenarios are both orthogonal and complete. This means that all the primitive behaviors contained within the use case appears in exactly one use case or user story. If there is overlap, that is, a primitive behavior appear as part of two scenarios, then the use case estimate is the sum of the user story estimates minus the overlapping behavior. This removes "double counting" of the common behavior. Since these are relative and approximate measures, such subtleties are generally ignored.

How it works...

Use case points or user story points are a relative measure of effort. The project velocity (refer to the *Measuring your success* recipe for more details) maps points to person-hours. Velocity is often unknown in the early stages of the project, but becomes better understood as the project progresses. The value of use case or user story points is that they remove the temptation of be overly (and *erroneously*) precise about estimated effort. All absolute work estimates assume an implied velocity, but in practice velocity varies based on team size, team skill, domain knowledge, work item complexity, tools and automation, development environment factors, and regulation and certification concerns.

Figure 1.23 shows the workflow for planning poker:

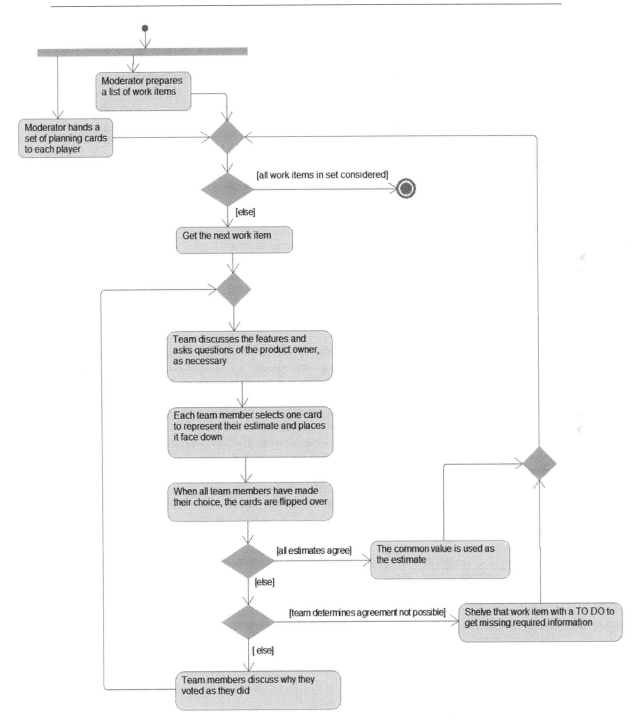

Figure 1.23 – Planning poker

The moderator prepares a list of work items

The moderator of the planning sessions prepares a list of work items that are generally epics, use cases, user stories, or scenarios. In addition to these common items, spikes, technical work items, defect repairs, and other work items may be regarded as part of the session as well.

The moderator hands a set of planning cards to each player

These "planning cards" have an effort estimate on one side, but are otherwise identical. Most commonly, a number in a Fibonacci sequence (1, 2, 3, 5, 8, 13, 21, 34, 55, 89, 144) or something similar is used.

Getting the next work item

Start with the first work item. To begin with, I recommend what appears to be the smallest work item, and this will often serve as a standard by which subsequent work items will be judged. As each work item is either estimated or shelved, go to the next.

The team discusses the features and asks questions of the product owner, as necessary

It is crucial to have a common understanding of what the work item entails. The product owner is the person who generally has the best understanding of the user's needs, but others may play this role for technical work items.

Each team member selects one card to represent their estimate and places it face down

The estimates are approximately linear, so that an estimate of "5" will be more than twice as much work as a work item estimate of "2", but less than twice the effort required for an estimate of "3". The cards are placed face down to ensure that the initial estimate of the work item is the unbiased opinion of the team member.

When all team members have made their choice, the cards are flipped over

Flipping the cards over exposes the estimates to the group.

The common value is used as the estimate

If the estimates all agree, then that value is used as the "job size" estimate for the work item, and the team moves on to the next work item.

Shelve that work item with a TO DO to get missing information that is required

If the team is unable to reach consensus after multiple voting rounds on a single work item, that item is shelved until it can be resolved. The underlying assumption is that there must be some crucial bit of misunderstanding or missing information needed. The team agrees to a task to identify the missing information and re-estimate this item in a later session.

Team members discuss why they voted as they did

If the estimates differ, then the team must share why they estimated as they did. This is particularly important for the lowest and highest estimated values.

Considerations

It is important that the relative size of the work items is consistent. If the average user story points is "8", and on average, a use case contains four user stories, then you would expect the average use case size to be about 39-55 points. If the average epic is split across three uses cases, you would expect the average epic estimate to be 144-377 (selecting a number only from the Fibonacci series). While strict adherence isn't crucial, good planning is made more difficult if you have a user story, a use case, and an epic with independent point scales.

Example

This example is for the user stories derived from the **Control Resistance** use case.

Use Case: Control Resistance

Purpose: Provide variable resistance to the rider to simulate on-road riding experience for ad hoc and planned workouts in resistance mode. In ERG mode, the power output is held constant independent of simulated incline or pedal cadence.

Description: This use case provides variable resistance to rider pedaling depending on a number of factors. The first is gearing. As with on-road cycling, a larger gear ratio results in a higher torque required to turn the pedals. The user can select gears from the emulated gearing (see *Use Case: Emulate Gearing*) to change the amount of torque required to turn the pedals. Next, the user can set the "incline" of the bike. The incline adds or subtracts the torque required based on the effort it would take to cycle up or down an incline. Lastly, the base level can be set as a starting point from which the previous factors may offset. By default, this is set by the estimated rider effort on a zero-incline smooth grade. These are all factors in "resistance mode", in which the power output varies as a function of the cadence, gearing, and incline, as described previously. In ERG mode, the power is held constant regardless of these factors. ERG mode is intended to enforce power outputs independent of rider pedal cadence. The power level in ERG mode can be manually set by the user or externally set by a training application. In all modes, the power level can be controlled in the range of 0 to 2,000 W.

Now, let's consider the user stories contained within this use case:

User story: Provide Basic Resistance

> *As a rider, I want basic resistance provided to the pedals so I can get*
> *a workout with an on-road feel in resistance mode.*

This means that for a given gear ratio and simulated incline, the ride feels a smooth and consistent resistance to pedaling.

User story: Set Resistance under User Control

> *As a rider, I want to set the resistance level provided to the pedals*
> *to increase or decrease the effort for a given gearing, cadence, and incline*
> *to simulate road riding.*

User story: Set Resistance under External Control

> *As a rider, I want the external training app to set the resistance to follow*
> *the app's workout protocol to get the desired workout.*

User story: ERG Mode

> *As a rider, I want to pedal at constant power regardless of variations in*
> *simulated terrain, cadence, or gearing to follow the prescribed power*
> *settings for their workout protocol.*

The other use cases and user stories will be similarly detailed. Refer to the recipes in *Chapter 2, System Specification*, for more details on use cases and user stories.

The team votes via planning poker for the efforts for each of these elements, negotiating when there is no agreement, until consensus on the efforts is reached. *Table 1.8* shows the results:

| Work Item Type | | | | |
Epic	Work Item Use Case	Work Item User Story	Spike or Technical Work Item	Job Size (User Story Points)
			Spike: Team availability	2
			Spike: Aggressive schedule	3
			Spike: Agile MBSE impact	3
Resist	Control resistance	Provide basic resistance		55
			Spike: Motor response lag time	8
			Spike: Robustness of main motor	5
Set up physical bike	Set up bike fit	Adjust seat height		3
Set up physical bike	Set up bike fit	Adjust seat reach		3
		Calibrate power output		8
Emulate gearing	Emulate front and rear gearing			34
Emulate gearing	Emulate mechanical gearing			34
Emulate gearing	Emulate basic gearing			89
Set up physical bike	Manually adjust bike fit			13

Epic	Work Item Use Case	Work Item User Story	Spike or Technical Work Item	Job Size (User Story Points)
Set up physical bike	Set up bike fit	Adjust handlebar height		3
Set up physical bike	Set up bike fit	Adjust handlebar reach		3
Monitor ride metrics		Monitor power		13
Monitor ride metrics		Monitor speed		5
Monitor ride metrics		Monitor distance		5
Monitor ride metrics		Monitor cadence		5
Communicate with apps	Communicate bluetooth low energy			34
Set up physical bike	Set up bike fit	Select crank length		5
Resist	Control resistance	Set resistance under rider control		21
Configure bike for rider	Connect personal data to app			21
Set up physical bike	Estimate bike fit with external parameters	Compute fit from professional fit data		1
Monitor ride metrics		Monitor incline		8
Communicate with Apps	Communicate with ANT+			34
Communicate with apps	Communicate with ANT FEC			55
Set up physical bike	Estimate bike fit with external parameters	Load GURU bike fit data		13
Set up physical bike	Estimate bike fit with external parameters	Load trek bike fit data		13

Epic	Work Item Use Case	Work Item User Story	Spike or Technical Work Item	Job Size (User Story Points)
Resist	Control resistance	ERG mode		55
	Manage personal data			5
Set up physical bike	Predict bike fit with camera image	Access camera image		2
Set up physical bike	Predict bike fit with camera image	Retrieve road bike dimensions from camera image		5
Set up physical bike	Predict bike fit with camera image	Compute fit parameters from road bike dimensions		2
Resist	Control resistance	Set resistance under external control		39
Emulate gearing	Emulate DI2 gearing			55
			Spike: USB robustness	5

Table 1.8 – Story point estimates for work items

Work item prioritization

This recipe is about the prioritization of work items in a backlog. There is some confusion as to the meaning of the term *priority*. Priority is a ranking of when some task should be performed with respect to other tasks. There are a variety of factors that determine priority and different projects may weight such factors differently. The most common factors influencing priority are as follows:

- Cost of delay: The cost of delaying the performance of the work item, which in turn is influenced by the following:

  a. Criticality: The importance associated with completing the work item

  b. Urgency: When the outcome or output of the work item completion is due

  c. Usefulness: The value to the outcome of the work item to the stakeholder

  d. Risk: How the completion of the work item affects the project risk

- Opportunity enablement: How the completion of the work item will enable stakeholder opportunity

- Cost: The cost or effort required to complete the work item

- Sensical sequencing: The preconditions of the work item and what other work items depend upon the completion of this work item

- Congruency: The consistency of the work item to the mission of the iteration to which it is assigned

- Availability of resources: The resources, including specialized resources, that are needed in order to complete this work item and their availability

Some priority schemes will be dominated by urgency, while others may be dominated by criticality or resource availability. The bottom line is that work item priority determines to which iteration a work item will be allocated from the project backlog and to a lesser degree when, within an iteration, the work item will be performed.

Purpose

The purpose of work item prioritization is to intelligently plan the work so as to achieve the product goals in an incremental, consistent fashion. Specifically, the goal of work item prioritization is to allocate work items to the iteration backlogs in a satisfactory manner.

Inputs and preconditions

A product backlog is created.

Outputs and post conditions

Work items in the product backlog are prioritized so that iteration planning can proceed.

How to do it...

There are many ways to perform prioritization. Some, such as the **MoSCoW** method, are qualitative. In this approach, work items are categorized into the following four groups:

- **Must**: A requirement that must be satisfied in the final solution for the product to be considered a success

- **Should**: Represents a high-priority work item that should be included in the final solution if possible

- **Could**: A work item that is desirable but not necessary for success

- **Won't**: A work item that the stakeholders have agreed to not implement now, but that might be considered in a future release

Priority poker is another means by which priority may be assigned. Priority poker is similar to planning poker used to estimate the work item effort. Planning poker is discussed in more detail in the *Estimating effort* recipe, and so won't be discussed here.

This recipe outlines the use of a prioritization technique known as **Weighted Shortest Job First** (**WSJF**), as defined by the **Scaled Agile Framework** (**SAFe**). The basic formulation is shown in the following equation:

$$WSJF = \frac{Cost\ of\ delay}{Job\ Duration}$$

Formula 1.1 - Weighted Shortest Job First

The SAFe definition of the cost of delay is provided in *Formula 1.2* . This equation differs from the original SAFe formulation through the addition of a project value term:

$$Cost\ of\ delay = Business\ value + Project\ value + Time\ criticality$$
$$+ Risk\ reduction\ or\ Opportunity\ enablement$$

Formula 1.2 - Cost of Delay

> **Note**
>
> You can read more on WSJF here: `scaledagileframework.com/wsjf`

Business value is either criticality or usefulness to the stakeholders, or a combination of the two. Project value, the term I added to the formula, refers to the value to the project. For example, a reduction in technical debt may not add direct value to stakeholders, but does provide value to the project. Time criticality, also known as *urgency*, refers to when the feature provides value to the stakeholder. Risk reduction is an improvement in the likelihood of project success, while opportunity enablement refers to business opportunities, such as new markets, that a feature will enable.

> **Note**
>
> **Must**, **Should**, **Could**, **Won't** prioritization as described in International Institute of Business Analysis (IIBA) Business Analysis Body of Knowledge (BABOK) Guide, `www.iiba.org/babok-guide.aspx`.

Each of the aspects of cost of delay is scaled using values such as a Fibonacci sequence (1, 2, 3, 5, 8, 21, 34, 55. 89, 144, ...) with larger values indicative of higher costs of delay. Since these are all relative measures, the summation provides a good quantitative idea of the cost of delay. For a given job size, a higher cost of delay results in a higher priority. For a given cost of delay, a larger job size reduces the priority.

Job duration is difficult to estimate until you know the resource loading, so we normally substitute job cost for job duration. Job cost is the topic of the *Estimating effort* recipe. WSJF performs a good first stab at determining priority, but it needs to be adjusted manually to take into account congruency with iteration missions and specialized resource availability. The workflow is outlined in *Figure 1.24*:

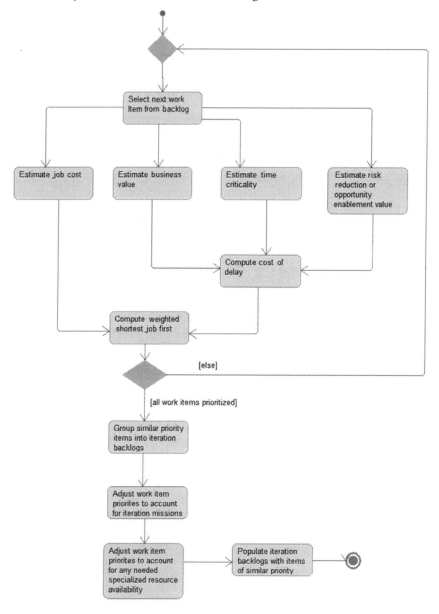

Figure 1.24 – Work item prioritization

Selecting the next work item from the backlog

Starting with the first work item, select the work item to prioritize.

Estimating the job cost

Estimate the cost of performing the work item. The details of how to do this are discussed in the *Estimating effort* recipe.

Estimating the business value

Whether you are considering the criticality of the work item or its usefulness, or both, estimate its business value. In this case, we are using relative measures with a Fibonacci sequence with the higher values corresponding to greater business value. Work items of similar business value should have the same value here.

Estimating time criticality

Estimate the time criticality of the work item, with more urgent work items having a higher value.

Estimating risk reduction or the opportunity enablement value

Estimate either the reduction of project risk or the enablement of business opportunity based on the approach taken in the previous two steps. Greater risk reduction or greater opportunity means higher value.

Computing the cost of delay

Compute the cost of delay as the sum of business value, time criticality, and risk reduction.

Computing the Weighted Shortest Job First

Compute WSJF as the cost of delay divided by the job cost.

Grouping similar priority items into the iteration backlog

The backlog for each iteration should contain elements of the same priority, depending on the availability of resources to perform the work. If there is capacity left over after allocating all elements of the same or similar priority, add work items from the next lowest priority. Similarly, if the accumulated cost of the set of work items of the same priority exceeds capacity, then move some to the next iteration backlog.

Adjusting work item priorities to account for iteration missions

Examine the work items for congruence to the mission of the iteration. If there is no congruence, then is there another iteration where the work item is more in line with the iteration purpose? If so, adjust the priority to match that of the more relevant iteration.

Adjusting work item priorities to adjust for any necessary specialized resource availability

Are there specialized resources required for the completion of a work item? This might be the availability of a **subject matter expert (SME)**, or the availability of computational or lab resources. Adjust the priority of work items to align with the availability of resources needed to accomplish the task.

Populating iteration backlogs with items of similar priority

Once the priorities have stabilized to account for all concerns, populate the iteration backlogs with the work items.

How it works...

Prioritization is the ranking of elements on the basis on their desired sequencing. There are many means for prioritization with varying degrees of rigor. I prefer the WSJF approach because it takes into account most of the important aspects that should affect priority, resulting in a quantitative measure of the cost of delay divided by the size of the job.

Figure 1.25 shows a graph of WSJF isoclines. All curves show how the resulting value of WSJF changes as the job size increases. Each separate curve represents a specific value for the cost of delay. You can see that the priority value diminishes rapidly as the size of the job grows. The practical effect of this is that higher-cost (in other words, higher-effort) tasks tend to be put off until later. Just be aware that this is a bit problematic. Since they require multiple iterations, there will be fewer iterations in which to schedule them:

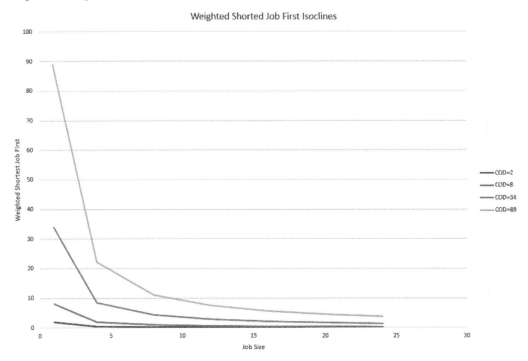

Figure 1.25 – WSJF isoclines

While this method is recommended by the SAFe literature, in practice, it must be modified so that you have congruence with the missions of the iterations. For example, it could happen that providing encrypted message transfer has a high WSJF value, while the creation of the base protocol stack has a lower value. Nevertheless, it makes no sense to work on the encryption design before you have a protocol in place over which the messages can be sent. Thus, you would likely raise the priority of the creation of the protocol stack and lower the priority of the encryption work to get "sensical sequencing." Encryption math can be quite complex and if the encryption SME isn't available for iteration 6, but is available for iteration 8, then it makes sense to adjust the priority of the encryption task to implement it when that expertise is available.

Example

Table 1.9 shows a worksheet that has a number of different kinds of work items, their previously estimated effort (job size), and the cost of delay terms. The spreadsheet sums up the terms to compute the **cost of delay (CoD)** column and then the **WSJF** column shows the computed WSJF value. The next column is the adjusted priority. This priority is generally the WSJF value, but some of these are adjusted to move the work item into an appropriate iteration. The last column shows in which iteration a work item is planned to be resolved:

	Work Item Type			Cost of Delay Terms						Priority		
Epic	Work Item Use Case	Work Item User Story	Spike or Technical Work Item	User Business Value	Project Value	Time Criticality	RR | OE	CoD	Job Size (user story points)	WSJF	Priority	Planned Iteration
			Spike: Team availability	1	55	1	21	78	2	39.00	39.00	0
			Spike: Aggressive schedule	1	1	34	34	70	3	23.33	23.33	0
			Spike: Agile MBSE impact	1	34	21	13	69	3	23.00	23.00	0
Resist	Control resistance	Provide basic resistance		55	1	21	1	78	55	1.42	1.42	1
			Spike: Motor response lag time	8	1	1	1	11	8	1.38	12.00	1
			Spike: Robustness of main motor	34	1	1	34	70	5	14.00	14.00	1
Set up physical bike	Set up bike fit	Adjust seat height		13	1	13	13	40	3	13.33	13.33	1
Set up physical bike	Set up bike fit	Adjust seat reach		13	1	8	13	35	3	11.67	11.67	2
		Calibrate power output		8	8	21	1	38	8	4.75	10.00	2
Emulate gearing	Emulate Front and rear gearing			34	1	21	1	57	34	1.68	19.00	2
Emulate gearing	Emulate mechanical gearing			21	1	21	1	44	34	1.29	10.00	2

Epic	Work Item Type / Work Item Use Case	Work Item User Story	Spike or Technical Work Item	Cost of Delay Terms / User Business Value	Project Value	Time Criticality	RR | OE	CoD	Job Size (user story points)	Priority / WSJF	Priority	Planned Iteration
Emulate gearing	Emulate basic gearing			34	1	34	1	70	89	0.79	10.00	2
Set up physical bike	Manually adjust bike fit			34	1	21	1	57	13	4.38	4.38	3
Set up physical bike	Set up bike fit	Adjust handlebar height		8	1	1	3	13	3	4.33	4.33	3
Set up physical bike	Set up bike fit	Adjust handlebar reach		5	1	1	3	10	3	3.33	3.33	3
Monitor ride metrics		Monitor power		34	1	1	1	37	13	2.85	2.85	3
Monitor ride metrics		Monitor speed		21	1	1	1	24	5	4.80	4.80	3
Monitor ride metrics		Monitor distance		21	1	1	1	24	5	4.80	4.80	3
			Spike: USB robustness	21	8	1	8	38	5	7.60	7.60	3
Monitor ride metrics		Monitor cadence		8	1	1	1	11	5	2.20	2.20	4
Communicate with apps	Communicate with low power Bluetooth			55	1	8	1	65	34	1.91	1.91	4
Set up physical bike	Set up Bike Fit	Select crank length		2	1	1	2	6	5	1.20	1.20	4
Resist	Control resistance	Set resistance under rider control		13	1	5	1	20	21	0.95	1.00	4
Configure bike for rider	Connect personal data to app			13	1	1	1	16	21	0.76	1.00	4
Set up physical bike	Estimate bike fit with external parameters	Compute fit from professional fit data		3	1	1	1	6	1	6.00	0.50	5
Monitor ride metrics		Monitor incline		13	1	1	1	16	8	2.00	0.50	5
Communicate with apps	Communicate with ANT+			34	1	5	1	41	34	1.21	0.50	5
Communicate with apps	Communicate with ANT FEC			34	1	13	1	49	55	0.89	0.89	5
Set up physical bike	Estimate bike fit with external parameters	Load GURU bike fit data		5	1	1	2	9	13	0.69	0.69	5
Set up physical bike	Estimate bike fit with external parameters	Load trek bike fit data		5	1	1	2	9	13	0.69	0.69	5

Epic	Work Item Type / Work Item Use Case	Work Item User Story	Spike or Technical Work Item	Cost of Delay Terms				CoD	Job Size (user story points)	Priority		Planned Iteration
				User Business Value	Project Value	Time Criticality	RR | OE			WSJF	Priority	
Resist	Control resistance	ERG mode		21	1	1	1	24	55	0.44	0.30	5
	Manage personal data			21	3	2	1	27	5	5.40	0.30	6
Set up physical bike	Predict bike fit with camera image	Access camera image		5	1	1	1	8	2	4.00	0.30	6
Set up physical bike	Predict bike fit with camera image	Retrieve road bike dimensions from camera image		8	1	1	1	11	5	2.20	0.30	6
Set up physical bike	Predict bike fit with camera image	Compute fit parameters from road bike dimensions		1	1	1	1	4	2	2.00	0.30	6
Resist	Control resistance	Set resistance under external control		21	1	5	1	28	39	0.72	0.30	6
Emulate gearing	Emulate DI2 gearing			13	1	5	1	20	55	0.36	0.30	6

Table 1.9 – Prioritized work items

Iteration 0

Iteration 0 refers to the work done before incremental development begins. This includes early product planning, getting the development team started up, setting up their physical and tooling environment, and making an initial architectural definition. All of this work is preliminary and most of it is expected to evolve over time as the project proceeds.

Purpose

The purpose of iteration 0 is to pave the way for the successful launch and, ultimately, the completion of the product.

Inputs and preconditions

The only inputs are the initial product and project concepts.

Outputs and post conditions

By the end of iteration 0, initial plans are in place and all that they imply for the product vision, the product roadmap, the release plan, and the risk management plan. This means that there is an initial product backlog developed by the end of iteration 0, at least enough that the next few iterations are scoped out. Iterations further out may be more loosely detailed but, as mentioned, their content will solidify as work progresses. Additionally, the team is selected and enabled with appropriate knowledge and skills to do the work, their physical environment is set up, and their tools and infrastructure are all in place. In short, the engineering team is ready to go in terms of developing the first increment and plans are in place to provide a project trajectory.

How to do it...

Iteration 0 is *the work that takes place before there is any work to do*. That is, it is the preparatory work that enables the team to deliver the product.

There are four primary areas of focus:

Focus	Work to be done	Outputs
Product	Create initial vision, product plan, and release plan	Product vision Product roadmap Release plan Risk management plan Initial product backlog
Team	Ready the team with the knowledge, skills, tools, and processes	Assembled team
Environment	Install, configure, and test tooling and workspaces	Team environment set up
Architecture	Define the initial high-level architecture with expectations of technology and design approaches	Architecture 0

Table 1.10 – Project focus areas

It is important not to try for high precision. Most traditional projects identify a final release date with a finalized budget, but these are often in error. It is better to plan by successive approximation. Realize that early on, the error in long-range forecasts is high because of things you do not know and because of things you know will change. As the project progresses, you gain knowledge of the product and the team's velocity, and so precision increases over time. These initial plans get the project started with a strong direction, but also with the expectations that those plans will evolve.

It is important to understand that you cannot do detailed planning in iteration 0 because you don't have a complete backlog and you haven't yet learned all the lessons the project has to teach you. That doesn't mean that you shouldn't do any planning; indeed, four of the outputs – the product vision, the product roadmap, the release plan, and the risk management plan – are all plans. However, they are all incorrect to some degree or other and those plans will require significant and ongoing modification, enhancement, and evolution. This is reflected in Douglass' Law #3:

Plan to replan.

> **Note**
>
> You can read more about The Laws of Douglass here: `https://www.bruce-douglass.com/geekosphere`.

We have discussed earlier in this chapter the product roadmap, the release plan, and the risk management plan. Their initial preparations are key ingredients to iteration 0. The workflow for iteration 0 is shown in *Figure 1.26*:

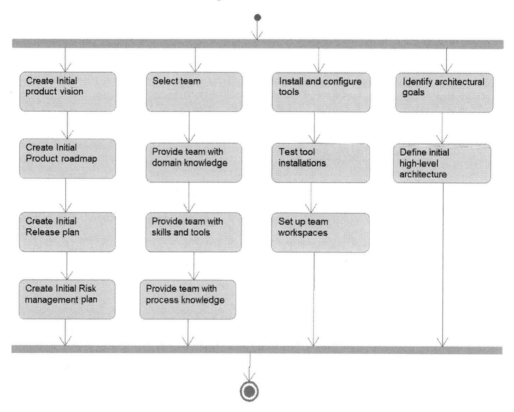

Figure 1.26 – Iteration 0

Creating an initial product vision

The product vision is a high-concept document regarding the product scope and purpose and the design approach to meet that purpose. It combines the company's business goals with the specific needs of the customer. It identifies how this product will differentiate itself from competing products and clarifies the value to both the company and the customers.

Creating an initial product roadmap

The product roadmap is a strategic plan that defines how the product will evolve over time. See the *Product roadmap* recipe in this chapter for further details.

Creating an initial release plan

The release plan is a tactical plan for how features will be developed in the next several product iteration cycles. The *Release plan* recipe discusses this in more detail.

Creating an initial risk management plan

The risk management plan is a strategic plan that identifies project risks and how and when they will be addressed by allocating spikes (experiments) during the iteration cycles. Refer to the *Managing risk* recipe for information on this plan.

Selecting the team

The team is the set of people who will collaborate on the development of the product. This includes engineers of various disciplines (systems, software, electronics, and mechanical, typically), testers, configuration managers, integrators, a product manager, and a process lead, sometimes known as a *scrum master*. There may be specialized roles as well, such as a safety czar, reliability czar, security czar, biomedical engineer, or aerospace engineer, depending on the product.

Providing the team with domain knowledge

Unless the team has prior experience in the domain, it will probably be useful to expose the team to the customer domain concepts and concerns. This will enable them to make better choices.

Providing the team with the requisite skills and tools

Any new technology, such as the use of Java or SysML, should be preceded by training and/or mentoring. The introduction of new tools, such as Jira for project tracking or Rhapsody for SysML modeling, should likewise involve training.

Providing the team with process knowledge

The team must understand the procedures and practices to be employed on the project to ensure good collaboration.

Installing and configuring tools

The tooling environment should be set up and ready for the team to use. This might include project enactment tools such as Rational Team Concert, in addition to modeling tools, compilers, editors, and so on.

Testing tool installations

This step verifies that the tools are properly installed and the infrastructure for the tools works. This is especially important in collaborative environments such as team clouds.

Setting up team workspaces

This action refers to the physical workspaces. It is common to co-locate teams where possible and this ensures that the teams have spaces where they can do individual "thought work", as well as collaborative spaces where they can work together.

Identifying architectural goals

Architecture, as we will see in the *Architecture 0* recipe, is the set of large-scale product organization and design optimization decisions. Goals for architectures are often focused around simplicity, understandability, testability, stability, extensibility, robustness, composability, safety, security, and performance. Frequently, these properties are in conflict; something easy to understand may not be scalable, for example. Thus, the architectural goals identify the relative importance of the goals with respect to the success of the project and the product.

Defining initial high-level architecture

This action defines the high-level architecture, congruent with the architectural goals identified in the previous step. This is known as Architecture 0, the subject of the *Architecture 0* recipe.

Example

For the example problem outlined in *Appendix A*, the roadmap, release plan, risk management plan, and Architecture 0 are developed in other recipes in this chapter and need not be repeated here. The other aspects are discussed here, however.

Creating an initial product vision and initial product roadmap

The initial product vision and roadmap are discussed in more detail in the *Product roadmap* recipe.

Creating the initial release plan

The release plan is discussed in more detail in the *Release plan* recipe.

Creating the initial risk management plan

The risk management plan is discussed in more detail in the *Managing risk* recipe.

Selecting the team

In our project, we select the systems, software, electronics, and mechanical engineers for the project. The team consists of 3 systems engineers, 2 mechanical engineers, 3 electronics engineers, and 10 software engineers. They will all be co-located on the fourth floor of the company's building. Each will have an individual office and there are two conference rooms allocated to the team.

Providing the team with domain knowledge

To provide the team with domain understanding, we bring in SMEs to discuss how they train themselves and others. The SMEs include professionals, personal trainers, and amateur cyclists and triathletes. Members of the focus group lead the team through some workouts on existing trainers to give them an understanding of what is involved in different kinds of training sessions. Some classwork sessions are provided as well to give the team members a basic understanding of the development and enactment of training plans, including the periodization of training, tempo workouts versus polarized training, and so on.

Installing and configuring tools

In addition to standard office tools, several engineering tools are installed and configured for the project:

- Systems engineers will use DOORS Next Generation for requirements, Rhapsody for SysML, and Cywin C++ for simulation, along with the Rhapsody Model Manager.

- Mechanical engineers will use AutoCAD for their mechanical designs.

- Electronics engineers will use SystemC for discrete simulation and Allegro Cadence for their designs.

- Software engineers will use Rhapsody for UML and code generation and Cygwin for C++, along with the Rhapsody Model Manager.

- The collaboration environment will use the Jazz framework with Rational Team Concert for project planning and enactment.

Testing tool installations

The IT department verifies that all the tools are properly installed, and can load, modify, and save sample work products from each. Specific interchanges between DOORS and Rhapsody are verified on the Jazz platform, and the Rhapsody Model Manager can successfully store and retrieve models.

Providing the team with the requisite skills and tools

The team has the following tasks:

- System engineers will receive week-long training on Rhapsody and SysML.

- Software engineers will receive week-long training on Rhapsody and UML.

- All engineers have used DOORS before and require no additional training.

Providing the team with process knowledge

The team will use the Harmony aMBSE process and the team will attend a 3-day workshop on the process. In addition, *A Priori Systems* will provide Agile and modeling mentoring for the team through at least the first four iterations.

Setting up team workspaces

Each engineer is provided with a configured computer connected to the company's network and can connect to the local Jazz team server to access the Jazz tooling – Rhapsody, DOORS Next Generation, Rational Team Concert, and Rhapsody Model Manager. It has the following tasks:

- Identify architectural goals.
- Define initial high-level architecture.

Both of these actions are discussed in more detail in the *Architecture 0* recipe.

Architecture 0

Architecture 0 is the set of strategic design optimization decisions for the system. Many different architectures can meet the same functional needs. What distinguishes them is their optimization criteria. One architecture may optimize worst case performance, while another may optimize extensibility and scalability, and yet another may optimize safety, all while meeting the same functional needs.

The Harmony process identifies five key views of architecture:

- **Subsystem and component view**: This view focuses on the largest scale pieces of the system, as well as their organization, relations, responsibilities, and interfaces.

- **Concurrency and resource view**: This view focuses on the concurrency units and management of resources within the system. Processes, tasks, threads, and the means for safely sharing resources across those boundaries are the primary concerns of this view.

- **Distribution view**: This view focuses on how collaboration occurs between different computational nodes within the system and how the subsystems share information and collaboration. Communication protocols and middleware make up the bulk of this view.

> **Note**
> Refer to the *Real-Time Agility* book for more details on the five key views of architecture.

- **Dependability view**: The three pillars of dependability are freedom from harm (safety), the availability of services (reliability), and protection against attack (security).

- **Deployment view**: Generally, subsystems are interdisciplinary affairs, consisting of some combination of software, electronic, and mechanical aspects. This view is concerned with the distribution of responsibility among the implementation of those disciplines (called *facets*) and the interfaces that cross engineering disciplinary boundaries.

Some recommendations for architecture in Agile-developed systems are shown in *Figure 1.27*:

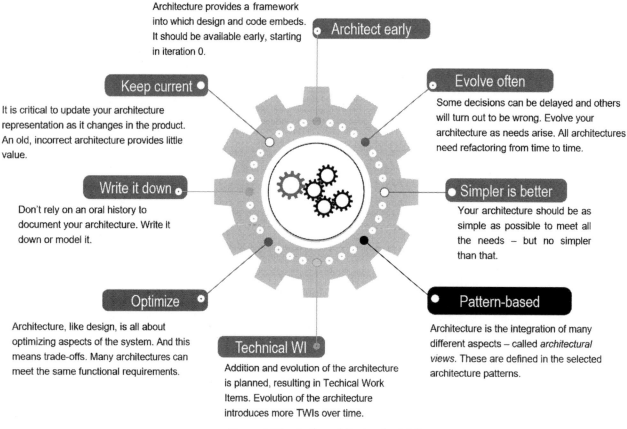

Figure 1.27 – Agile architectural guidelines

Purpose

Because architecture provides, among other things, the large-scale organization of design elements, as engineers develop those design elements, Architecture 0 provides a framework into which those elements fit. It is fully expected that Architecture 0 is minimalist, and therefore incomplete. It is expected that the architecture will change and evolve through the development process, but it is an initial starting point.

Inputs and preconditions

A basic idea of the functionality and use of the system is necessary to develop the initial architectural concept. Thus, the preconditions for the development of Architecture 0 are the product vision and at least a high-level view of the epics, use cases, and user stories of the system.

Outputs and post conditions

The output is a set of architecture optimization criteria and an initial set of concepts from the different architectural views. This may be textual, but I strongly recommend this to be in the form of a SysML architectural model. This model may have a number of different diagrams showing different aspects of the architecture. It is common, for example, to have one or more diagrams for each architectural view. In Architecture 0, many of these will be missing and will be elaborated as the project proceeds.

How to do it...

Architecture 0 is an incomplete, minimalist set of architectural concepts. Some thought is given to architectural aspects that will be given later, if only to assure ourselves that they can be integrated smoothly when they are developed. Again, it is expected that the architecture will be elaborated, expanded, and refactored as the product progresses. *Figure 1.28* shows the basic workflow:

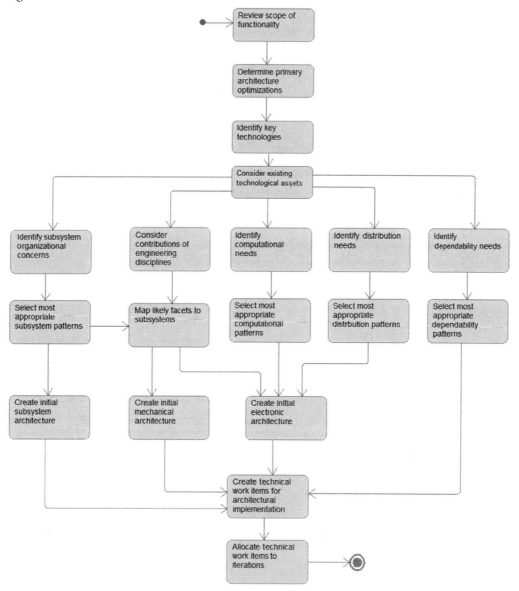

Figure 1.28 – Architecture 0

Reviewing the scope of functionality

Determining primary architectural optimizations

Selecting a design is an exercise in balancing competing optimization concerns. This step identifies and ranks the most important architectural considerations, such as worst-case performance, average performance, bandwidth, throughput, scalability, extensibility, maintainability, manufacturability, testability, and certifiability, to name a few.

Identifying key technologies

It is common that one or more key technological ideas dominate the vision of the product. Electric cars, for example, have electric motors and electronic means to power them. While not overly constraining the solutions here, it is important to at least identify the key technologies to constrain the solution space.

Considering existing technological assets

Unless this is the very first time an organization has developed a given type of product, there is likely some "prior art" that should be considered for inclusion in the new product. The benefits and costs can be considered of employing the organization's existing technological intellectual property versus creating something entirely new.

Identifying subsystem organizational concerns

Subsystems are the largest-scale pieces of the system and thus serve as the primary organization units holding elements of designs from downstream engineering. This step considers the pros and cons of different subsystem allocations and organizations. A good subsystem should offer the following benefits:

- **Coherence**: It provides a small number of services.
- **Internally tightly coupled**: Highly co-dependent elements should generally reside in the same subsystem.
- **Externally loosely coupled**: Subsystems should stand on their own with their responsibilities, but collaborate in well-defined ways with other subsystems.
- **Collaboration with interfaces**: The ability to interact with other subsystems in well-defined ways with a small number of interfaces.

Considering the contributions of engineering disciplines

The aspects of a design from a single engineering discipline are called a *facet*. There will typically be software facets, electronic facets, mechanical facets, hydraulic facets, pneumatic facets, and so on. The set of facets and their interactions is known as the *deployment architecture*, an important view of the system architecture. Early on, there may be sufficient information for engaging engineers of these disciplines and giving consideration to how they are likely to contribute to the overall design.

Identifying computational needs

Computational needs affect both software and electronics disciplines. If the system is an embedded system – the primary case considered in this book – then the computational hardware must be selected or developed with the particular system in mind. These decisions can have a huge impact on performance and the ability of the software to deliver computational functionality. The software architectural concerns of the selection of thread models is not considered here, as it is solely a software concern. Nevertheless, the system must have adequate computational resources and early estimates must be made to determine the number and type of CPUs and memory.

Identifying distribution needs

Networks such as 1553 or CAN buses and other connection technologies, as well as possible middleware choices, including AUTOSAR, CORBA, and DDS, are the focus of this step.

Identifying dependability needs

This step is crucial for safety-critical, high-reliability, or high-security systems. The initial concepts for managing dependability concerns must be considered early for such high dependability systems and may be saved for later iterations for systems in which these are of minimal concern.

Selecting the most appropriate subsystem patterns

There are many organizational schemes for subsystem architecture, such as the layered pattern, microkernel pattern, and channel pattern that provide different optimizations.

Mapping likely facets to subsystems

Facets are the contributions to an overall design from specific engineering disciplines, such as software, electronics, and mechanical engineering. We recommend that subsystem teams are interdisciplinary and contain engineers from all relevant disciplines. This step is focused on early concept deployment architecture only.

Selecting the most appropriate computational patterns

Computational patterns concentrate on proposed computational approaches. While largely a software concern, electronics plays a key role in delivering adequate computation power and resources. This is especially relevant when the computation approach is considered a key technology, as it is for autonomous learning systems, or easy-to-certify cyclic executives for safety-critical systems.

Selecting the most appropriate distribution patterns

There are many ways to wire together distributed computing systems with networks, buses, and other communication links, along with supporting middleware. This architectural view focuses on that aspect of the system design. This impacts not just the software, but the electronic and, to a lesser degree, the mechanical designs.

Selecting the most appropriate dependability patterns

Different patterns support different kinds of optimizations for safety, reliability, and security concerns. If these aspects are crucial, they may be added to Architecture 0 rather than leaving them for later design. Deciding to *make the product safe/reliable/secure* late in the development cycle is a recipe for project failure.

Creating an initial subsystem architecture

This aspect is crucial for the early design work so that the design elements have a place to be deployed. Subsystems that are not needed for early iterations can be more lightly sketched out than ones that are important for the early increments.

Creating an initial mechanical architecture

The initial mechanical architecture provides a framework for the development of physical structures, wiring harnesses, and moving mechanical parts.

Creating an initial electronics architecture

The initial electronics architecture provides a framework for the development of both the analog electronics, such as power management, motors, and actuators, as well as the digital electronics, including sensors, networks, and computational resources.

Creating technical work items for architectural implementation

A skeletal framework for the architecture is provided in Architecture 0, but beyond this architectural implementation, work results in technical work items that are placed in the backlog for development in upcoming iterations.

Allocating technical work items to iterations

Initial allocation of the technical work items is done to support the product roadmap and, if available, the release plan. These elements may be reallocated later as the missions of the iterations evolve.

Example

Reviewing the scope of functionality

The Pegasus is a high-end smart cycling trainer that provides fine-grained control over bike fit, the high-fidelity simulation of road feel, structured workouts, and interactions with popular online training apps. Read the contents of the *Appendix* to review the functionality of the system.

Determining the primary architectural optimizations

The primary optimization concerns are determined to be the following:

- **Recurring costs**: The costs per shipped item.
- **Robustness**: The maintenance effort and the cost of ownership should be low.
- **Controllability**: Fine-grained control of power over a broad range.
- **Enhanceability**: The ability to upgrade via OTA to add new sensors, capabilities, and training platforms is crucial.

Identifying key technologies

There are a number of key technologies crucial to the acceptance and success of the system:

- Bluetooth Low Energy (BLE) smart capabilities for interacting with common sensors and app-hosting clients (Windows, iPad, iPhone, and Android)

- ANT+ for connecting to common sensors

- IEEE 802.11 wireless networking

- Electronic motors to provide resistance

Considering existing technological assets

This is a new product line for the company and so there are no relevant technological assets.

Identifying subsystem organizational concerns

To improve manufacturability, we want to internalize cabling as well as minimize the number of wires. This means that we would like to co-locate the major electronics components to the greatest degree possible. However, user controls must be placed within convenient reach. Care must also be taken for adequate electric shock protection as users are likely to expose the system to corrosive sweat.

Selecting the most appropriate subsystem patterns

We select the *Hierarchical Control Pattern* and *Channel Pattern* as the most applicable for our systems architecture.

> **Note**
>
> You can read more on the *Hierarchical Control Pattern* and *Channel Pattern* here: *Real-Time Design Patterns, Addison-Wesley, by Bruce Powel Douglass, 2003.*

Creating an initial subsystem architecture

Figure 1.29 shows the operational context of the Pegasus Indoor Training Bike. This is captured in a **Block Definition Diagram (BDD)** in the architectural design package of the model:

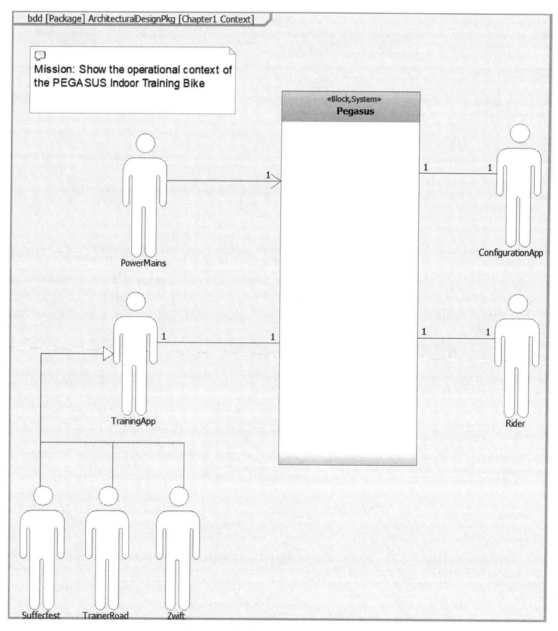

Figure 1.29 – Pegasus context diagram

Next, *Figure 1.30* shows the set of subsystems. This diagram is like a high-level parts list and is very common in system designs in SysML:

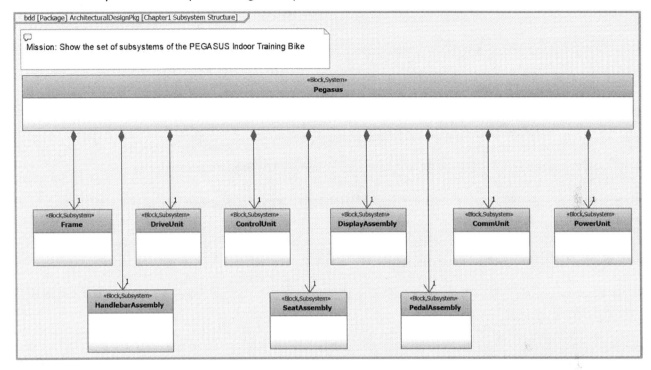

Figure 1.30 – Pegasus subsystems

Perhaps more interesting is *Figure 1.31*, which shows how the subsystems connect to one another on an **Internal Block Diagram (IBD)**. This is also a commonly used architectural view in SysML models. Specifically, this diagram shows the primary functional or dynamic interfaces.

I follow a convention in my architectural models in which dynamic connections – that is, ones that support runtime continuous or discrete flow – use ports, but static connections, such as when parts are bolted together, are shown using connectors with the «static» stereotype. I find this a useful visual distinction in my systems architecture diagrams.

Thus, the relation between the **Frame** and the **Drive Unit** is an association, but the relation between the **Pedal Assembly** and the **Drive Unit** employs a pair of ports, as there are runtime flows between the pedals and the drive motor during system operation:

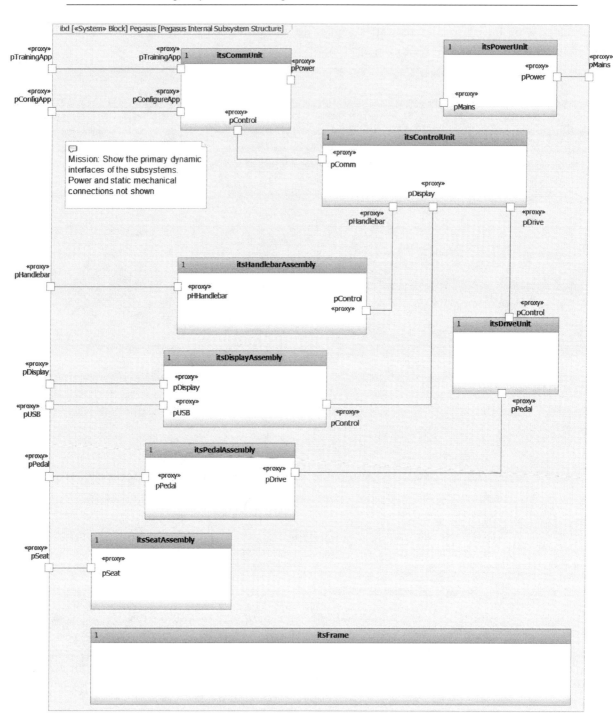

Figure 1.31 – Pegasus connected architecture – primary dynamic interfaces

Considering the contributions of engineering disciplines

The electronics will provide the interfaces to the user for control of the trainer as well as physical protocols for app communication. It will also provide the resistance via the application of torque from the electronic motor.

The mechanical design will provide the bike frame and all the bike fit adjustments. The pedals will accept torque from the user and provide resistance to applied force via the crank arms. Additionally, the weighted flywheel will smooth out resistance under load by providing an inertial load. Finally, mechanical design will provide all the cable routing.

The software will provide the "smarts" and use the electronics to receive and process user input from controls and inputs from connected apps, as well as from the pedals. The software will also be responsible for messages to the apps for measured sensor data.

Mapping likely facets to subsystems

Facets, you will remember, are the contributions engineering disciplines make to the system design. *Table 1.10* shows the initial concept for mapping the engineering facets to the subsystem architecture. This will result, eventually, in a full deployment architecture, but for now it just highlights our current thinking about how the work from the engineering disciplines will map to the subsystems:

Subsystem	Mechanical	Electronics	Software
Frame	Mechanical only		
Handlebar Assembly	Mechanical only		
Drive Unit	Housing for motor, flywheel, and drive train	Motor electronics	Discrete outputs from control unit software (SW) controlled
Control Unit	Cabling and mounting	Primary CPU, memory, and electronic resources for SW, persistence storage for SW	Control motor, process incoming sensor and power data, process communications with apps, OTA updates
Seat Assembly	Mechanical only		
Display Assembly	Cabling and mounting	Display and buttons, USB connectors (future expansion)	User I/O management, USB interface support
Pedal Assembly	Crank arms, LOOK-compatible shoe mount, connects to drive train	Power sensor in the pedal assembly	Discrete inputs to SW in control unit
Comm Unit	Cabling and mounting	802.11, Bluetooth (BLE) Smart, ANT+	SW in control unit controls and mediates communications, from sensors and external apps
Power Unit	Cabling and mounting	Converts wall power to internal power and distributes where needed	

Table 1.11 – Initial deployment architecture

Identifying computational needs

At a high level, the primary computational needs are as follows:

- To receive and process commands to vary the resistance, either from internal loads, user inputs, or app control
- To actively control the resistance provided by the motor
- To monitor connected Bluetooth and ANT+ sensors, such as from heart rate straps
- To send sensor data to connected apps
- To update the user display when necessary
- To perform OTA updates

Selecting the most appropriate computational patterns

An asymmetric dual processor architecture is selected with a single primary CPU in the control unit and a secondary processor to manage communications.

Identifying distribution needs

All communication needs will be performed by a (proposed) 16-bit communication processor housed in the comm unit; all other SW processing will be performed by the control unit on the primary CPU.

Selecting the most appropriate distribution patterns

To facilitate timely distribution of information within the system, an internal serial interface, such as RS232, is deemed adequate.

Identifying dependability needs

The primary safety concern is electric shock caused by faulty wiring, wear, or corrosion. Reliability needs focus on resistance to corrosion due to sweat, and the durability of the main drive motor. Security is determined to not be a significant concern.

Selecting the most appropriate dependability patterns

The single-channel protected pattern is selected as the most appropriate.

Creating an initial electronics architecture

The power interfaces are shown in *Figure 1.32*:

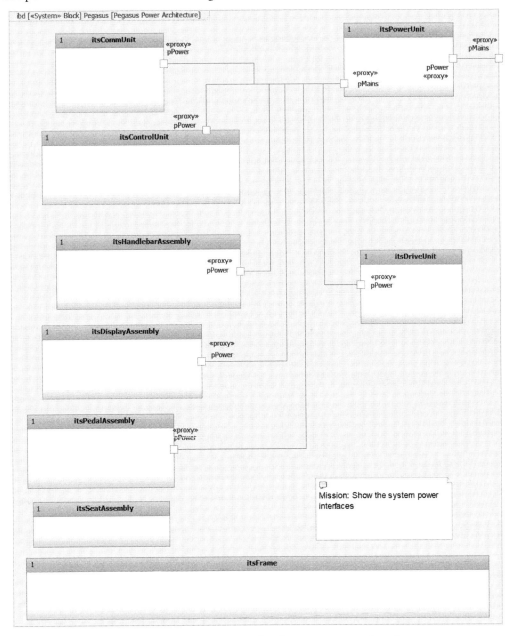

Figure 1.32 – Pegasus connected architecture – power interfaces

In addition, the drive unit hosts the primary motor to provide resistance to pedaling.

Creating an initial mechanical architecture

The internal mechanical connections are shown in *Figure 1.33*:

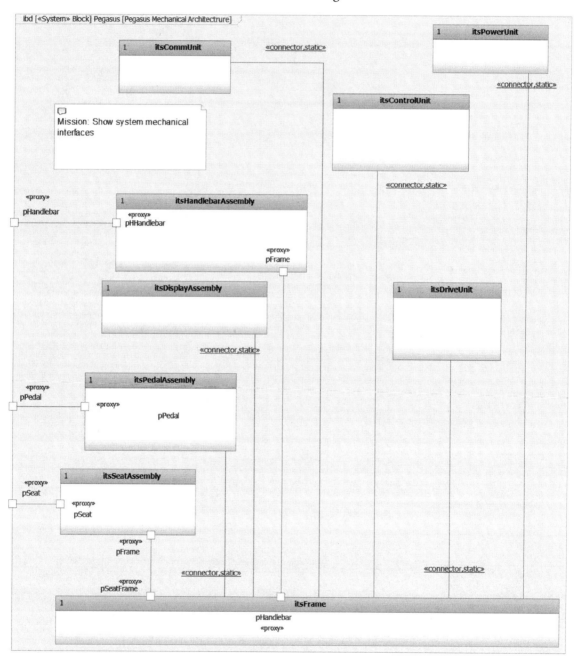

Figure 1.33 – Pegasus connected architecture – mechanical interfaces

The seat and handlebars are adjustable by the user and pedals can be added or removed, and there is a spot provided for the rider to *clip in* when they get on the bike. Thus, these connections use ports. The other connections are places where pieces are bolted together and do not vary during operation, except under catastrophic mechanical failure, so connectors represent these connections.

Creating technical work items for the architectural implementation

We identify the following technical work items in Architecture 0:

Mechanical technical work items:

- CAD frame design
- Hand-built frame
- Factory-built frame

Electronic technical work items:

- Motor simulation platform
- Hand-built motor
- Factory-built motor electronics
- CPU selection
- Simulated digital electronics platform
- Hand-built digital electronics platform
- Factory-built digital electronics platform

Allocating technical work items to the iterations

Allocation of such technical work items is discussed in detail in the *Iteration plan* recipe.

Additional note

Note that this is not a fully fleshed-out architecture. We know that in principle, for example, the pedals and the drive unit have flows between them because the pedals must provide more resistance when the main motor is producing greater resistance, but we don't yet know if this is a mechanical power flow, perhaps via a chain, or an electronic flow or discrete software messages to active resistance motors at the site of the pedals. I did add a power interface to the **Pedal Assembly**. If it turns out that it isn't needed, it can be removed. That's a job for later iterations to work out.

I also didn't attempt to detail the interfaces – again, deferring that for later iterations. But I did add the ports and connectors to indicate the architectural intent. That is why the default **StubInterfaceBlock** (provided by default by Rhapsody) is shown as the proxy port type in the diagrams.

Organizing your models

Packages are the principal mechanism for organizing models. In fact, a *model* is just a kind of package in the underlying SysML metamodel. Different models used for different purposes are likely to be organized in different ways. This recipe focuses on models for systems engineering to specifically support requirements capture, use case and requirements analysis, architectural trade studies, architectural design, and the handoff of relevant systems model data to the subsystem teams. In this recipe, we create not only the systems model, but the federation of models used in systems engineering.

Purpose

Good organization is surprisingly important. The reasons for this include the following:

- Group information to facilitate access and use.

- Support concurrent model use by different team members performing different tasks.

- Serve as the basis for configuration management.

- Allow for relevant portions of models to be effectively reused.

- Support team collaboration on common model elements.

- Allow for the independent building, simulation, and verification of model aspects.

Inputs and preconditions

The product vision and purpose is the primary input for the systems engineering model. The handoff model is created once the architecture is stable for the iteration and is the primary input for the subsequent shared model and subsystem models.

Outputs and post conditions

The outputs are the shells of the systems, shared, and subsystem models. The systems model is populated with the system requirements, if they exist. The shared model is initially populated with (references to) the system requirements, (logical) system interfaces, and a (logical) data schema from the systems model. A separate subsystem model is created for each subsystem and is initially populated with a reference to its subsystem requirements from the systems model, and the physical interfaces and data schema from the shared model.

How to do it...

Figure 1.34 is the workflow for creating and organizing the systems model. By the end, you'll have logical places for the MBSE work, and your team will be able to work more or less independently on their portions of the effort:

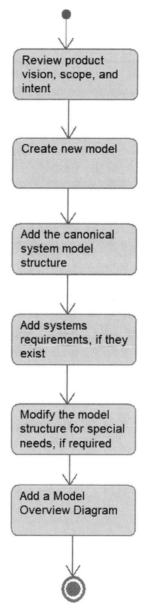

Figure 1.34 – Organizing the systems engineering model

Reviewing the product vision, scope, and intent

Every product has a vision that includes its scope and intent. Similarly, every model you create has a scope, purpose, and level of precision. A model's scope determines what goes into the model and what is outside of it. A common early failure of modeling happens when you don't have a well-defined purpose for a model.

The purpose of the model is important because it determines the perspective of the model. George Box is famously attributed the quote "All models are wrong, but some are useful." What I believe this means is that *every model is an abstraction of reality*. A model fundamentally represents information useful to the purpose of the model and ignores system properties that are not useful. The purpose of the model, therefore, determines what aspects of the product and its context will be represented and how.

The level of precision of the model is something often overlooked but is also important. It is too often the case that you will see requirements such as the following:

The aircraft will adjust the rudder control surface to ±30 degrees.

That's fine as far as it goes, but what does it mean to achieve a value of +15 degrees? Is 14.5 degrees close enough? How about 14.9? 14.999? How quickly will the position of the rudder be adjusted? If it took a minute, would that be OK? Maybe 1.0 second? 100 ms? The degree to which you care about how close is "close enough" is the precision of the model and different needs have different levels of required precision.

The bottom line is, know *what* you are modeling, *why* you are modeling it, and *how close to reality* you must come to achieve the desired value from your model. In this case, the model is of the requirements, their analyses, supporting analyses leading to additional requirements, and the architecture structure.

Creating a new model

In whatever tool you are using, create a blank, empty model.

Adding the canonical system model structure

This is the key step for this recipe. The author has consulted on literally hundreds of systems engineering projects over the years and the **Subsystem Model** organization shown in *Figure 1.35* has emerged as a great starting point. You may well make modifications, but this structure is so common that I call it the *system canonical organization*. It serves the purpose of MBSE well:

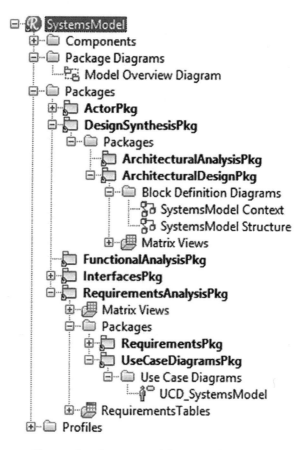

Figure 1.35 – Systems model canonical structure

The main categories in *Figure 1.35* are packages that will hold the modeled elements and data. The main packages are the following:

- **Actor Package**: This package holds the actors – elements that represent objects that interact with the system in ways that you care about.

- **Design Synthesis Package**: This holds all design-related information for the systems model.

- **Architectural Analysis Package**: This holds architectural analyses, such as trade studies, usually in one nested package per analysis.

- **Architectural Design Package**: This holds the architectural design, the system and subsystem blocks, and their relations. Later in the process, it will hold the subsystem specifications, one (nested) package per subsystem.

- **Functional Analysis Package**: This holds the use case analyses, one (nested) package per use case analyzed.

- **Interfaces Package**: This holds the logical system and subsystem interfaces as well as the logical data schema for data and flows passed via those interfaces.

- **Requirements Analysis Package**: This holds all the requirements information.

- **Requirements Package**: This holds the requirements, either directly (most common) or as remote resources in the Jazz environment.

- **Use Case Diagrams Package**: This holds the system use cases and use case diagrams.

Note that while this organization is labeled *canonical*, it is common to have minor variants to the structure.

Adding systems requirements, if they exist

It is not uncommon that you're handed an initial set of system requirements. If so, they can be imported or referenced. If they are added later, this is where they go.

Modifying the model structure for special needs, if required

You may identify special tasks or model information that you need to account for, so it's OK to add additional packages as needed.

Adding a model overview diagram

I like every model to contain a *model overview diagram*. This diagram is placed at the "outermost level" and serves as a brief introduction to the model purpose, content, and organization. It commonly has hyperlinks to tables and diagrams of particular interest. The lower left-hand corner of *Figure 1.36* has a comment with hyperlinks to important diagrams and tables located throughout the model. This aids model understanding and navigation, especially in large and complex models:

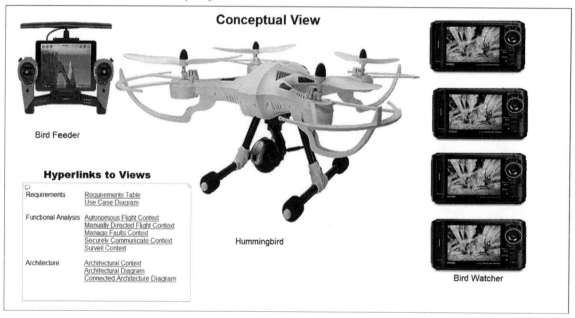

Aviary System of Systems Model Overview

This model is an overview of the Aviary Enterprise system which consists of 3 parts, each of which is detailed in its own, unconnected, model:

- Hummingbird - done aircraft
- Bird Feeder - Pilot controller
- Bird Watcher - independent video stream viewer

This model, however, is solely focused on the SoS structure. It does identify the primary systems which compose it, but that is as far as it goes. For more detail on the individual systems, see the model for the corresponding element.

Figure 1.36 – Example model overview diagram

Once systems engineering work is complete and the time arrives to hand off to downstream engineering, more models must be created. In this case, the input is the systems model, and the output is the shared model and a set of subsystem models. The shared model contains information common to more than one subsystem – specifically the physical system and subsystem interfaces and the corresponding physical data schema used by those interfaces. The details in terms of elaborating upon these models are provided in greater detail in *Chapter 4, Handoff to Downstream Engineering,* but their initial construction is shown in *Figure 1.37*:

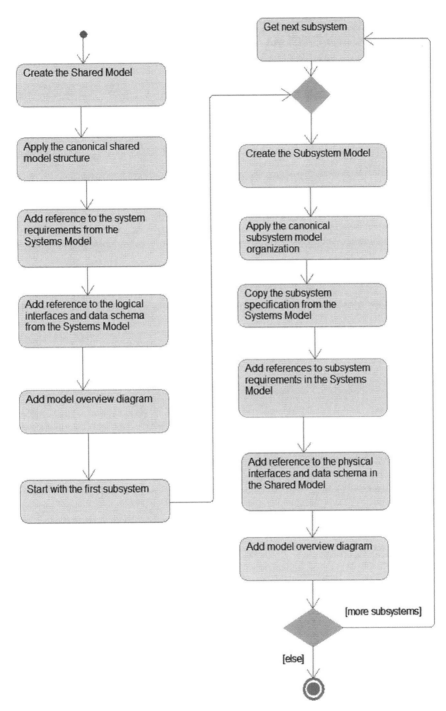

Figure 1.37 – Organizing the shared and subsystem models

Creating the shared model

This task creates an empty **Shared Model**. This model will hold the information shared by more than one subsystem; that is, each subsystem model will have a reference to these common interface and data definitions and elements.

Applying the canonical shared model structure

The purpose of the shared model is two-fold. First, using the logical interfaces and data schema as a starting point, derive the physical interfaces and data schema, a topic of *Chapter 4, Handoff to Downstream Engineering*. Secondly, the **Shared Model** serves as a common repository for information shared by multiple subsystems. The organization shown in *Figure 1.38* does precisely that:

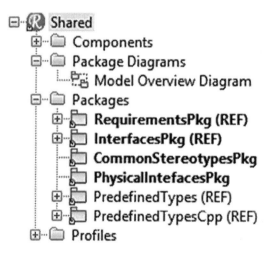

Figure 1.38 – Shared model canonical structure

The **Requirements** and **Interfaces** packages in *Figure 1.38* reference the systems model packages of the same name. In this way, those elements are visible to support the work in the shared model. The **Physical Interfaces** package holds the physical interfaces and data schema to be used by the subsystems. The **Common Stereotypes** package holds stereotypes that are either used in the **Physical Interfaces** package or are created for multiple subsystems to use.

Adding references to the system requirements

As shown in the preceding screenshot, the **Requirements** package of the systems model is referenced so that the requirements are available to view, but also so that the physical interfaces and data schema can trace to them, so as to provide a full traceability record.

Adding references to the logical interfaces and data schema

The logical interfaces and related logical data schema specify logical properties of those elements without specifying physical implementation details. The *Creating the logical data schema* recipe from *Chapter 2, System Specification,* goes into the creation of those elements. By referencing these elements in the shared model, the engineer has visibility of them but can also create trace links from the physical interfaces and data schema to them.

Adding a model overview diagram

As in the systems model organization, every model should have a model overview diagram to serve as a table of contents and introduction to the model.

Creating the subsystem model

Commonly, each subsystem has its own interdisciplinary team, so the creation of a subsystem model per subsystem provides each team with a modeling workspace for their efforts.

Applying the canonical subsystem model organization

Figure 1.39 shows the canonical organization of a subsystem model. Remember that each subsystem team has their own, with the same basic organization:

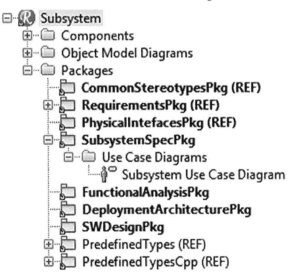

Figure 1.39 – Subsystem model canonical structure

The **Common Stereotypes** and **Physical Interfaces** packages are referenced from the shared model, while the **Requirements** package is referenced from the systems model.

We would like to think that the requirements and use cases being handed down to the subsystem team are perfect; however, experience shows us that we would be wrong. First, there may be additional elaboration work necessary at the subsystem level to understand those subsystem requirements. Furthermore, discipline-specific requirements must be derived from the subsystem requirement so that the electronics, mechanical, and software engineers clearly understand what they need to do. That work is held in the **Subsystem Spec** package. If we create additional, more detailed, use cases, they will be analyzed in the **Functional Analysis** package in the same way that the system use cases are analyzed in the systems model.

The **Deployment Architecture** package is where the identification of the facets and the allocation of responsibilities to the engineering disciplines takes place. To be clear, this package does not detail the internal structure of the facets; the electronics architecture, for example, is not depicted in this package, but the electronics facet as a black box entity is. Furthermore, the interfaces between the electronics, software, and mechanical facets are detailed here as well.

Lastly, the **SW Design** package is where the design and implementation of the software will be done. It is expected that the software will continue to work in the model, but that the other facets will not. For electronics and mechanical design, we expect that they will use their own separate tools and this model will serve only as a specification of what needs to be done in those facets. It is possible that the electronics design could be done here, using SysML or UML and then generating SystemC, for example, but that is fairly rare. SysML and UML are poorly suited to capturing mechanical designs, as they don't have any underlying metamodel for representing or visualizing geometry.

Copying the subsystem specification

The subsystem package is *copied* (rather than referenced) from the systems model. This model holds the subsystem details, such as subsystem functions and use cases. Of course, the name of this package in *Figure 1.39* is misleading; if the name of the subsystem was **Avionics Subsystem**, then the name of this package would be **Avionics Subsystem Package**, or something similar.

In a practical sense, I prefer to copy rather than reference the subsystem package from the systems model because that isolates the subsystem model from subsequent changes to that package in the systems model that may take place in later iterations. The subsystem team may then explicitly re-import that changed subsystem model at times of its own choosing. If the subsystem package is added by reference, then whenever the systems team modifies it, the changes are reflected in the referencing subsystem model. This can also be handled by other means, such as referencing versions of the systems model in the configuration management set, but I find this conceptually easier. However, if you prefer to have a reference rather than a copy, that's an acceptable variation point in the recipe.

Adding references to the subsystem requirements

The **Requirements** package in the systems model also holds the derived subsystem requirements (see *Chapter 2, System Specification*). Thus, referencing the **Requirements** package from the systems model allows easy access to those requirements.

Adding references to the physical interfaces and data schema

Logical interfaces serve the needs of systems engineering well, for the most part. However, since the subsystem team is developing the physical subsystem, they need to know the actual bit-level details of how to communicate with the actors and other subsystems; they must reference the physical interfaces from the shared model.

Adding a model overview diagram

As before, each model should have a model overview diagram to serve as a table of contents and introduction to the model.

How it works...

At the highest level, there is a federated set of models defined here. The systems model holds the engineering data for the entire set, and this information is almost exclusively at the logical level of abstraction. This means that the important logical properties of the data are represented, such as the extent and precision of the data, but its physical properties are not. Thus, we might represent an element such as a **Radar Track** in the systems model as having a value property of range with an extent of 10 meters to 300 kilometers and a precision of ± 2 meters. Those are logical properties. However, the physical schema might represent the value as a scaled integer with 100 * the value for transmission over the 1553 avionics bus. Thus, a range of 123 kilometers would be transmitted as an integer value of 12,300. This representation is a part of the physical data schema that realizes the logical properties.

Beyond the systems model, the shared model provides a common repository for information shared by multiple subsystems. During systems engineering work, this is limited to the physical interfaces and associated physical data schema. Later, in downstream engineering, other shared subsystem design elements might be shared, but that is beyond our scope of concern.

Lastly, each subsystem has its own subsystem model. This is a model used by the interdisciplinary subsystem team. For all team members, this model serves as a specification of the system and the related engineering facets. Remember that a facet is defined to be the contribution to a design specific to a single engineering discipline, such as software, electronics, or mechanical design. Software work is expected to continue in the model, but the other disciplines will likely design in their own specific tools.

Example

Figure 1.40 shows the initial organization of the **Pegasus System Model**, with Architecture 0 already added (see the *Architecture 0* recipe). I've filled in a few other details, such as adding an empty use case diagram, a use case requirements trace matrix, and a subsystem requirements trace matrix, to illustrate how the model will be elaborated over time:

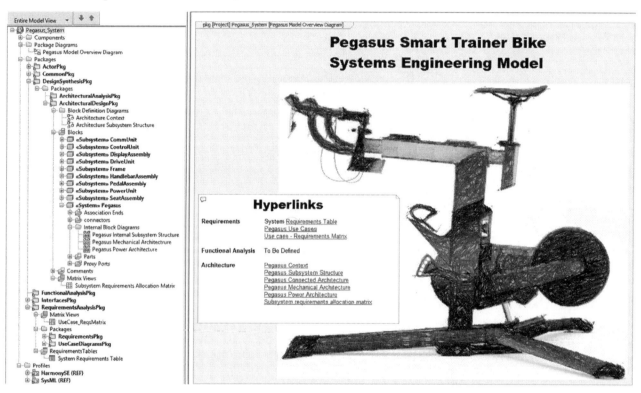

Figure 1.40 – Pegasus system mode – overview diagram

The following models are *not* created early in the MBSE process but rather later, once the Pegasus architecture work is complete and the work developing the handoff to downstream engineering is underway.

Astute readers may notice the **HarmonySE** profile in the model. This is an IBM Rhapsody-specific profile that provides some automation and support for systems engineering, including the automatic creation of the systems model organization. For more information, see the description of the profile in the *Harmony aMBSE Deskbook* available here: https://www.bruce-douglass.com/papers.

Figure 1.41 shows the model overview diagram for the shared model, as it is developed in *Chapter 4, Handoff to Downstream Engineering*. The upper packages are actually owned by the SE model, but used by reference within the shared model. The lower packages hold the physical interface and related data schema and are provided to the subsystem models.

The astute reader will note that the browser shows a list of all the relevant models in the system, including the systems model, the shared model, and the subsystem models. Rhapsody allows you to load multiple models (Rhapsody projects), although only one can be edited at a time:

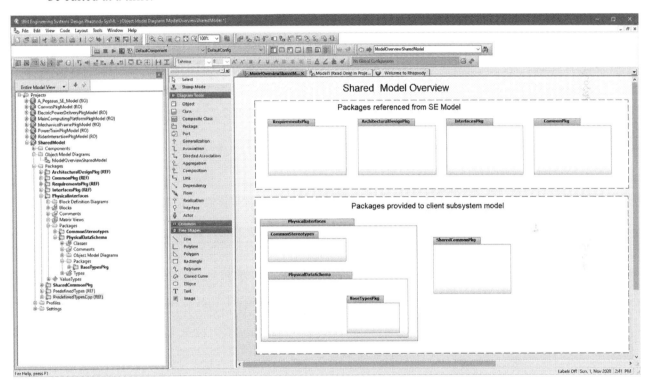

Figure 1.41 – Pegasus shared model

Let's now have a look at *Figure 1.42*:

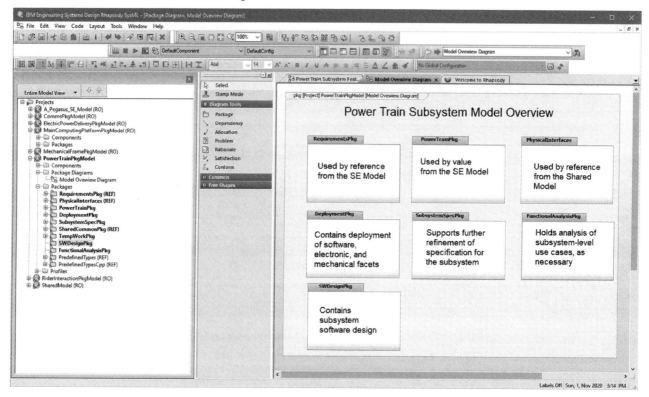

Figure 1.42 – Power train subsystem model

This screenshot shows the power train subsystem model based on the canonical form for that kind of model.

2

System Specification

This chapter contains recipes related to capturing and analyzing requirements. The first four recipes are alternative ways to achieve essentially the same thing. Functional analysis generates high-quality requirements, use cases, and user stories, all of which are means to understand what the system must consist of.

By *high-quality requirements*, I mean requirements focused around a use case that are demonstrably the following:

- Complete
- Accurate
- Correct
- Consistent
- Verifiable

The problem with textual requirements is that natural language is ambiguous, imprecise, and only weakly verifiable. Keeping text human-readable is very useful, especially for non-technical stakeholders, but is insufficient to ensure we are building the right system. The recipes covered in this chapter are as follows:

- Functional analysis with scenarios
- Functional analysis with activities
- Functional analysis with state machines
- Functional analysis with user stories
- Model-based safety analysis
- Model-based threat analysis
- Specifying logical system interfaces
- Creating the logical data schema

Why aren't textual requirements enough?

There are many reasons why textual requirements by themselves fail to result in usable, high-quality systems.

First, it is difficult to ensure all the following functionality is present:

- All normal (sunny day) functionality
- All edge cases
- All variations of inputs, sequences, and timings
- All exception, error, and fault cases
- Qualities of service, such as performance, range, precision, timing, safety, security, and reliability
- All stakeholders appropriately represented

Getting that much is a daunting task indeed. But even beyond that, there is an *air gap* between realizing a possibly huge set of *shall* statements and actually meeting the stakeholder needs. The stakeholder believes that if the system performs a specific function, then in practice, their needs will be met. Experience has shown that is not always true. Customers often ask for features that don't address their true needs. Further, requirements are volatile and interact in often subtle but potentially catastrophic ways.

We address this issue by capturing requirements both in textual and formal means via modeling. The textual requirements are important because they are human-readable by anyone even without modeling training. The model representation of the requirement is more formal and lends itself to more rigorous thought and analysis. In general, both are necessary.

Definitions

Before we get into the recipes, let's agree on common terms:

- **Requirement**: A *stakeholder requirement* is a statement of what a stakeholder needs. A *system requirement* is a statement of what the system must do to satisfy a stakeholder need. We will focus on system requirements in this chapter. Normally, requirements are written in an active voice using the *shall* keyword to indicate a normative requirement, as in the following example:

  The system shall move the robot arm to comply with the user directive.

- **Actor**: An *actor* is an element outside the scope of the system we are specifying that has interactions with the system that we care about. Actors may be human users, but they can also be other systems, software applications, or environments.

- **Use Case**: A use case is a collection of scenarios and/or user stories around a common usage of a system. One may alternatively think of a use case as a collection of requirements around a usage-centered capability of the system. Still another way to think about use cases is that they are a sequenced set of system functions that execute in a coherent set of system-actor interactions. These all come down to basically the same thing. In practice, a use case is a named usage of a system that traces to anywhere between 10-100 requirements and 3-25 scenarios or user stories.

- **Activities**: An activity diagram in SysML is a composite behavior of some portion of a system. Activities are defined in terms of sequences of actions which, in this context, correspond to either a system function, an input, or an output.

  Activities can model the behavior of use cases. Activities are said to be *fully constructive* in the sense that they model all possible behavior of the use case.

- **State Machines**: A state machine in SysML is a composite behavior of a system element, such as a block or use case. In this context, a state machine is a *fully constructive* behavior focusing on conditions of the system (states) and how the system changes from state to state, executing system functions along the way.

- **Scenarios**: A scenario is an interaction of a set of elements in a particular case or flow. In this usage, a scenario represents a partially complete behavior showing the interaction of the actors with the system as it executes a use case. The reason that it is partially complete is that a given scenario only shows one or a very small number of possible flows within a use case. Scenarios are roughly equivalent to user stories. In SysML, scenarios are generally captured using sequence diagrams.

- **User Story**: A user story is a statement about system usage from a user or actor's point of view that achieves a user goal. User stories describe singular interactions and so are similar in scope to scenarios. User stories use a canonical textual formulation such as *As a <user> I want <feature> so that <output or outcome>*.

Here's an example:

> *As a pilot, I want to control the rudder of the aircraft using foot pedals so that I can set the yaw of the aircraft.*

User stores tend to be most beneficial for simpler interactions, as complex interactions are difficult to write out in understandable text. Scenarios are generally preferred for complex interactions or when there is a lot of precise detail that must be specified. Consider the following somewhat unwieldy user story:

> *As a navigation system, I want to measure the position of the aircraft in 3 dimensions with an accuracy of +/- 1 m every 0.5s so that I can fly to the destination.*

And that's still a rather simple scenario.

Functional analysis with scenarios

As stated in the chapter introduction, functional analysis is a means to both capture and improve requirements through analysis. In this case, we'll begin with scenarios as a way to elicit the scenarios from the stakeholder and create the requirements from those identified interactions. We then develop an executable model of the requirements that allows us to verify that the requirements interact how we expect them to, identify missing requirements, and perform *what-if* analyses for additional interactions.

Purpose

The purpose of this recipe is to create a high-quality set of requirements by working with the stakeholders to identify and characterize interactions of the system with its actors. This is particularly effective when the main focus of the use case is the interaction between the actors and the system or when trying to gather requirements from non-technical stakeholders.

Inputs and preconditions

The input is a use case naming a capability of the system from an actor-use point of view.

Outputs and postconditions

There are several outcomes, the most important of which is a set of requirements accurately and appropriately specifying the behavior of the system for the use case. Additional outputs include an executable use case model, logical system interfaces to support the use case behavior, along with a supporting logical data schema and a set of scenarios that can be used later as specifications of test cases.

How to do it

Figure 2.1 shows the workflow for this recipe. There are many steps in common with the next two recipes:

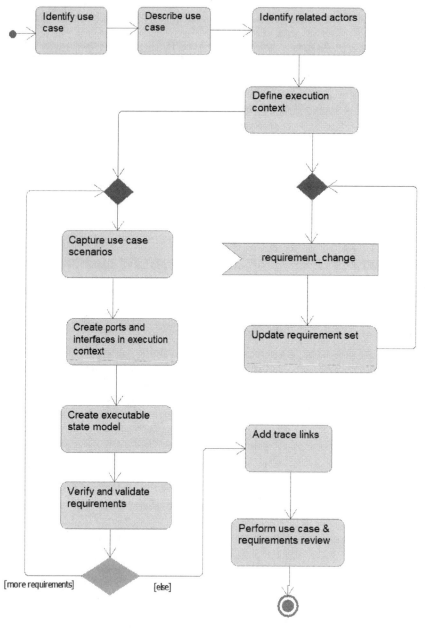

Figure 2.1 – Functional analysis with scenarios

Identify the use case

This first step is to identify the generic usage of which the scenarios of interest, user stories, and requirements are aspects.

Describe the use case

The description of the use case should include its purpose, and a general description of the flows, preconditions, postconditions, and invariants (assumptions). Some modelers add the specific actors involved, user stories, and scenarios, but I prefer to use the model itself to contain those relations.

Identify related actors

The related actors are those people or systems outside our scope that interact with the system while it executes the current use case. These actors can send messages to the system, receive messages from the system, or both.

Define the execution context

The execution context is a kind of modeling *sandbox* that contains an executable component consisting of executable elements representing the use case and related actors. The recommended way to achieve this is to create separate blocks representing the use case and the actors, connected via ports. Having an isolated simulation sandbox allows different systems engineers to progress independently on different use case analyses.

Capture use case scenarios

Scenarios are singular interactions between the system and the actors during the execution of the use case. When working with non-technical stakeholders, it is an effective way to understand the desired interactions of the use case. We recommend starting with normal, *sunny day* scenarios before progressing to edge case and exceptional *rainy day* scenarios. It is important to understand that every message identifies or represents one or more requirements.

Create ports and interfaces in the execution context

Once we have a set of scenarios, we've identified the flows from the use case to the actors and from the actors to the system. By inference, this identifies ports relating the actors and the system, and the specific flows within the interfaces that define them.

Create an executable state model

This step creates what I call the *normative state machine*. Executing this state machine can recreate each of the scenarios we drew in the *Capture use case scenarios* section. All states, transitions, and actions represent requirements. Any state elements added only to assist in the execution that do not represent requirements should be stereotyped *«non-normative»* to clearly identify this fact. It is also common to create state behavior for the actors in a step known as *instrumenting the actor* to support the execution of the use case in the execution context.

Verify and validate requirements

Running the execution context for the use case allows us to demonstrate that our normative state machine in fact represents the flows identified by working with the stakeholder. It also allows us to identify flows and requirements that are missing, incomplete, or incorrect. These result in **Requirements_change** change requests to fix the identified requirement defects.

Requirements_change

Parallel to the development and execution of the use case model, we maintain the textual requirements. This workflow event indicates the need to fix an identified requirement defect.

Update the requirements set

In response to an identified requirement defect, we fix the textual requirements by adding, deleting, or modifying requirements. This will then be reflected in the updated model.

Add trace links

Once the use case model and requirements stabilize, we add trace links using the *«trace»* relation or something similar. This is generally a backtrace to stakeholder requirements as well as forward links to any architectural elements that might already exist.

Perform the use case and requirements review

Once the work has stabilized, a review for correctness and compliance with standards may be done. This allows subject matter experts and stakeholders to review the requirements, use case, states, and scenarios for correctness and for quality assurance staff to ensure compliance with modeling and requirements standards.

Let's have a look at an example.

Identify the use case

This example will examine the *Emulate Basic Gearing* use case. The use case is shown in *Figure 2.2*:

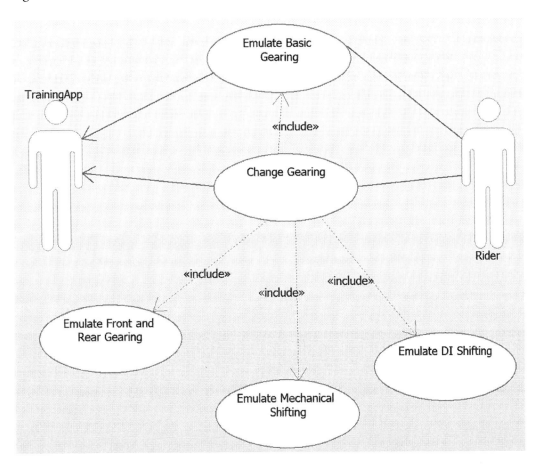

Figure 2.2 – Emulate Basic Gearing use case

Describe the use case

All model elements deserve a useful description. In the case of a use case, we typically use the format shown here:

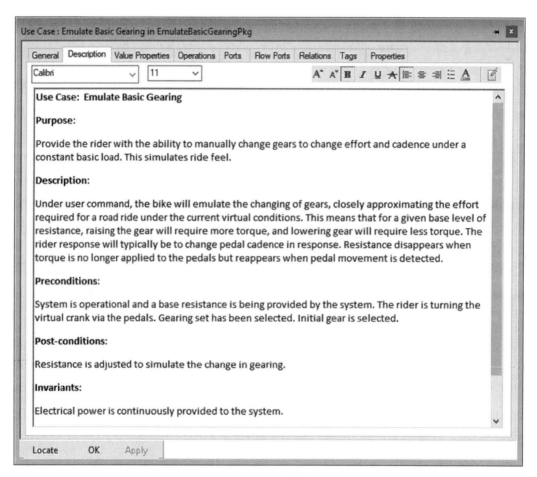

Figure 2.3 – Use case description

Identify related actors

The related actors in this example are the **Rider** and the **Training App**. The rider signals the system to change the gearing via the gears control and receives a response in terms of changing resistance. The training app, when connected, is notified of the current gearing so that it can be displayed. The relation of the actors to the use case is shown in *Figure 2.2*.

Define the execution context

The execution context creates blocks that represent the actors and the use case for the purpose of the analysis. In this example, the following naming conventions are observed:

- The block representing the use case has the use case name (with white space removed) preceded by Uc_. Thus, for this example, the use case block is named **Uc_EmulateBasicGearing**.

- Blocks representing the actors are given the actor name preceded with a and an abbreviation of the use case. For this use case, the prefix is aEBG_ so the actor blocks are named **aEBG_Rider** and **aEBG_TrainingApp**.

- The interface blocks are named as *<use case block>_<actor block>*. The names of the two interface blocks are **iUc_EmulateBasicGearing_aEBG_Rider** and **iUc_EmulateBasicGearing_aEBG_TrainingApp**. The normal form of the interface block is associated with the proxy port on the use case block; the conjugated form is associated with the corresponding proxy port on the actor block.

All these elements are shown in the **Internal Block Diagram** (**IBD**) in *Figure 2.4*:

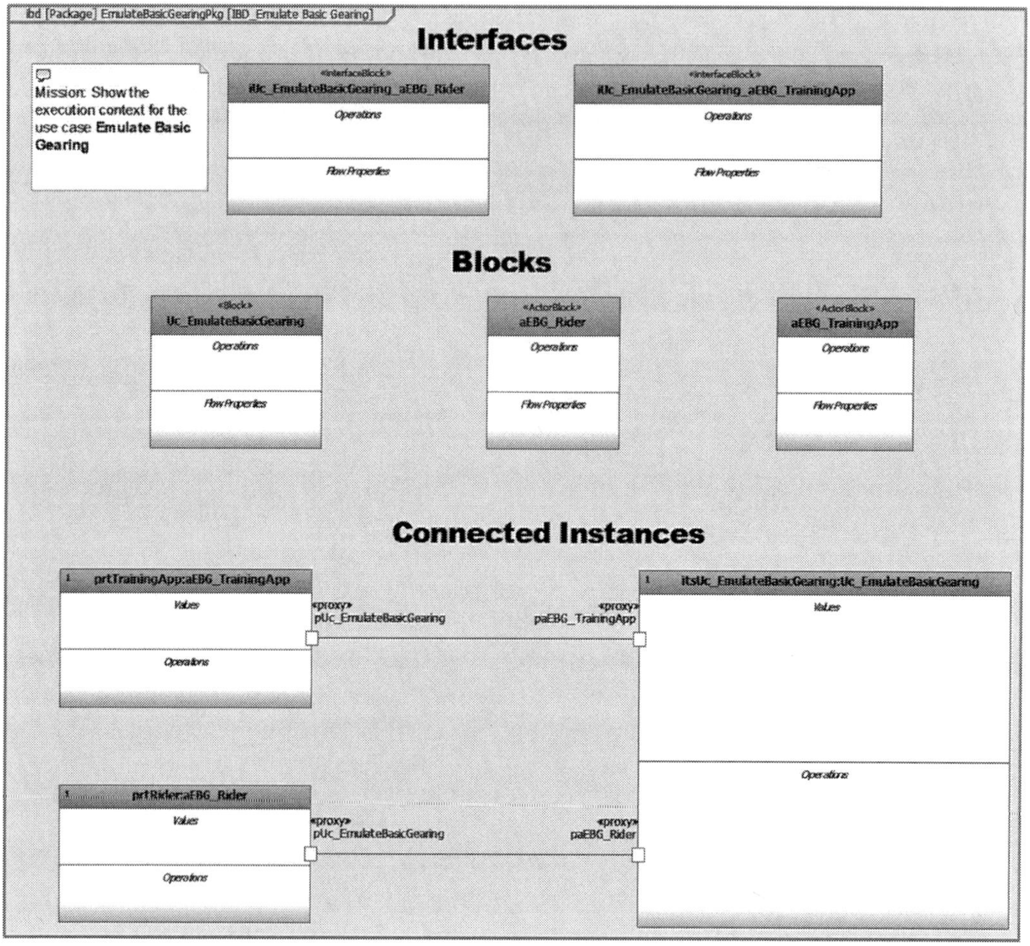

Figure 2.4 – Emulate Basic Gearing execution context

Capture use case scenarios

Scenarios here are captured to show the interaction of the system with the actors using this use case. Note that continuous flows are shown as flows with the *«continuous»* stereotype. This resistance at a specific level is applied continuously until the level of resistance is changed. As is usual in use case analysis, messages between the actors are modeled as events and invocations of system functions on the use case lifeline are modeled as operations.

The first scenario (*Figure 2.5*) shows normal gear changes from the rider. Note that the *messages to self* on the use case block lifeline indicate system functions identified during the scenario development:

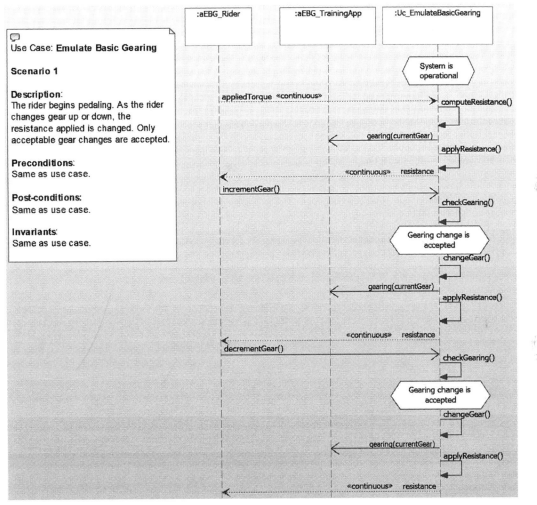

Figure 2.5 – Emulate Basic Gearing scenario 1

The next scenario shows what happens when the rider tries to increment the gearing beyond the maximum gearing allowed by the current configuration. It is shown in *Figure 2.6*:

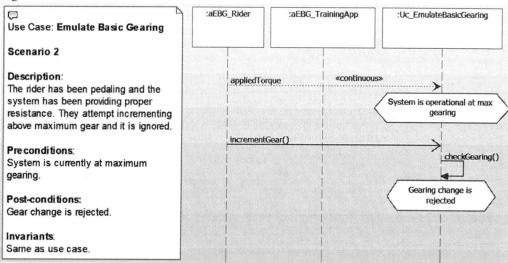

Figure 2.6 – Emulate Basic Gearing scenario 2

The last scenario for this use case shows the rejection of a requested gear change below the provided gearing:

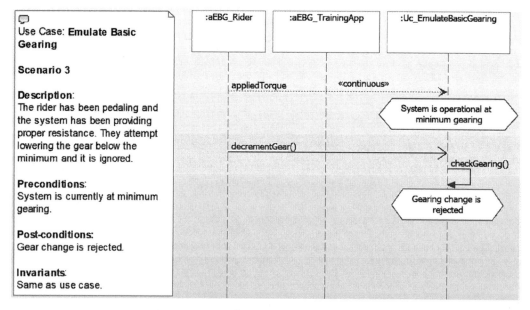

Figure 2.7 – Emulate Basic Gearing scenario 3

Based on these sequences, we identify the following requirements:

- The system shall respond to applied pedal torque with resistance calculated from the base level of resistance, current gearing, and applied torque to simulate pedal resistance during road riding.

- The system shall send the current gearing to the training app when the current gearing changes.

- The system shall respond to a rider-initiated increase in gear by applying the new level of gearing provided that it does not exceed the maximum gearing of the gearing configuration.

- The system shall respond to a ride-initiated decrease in gear by applying the new level of gearing provided that it does not exceed the minimum gearing of the gearing configuration.

Create ports and interfaces in the execution context

It is a simple matter to update the ports and interface blocks to contain the messages going between the actors and the use case. The sequence diagrams identify the messages between the use case and actor blocks, so the interface blocks must support those specific flows (*Figure 2.8*):

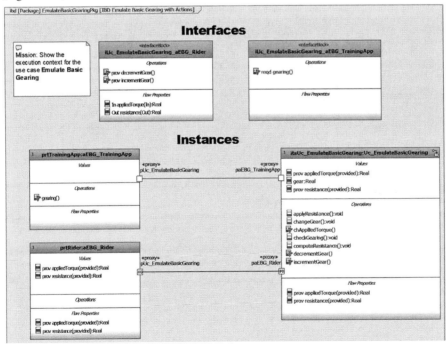

Figure 2.8 – Emulate Basic Gearing ports and interfaces

Create an executable state model

This step constructs the normative state machine for the use case as well as instrumenting the actors with their own state machines. The state machine of the use case block is the most interesting because it represents the requirements. *Figure 2.9* shows the state machine for the **Emulate Basic Gearing** use case:

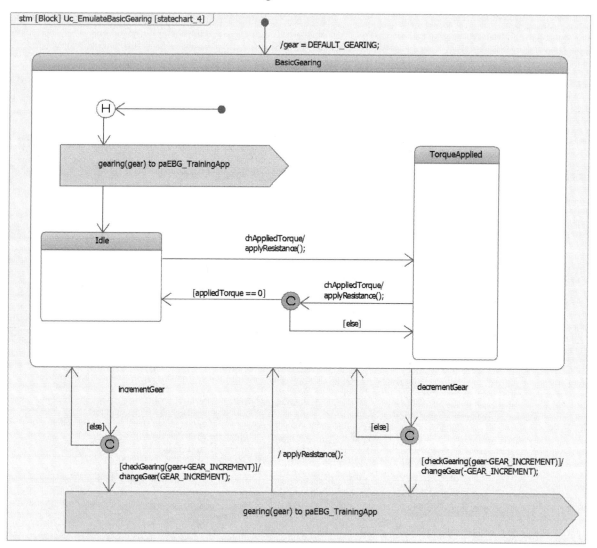

Figure 2.9 – Emulate Basic Gearing state machine

To support the execution, the system functions must be elaborated enough to support the execution and simulation. These system functions include `applyResistance()`, `checkGearing()`, and `changeGear()`. *Figure 2.10* shows their simple implementation:

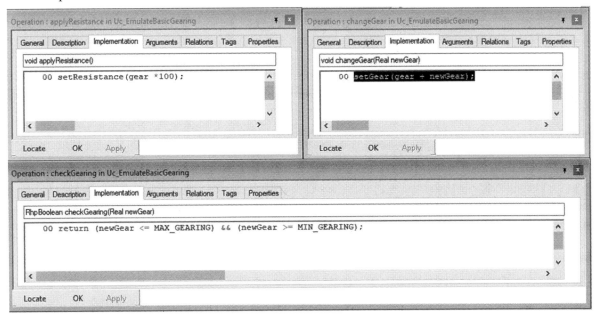

Figure 2.10 – Emulate Basic Gearing system functions

The system variable **gear** is represented as a **Real** (from the SysML value type library), representing the gear multiplier, in a fashion similar to gear-inches, a commonly used measure in cycling. The flow properties **appliedTorque** and **resistance** are likewise implemented as **Reals**.

The state machines for the actor blocks are even simpler than those of the use case block. *Figure 2.11* shows the **Rider** state machine:

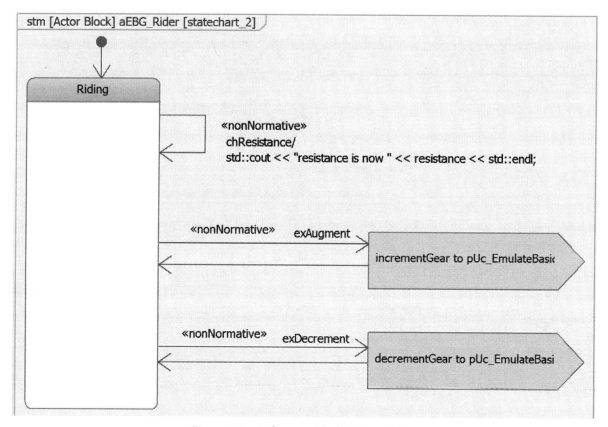

Figure 2.11 – Rider actor block state machine

Figure 2.12 shows the **TrainingApp** state machine and the implementation of its `displayGearing()` function:

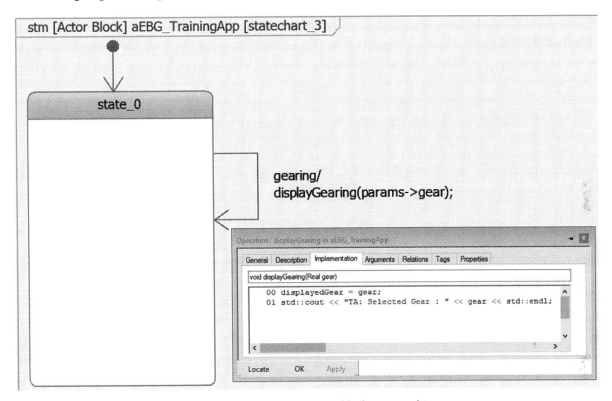

Figure 2.12 – TrainingApp actor block state machine

Lastly, some constants are defined. **DEFAULT_GEARING** is set to the same value as **MIN_GEARING**; in this case, 30 gear-inches. **MAX_GEARING** is set to about the same as a 53x10 gearing, 140. The **GEAR_INCREMENT** is used for incrementing or decrementing the gearing and is set to 5 gear-inches for the purpose of simulation.

Verify and validate requirements

To facilitate control of the execution, a panel diagram is created. The buttons insert events in the relevant objects and the text boxes display and support modification of the value and flow properties. A panel diagram is a useful feature of the IBM Rhapsody modeling tool used to create these models:

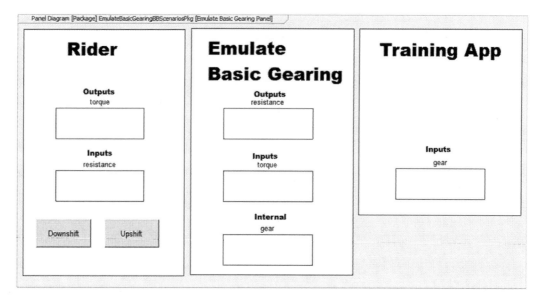

Figure 2.13 – Emulate Basic Gearing panel diagram

The execution of the state model recreates the sequence diagrams. *Figure 2.14* shows the recreation of Scenario 1 (*Figure 2.5*) by the executing model. The creation of such sequence diagrams automatically from execution is another useful Rhapsody feature:

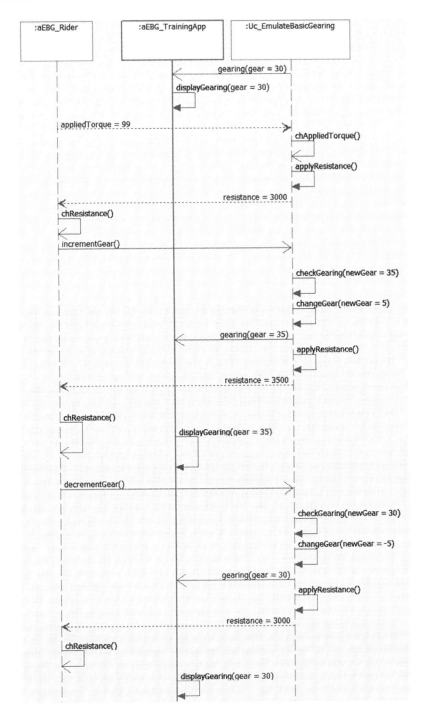

Figure 2.14 – Animated sequence diagram from model execution

While in review, the project lead notices that there is no requirement to display the initial starting value for the gearing, before a specific gear has been selected. Additionally, we see that the requirement to notify the training app was missing. These are identified as missing requirements that must be added.

Requirements_change

In this example, we notice that we omitted a requirement to update the rider display of the gearing. The change has already been made to the state machine.

Update requirement set

We add the following requirements to the requirements set:

- The system shall display the currently selected gear.

- The system shall default to the minimum gear during initialization.

Add trace links

In this case, we ensure there are trace links back to stakeholder requirements as well as from the use case to the requirements. This is shown in the use case diagram in *Figure 2.15*. The newly identified requirements are highlighted with a bold border:

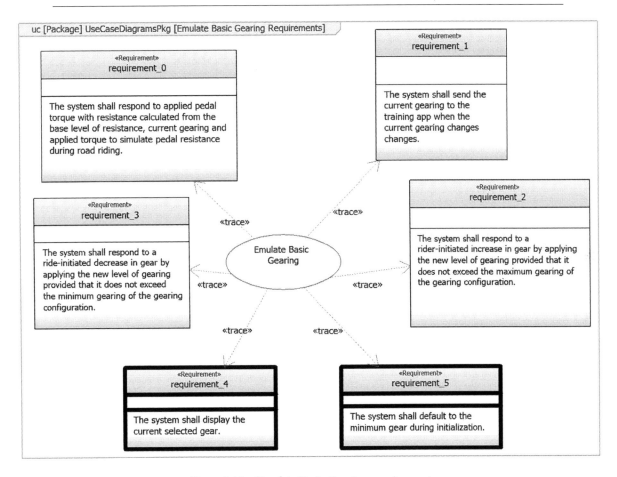

Figure 2.15 – Emulate Basic Gearing requirements

Perform a use case and requirements review

The requirements model can now be reviewed by relevant stakeholders. The work products that should be included in the review include all the diagrams shown in this section, the requirements, and the executing model. The use of the executing model allows a what-if examination of the requirements set to be easily done during the review. Such questions as *What happens to the gearing if the rider turns the system off and back on?* or *What is absolute maximum gearing to be allowed?* can be asked. The simulation of the model allows the questions to either be answered by running the simulation case or can be identified as an item that requires resolution.

Functional analysis with activities

Functional analysis can be performed in a number of subtly different ways. In the previous recipe, we started with the sequence diagram to analyze the use case. That is particularly useful when the interesting parts of the use case are the interactions. The workflow in this recipe is slightly different, although it achieves exactly the same objectives. This workflow starts with the development of an activity model and generates scenarios from that. In this recipe, just as in the previous one, when the work is all complete, it is the state machine that forms the normative specification of the use case; the activity diagram is used as a stepping stone along the way. The objective of the workflow, as with the previous recipe, is to create an executable model to identify and fix defects in the requirements, such as missing requirements, or requirements that are incomplete, incorrect, or inaccurate. Overall, this is the most favored workflow among model-based systems engineers.

Purpose

The purpose of the recipe is to create a set of high-quality requirements by identifying and characterizing the key system functions performed by the system during the execution of the use case capability. This recipe is particularly effective when the main focus of the use case is a set of system functions and not the interaction of the system with the actors.

Inputs and preconditions

A use case naming a capability of the system from an actor-use point of view.

Outputs and postconditions

There are several outcomes, the most important of which is a set of requirements accurately and appropriately specifying the behavior of the system for the use case. Additional outputs include an executable use case model, logical system interfaces to support the use case behavior and a supporting logical data schema, and a set of scenarios that can be used later as specifications of test cases.

How to do it...

Figure 2.16 shows the workflow for this recipe. It is similar to the previous recipe. The primary difference is that rather than beginning the analysis by creating scenarios with the stakeholders, it begins by creating an activity model of the set of primary flows from which the scenarios will be derived:

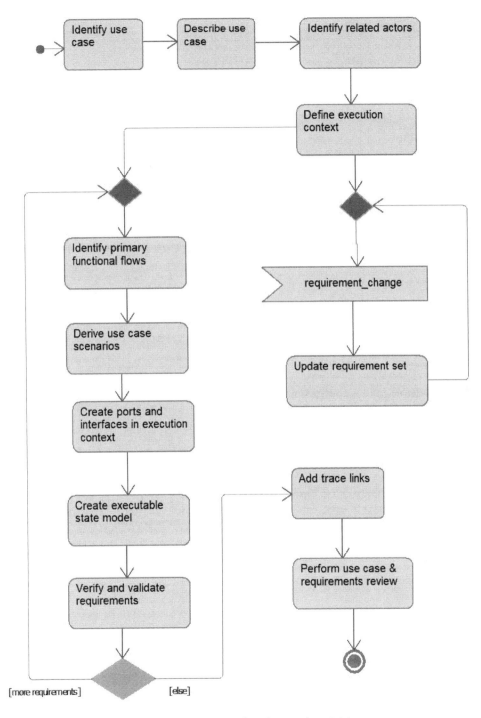

Figure 2.16 – Functional analysis with activities

Identify the use case

This first step is to identify the generic usage of which the scenarios of interest, user stories, and requirements are aspects.

Describe the use case

The description of the use case should include its purpose, general description of the flows, preconditions, postconditions, and invariants (assumptions). Some modelers add the specific actors involved, user stories, and scenarios, but I prefer to use the model itself to contain those relations.

Identify related actors

The related actors are those people or systems outside our scope that interact with the system while it executes the current use case. These actors can send messages to the system, receive messages from the system, or both.

Define the execution context

The execution context is a kind of modeling *sandbox* that contains an executable component consisting of executable elements representing the use case and related actors. The recommended way to achieve this is to create separate blocks representing the use case and the actors, connected via ports. Having an isolated simulation sandbox allows different systems engineers to progress independently on different use case analyses.

Identify primary functional flows

The activity model identifies the functional flows of the system while it executes the use case capability. These consist of a sequenced set of actions, connected by control flows, with control nodes (notably, decision, merge, fork, and join nodes) where appropriate. In this specific recipe step, the focus is on the primary flows of the system – also known as *sunny day* flows – and less on the secondary and fault scenarios (known as *rainy day* scenarios). The actions are either system functions, reception of messages from the actors, sending messages to the actors, or waiting for timeouts.

This activity model is not complete in the sense that it will not include all possible flows within the use case. The later *Create executable state model* recipe step will include all flows, which is why the state machine, rather than the activity model, is the normative specification of the use case. This activity model allows the systems engineer to begin reasoning about the necessary system behavior. Most systems engineers feel very comfortable with activity models and prefer to begin the analysis here rather than with the scenarios or with the state machine.

Derive use case scenarios

The activity model identifies multiple flows, as indicated by control nodes, such as decision nodes. A specific scenario takes a singular path through the activity flow so that a single activity model results in multiple scenarios. The scenarios are useful because they are easy to review with non-technical stakeholders and because they aid in the definition of the logical interfaces between the system and the actors.

> **Note**
>
> The activity diagram *can* be made complete, but it is usually easier to do that with a state machine. If you prefer to work entirely in the activity diagram, then evolve the activity model to be executable rather than develop a state machine for this purpose.

Create ports and interfaces in the execution context

Once we have a set of scenarios, we've identified the flow from the use case to the actors and from the actors to the system. By inference, this identifies ports relating the actors and the system, and the specific flows within the interfaces that define them.

Create an executable state model

This step identifies what I call the *normative state machine*. Executing this state machine can recreate each of the scenarios we drew in the *Capture use case scenarios* section. All states, transitions, and actions represent requirements. Any state elements added only to assist in the execution but that do not represent requirements should be stereotyped «**non-normative**» to clearly identify this fact. It is also common to create state behavior for the actors in a step known as *instrumenting the actor* to support the execution of the use case in the execution context.

Verify and validate requirements

Running the execution context for the use case allows us to demonstrate that our normative state machine in fact represents the flows identified by working with the stakeholder. It also allows us to identify flows and requirements that are missing, incomplete, or incorrect. These result in **Requirements_change** change requests to fix the identified requirements defects.

Requirements_change

Parallel to the development and execution of the use case model, we maintain the textual requirements. This workflow event indicates the need to fix an identified requirements defect.

Update requirement set

In response to an identified requirements defect, we fix the textual requirements by adding, deleting, or modifying requirements. This will then be reflected in the updated model.

Add trace links

Once the use case model and requirements stabilize, we add trace links using the *«trace»* relation or something similar. This generally means backtraces to stakeholder requirements as well as forward links to any architectural elements that might already exist.

Perform the use case and requirements review

Once the work has stabilized, a review for correctness and compliance with standards may be done. This allows subject matter experts and stakeholders to review the requirements, use case, activities, states, and scenarios for correctness and for quality assurance staff to ensure compliance with modeling and requirements standards.

Example

Let's see an example here.

The example used for this recipe is the **Control Resistance** use case, shown in *Figure 2.17* along with some other use cases:

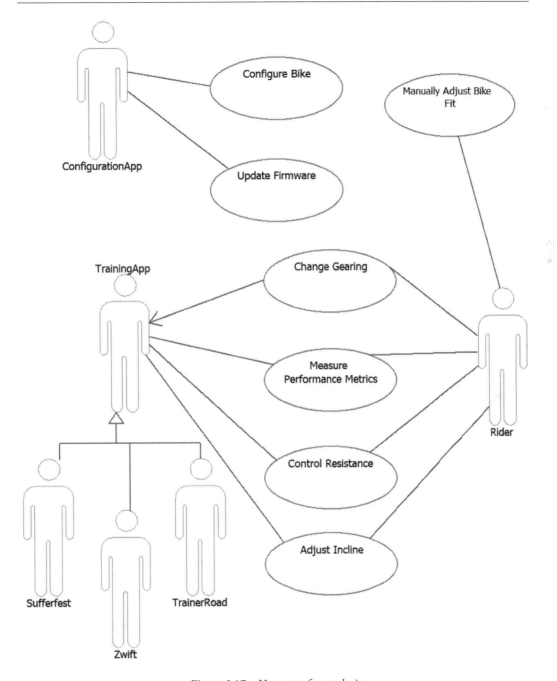

Figure 2.17 – Use cases for analysis

Describe the use case

All model elements deserve a useful description. In the case of a use case, we typically use the format shown in *Figure 2.18*:

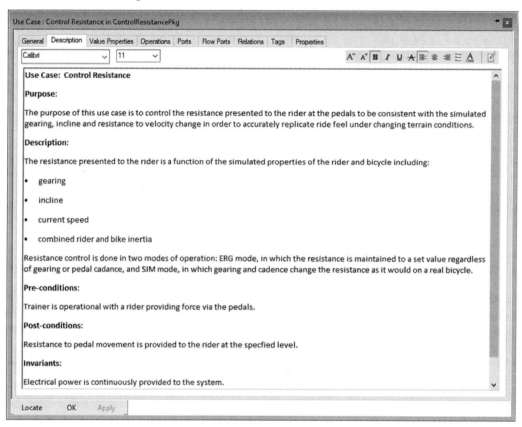

Figure 2.18 – Control Resistance use case description

Identify related actors

The related actors in this example are the **Rider** and the **Training App**. The rider signals the system to change the gearing via the gears control and receives a response in terms of changing resistance as well as setting resistance mode to ERG or SIM mode. The training app, when connected, is notified of the current gearing so that it can be displayed, provides a simulated input of incline, and can, optionally change between SIM and ERG modes. The relation of the actors to the use case is shown in *Figure 2.17*.

Define the execution context

The execution context creates blocks that represent the actors and the use case for the purpose of the analysis. In this example, the following naming conventions are observed:

- The block representing the use case is has the use case name (with white space removed) preceded by Uc_. Thus, for this example, the use case block is named **Uc_ControlResistance**.

- Blocks representing the actors are given the actor name preceded with a and an abbreviation of the use case. For this use case, the prefix is aCR_ so the actor blocks are named **aCR_Rider** and **aCR_TrainingApp**.

- The interface blocks are named as *<use case block>_<actor block>*. The names of the two interface blocks are **iUc_ControlResistance_aCR_Rider** and **iUc_ControlResistance_aCR_TrainingApp**. The normal form of the interface block is associated with the proxy port on the use case block; the conjugated form is associated with the corresponding proxy port on the actor block.

All these elements are shown on the IBD in *Figure 2.19*:

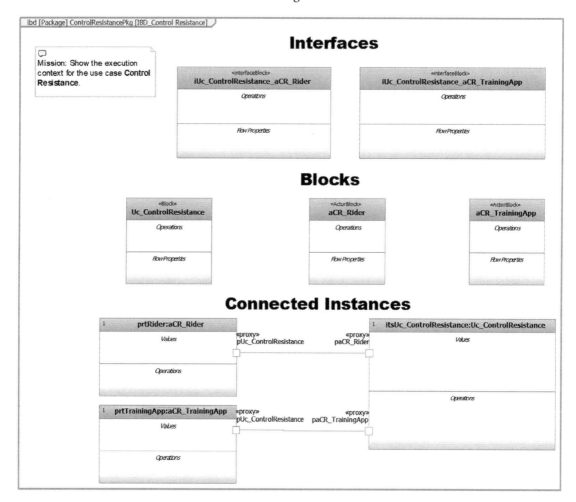

Figure 2.19 – Control resistance execution context

Identify the primary functional flow

This step creates an activity model for the primary flows in the use case. The flow consists of a set of steps sequenced by control flows and mediated by a set of control nodes. In this example, we will only consider SIM mode to keep the content short and easy to understand. In SIM mode, we simulate the outside riding experience by measuring the position, speed, and force applied to the pedal, and compute the (simulated) bike inertia, speed, acceleration, and drag. From that and the currently selected gear, the system computes and applies resistance to the pedal's movement. The high-level flow is shown in *Figure 2.20*:

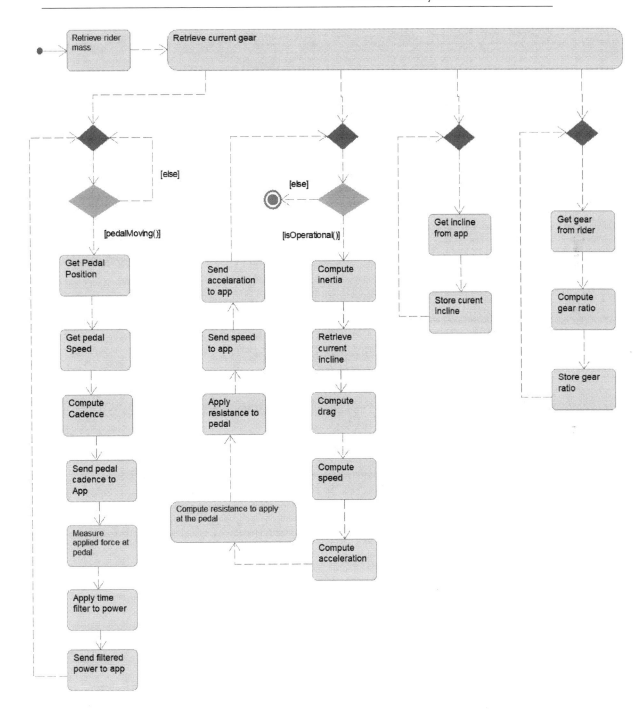

Figure 2.20 – Activity flow for Compute Resistance

Directly from the activity diagram, we can identify a number of requirements, shown in tabular form in *Table 2.1*:

ID	Specification
AcceptInclneReq	The system shall accept road incline from the connected training app.
AcceptInclnieReq	The system shall accept simulated incline from the connected training app throughout a training session.
ApplyResistanceReq	The system shall compute and apply resistance to pedal movement based on simulated inertia, speed, acceleration, and rider power input.
ComputeDragReq	The system shall compute simulated drag based on computed rider inertia and simulated road incline.
ComputeSpeedReq	The system shall compute simulated road speed based on computed inertia, current simulated speed and acceleration, and rider-applied force to the pedal.
FilterPowerReq	The system shall provide time-filtering of power, supporting 0, 1-second, 3-second, and 5-second power averaging, settable by the rider.
GearStorageReq	The system shall store the current gear persistently so that the last gear is retained across power cycles and resets.
MeasureForceReq	The system shall measure the force applied by the rider to the pedals.
MonitorPedalSpeedReq	The system shall monitor pedal position and speed.
PedalCadenceReq	The system shall compute pedal cadence.
SendCadenceReq	The system shall send pedal cadence to the associated training app, when connected.
SendPowerReq	The system shall send filtered power to the training app, if connected.
SendSpeedReq	The system shall send computed speed and acceleration to the connected training app, if any.
StoreGearRealtimeReq	The system shall store gear ratios from the gear settings.
WeigfhtReq	The system shall store the rider weight for the computation of pedal resistance.

Table 2.1 – Control Resistance requirements (first cut)

Derive use case scenarios

The activity flow in *Figure 2.20* can be used to create scenarios in sequence diagrams. It is typical to create a set of scenarios such that each control flow is shown at least once. This is called the *minimal spanning set* of scenarios. In this case, because of the nature of parallelism, a high-level scenario (*Figure 2.21*) is developed with the more detailed flows put on the reference scenarios:

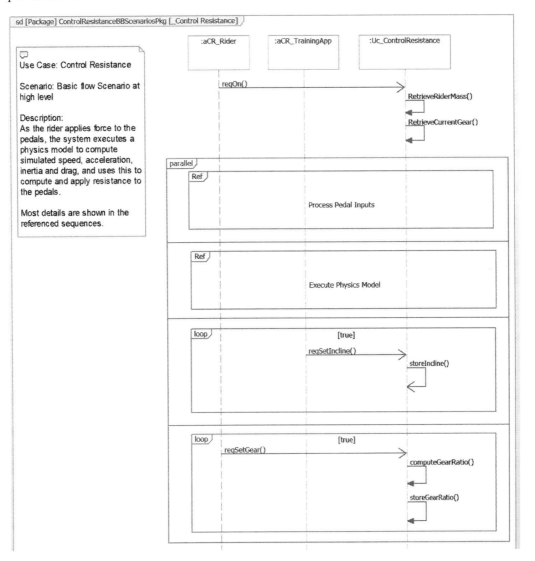

Figure 2.21 – Compute Resistance main scenario

The first reference scenario (*Figure 2.22*) reflects the inputs, gathered via system sensors, of the pedal status. This part of the overall scenario flow provides the necessary data for the computation of resistance:

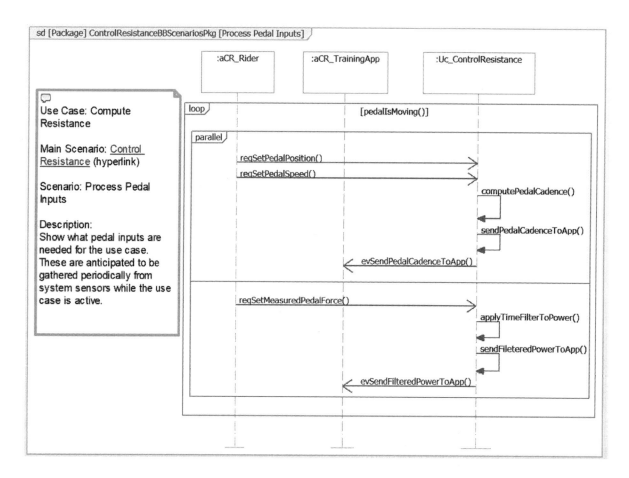

Figure 2.22 – Process Pedal Inputs scenario

The third scenario outlines the execution of the physics model *per se.* This scenario outlines how the simulated bike speed, acceleration, and drag are computed, and these outputs are then used to compute the resistance the system will apply to the pedal. It is important to note that this is not intended to provide a design but rather to identify and characterize the system functions that must be part of the design:

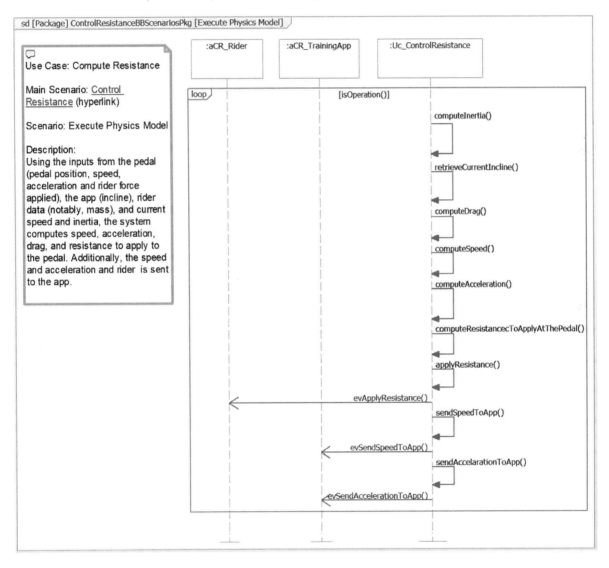

Figure 2.23 – Execute Physics Model scenario

Create ports and interfaces in the execution context

Now that we have defined some interactions between the system and the actors, we can make the interfaces to support those message exchanges. This is shown in the IBD in *Figure 2.24*:

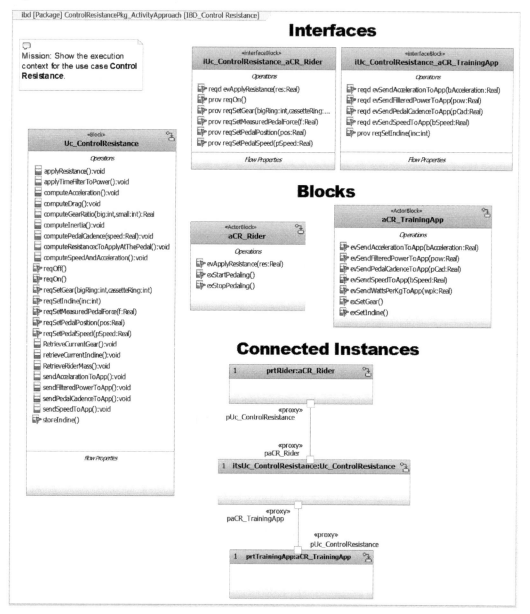

Figure 2.24 – Compute Resistance Interfaces

Create an executable state model

Figure 2.25 shows the state machine for the **Control Resistance** use case:

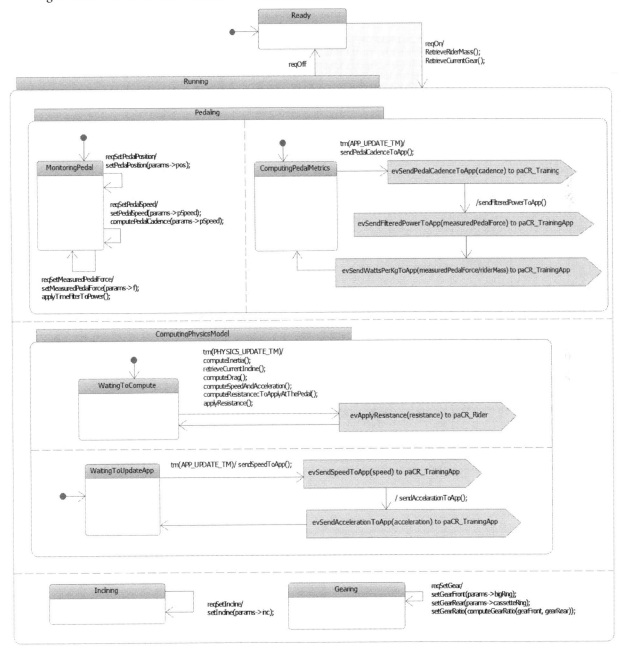

Figure 2.25 – Control Resistance use case state machine

Astute readers will note that event parameters for sending between the actors and the use case have been added. For example, **evSendFileteredPowerToApp** now passes **measuredPedalForce**, of type **Real**, to the **Training App**.

To complete the execution, we need to create (simple) implementations for the system functions referenced in the state machine, and create simple state models for the actors to support the simulation. The details of the implementation are not provided here but are available in the downloadable model:

- `setPedalPosition()`
- `setPedalSpeed()`
- `computePedalCadence()`
- `setMeasuredPedalForce()`
- `applyTimeFilterToPower()`
- `computeInertia()`
- `retrieveCurrentIncline()`
- `computeDrag()`
- `computeSpeed()`
- `computeAcceleration()`
- `computeResistancecToApplyAtThePedal()`
- `applyResistance()`
- `storeIncline()`
- `computeGearRatio()`
- `storeGearRatio()`

A few of these functions, while they must be elaborated in the actual design, can have empty implementations in the simulation:

- `sendPedalCadenceToApp()`
- `sendFilteredPowerToApp()`
- `sendSpeedToApp()`
- `sendAccelerationToApp()`

Also, to support simulation, the following value properties are defined:

- `gearFront: int` – this is the number of teeth in the front (simulated) chainring.
- `gearRear: int` – this is the number of teeth in the rear (simulated) cassette ring.
- `gearRatio: Real` – this is the ratio **gearFront/gearRear**.
- `incline: int` – this is the simulated incline on the bike, from -15 to +20 degrees.
- `measuredPedalForce: Real` – this is the force on the pedals provided by the rider.
- `pedalPosition: Real` – this is the position, in degrees, of the pedal.
- `pedalSpeed: Real` – this is the angular speed of the pedal movement.
- `cadence: int` – this is the pedal RPM (derived directly from pedal speed).

Lastly, we need to define the value properties `APP_UPDATE_TM` and `PHYSICS_UPDATE_TM`. In the real world these would run quickly, but we might slow them down for debugging and simulation on the desktop. Here, we'll set `APP_UPDATE_TM` to 10,000 ms and `PHYSICS_UPDATE_TM` to 5,000 ms.

We also need to *instrument the actors* for simulation support. A simple state behavioral model for the **aCR_Rider** is shown in *Figure 2.26*:

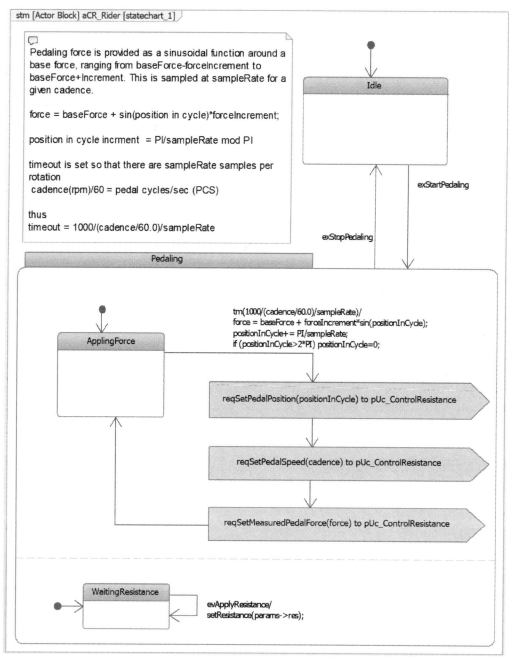

Figure 2.26 – Ride state machine

The state machine for the Training App is shown in *Figure 2.27*:

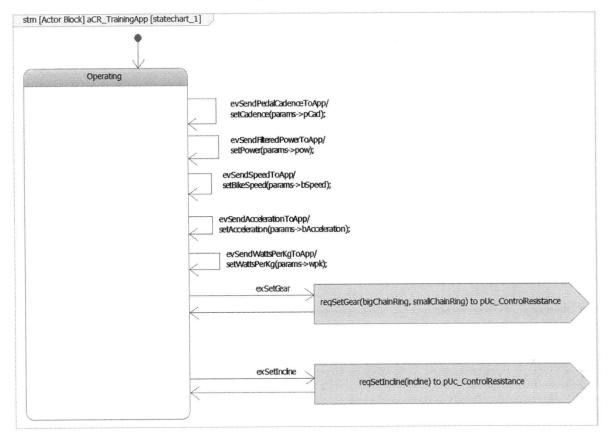

Figure 2.27 – State machine for the Training App for the Control Resistance use case

Verify and validate requirements

The simulation is not meant to be a high-fidelity physics simulation of all the forces and values involved, but instead aims to be a medium-fidelity simulation to help validate the set of requirements and to identify missing or incorrect ones. A control panel was created to visualize the behavior and input the values (*Figure 2.28*):

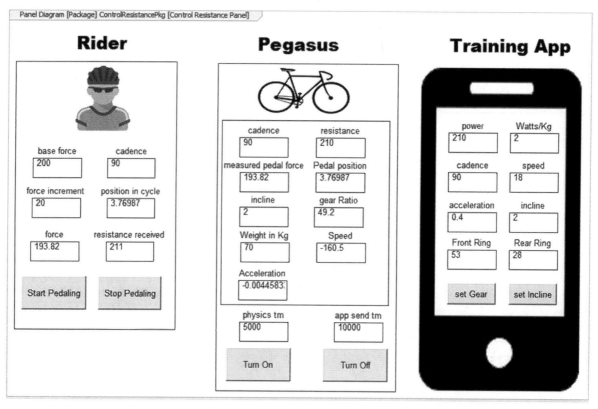

Figure 2.28 – Control Resistance panel diagram

Simulation of difference scenarios results in many sequence diagrams capturing the behavior, such as the (partial) one shown in *Figure 2.29*:

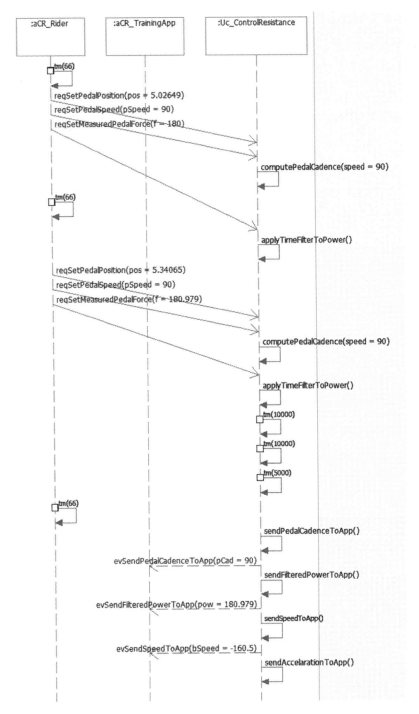

Figure 2.29 – A (partial) animated sequence diagram example of the Control Resistance use case

Requirements_change

A number of minor requirements defects are identified and flagged to be added to the requirements set.

Update the requirements set

The creation and execution of the use case simulation uncovers a couple of new requirements related to timing:

- The system shall update the physics model frequently enough to provide the rider with a smooth and road-like experience with respect to resistance.

- The system shall update the training app with the pedal cadence at least every 1.0 seconds.

- The system shall update the training app with rider-filtered power output at least every 0.5 seconds.

- The system shall update the training app with the simulated bike speed at least every 1.0 seconds.

Also, we discover a missing data transmission to the training app:

- The system shall send the current power in watts per kilogram to the training app for the current power output at least every 1.0 seconds.

Add trace links

The trace links are updated in the model. This is shown in matrix form in the following screenshot:

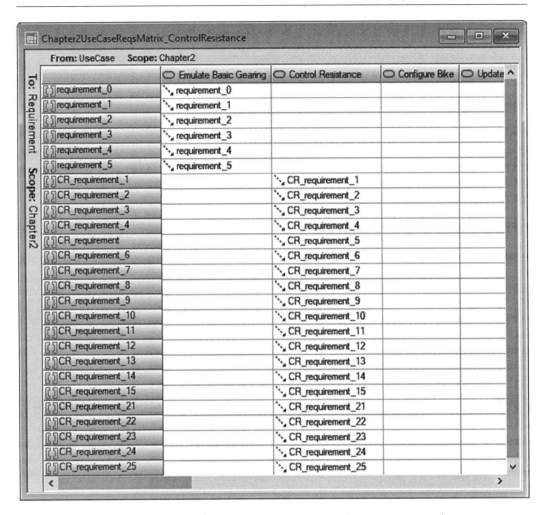

Figure 2.30 – Control Requirements use case requirements trace matrix

Perform a use case and requirements review

The requirements model can now be reviewed by relevant stakeholders. The work products that should be included in the review include all the diagrams shown in this section, the requirements, and the executing model. The use of the executing model allows a what-if examination of the requirements set to be easily done during the review. Such questions as *How quickly does the resistance control need to be updated to simulate the road riding experience?* or *What is the absolute maximum resistance supported to be allowed?* can be asked. Simulation of the model allows the questions to either be answered by running the simulation case or can be identified as an item that requires resolution.

Functional analysis with state machines

Sometimes, beginning with the state machine is the best approach for use case analysis. This is particularly true when the use case is obviously *modal* in nature, with different operational modes. This approach generally requires systems engineers who are very comfortable with state machines. This recipe is much like the previous use case analyses and can be used instead; the output is basically the same for all three of these recipes. The primary differences are that no activity diagram is created and the sequence diagrams are created from the executing use case state behavior.

Purpose

The purpose of the recipe is to create a set of high-quality requirements by identifying and characterizing the key system functions performed by the system during the execution of the use case capability. This recipe is particularly effective when the use case is clearly modal in nature and the systems engineers are highly skilled in developing state machines.

Inputs and preconditions

A use case naming a capability of the system from an actor-use point of view.

Outputs and postconditions

There are several outcomes, the most important of which is a set of requirements accurately and appropriately specifying the behavior of the system for the use case. Additional outputs include an executable use case model, logical system interfaces to support the use case behavior and a supporting logical data schema, and a set of scenarios that can be used later as specifications of test cases.

How to do it...

Figure 2.31 shows the workflow for this recipe. It is similar to the previous recipe. The primary difference is that rather than beginning the analysis by creating scenarios with the stakeholders, it begins by creating an activity model of the set of primary flows from which the scenarios will be derived:

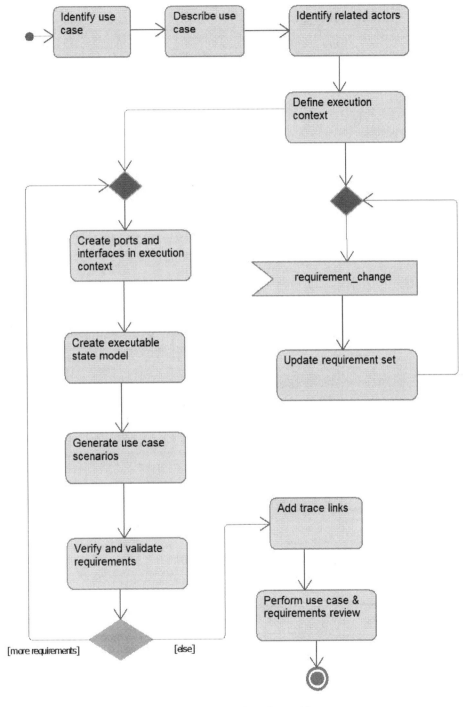

Figure 2.31 – Functional analysis with states

Identify the use case

This first step is to identify the generic usage of which the scenarios of interest, user stories, and requirements are aspects.

Describe the use case

The description of the use case should include its purpose, a general description of the flows, preconditions, postconditions, and invariants (assumptions). Some modelers add the specific actors involved, user stories, and scenarios, but I prefer to use the model itself to contain those relations.

Identify related actors

The related actors are those people or systems outside our scope that interact with the system while it executes the current use case. These actors can send messages to the system, receive messages from the system, or both.

Define the execution context

The execution context is a kind of modeling sandbox that contains an executable component consisting of executable elements representing the use case and related actors. The recommended way to achieve this is to create separate blocks representing the use case and the actors, connected via ports. Having an isolated simulation sandbox allows different systems engineers to progress independently on different use case analyses.

Create ports and interfaces in the execution context

Once we have a set of scenarios, we've identified the flow from the use case to the actors and from the actors to the system. By inference, this identifies ports relating the actors and the system, and the specific flows within the interfaces that define them.

Create executable state model

This step identifies what I call the *normative state machine*. Executing this state machine can recreate each of the scenarios we drew in the *Capture use case scenarios* section of the *Functional analysis with scenarios* recipe. Almost all states, transitions, and actions represent requirements. Any state elements added only to assist in the execution that do not represent requirements should be stereotyped «*non-normative*» to clearly identify this fact. It is also common to create state behavior for the actors in a step known as *instrumenting the actor* to support the execution of the use case in the execution context.

Generate use case scenarios

The state model identifies multiple flows, driven by event receptions and transitions, executing actions along the way. A specific scenario takes a singular path through the state flow so that a single state machine model results in multiple scenarios. The scenarios are useful because they are easy to review with non-technical stakeholders and because they aid in the definition of the logical interfaces between the system and the actors. Because the state machine is executable, it can be automatically created from the execution of the state machine, provided that you are using a supportive tool.

Verify and validate requirements

Running the execution context for the use case allows us to demonstrate that our normative state machine in fact represents the flows identified by working with the stakeholder. It also allows us to identify flows and requirements that are missing, incomplete, or incorrect. These result in **Requirements_change** change requests to fix the identified requirements' defects.

Requirements_change

Parallel to the development and execution of the use case model, we maintain the textual requirements. This workflow event indicates the need to fix an identified requirement's defect.

Update the requirement set

In response to an identified requirements defect, we fix the textual requirements by adding, deleting, or modifying requirements. This will then be reflected in the updated model.

Add trace links

Once the use case model and requirements stabilize, we add trace links using the «*trace*» relation or something similar. These are generally backtraces to stakeholder requirements as well as forward links to any architectural elements that might already exist.

Perform a use case and requirements review

Once the work has stabilized, a review for correctness and compliance with standards may be done. This allows subject matter experts and stakeholders to review the requirements, use case, states, and scenarios for correctness, and for quality assurance staff to ensure compliance with modeling and requirements standards.

Example

Let's see an example.

The example used for this recipe is the *Emulate Front and Rear Gearing* use case. This use case is shown in *Figure 2.32*, along with some closely related use cases:

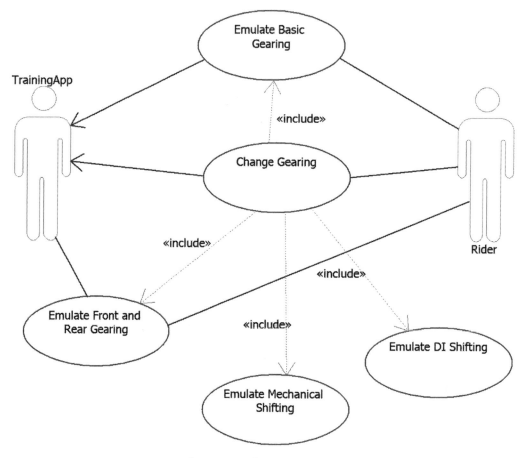

Figure 2.32 – Emulate Front and Rear Gearing use case in context

Describe the use case

All model elements deserve a useful description. In the case of a use case, we typically use the format shown in *Figure 2.33*:

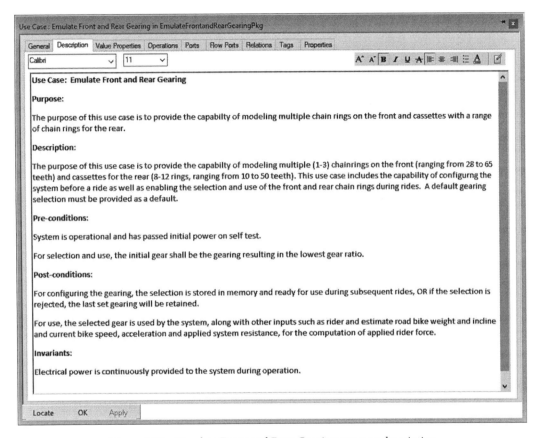

Figure 2.33 – Emulate Front and Rear Gearing use case description

Identify related actors

The related actors in this example are the **Rider** and the **Training App**. The rider signals the system to change the gearing via the gears control and receives a response in terms of changing resistance as well as setting the resistance mode to ERG or SIM mode. The training app, when connected, is notified of the current gearing so that it can be displayed, provides a simulated input of incline, and can optionally change between SIM and ERG modes. The relation of the actors to the use case is shown in *Figure 2.32*.

Define the execution context

The execution context creates blocks that represent the actors and the use case for the purpose of the analysis. In this example, the following naming conventions are observed:

- The block representing the use case has the use case name (with white space removed) preceded by Uc_. Thus, for this example, the use case block is named **Uc_EmulateFrontandRearGearing**.

- Blocks representing the actors are given the actor name preceded with a and an abbreviation of the use case. For this use case, the prefix is aEFRG_, so the actor blocks are named **aEFRG_Rider** and **aEFRG_TrainingApp.**

- The interface blocks are named as *<use case block>_<actor block>*. The names of the two interface blocks are **iUc_EmulateFrontandRearGearing_aEFRG_Rider** and **iUc_EmulateFrontandRearGearing_aEFRG_TrainingApp**. The normal form of the interface block is associated with the proxy port on the use case block; the conjugated form is associated with the corresponding proxy port on the actor block.

All these elements are shown in the IBD in *Figure 2.34*:

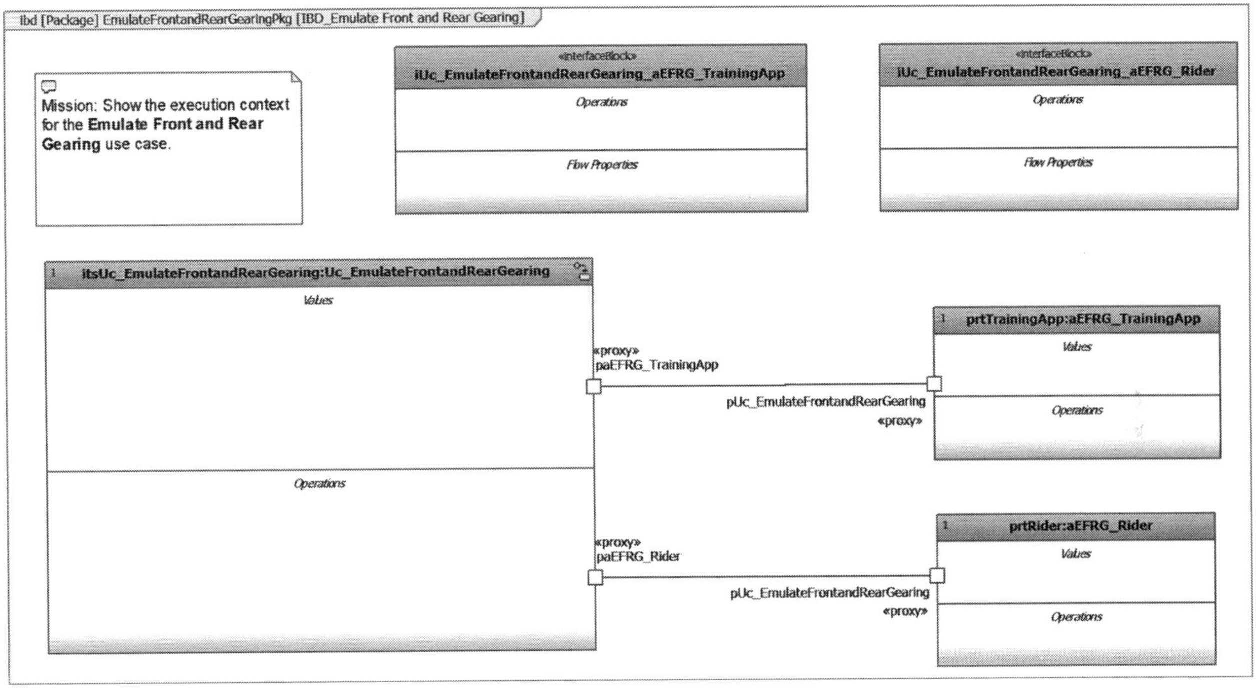

Figure 2.34 – Emulate Front and Rear Gearing use case execution context

Create ports and interfaces in the execution context

The (empty) ports and interfaces are added between the use case block and the actor blocks, as shown in *Figure 2.34*. These will be elaborated as the development proceeds in the next step.

Create an executable state model

Figure 2.35 shows the state machine for the **Emulate Front and Rear Gearing** use case. It is important to remember that the state machine is a restatement of textual requirements in a more formal language and *not* a declaration of design. The purpose of creating this state machine during this analysis is to identify requirement defects, not to design the system:

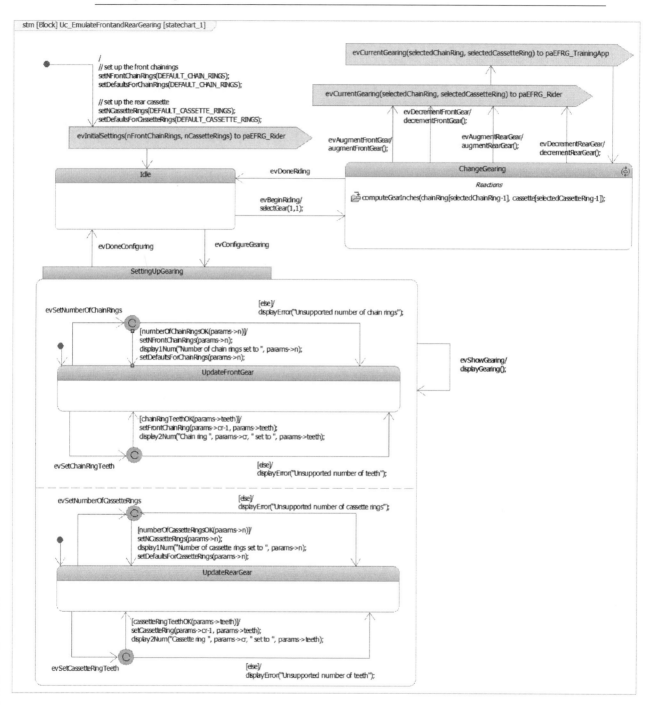

Figure 2.35 – State machine for Emulate Front and Rear Gearing

The use case block contains a number of system functions, value properties, and constants. These are shown in *Table 2.2*:

Feature	Description
System Functions	
augmentFrontGear	If permitted, augments the selected front gear by one
augmentRearGear	If permitted, augments the selected rear cassette gear by one
cassetteRingTeethOK	Returns TRUE if the number of teeth to set to the selected cassette ring is OK
chainRingTeethOK	Returns TRUE if the number of teeth to set to the selected chain ring is OK
computeGearInches	Sets the gearInches value property to the computed gear inches for the currently selected gearing
decrementFrontGear	If permitted, decrements the selected front cassette gear by one
decrementRearGear	If permitted, decrements the selected rear gear by one
display1Num	Displays a string and a number
display2Num	Displays two strings and two numbers
displayError	Displays an error message
numberOfCassetteRingsOK	Returns TRUE if the number of cassette rings being defined is OK
numberOfChainRingsOK	Returns TRUE if the number of front chain rings is OK
selectGear	Selects the front and rear rings as the current gearing
setCassetteRing	Defines the specified teeth for the specified cassette ring
setDefaultsForCassetteRings	Sets up the default gearing for the cassette rings
setDefaultsForChainRings	Sets up the default gearing for the front chain ring
setFrontChainRing	Specifies the number of teeth for the specified chain ring

Feature	Description
Value Properties	
`cassette`	A collection (array) of cassette rings, represented by the position (index) and number of teeth
`chainRing`	A collection (array) of chain rings, represented by the position (index) and number of teeth
`gearInches`	Real value computed by the gear ratio and the diameter of the wheel; specifies the mechanical advantage of the currently selected gearing
`nCassetteRings`	The number of defined cassette rings to be emulated
`nFrontChainRings`	The number of defined front chain rings to be emulated
`selectedCassetteRing`	The currently selected cassette ring while riding
`selectedChainRing`	The currently selected chain ring while riding
Named Constants	
`DEFAULT_CASSETTE_RINGS`	The default number of cassette rings (12)
`DEFAULT_CHAIN_RINGS`	The default number of chain rings (2)
`MAX_CASSETTE_RING_TEETH`	The maximum number of teeth in any cassette ring (50)
`MAX_CASSETTE_RINGS`	The maximum number of cassette rings (12)
`MAX_CHAIN_RING_TEETH`	The maximum number of teeth a chain ring (70)
`MAX_CHAIN_RINGS`	The maximum number of chain rings (3)
`MIN_CASSETTE_RING_TEETH`	The minimum number of cassette ring teeth (10)
`MIN_CHAIN_RING_TEETH`	The minimum number of chain ring teeth (20)

Table 2.2 – Emulate Front and Rear Gearing use case features

The behavior of the operations on the state machine are system functions. These must be elaborated for the purpose of simulation, and trace to requirements. For example, *Figure 2.36* shows the behavior for the system functions that set up the defaults for the gearing for the rear cassette and front chain rings and the function that computes the gear inches when the gear is changed. This can be done in the action language used for the model (C++ in this case) or in activity diagrams. For this example, I used activity diagrams:

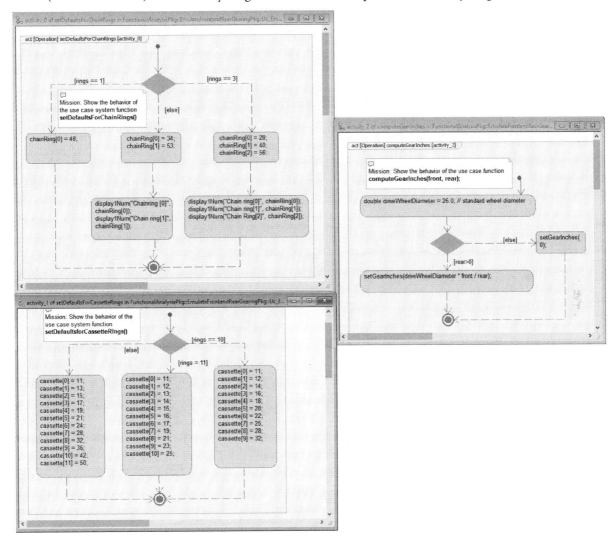

Figure 2.36 – Setting the defaults for Emulate Front and Rear Gearing

To support the simulation, the actor block **aEFRG_Rider** was instrumented with a state machine to interact with the use case block. This is shown in the following screenshot:

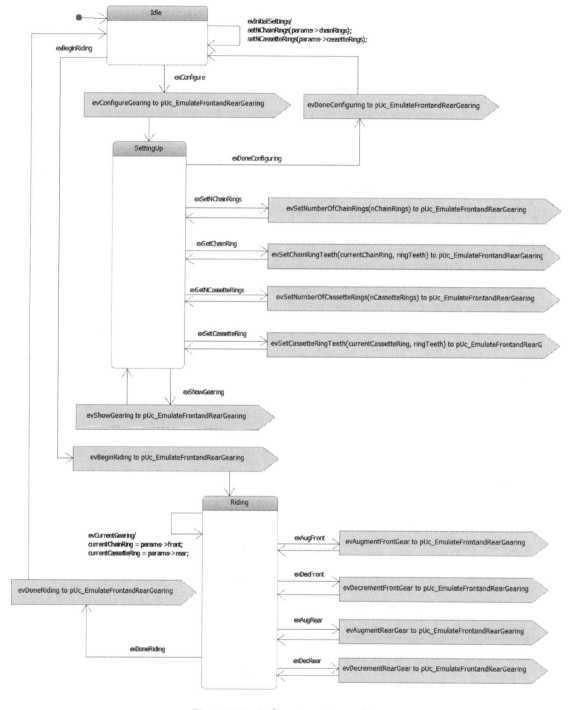

Figure 2.37 – Rider actor state machine

Generate use case scenarios

Scenarios are specific sequenced interaction sets that identify sequencing, timing, and values of different example users of a system. Sequence diagrams are generally easy to understand, even for non-technical stakeholders. In this recipe, sequences are created by exercising the use case state machine by changing the inputs to exercise different transition paths in the state machine. It is important to understand that there are usually an infinite set of possible scenarios, so we must constrain ourselves to consider a small representative set. The criteria we recommend is the *minimal spanning set*; this is a set of scenarios such that each transition path and action is executed at least once. More scenarios of interest can be added, but the set of sequences should at least meet this basic criterion.

Let's consider two different scenarios. The first (*Figure 2.38*) focuses on setting up the gearing for the bike prior to riding:

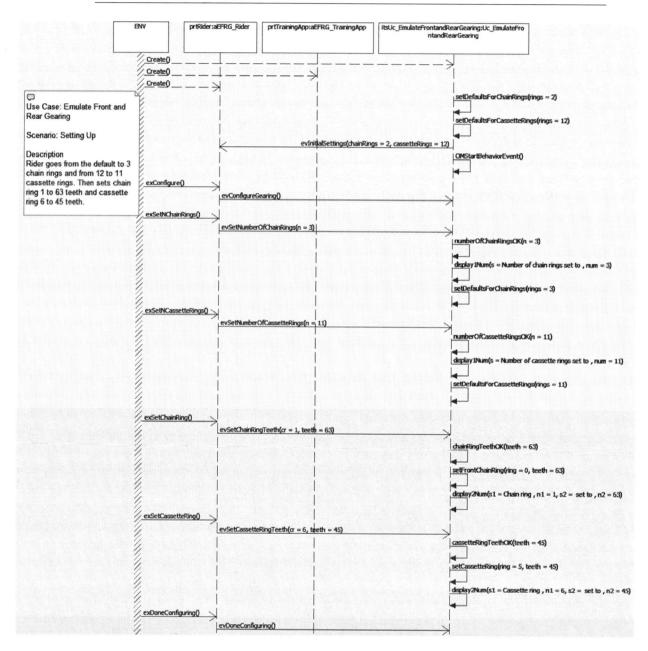

Figure 2.38 – Scenario for the gearing setup

The second scenario shows the rider changing gears while riding in *Figure 2.39*:

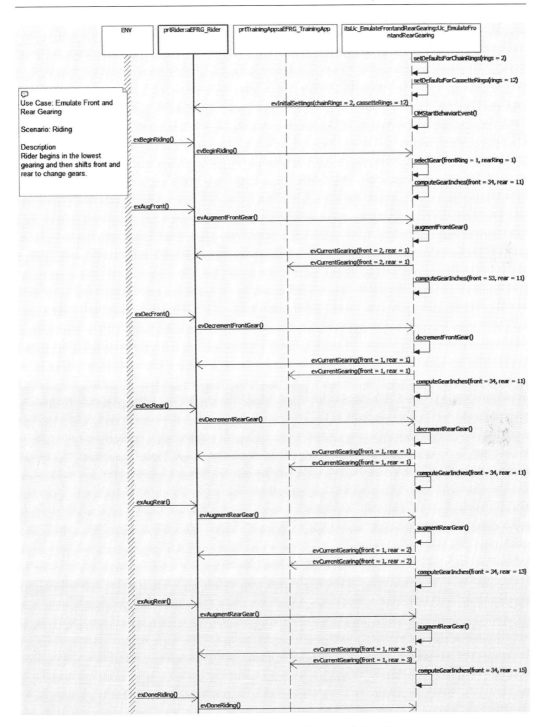

Figure 2.39 – Scenario for gear changes while riding

Verify and validate requirements

The creation of the state machines in the previous section and their execution allows us to identify missing, incorrect, or incomplete requirements. The panel diagram in *Figure 2.40* allows us to drive different scenarios and to perform *what if* analyses to explore the requirements:

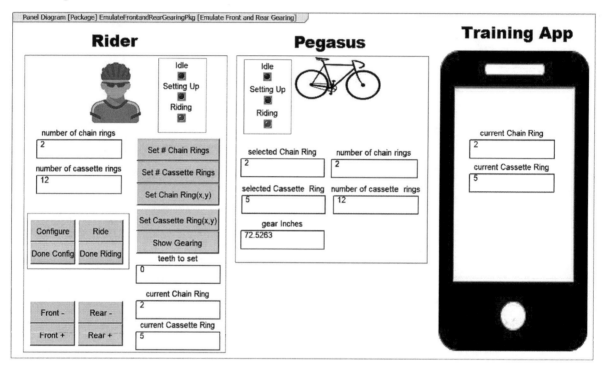

Figure 2.40 – Emulate Front and Rear Gearing panel diagram

Requirements_change

Parallel to the development and execution of the use case model, we maintain the textual requirements. This workflow event indicates the need to fix an identified requirement's defect.

Update the requirement set

In this example, we'll show the requirements in a table in the modeling tool. *Figure 2.41* shows the newly added requirements:

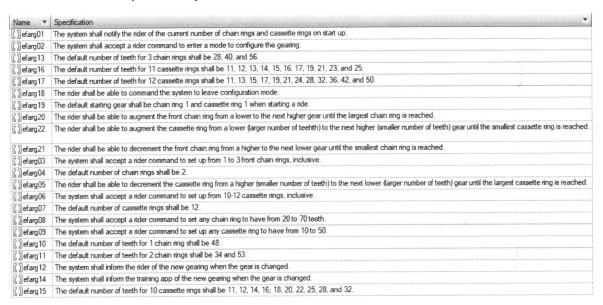

Name	Specification
efarg01	The system shall notify the rider of the current number of chain rings and cassette rings on start up.
efarg02	The system shall accept a rider command to enter a mode to configure the gearing.
efarg13	The default number of teeth for 3 chain rings shall be 28, 40, and 56.
efarg16	The default number of teeth for 11 cassette rings shall be 11, 12, 13, 14, 15, 16, 17, 19, 21, 23, and 25.
efarg17	The default number of teeth for 12 cassette rings shall be 11, 13, 15, 17, 19, 21, 24, 28, 32, 36, 42, and 50.
efarg18	The rider shall be able to command the system to leave configuration mode.
efarg19	The default starting gear shall be chain ring 1 and cassette ring 1 when starting a ride.
efarg20	The rider shall be able to augment the front chain ring from a lower to the next higher gear until the largest chain ring is reached.
efarg22	The rider shall be able to augment the cassette ring from a lower (larger number of teehth) to the next higher (smaller number of teeth) gear until the smallest cassette ring is reached.
efarg21	The rider shall be able to decrement the front chain ring from a higher to the next lower gear until the smallest chain ring is reached.
efarg03	The system shall accept a rider command to set up from 1 to 3 front chain rings, inclusive.
efarg04	The default number of chain rings shall be 2.
efarg05	The rider shall be able to decrement the cassette ring from a higher (smaller number of teeth) to the next lower (larger number of teeth) gear until the largest cassette ring is reached.
efarg06	The system shall accept a rider command to set up from 10-12 cassette rings, inclusive.
efarg07	The default number of cassette rings shall be 12.
efarg08	The system shall accept a rider command to set any chain ring to have from 20 to 70 teeth.
efarg09	The system shall accept a rider command to set up any cassette ring to have from 10 to 50.
efarg10	The default number of teeth for 1 chain ring shall be 48.
efarg11	The default number of teeth for 2 chain rings shall be 34 and 53.
efarg12	The system shall inform the rider of the new gearing when the gear is changed.
efarg14	The system shall inform the training app of the new gearing when the gear is changed.
efarg15	The default number of teeth for 10 cassette rings shall be 11, 12, 14, 16, 18, 20, 22, 25, 28, and 32.

Figure 2.41 – Emulate Front and Rear Gearing requirements

Add trace links

Now that we've identified the requirements, we can add them to the model and add trace links to the **Emulate Front and Rear Gearing** use case. This is shown in the table in *Figure 2.42*:

	Emulate Basic Gearing	Control Resistance	Emulate Front and Rear Gearing
From: UseCase Scope: Chapter2			
requirement_0	requirement_0		
requirement_1	requirement_1		
requirement_2	requirement_2		
requirement_3	requirement_3		
requirement_4	requirement_4		
requirement_5	requirement_5		
CR_requirement_1		CR_requirement_1	
CR_requirement_2		CR_requirement_2	
CR_requirement_3		CR_requirement_3	
CR_requirement_4		CR_requirement_4	
CR_requirement		CR_requirement_5	
CR_requirement_6		CR_requirement_6	
CR_requirement_7		CR_requirement_7	
CR_requirement_8		CR_requirement_8	
CR_requirement_9		CR_requirement_9	
CR_requirement_10		CR_requirement_10	
CR_requirement_11		CR_requirement_11	
CR_requirement_12		CR_requirement_12	
CR_requirement_13		CR_requirement_13	
CR_requirement_14		CR_requirement_14	
CR_requirement_15		CR_requirement_15	
CR_requirement_21		CR_requirement_21	
CR_requirement_22		CR_requirement_22	
CR_requirement_23		CR_requirement_23	
CR_requirement_24		CR_requirement_24	
CR_requirement_25		CR_requirement_25	
efarg01			efarg01
efarg02			efarg02
efarg13			efarg13
efarg16			efarg16
efarg17			efarg17
efarg18			efarg18
efarg19			efarg19
efarg20			efarg20
efarg22			efarg22
efarg21			efarg21
efarg03			efarg03
efarg04			efarg04
efarg05			efarg05
efarg06			efarg06
efarg07			efarg07
efarg08			efarg08
efarg09			efarg09
efarg10			efarg10
efarg11			efarg11
efarg12			efarg12
efarg14			efarg14
efarg15			efarg15

(Left margin labels: To: Requirement   Scope: RequirementsAnalysisPkg)

Figure 2.42 – Emulate Front and Rear Gearing requirements trace

Perform a use case and requirements review

With the analysis complete and the requirements added, a review can be conducted to evaluate the set of requirements. This review typically includes various subject matter experts in addition to the project team.

Functional analysis with user stories

The other functional analysis recipes in this chapter are fairly rigorous and use executable models to identify missing and incorrect requirements. User stories can be used for simple use cases that don't have complex behaviors. In the other functional analysis recipes, the validation of the use case requirements can use a combination of subject matter expert review, testing, and even formal mathematical analysis prior to their application to the system design. User stories only permit validation via review and so are correspondingly harder to verify as complete, accurate, and correct.

A little bit about user stories

User stories are approximately equivalent to scenarios in that both scenarios and user stores describe a singular path through a use case. Both are *partially constructive* in the sense that individually, they only describe part of the overall use case. User stories do it with natural language text while scenarios do it with SysML sequence diagrams. The difference between user stories and scenarios is summarized in *Figure 2.43*:

User Story

They often are cast in a standardized form:

"As a " <user> "I want" <feature> "so that " <reason>

For example,

As a pilot, **I want the pedal to control the rudder in a range of -30 to +30 degrees** so that I can steer left or right.

- Simple
- No special tools needs
- Easy to review with stakeholders

- It may be difficult or impossible to write a user story for a complex interaction
- It is difficult to state qualities of service within a user story

Scenario

Supported in UML, scenarios show the user story as a set of message interactions and services among a set of roles, once of which is the system.

- Can represent far more complex interactions than textual user stores
- Supported by many UML/SysML tools
- Can support model-based trace to requirements and design elements with summary table generation
- QoS requirements can be added as annotations and constraints

- Requires a tool (although simple drawing tools can be used)
- A little bit more complex to read and understand
- Not in 'natural language'

Figure 2.43 – User story or scenarios

User stories have a canonical form:

As a <user> I want <feature> so that <reason>|<outcome>

A few examples of user stores are provided in *Chapter 1, Basics of Agile Systems Modeling,* in the *Estimating effort* recipe. Here's one of them.

User Story: Set Resistance Under User Control

As a rider, I want to set the resistance level provided to the pedals to increase or decrease the effort for a given gearing, cadence, and incline so that the system simulates the road riding effort.

Each user story represents a small set of requirements. A complete set of user stories includes almost all requirements traced by the use case.

In SysML, we represent user stories as stereotypes of use cases and use *«include»* relations to indicate the use case to which the user story applies. The stereotype adds the **acceptance_criteria** tag to the user story so that it is clear what it means to satisfy the user story. An example relating a use case, user stories, and requirements is shown in *Figure 2.44*:

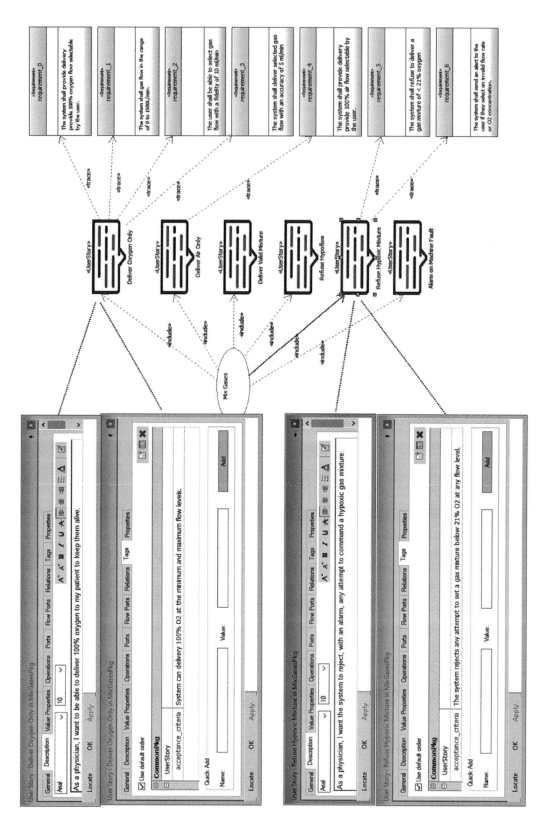

Figure 2.44 – User stories as a stereotype of a use case

Here are some guidelines for developing good user stories:

- **Focus on the users**: Avoid discussing or referencing design, but instead focus on the user-system interaction.

- **Use personae to discover the stories**: Most systems have many stakeholders with needs to be met. Each user story represents a single stakeholder role. Represent all the users with the set of user stories.

- **Develop user stories collaboratively**: User stories are a lightweight analytic technique and can foster good discussions among the product owner and stakeholder, resulting in the identification of specific requirements.

- **Keep the stories simple and precise**: Each story should be easy to understand; if it is complex, then try to break it up into multiple stories.

- **Start with epics or use cases**: User stories are small, finely grained things, while epics and use cases provide a larger context.

- **Refine your stories**: As your understanding deepens and requirements are uncovered, the user stories should be updated to reflect this deeper understanding.

- **Be sure to include acceptance criteria**: Acceptance criteria complete the narrative by providing a clear means by which the system design and implementation can be judged to appropriately satisfy the user need.

- **Stay within the scope of the owning epic or use case**: While it is true that in simple systems, user stories may not have an owner epic or use case, most will. When there is an owner epic or use case, the story must be a subset of that capability.

- **Cover all the stories**: The set of user stories should cover all variant interaction paths of the owning epic or use case.

- **Don't rely solely on user stories**: Because user stories are a natural language narrative, it isn't clear how they represent all the quality of service requirements. Be sure to include safety, reliability, security, performance, and precision requirements by tracing the user story to those requirements.

Purpose

User stories are a lightweight analytic technique for understanding and organizing requirements. Most commonly, these are stories within the larger capability context of an epic or use case. User stories are approximately equivalent to a scenario.

Inputs and preconditions

A use case naming a capability of the system from an actor-use point of view.

Outputs and postconditions

The most important outcome is a set of requirements accurately and appropriately specifying the behavior of the system for the use case and acceptance criteria in terms of what it means to satisfy them.

How to do it...

Figure 2.45 shows the workflow for this recipe. It is a more lightweight and more informal approach than the preceding recipes but may be useful for simple use cases. Note that unlike previous recipes, it does not include a behavioral specification in formal language such as activities or state machines:

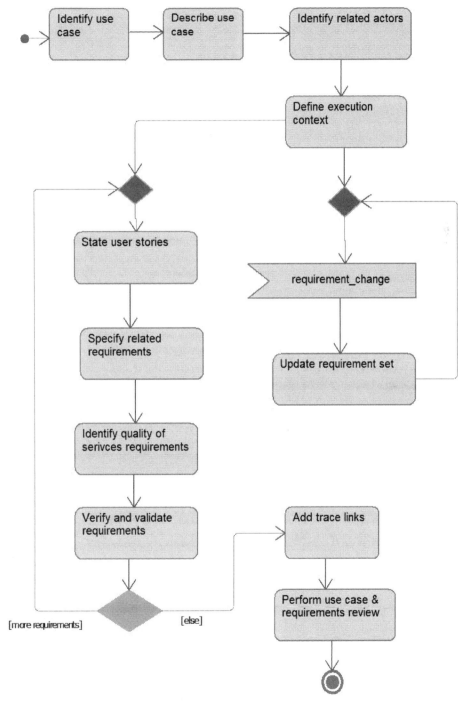

Figure 2.45 – Functional analysis with user stories

Identify the use case

This first step is to identify the generic usage of which the scenarios of interest, user stories, and requirements are aspects.

Describe the use case

The description of the use case should include its purpose, a general description of the flows, preconditions, postconditions, and invariants (assumptions). Some modelers add the specific actors involved, user stories, and scenarios, but I prefer to use the model itself to contain those relations.

Identify related actors

The related actors are those people or systems outside our scope that interact with the system while it executes the current use case. These actors can send messages to the system, receive messages from the system, or both.

State the user stories

This step includes more than creating the **As a <role> ...** statements. It also includes creating *«include»* relations from the owning use case and the addition of acceptance criteria for each user story. If this is the first time this is being done, you will also have to create a *«user story»* stereotype that applies to use cases to be able to create the model elements.

Specify the related requirements

User stories are a way to capture required system behavior from the actor's perspective. They generally represent a small number of textual system requirements. This step enumerates them.

Identify the quality of service requirements

It is very common to forget to include various kinds of qualities of service. This step is an explicit reminder to specify *how well* the services are provided. Common qualities of service include safety, security, reliability, performance, precision, fidelity, and accuracy.

Verify and validate the requirements

For this recipe, validating the requirements is done with a review with the relevant stakeholders. This should involve looking at the use, the set of user stories, the user stories themselves and their acceptance criteria, and the functional and quality of service requirements.

Requirements_change

Parallel to the development and execution of the use case model, we maintain the textual requirements. This workflow event indicates the need to fix an identified requirement's defect.

Update the requirement set

In response to an identified requirement's defect, we fix the textual requirements by adding, deleting, or modifying requirements. This will then be reflected in the updated model.

Add trace links

Once the use case model and requirements stabilize, we add trace links using the *«trace»* relation or something similar. These are generally backtraces to stakeholder requirements as well as forward links to any architectural elements that might already exist.

Perform a use case and requirements review

Once the work has stabilized, a review for correctness and compliance with standards may be done. This allows subject matter experts and stakeholders to review the requirements, use case, and user stories for correctness, and for quality assurance staff to ensure compliance with modeling and requirements standards.

Example

Here's an example.

Identify the use case

For this recipe, we will analyze the **Emulate DI Shifting** use case. In many ways, this use case is an ideal candidate for user stories because the use case is simple and not overly burdened with quality of service requirements.

Describe the use case

The use case description is shown in *Figure 2.46*:

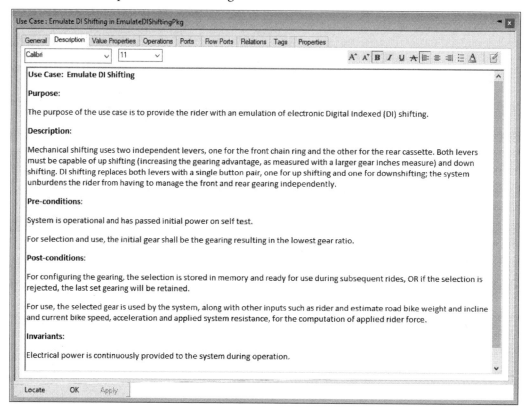

Figure 2.46 – Description of the Emulate DI Shifting use case

> **Note**
>
> Interested readers can learn more about DI shifting here: `https://en.wikipedia.org/wiki/Electronic_gear-shifting_system`

Identify related actors

The only actor in this use case is the **Rider**, as shifting gears is one of the three key ways that the **Rider** interacts with the system (the other two being pedaling and applying the brakes).

State the user stories

Figure 2.47 shows the three identified user stories for the use case: using buttons to shift gears, handling gearing cross-over on upshifting, and handling gearing cross-over on downshifting. Note this diagram is very similar to *Figure 2.44*; however, rather than use an icon for the user stories, this diagram uses standard SysML notation. Additionally, the canonical form of the user story in the description and the acceptance criteria in the tag are exposed in comments:

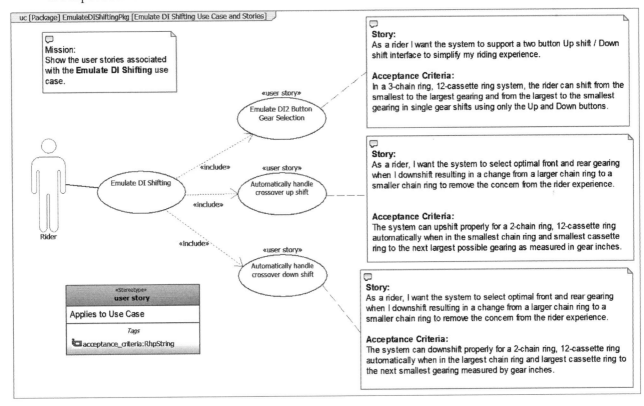

Figure 2.47 – Emulate DI Shifting user stories

Specify the related requirements

As these are simple user stories, there are a small number of functional requirements. See *Figure 2.48*:

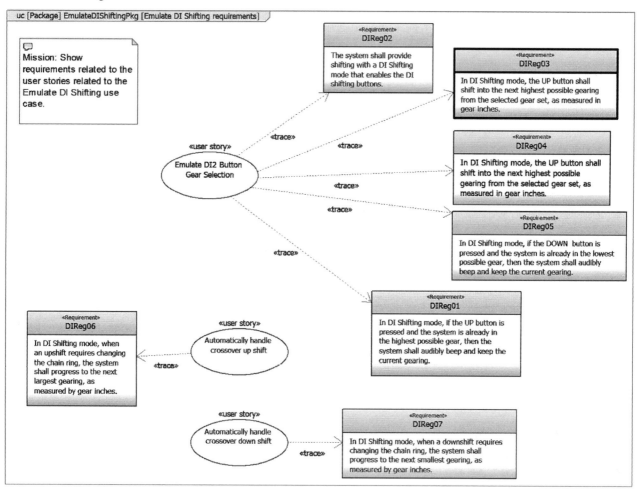

Figure 2.48 – Emulate DI Shifting functional requirements

Identify the quality of service requirements

The previous step specified a small number of requirements but didn't clarify how well these system functions are to be performed. Most notably, performance and reliability requirements are missing. These are added in *Figure 2.49*, shown this time in a requirements table:

Name	Specification
DIReg01	In DI Shifting mode, if the UP button is pressed and the system is already in the highest possible gear, then the system shall audibly beep and keep the current gearing.
DIReg02	The system shall provide shifting with a DI Shifting mode that enables the DI shifting buttons and disables the shifting levers.
DIReg03	In DI Shifting mode, the UP button shall shift into the next highest possible gearing from the selected gear set, as measured in gear inches.
DIReg04	In DI Shifting mode, the UP button shall shift into the next highest possible gearing from the selected gear set, as measured in gear inches.
DIReg05	In DI Shifting mode, if the DOWN button is pressed and the system is already in the lowest possible gear, then the system shall audibly beep and keep the current gearing.
DIReg06	In DI Shifting mode, when an upshift requires changing the chain ring, the system shall progress to the next largest gearing, as measured by gear inches.
DIReg07	In DI Shifting mode, when a downshift requires changing the chain ring, the system shall progress to the next smallest gearing, as measured by gear inches.
DIQoSReq01	In DI Mode, shifts shall be executed in less than 400 ms or 1/4 pedal stroke, whichever is longer in time.
DIQosReq02	The DI shifting button shall perform reliably for at least 100,000 presses.
DIQoSReq03	In DI Shifting mode, gear shifts may be taken regardless of current power load being applied to the gears, from 0W to the maximum load allowed.

Figure 2.49 – Emulate DI Shifting quality of service and functional requirements

Verify and validate the requirements

The next step is to validate the user stories and related requirements with the stakeholders to ensure their correctness, and look for missing, incorrect, or incomplete requirements.

Requirements_change

During this analysis, a stakeholder notes that nothing is said about how the system transitions between mechanical shifting and DI shifting. The following requirements are added:

- The system shall enter DI Shifting Mode by selecting that option in the Configuration App.

- Once DI Shifting Mode is selected, this selection shall persist across resets, power resets, and software updates.

- Mechanical shifting shall be the default on startup or after a factory-settings reset.

- The system shall leave DI Shifting mode when the user selects the **Mechanical Shifting** option in the Configuration App.

Update the requirements set

The requirements are updated to reflect the stakeholder input from earlier.

Add trace links

Trace links from both the use case and user stories to the requirements are added. These are shown in diagrammatic form in *Figure 2.50*. Note: the figure does not show that the **Emulate DI Shifting** use case traces to all these requirements just to simplify the diagram:

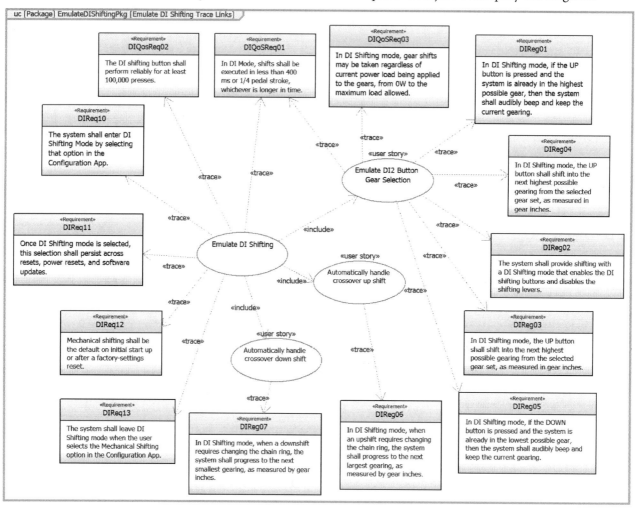

Figure 2.50 – Emulate DI Shifting trace links

Perform a use case, user story, and requirements review

With the analysis complete and the requirements added, a review can be conducted to evaluate the set of requirements. This review typically includes various subject matter experts in addition to the project team.

Model-based safety analysis

The term *safety* can be defined as *freedom from harm*. Safety is one of the three pillars of the more general concern of *system dependability*. Safety is generally considered with respect to the system causing or allowing physical harm to persons, up to and including death. Depending on the industry, different systems must conform to different safety standards, such as DO-178 (airborne software), ARP4761 (aerospace systems), IEC 61508 (electronic systems), ISO 26262 (automotive safety), IEC 63204 (medical), IEC 60601 (medical), and EN50159 (railway), just to name a few. While there is some commonality among the standards, there are also a number of differences that you must take into account when developing systems to comply with those standards.

This recipe provides a generic workflow applicable to all these standards, but you may want to tailor it for your specific needs. Note that we recommend this analysis is done on a per-use case basis so that the analysis of each relevant use case includes safety requirements in addition to the functional and quality of service requirements.

A little bit about safety analysis

Some key terms for safety analysis are as follows:

- **Accident** – A loss of some kind, such as injury, death, equipment damage, or financial. Also known as a *mishap*.
- **Risk** – The product of the likelihood of an accident and its severity.
- **Hazard** – A set of conditions and/or events that inevitably results in an accident.
- **Fault tolerance time** – the period of time a system can manifest a fault before an accident is likely to occur.
- **Safety control measure** – An action or mechanism that improves systems safety either by 1) reducing an accident, hazard, or risk's likelihood or 2) reducing its severity.

The terms *faults*, *failures*, and *errors* are generally used in one of three ways, depending on the standard employed:

- Faults lead to failures, which lead to errors:

  a. Fault – An incorrect step, process, or data.

  b. Failure – The inability of a system or component to perform its required function.

  c. Error – A discrepancy between an actual value or action and the theoretically correct value or action.

d. A fault at one level can lead to a failure one level up.

- Faults are actual behaviors that are in conflict with specified or desired behaviors:

  a. Fault – Either a failure or an error.

  b. Failure – An event that occurs at a point in time when a system or component performs incorrectly.

  - Failures are *random* and may be characterized with a probability distribution.

  c. Error – A condition in which a system or component systematically fails to achieve its required function.

  - Errors are *systematic* and always exist, even if they are not manifest.

  - Errors are the result of requirement, design, implementation, or deployment mistakes, such as a software bug.

  d. Manifest – When a fault is visible. Faults may be manifest or latent.

- Faults are undesirable anomalies in systems or software (ARP-4761):

  Failure – A loss of function or a malfunction of a system

  Error – The occurrence arising as a result of an incorrect action or decision by personnel operating or maintaining a system, or a mistake in the specification, design, or implementation

The most common way to perform the analysis is with a **Fault Tree Analysis (FTA)** diagram. This is a causality diagram that relates normal conditions and events, and abnormal conditions and events (such as faults and failures), with undesirable conditions (hazards). A *Hazard Analysis* is generally a summary of the safety analysis from one or more FTAs.

FTA

An FTA diagram connects nodes with logic flows to aid understanding of the interactions of elements relevant to the safety concept. Nodes are either events, conditions, outcomes, or logical operators, as shown in *Figure 2.51*. See `https://www.sae.org/standards/content/arp4761/` for a good discussion of FTA diagrams:

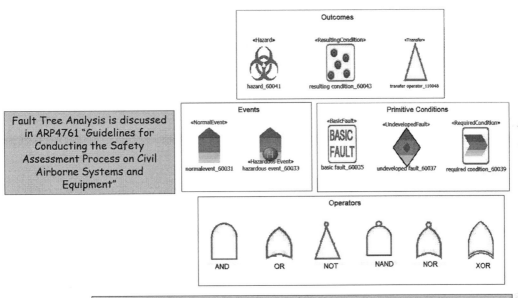

Figure 2.51 – FTA elements

The logical operators take one or more inputs and produce a singular output. The **AND** operator, for example, produces a **TRUE** output if both its inputs are **TRUE**, while the **OR** operator returns **TRUE** if either of its inputs is **TRUE**. There is also a **TRANSFER** operator, which allows an FTA diagram to be broken up into subdiagrams.

Figure 2.52 shows an example FTA diagram. This diagram shows the safety concerns around an automotive braking system. The hazard under consideration is **Failure to Brake**. The diagram shows that this happens when the driver intends to brake and at least one of three conditions is present: a pedal input fault, an internal fault, or a wheel assembly fault:

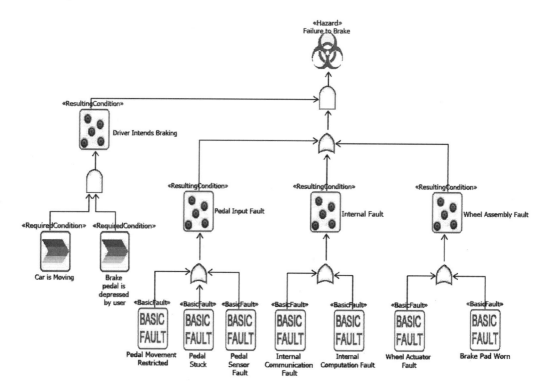

Figure 2.52 – Example FTA diagram

Cut sets

A *cut* is a collection of faults that, taken together, can lead to a hazard. A *cut set* is the set of such collections such that all possible paths from the primitive conditions and events to the hazard have been accounted for. In general, if you consider n primitive conditions as binary (present or non-present), then there are 2^n cuts that must be examined. Consider the simple FTA in *Figure 2.53*. The primitive conditions are marked as *a* though *e*:

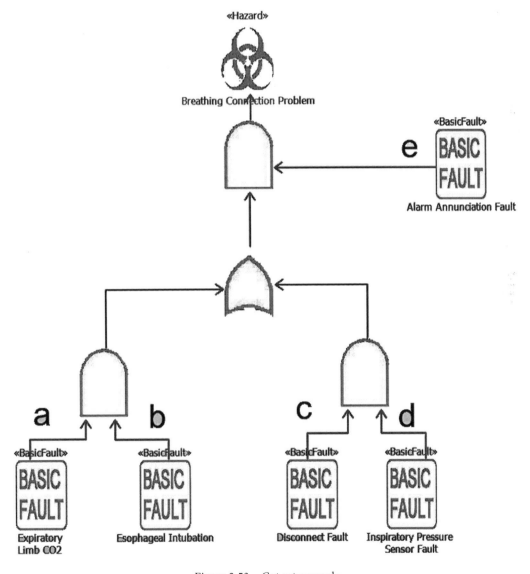

Figure 2.53 – Cut set example

With 5 primitive conditions, 32 prospective cut sets should be considered, of which only 3 can lead to the hazard manifestation, as shown in *Figure 2.54*. Only these three need to be subject to the addition of a safety measure:

Basic Fault/ Condition	a	b	c	d	e	Hazard
1	T	T	F	F	T	T
2	F	F	T	T	T	T
3	T	T	T	T	T	T
4	T	F	F	F	T	F
5	F	T	F	F	T	F
6	F	F	T	F	T	F
7	F	F	F	F	T	F
8	T	T	T	T	F	F
9	F	T	T	T	F	F
10	F	F	T	T	F	F
(22 more…)						

Figure 2.54 – Cut sets example (2)

Hazard analysis

There is normally one FTA diagram per identified hazard, although that FTA diagram can be decomposed into multiple FTA diagrams via the transfer operator. A system, however, normally has multiple hazards. These are summarized into a hazard analysis. A hazard analysis summarizes the hazard-relevant metadata, including the hazard name, description, severity, likelihood, risk, tolerance time, and possibly, related safety-relevant requirements and design elements.

UML Dependability Profile

I have developed a UML Dependability Profile that can be applied to UML and SysML models in the Rhapsody tool. It is free to download from `https://www.bruce-douglass.com/safety-analysis-and-design`. The ZIP repository includes instructions on the installation and use of the profile. All the FTA diagrams in this recipe were created in Rhapsody using this profile.

Purpose

The purpose of this recipe is to create a set of safety-relevant requirements for the system under development by analyzing safety needs.

Inputs and preconditions

A use case naming a capability of the system from an actor-use point of view that has been identified, described, and for which relevant actors have been identified. Note: this recipe is normally performed in parallel with one of the functional analysis recipes from earlier in this chapter.

Outputs and postconditions

The most important outcome is a set of requirements specifying how the system will mitigate or manage the safety concerns of the system. Additionally, a safety concept is developed identifying the needs for a set of safety control measures, which is summarized in a hazard analysis.

How to do it...

Figure 2.55 shows the workflow for the recipe:

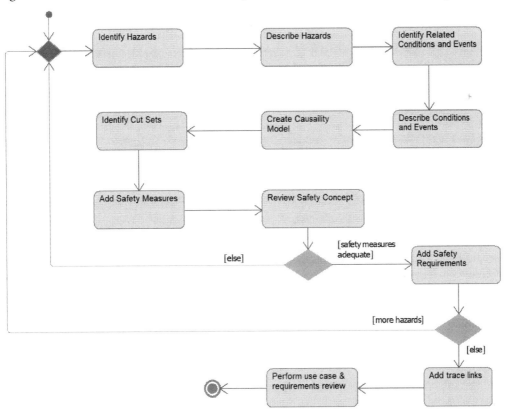

Figure 2.55 – Model-based safety analysis workflow

Identify the hazards

A hazard is a condition that can lead to an accident. This step identifies the hazards relevant to the use case under consideration that could arise from the system behavior in its operational context.

Describe the hazards

Hazards are specified by their safety-relevant metadata. This generally includes the hazard name, description, likelihood, severity, risk, and safety integrity level, adopted from the relevant safety standard.

Identify related conditions and events

This step identifies the conditions and events related to the hazard, including the following:

- Required conditions
- Normal events
- Hazardous events
- Fault conditions
- Resulting conditions

Describe conditions and events

Each condition and event should be described. A typical set of aspects of such a description includes the following:

- Overview
- Effect
- Cause
- Current controls
- Detection mechanisms
- Failure mode
- Likelihood or **Mean Time Between Failure** (**MTBF**)
- Severity
- Recommended action
- Risk priority (product of likelihood and severity or MTBF/severity)

Create a causality model

This step constructs an FTA connecting the various nodes with logic flows and logic operators flowing from primitive conditions up to resulting conditions and, ultimately, to the hazard.

Identify cut sets

Identify the relevant cuts from all possible cut sets to ensure that each is safe enough to meet the safety standard being employed. This typically requires the addition of safety measures, as discussed in the next step.

Add safety measures

Safety measures are technical means or usage procedures by which safety concerns are mitigated. All safety measures either reduce the likelihood or the severity of an accident. In this analysis, care should be taken to specify the effect of the measures rather than their implementation, as much as possible. Design-level hazard analysis will be conducted later to ensure the adequacy of the design realization of the safety measures specified here.

Review the safety concept

This step reviews the analysis and the set of safety measures to ensure their adequacy.

Add safety requirements

The safety requirements specify what the design, context, or usage must meet in order to be adequately safe. These requirements may be specially annotated to indicate their safety relevance or may just be treated as requirements that the system must satisfy.

Example

Let's see an example.

The Pegasus example problem isn't ideal for showing safety analysis because it isn't a safety-critical system. For that reason, we will use a different example for this recipe.

Problem statement – medical gas mixer

The **Medical Gas Mixer** (**MGM**) takes in gas from wall supplies for O_2, He, N_2, and air and mixes them and delivers a flow to a medical ventilator. When operational, the flow must be in the range of 100 ml/min to 1,500 ml/min with a delivered O_2 percentage (known as the *Fraction of Delivered Oxygen*, or FiO_2) of no less than 21%. The flows from the individual gas sources are selected by the physician via the ventilator's interface.

Neonates face an additional hazard of *hyperoxia* – too much oxygen in the blood, as this can damage their retinas and lungs.

In this example, the focus of our analysis is the **Mix Gases** use case.

Identify the hazards

The fundamental hazard of this system is *hypoxia* – delivering too little oxygen to sustain health. The average adult breathes about 7-8 liters of air per minute, resulting in a delivered oxygen flow of around 1,450 ml O_2/minute. For neonates, required flow can be as low as 40 ml O_2/minute, while for large adults the need might be as high as 4,000 ml O_2/minute at rest.

Describe the hazards

The *«Hazard»* stereotype includes a set of tags for capturing the hazard metadata. This is shown in *Figure 2.56*:

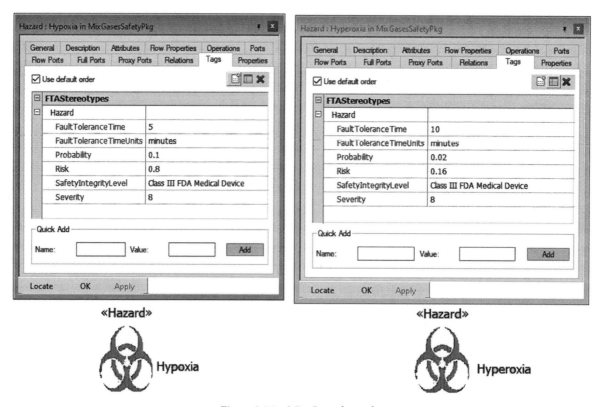

Figure 2.56 – Mix Gases hazards

Identify related conditions and events

For the rest of this example, we will focus exclusively on the **Hypoxia** hazard. There are two required conditions (or assumptions/invariants): first, that the gas mixer is in operation and second, that there is a physician in attendance. This latter assumption means that the physician can be part of the *safety loop*.

There a number of faults that are relevant to the **Hypoxia** hazard:

- The gas supply runs out of either air or O_2, depending on which is selected.
- The gas supply valve fails for either air or O_2, depending on which is selected.
- The patient is improperly intubated.
- A fault in the breathing circuit, such as disconnected hoses or leaks.
- The ventilator commands an FiO_2 level that is too low.
- The ventilator commands a total flow of the specified mixture that is too low.

Describe conditions and events

The *«BasicFault»* stereotype provides tags to hold fault metadata. The metadata for three of these faults, **Gas Supply Valve Fault**, **Improper Intubation**, and **Commanded FiO2Too Low** are shown in *Figure 2.57*. Since the latter has more primitive underlying causes, it will be changed to a **Resulting Condition** and the primitive faults added as follows:

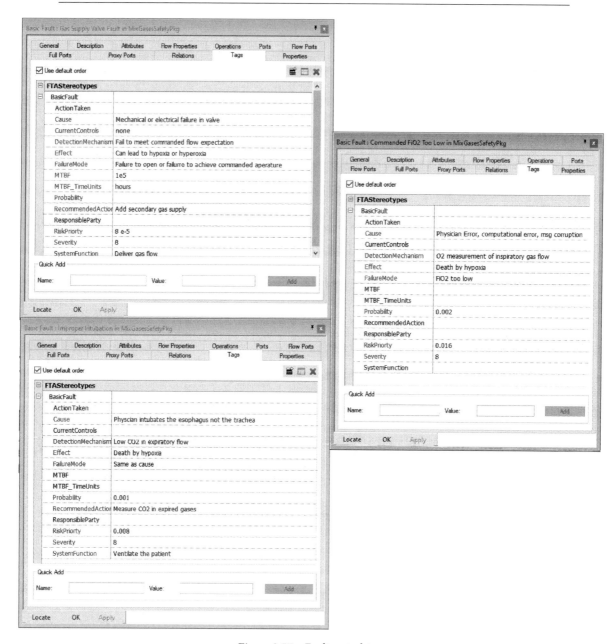

Figure 2.57 – Fault metadata

Create a causality model

Figure 2.58 shows the initial FTA. This FTA doesn't include any safety mechanisms, which will be added shortly. Nevertheless, this FTA shows a causality tree linking the faults to the hazard with a combination of logic operators and logic flows:

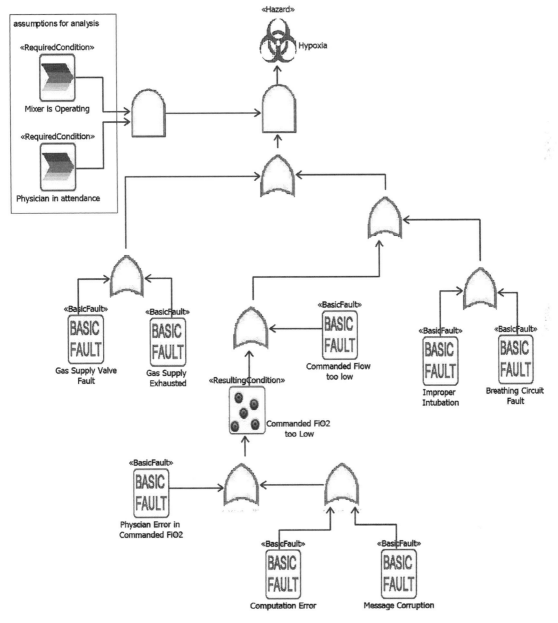

Figure 2.58 – Initial FTA

Identify cut sets

There are 10 primitive fault elements, so there are potentially 2^{10} (1,024) cuts in the cut set, although we are only considering cases in which the assumptions are true, so that immediately reduces the set to 2^8 (256) possibilities. All of these are ORed together so it is enough to independently examine just the 8 basic faults.

Add safety measures

Adding a safety measure reduces either the likelihood or the severity of the outcome of a fault to an acceptable level. This is done on the FTA by creating *anding-redundancy*. This means that for the fault to have its original effect *both* the original fault must occur *and* the safety measure must fail. The likelihood of both failing is the product of their probabilities. For example, if the **Gas Supply Valve Fault** has a probability of 8×10^{-5} and we add a safety measure of a gas supply backup that automatically kicks in that has a probability of failure of 2×10^{-6}, then the resulting probability of both failing is 16×10^{-11}. Acceptable probabilities of hazards can be determined from the safety standard being used.

For the identified faults, we will add the following safety measures:

- Gas Supply Valve Fault safety measure: Secondary Gas Supply

- Gas Supply Exhausted fault safety measure: Secondary Gas Supply

- Improper Intubation fault safety measures: CO_2 Sensor on Expiratory Flow and Alarm On Fault

- Breathing Circuit Fault safety measures: Inspiratory Limb Flow Sensor and Alarm On Fault

- Physician Error In Commanded O_2 safety measures: Range Check Commanded O_2 and Alarm On Fault

- Computation Error fault safety measures: Secondary Parallel Computation and Alarm On Fault

- Message Corruption fault safety measure: Message CRC

- Commanded Flow Too Low fault safety measures: Inspiratory Limb Flow Sensor and Alarm On Fault

Adding these results in a more detailed FTA. To ensure readability, transfer operators are added to break up the diagram by adding a sub-diagram for **Commanded FiO$_2$ Too Low**. *Figure 2.59* shows the high-level FTA diagram with safety measures added. Note that they are added in terms of what happens when they fail. Failure of safety measures is indicated with a red bold font for emphasis.

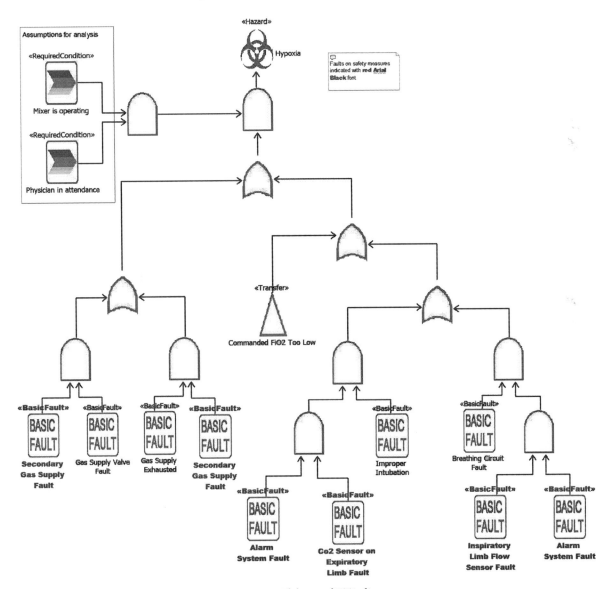

Figure 2.59 – Elaborated FTA diagram

Note also the use of the transfer operator to connect this diagram with the more detailed one for the sub-diagram shown in *Figure 2.60*:

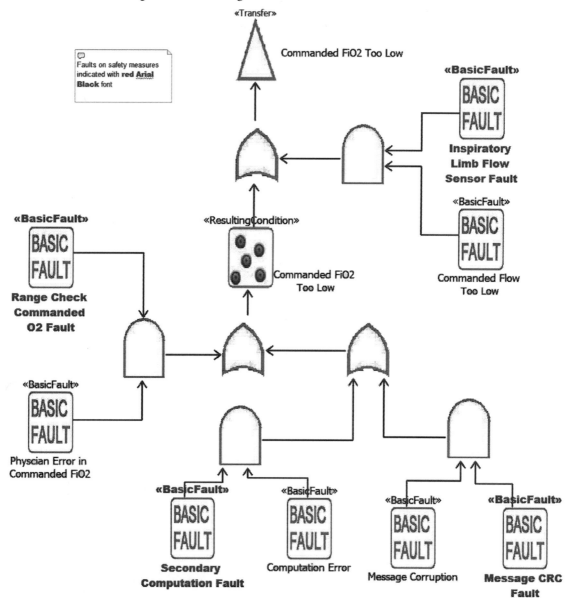

Figure 2.60 – Commanded FIO$_2$ flow Too Low FTA

Review the safety concept

The set of safety measures addresses all the identified safety concerns.

Add safety requirements

Now that we have identified the safety measures necessary to develop a safe system, we must create the requirements that mandate their inclusion. These are shown in *Figure 2.61*:

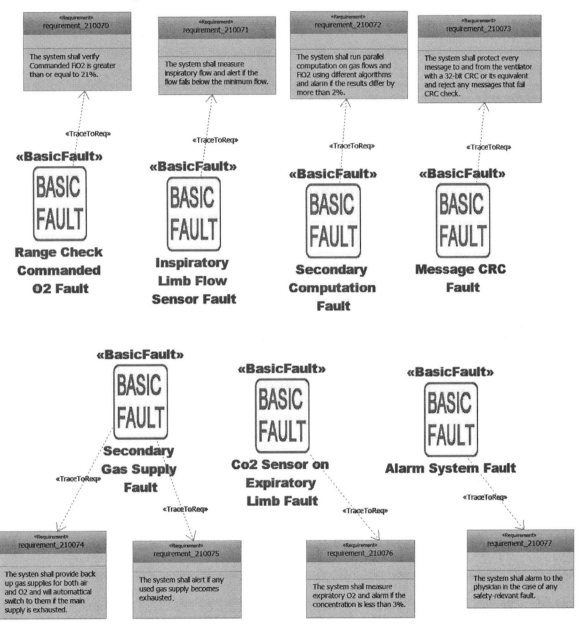

Figure 2.61 – Safety requirements

Model-based threat analysis

It used to be that most systems were isolated and disconnected; the only way to attack such a system required a physical presence. Those days are long gone.

These days, most systems are internet-enabled and connected via apps to cloud-based servers and social media. This presents opportunities to attack these systems, compromise their security, violate their privacy, steal their information, and cause damage through malicious software.

Unfortunately, little has been done to protect systems in a systematic fashion. The most common response I hear when consulting is " *Security. Yeah, I need me some of that,"* and the issue is ignored thereafter. Sometimes, some thought is given to applying security tests *ex post facto,* or perhaps doing some code scans for software vulnerabilities, but very little is done to methodically analyze a system from a cyber-physical security posture standpoint. This recipe addresses that specific need.

Basics of cyber-physical security

Security is the second pillar of dependability. The first, safety, was discussed in the previous recipe. Reliability, the remaining pillar, is discussed in the next recipe. Key concepts for a systematic approach to cyber-security needs are as follows:

Security – Resilience to attack.

Asset – A security-relevant feature of a system that the system is responsible for protecting. Assets have the following properties:

- Access Level Permitted
- Accountability
- Asset Kind:

  a. Actor

  b. Information Asset

  c. Current Asset

  d. Resource Asset

     e. Physical Asset

     f. Service Asset

     g. Security Asset

     h. Tangible Asset

     i. Intangible Asset

- Availability
- Clearance Required
- ID
- Integrity
- Value

Asset Context – The system or extra-system elements enshrouding one or more assets; a safe in which money is kept is a simple example of an asset context. An asset context may be decomposed into contained asset context elements.

Security field – The set of assets, asset contexts, vulnerabilities, and countermeasures for a system (also known as the system security posture).

Vulnerability – A weakness in the security field of an asset that may be exploited by an attack.

Threat – The means by which a vulnerability of the security field of an asset may be exploited.

Attack – The realization of a threat invoked by a threat agent.

Attack chain – A type of attack that is composed of sub-attacks, sometimes known as a *cyber killchain*. Most modern attacks are of this type.

Threat agent – A human or automated threat source that invokes an attack, typically intentionally.

Security countermeasure – A means by which a vulnerability is protected from attack. Countermeasures may be passive or active, and may be implemented by design elements, policies, procedures, labeling, training, or obviation. Countermeasure types include the following:

- Access control
- Accounting
- Active detection
- Authentication
- Recovery
- Boundary control
- Backup
- Encryption
- Deterrence
- Obviation
- Nonrepudiation
- Policy action
- Response
- Scanning detection

Role – A part a person plays in a context, such as a user, administrator, or trusted advisor.

Authenticated role – A role with explicit authentication, which typically includes a set of permissions.

Permission – The right or ability to perform an action that deals with an asset. A role may be granted permissions to perform different kinds of access to an asset.

Access – A type of action that can be performed on a resource. This includes the following:

- No access
- Unrestricted access
- Read access
- Modify access
- Open access
- Close access
- Entry access
- Exit access
- Create access
- Delete access
- Remove access
- Invoke access
- Configure access
- Interrupt access
- Stop access

Security violation – The undesired intrusion into, interference with, or theft of an asset; this may be the result of an attack (intentional) or a failure (unintentional).

Risk – The possibility of an undesirable event occurring or an undesirable situation manifesting. Risk is the product of (at least) two values: likelihood and severity. Severity in this case is a measure of the asset value.

Risk Number – The numeric value associated with a risk (likelihood multiplied by severity).

Modeling for security analysis

The UML Dependability Profile used in the previous recipe also includes cyber-physical threat modeling using the previously mentioned concepts. The security information can be captured and visualized in a number of diagrammatic and tabular views. It may be downloaded at `https://www.bruce-douglass.com/safety-analysis-and-design`.

Security Analysis Diagram

The **Security Analysis Diagram** (**SAD**) is a logical causality diagram very similar to the FTA diagram used in the previous recipe. A SAD shows how assets, events, and conditions combine to express vulnerabilities, how countermeasures address vulnerabilities, and how attacks cause security violations. The intention is to identify when and where countermeasures are or should be added to improve system security. This diagram uses logical operations (AND, OR, NOT, XOR, and so on) to combine the presence of assets, asset context, situations, and events. *Figure 2.62* shows a typical SAD. You can identify the kind of element by the stereotype, such as «*Asset*», «*Asset Context*», «*Countermeasure*», «*Vulnerability*», and «*Threat*»

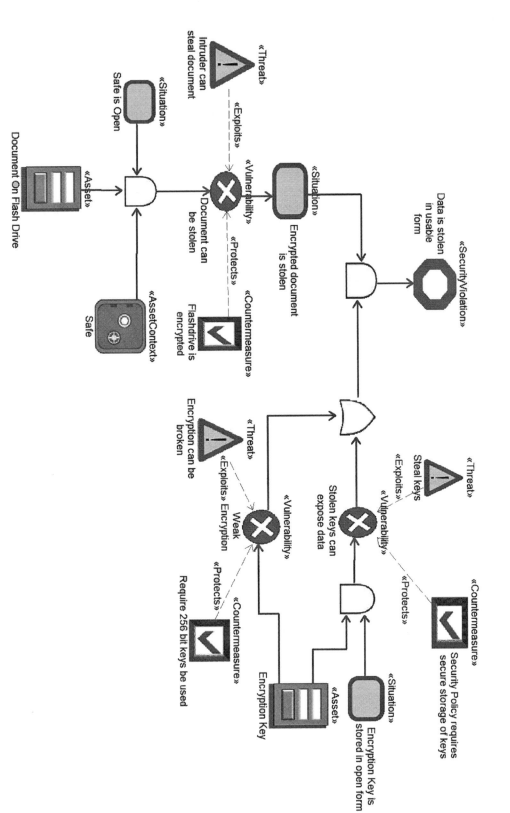

Figure 2.62 – A typical SAD

Asset diagram

Another useful diagram is the asset diagram. The asset diagram is meant to show the relationships between assets, asset contexts, vulnerabilities, countermeasures, supporting security requirements, and security-relevant design elements. *Figure 2.63* shows an asset diagram in use:

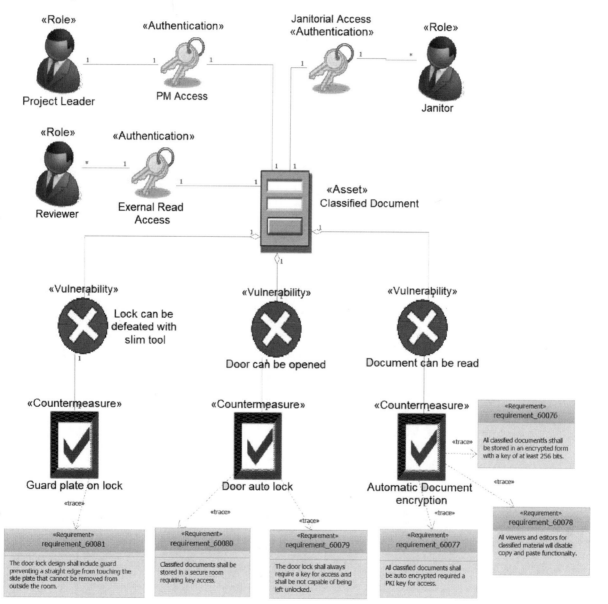

Figure 2.63 – Asset diagram

Attack flow diagram

The last diagram of particular interest is the attack flow diagram. It is a specialized activity diagram with stereotyped actions to match the canonical attack chain, shown in *Figure 2.64*:

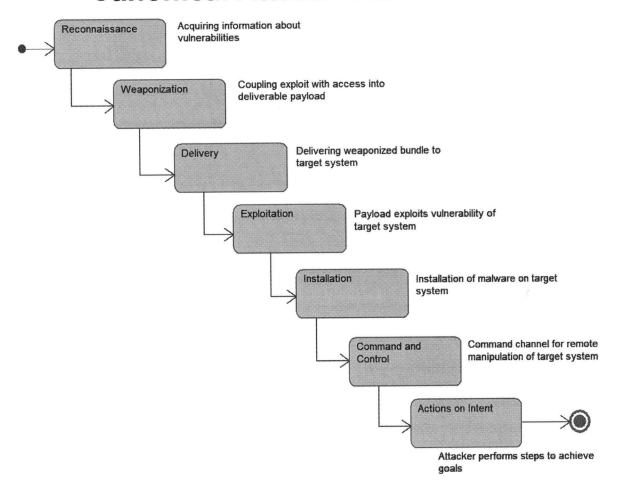

Figure 2.64 – Canonical attack chain

The purpose of this diagram is to allow us to reason about how attacks unfold so that we can identify appropriate spots to insert security countermeasure actions. *Figure 2.65* shows an example of its use:

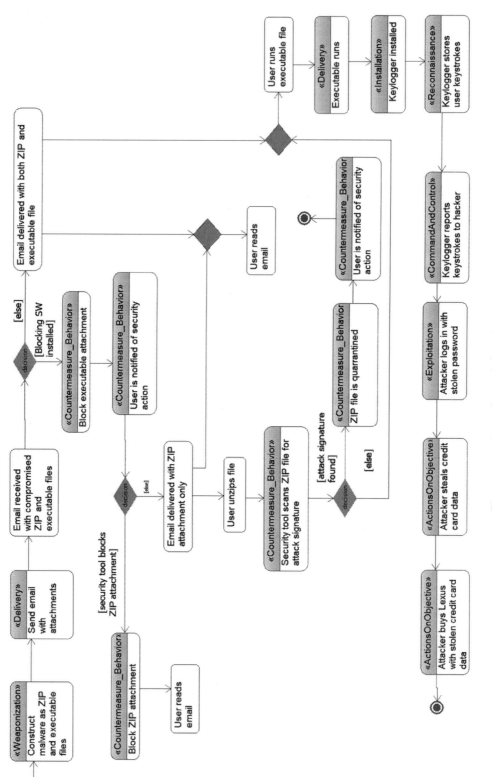

Figure 2.65 – Example attack flow diagram

The stereotyped actions either identify the action as a part of the attack chain or identify the action as a countermeasure. The actions without stereotypes are normal user actions.

Tabular views

Tables and matrices can easily be constructed to summarize the threat analysis. The Security Posture Table, for example, is a tabular summary for assets, asset context, vulnerabilities, and countermeasures and their important security-relevant metadata, including **Name**, **Description**, **Risk Number**, **Severity**, **Probability**, **Consequence**, and **Impact**.

Purpose

The purpose of this recipe is to identify system assets subject to attack, how they can be attacked, and where to best apply countermeasures.

Inputs and preconditions

A use case naming a capability of the system from an actor-use point of view that has been identified, described, and for which relevant actors have been identified. Note: this recipe is normally performed in parallel with one of the functional analysis recipes from earlier in this chapter.

Outputs and postconditions

The most important outcome is a set of requirements specifying how the system will mitigate or manage the security concerns of the system. Additionally, a security posture concept is identifying the need for a set of security control measures, which is summarized in a cyber-physical threat analysis.

How to do it...

The workflow for this recipe is shown in *Figure 2.66*:

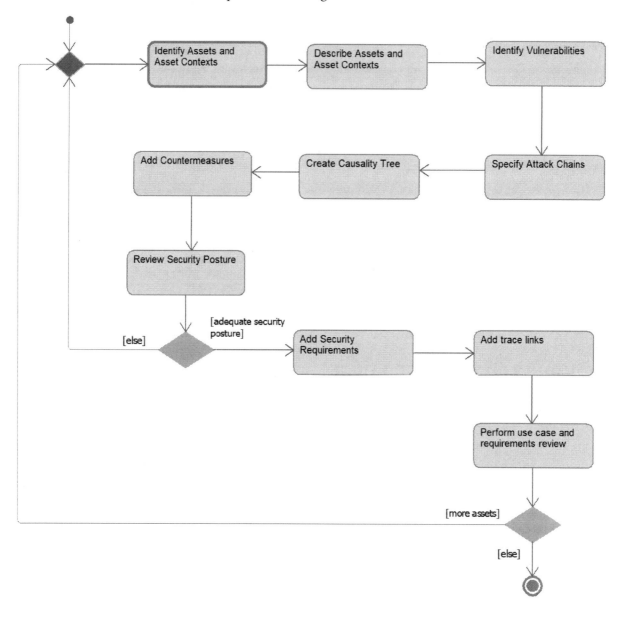

Figure 2.66 – Security analysis workflow

Identify assets and asset contexts

Assets are system or environmental features of value that the system is charged to protect. Assets can be classified as being one of several types, including the following:

- **Information**: Information of value, such as a credit card number

- **Currency**: Money, whether in physical or virtual form

- **Resource**: A capability, means, source, system, or feature of value, such as access to GPS for vehicle navigation

- **Physical**: A tangible resource that can be physically compromised, threatened, or damaged, such as a gas supply for a medical ventilator

- **Service**: A behavior of the system that provides value, such as delivering cardiac therapy

- **Security**: A security measure that can be compromised as a part of an attack chain, such as a firewall

Of course, these categories overlap to a degree, so categorize your assets in a way that makes sense to you and your stakeholders.

Assets are system or environmental features that have value that your system is responsible for protecting. Create one or more asset diagrams to capture the assets and asset contexts. You can optionally add access roles, permissions, and vulnerabilities, but the primary purpose is to identify and understand the assets.

Describe assets and asset contexts

Assets have a number of properties you may want to represent. At a minimum, you want to identify the asset kind and the value of the asset. Asset value is important because you will be willing to spend greater cost and effort to protect more valuable assets. You may also want to specify the asset availability, clearance, or access level required.

Identify vulnerabilities

Vulnerabilities are weaknesses in the system security field; in this context, we are especially concerned with vulnerabilities specific to assets and asset contexts. If you are using known technology, then sources such as the **Common Vulnerability Enumeration** (**CVE**) or **Common Weakness Enumeration** (**CWE**) are good sources of information.

> **Note**
> Refer to `https://cve.mitre.org/cve/` and `https://cwe.mitre.org/` for further reading.

Specify attack chains

Most attacks are not a single action, but an orchestrated series of actions meant to defeat countermeasures, gain access, compromise a system, and then perform *actions on objective* to exploit the asset. Use the attack flow diagram or attack scenario diagrams to model and understand how an attack achieves its goals and where countermeasures might be effective.

Create a causality tree

Express your understanding of the causal relations between attacks, vulnerabilities, and countermeasures on security analysis diagrams. These diagrams are similar to FTAs and are used in safety analysis.

Add countermeasures

Once a good understanding is achieved of the assets, their vulnerabilities, the attack chains used to penetrate the security field, and the causality model, you're ready to identify what security countermeasures are appropriate and where in the security field they belong.

Review the security posture

Review the updated security posture to ensure that you've identified the correct set of vulnerabilities, attack vectors, and countermeasures. It is especially important to review this in the context of the CVE and CWE.

Add security requirements

When you're satisfied that the proposed countermeasures, add requirements for them. As with all requirements, these should specify what needs to be done and not specifically how, since the latter concern is one of design.

Add trace links

Add trace links from your security analysis to the newly added requirements, from the associated use case to the requirements, and from the use case to the security analysis. If an architecture already exists, also add trace links from the architectural elements to the security requirements, as appropriate.

Perform a use case and requirements review

This final step of the recipe reviews the set of requirements for the use case, including any requirements added as a result of this recipe.

Next, let's see an example.

Example

For this example, we'll consider the use case **Measure Performance Metrics**. This use case is about measuring metrics such as heart rate, cadence, power, (virtual) speed, and (virtual) distance and uploading them to the connected app. The use case is shown in *Figure 2.67*:

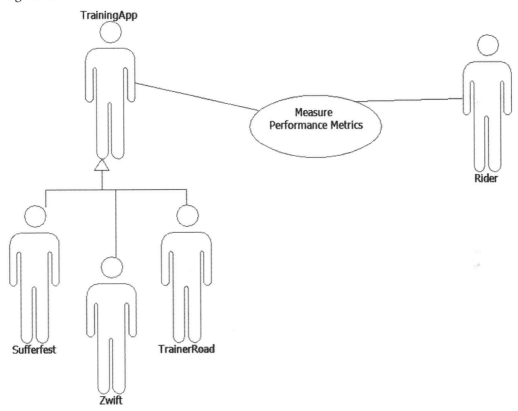

Figure 2.67 – Measure Performance Metrics use case

Identify assets and asset contexts

There are two kinds of assets that might be exposed; the login ID and password used during the connection to the app and the rider's privacy-sensitive performance data. The assets of concern are the **Ride Login Data** and **Rider Performance Metrics**.

Other use cases potentially expose other assets, such as the **Update Firmware** use case exposing the system to malware, but those concerns would be dealt with during the analysis of the latter use case.

Describe assets and asset contexts

The asset metadata is captured during the analysis. It is shown in *Figure 2.68*. Both assets are of the **INFORMATION_ASSET** asset kind. The **Rider Login Data** is a high-valued asset, while the **Rider Performance Data** is of medium value:

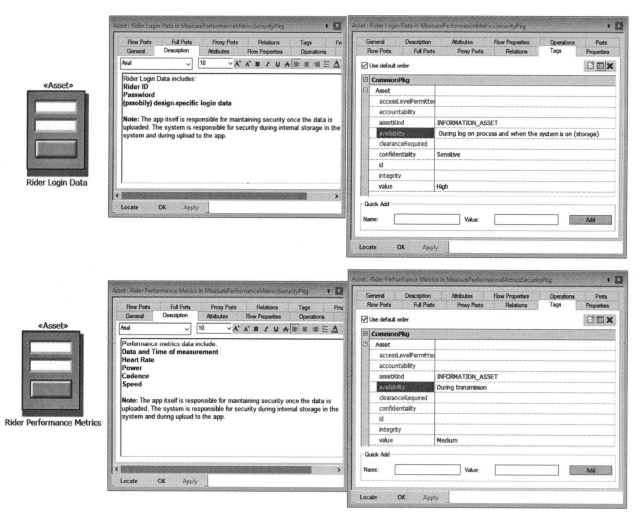

Figure 2.68 – Asset metadata

Identify vulnerabilities

Next, we look to see how the assets express vulnerabilities. We can identify three vulnerabilities that apply to both assets: impersonation of a network, impersonation of the connected app, and sniffing the data as it is sent between the system and the app. See *Figure 2.69*:

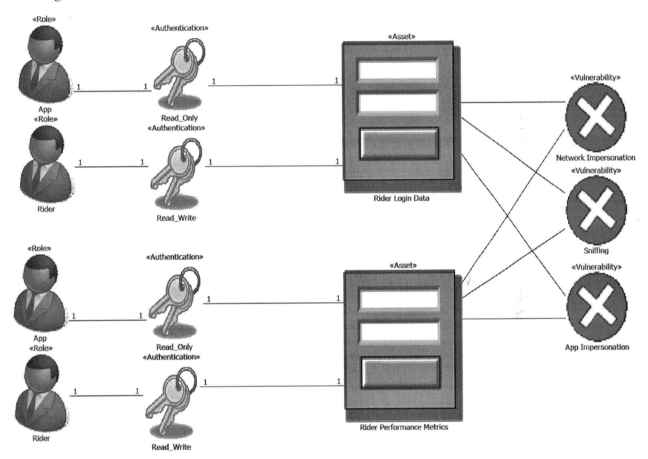

Figure 2.69 – Asset vulnerabilities

Specify attack chains

Figure 2.70 shows the attack chain for the **Measure Performance Metrics** use case. These attack chains show the normal processing behavior along with the attack behaviors of the adversary and the mitigation behaviors of the system:

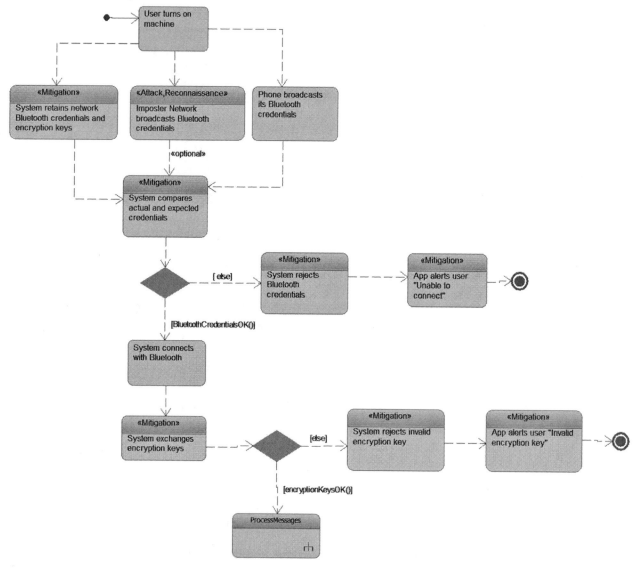

Figure 2.70 – Measure Performance Metrics attack chain

The attack chain is further decomposed into a call behavior, shown in *Figure 2.71*:

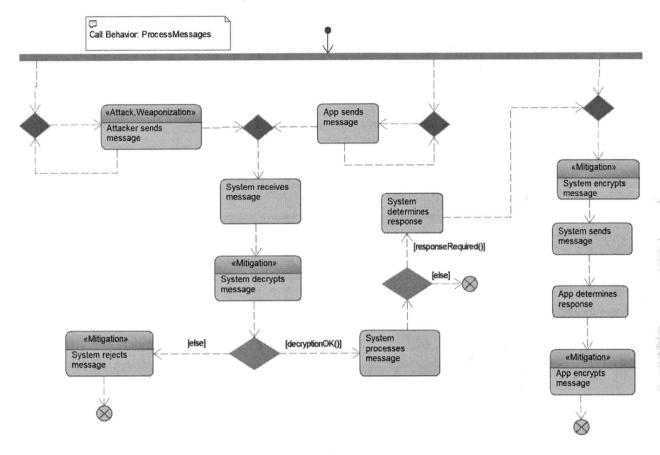

Figure 2.71 – Process Messages attack chain

Create a causality tree

Now that we've identified and characterized the assets, vulnerabilities, and attacks, we can put together a causality model. This is shown in *Figure 2.72* for compromising login data and credentials:

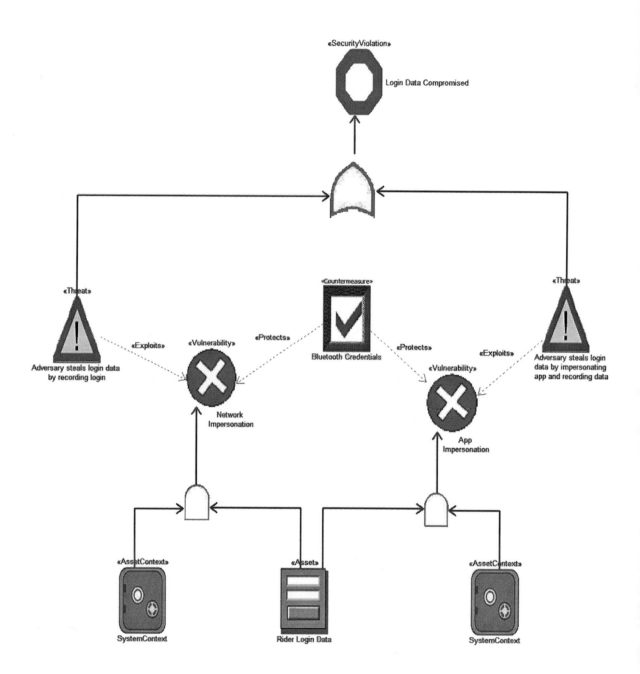

Figure 2.72 – SAD for rider login data

We also have a casualty model in *Figure 2.73* for the rider metric data:

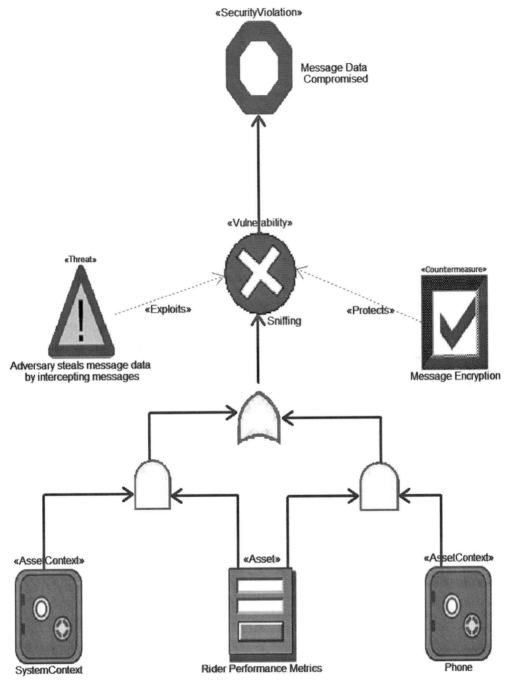

Figure 2.73 – SAD for rider metric data

Add countermeasures

We can see in the previous two figures that our causality diagram has identified two security countermeasures: the use of credentials for Bluetooth connections and the addition of encryption for message data.

Review the security posture

In this step, we review our security posture. The security posture is the set of assets, asset contexts, vulnerabilities, and countermeasures. In this case, the assets are the rider login data and the rider metrics data. The login data includes the username and password. The metrics data includes all the metrics gathered, including speed, distance, elapsed time, date and time of workout, power, cadence, and heart rate.

There are two asset contexts: the system itself and the phone hosting the app. The latter context is out of the system's scope and we have limited ability to influence its security, but we can require the use of the protections it provides. Notably, this includes Bluetooth credentials and the encryption of data during transmission. Other use cases may allow us better control over the security measures in this asset context. For example, the **Configure System** use case uses a configuration app of our own design that we can ensure stores data internally in encrypted form; we have no such control over the third-party training apps.

We have identified three vulnerabilities. During login, the system can be compromised either by network or app impersonation. By pretending to be a trusted conduit or trusted actor, an adversary can steal login information. We address these concerns with two explicit countermeasures: message encryption and the use of credentials. Security could be further enhanced by requiring multi-factor authentication, but that was not considered necessary in this case. During rides, the system transmits metric data to the app for storage, display, and virtual simulation. An adversary could monitor such communications and steal that data. This is addressed by encrypting messages between the system and the app.

Add security requirements

The security requirements are simply statements requiring the countermeasure design and implementation. In this case, there are only two such requirements:

- The system shall require the use of a Bluetooth credentials agreement between the system and the app to permit message traffic.

- The system shall encrypt all traffic between itself and the app with at least 128-bit encryption.

Add trace links

The new requirements trace to the **Measure Performance Metrics** use case. Further, trace links are added from the countermeasures to the requirements, linking our analysis to the requirements.

Perform a use case and requirements review

We can now review the use case, functional analysis, and dependability analyses for completeness, accuracy, and correctness.

Specifying logical system interfaces

System interfaces identify the sets of services, data, and flows into and out of a system. By *logical interfaces*, we mean abstract interfaces that specify the content and precision of the flows but not their physical realization. For example, a system interface to a radar might include a message **herezaRadarTrack(r: RadarTrack)** as a SysML event carrying a radar track as a parameter without specifying what communication means will be used, let alone the bit-mapped structure of the 1553 Bus message. Nevertheless, the specification of the interface allows us to consider the set of services requested from the system by actors, the set of services needed by the system from the actors, and the physical flows across the system boundary.

The initial set of interfaces are a natural outcome of our use case analysis. Each use case characterizes a set of interactions of the system with a group of actors for a similar purpose. These interactions necessitate system interfaces. This recipe will focus on the identification of these interfaces and the identification of the data and flows that they carry; the actual definition of these data elements is described in the last recipe in this chapter, *Creating the logical data schema*.

The logical interfaces from a single use case analysis are only a part of the entire set of system interfaces. The set interfaces from multiple use cases are merged together during system architecture definition. This topic is discussed in the recipes of the next chapter, *Chapter 3, Developing System Architectures*. Those are still logical interfaces, however, and abstract away implementation detail. The specification of physical interfaces from their logical specification is described in *Chapter 4, Handoff to Downstream Engineering*.

A note about SysML ports and interfaces

SysML supports a few different ways to model interfaces and this is intricately bound up with the topic of ports. SysML has the *standard port* (from UML), which is typed by an *interface*. An interface is similar to an abstract class; it contains specifications of services but no implementation. A block that realizes an interface must provide an implementation for each operation specified within that interface. UML ports are typed by the interfaces they support. A port may either *provide* or *require* an interface. If an interface is *provided* by the system, that means that the system must provide an implementation that realizes the requested services. If an interface is *required*, then the system can request an actor to provide those services. These services can be synchronous calls or asynchronous event receptions and can carry data in or out, as necessary. Note that the difference between *provided* and *required* determines where the services are implemented and not the direction of the data flow.

These interfaces are fundamentally about services that can, incidentally, carry data. SysML also defines *flow ports*, which allow data or flow to be exchanged without services being explicitly involved. Flow ports are bound to a single data or flow element and have an explicit flow direction, either into or out from the element. Block instances could bind flow ports to internal value properties and connect them to flow ports on other blocks that were identically typed.

SysML 1.3 and later versions deprecate the standard and flow ports and add the *proxy port*. Proxy ports essentially combine both the standard ports and flow ports. The flows specified as sent or received by a proxy part are defined to be *flow properties* rather than value properties, a small distinction in practice. More importantly, proxy ports are not typed by *interfaces* but rather by *interface blocks*. Interface blocks are more powerful than interfaces in that they can contain nested parts and proxy ports themselves. This allows the modeling of some complex situations that are difficult with simple interfaces. With proxy ports, gone are the *lollipop* and the *socket* notations; they are replaced by the port and port conjugate (~) notation. In short, standard ports use interfaces, but with proxy ports use interface blocks. The examples in this book exclusively use proxy ports and interface blocks and not standard ports.

Note

To be clear, **deprecated** means that the use of these ports is **discouraged** but they are still part of the standard, so feel free to use them.

This recipe specifically refers to the identification and specification of logical interfaces during use case specification, as experience has shown this is a highly effective means for identifying the system interfaces.

Continuous flows

Systems engineering must contend with something that software development does not: continuous flows. These flows may be information but are often physical in nature, such as materiel, fluids, or energy. SysML extends the discrete nature of UML activities with the *«continuous»* stereotype for continuous flows. The *«stream»* stereotype (from UML) refers to object flows (*tokens*) that arrive as a series of flow elements at a given rate. *«continuous»* is a special case where the time interval between streaming flow elements approaches zero. In practice, *«stream»* is used for a flowing stream of discrete elements, often at a rate specified with the SysML *«rate»* stereotype, while *«continuous»* is used for truly continuous flows. An example of *«stream»* might be a set of discrete images sent from a video camera at a rate of 40 frames per second. An example of *«continuous»* flow might be water flowing through a pipe or the delivery of electrical power.

In my work, I use these stereotypes on flows in sequence diagrams as well. I do this by applying the stereotypes to messages and through the use of a *continuous* interaction operator. An example is shown in *Figure 2.74*:

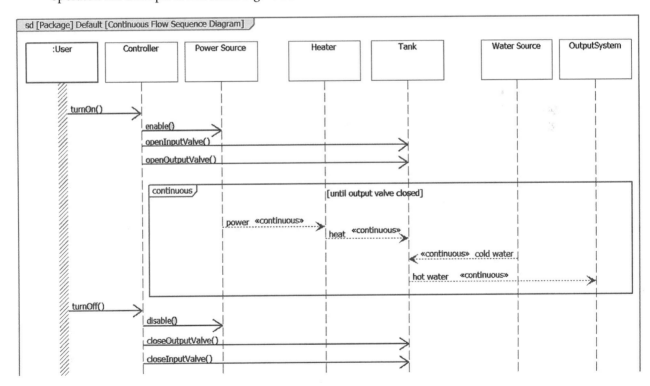

Figure 2.74 – Continuous flows on sequence diagrams

The figure shows flows (messages with dash lines) marked with the *«continuous»* stereotype. This indicates that the flow is continuous throughout its execution context. That context can be the entire diagram or limited to an interaction operator, as it is in this case. Within a context, there is no ordering among *«continuous»* flows; this is in contrast to the normal *partial ordering* semantics of SysML sequence diagrams in which *lower in the diagram* corresponds (roughly) to *later in time*. However, *«continuous»* flows are active throughout their execution context, and so the ordering of continuous flows is inherently meaningless (although the ordering of non-continuous messages is still in force).

The use of the *«continuous»* interaction operator emphasizes the unordered nature of the flows. Any events with the interaction operator still operate via the normal partial ordering semantics.

Purpose

The purpose of this recipe is to identify the exchange of services and flows that occur between a system and a set of actors, especially during use case analysis.

Inputs and preconditions

The precondition is that a use case and set of associated actors have been identified.

Outputs and postconditions

Interfaces or interface blocks are identified, and well as which actors must support which interfaces or interface blocks.

How to do it...

Figure 2.75 shows the workflow for this recipe. This overlaps with some of the other recipes in this chapter but focuses specifically on the identification of the system interfaces:

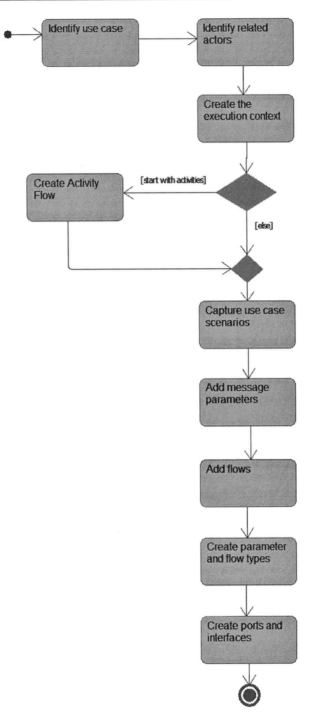

Figure 2.75 – Specify logical interfaces workflow

Identify the use case

This first step is to identify the generic usage of the system that will use the to-be-identified system interfaces.

Identify related actors

The related actors are those people or systems outside our scope that interact with the system while it executes the current use case. These actors can send messages to the system, receive messages from the system, or both using the system interfaces.

Create the execution context

The use case execution context is a kind of modeling *sandbox* that contains an executable component consisting of executable elements representing the use case and related actors. The recommended way to achieve this is to create separate blocks representing the use case and the actors, connected via ports. Having an isolated simulation sandbox allows different systems engineers to progress independently on different use case analyses.

Create the activity flow

This step is optional but is a popular way to begin to understand the set of flows in the use case. This step identifies the actions – event reception actions, event send actions, and internal system functions – that define the set of flows of the use case.

Capture the use case scenarios

Scenarios are singular interactions between the system and the actors during the execution of the use case. When working with non-technical stakeholders, they are an effective way to understand the desired interactions of the use case. We recommend starting with normal, *sunny day* scenarios before progressing to edge cases and exceptional *rainy day* scenarios. It is important to understand that every message identifies or represents one or more requirements and results in messages that must be supported in the derived interfaces. If the *create the activity flow* task is performed, then the sequence diagrams can be derived from those flows.

> **Recommendation:**
> Use asynchronous events for all *actor > system* and *system > actor* service invocations. This specifies the logical interfaces and so the underlying communication mechanism should be abstracted away. Later, in the definition of the physical interfaces and data schema, these can be specified in a technology-specific fashion.

Add message parameters

These events often carry data. This data should be explicitly modeled as event arguments.

Add flows

Use UML flows to indicate discrete flows of information, materiel, fluids, or energy exchanges between the system and an actor that are not intimately bound to a service request. Stereotype these flows as *«continuous»* when appropriate, such as the flows of energy or fluids.

Create parameter and flow types

The event arguments must be typed by elements in the logical data schema (see the *Creating the logical data schema* recipe). The same is true for flow types. Because these types are specifications, they will include not only some (logical) base type, but also units, ranges, and other kinds of metadata.

Create ports and interfaces

Based on the defined interaction of the system with the actors while executing the use case, add ports between the actor and use case blocks and type these ports with interface blocks. These interface blocks will enumerate the services and flows going between the actors and the system. Technically speaking, this can be done using UML standard ports and SysML flow ports, or the more modern SysML 1.3 proxy ports.

Example

We will now look at an example.

This example will use the **Control Resistance** use case, but we will follow a different approach than we used for this use case in the *Functional analysis with activities* recipe, just to demonstrate that there are alternative means to achieve similar goals in MBSE.

Identify the use case

The **Control Resistance** use case focuses on how resistance is applied to the pedals in response to simulated gearing, conditions, and user-applied force. The description is shown in *Figure 2.18*.

Identify related actors

There are three actors for this use case: **Rider**, **Training App**, and **Power Source**. The **Rider** provides power to and receives resistance from the pedals. The **Training App** is sent the rider power information. The **Power Source** provides electric power to run the system motors and digital electronics.

Create the execution context

Creating the execution context creates blocks that represent the actors and the use case for the purpose of analysis and simulation. They contain proxy ports that will be defined by the interfaces identified in this workflow:

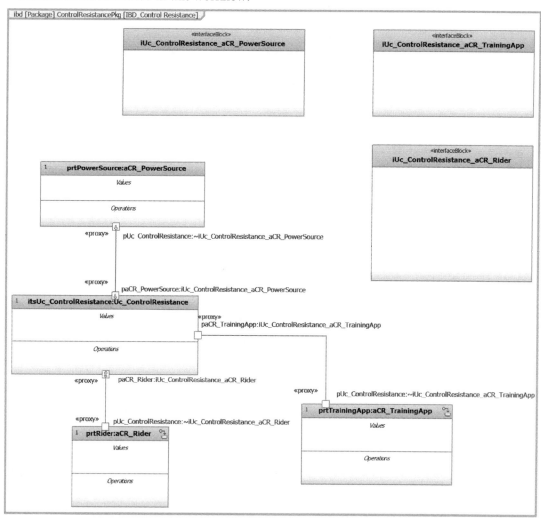

Figure 2.76 – Control Resistance execution context for interface definition

Create the activity flow

The activity flow shows the object and control flows for the use case. In this example, we will show continuous flows in addition to discrete flows. The activity is decomposed into three diagrams. The top level is shown in *Figure 2.77*. This diagram shows the distribution of electric power on the left. This section contains an interruptible region that terminates the entire behavior when an **evPowerOff** event is received. The center part, containing the **Determine Base Pedal Resistance** *call behavior*, does the bulk of the functional work of the use case. Note that it takes the computed base resistance on the pedal and adjusts it for its current angular position. On the right, the **Training App** is updated periodically with bike data.

Discrete events, such as turning the system on and off or changing the gears, are simple to model in the activity diagrams; they can easily be modeled as either *event receptions* for incoming events or *send actions* for outgoing events. Of course, these events can carry information as arguments as needed.

It is somewhat less straightforward to model continuous inputs and outputs. What I have done here is use an *object node*, stereotyped as both «*external*» and «*continuous*» for such flows. An example of a continuous flow coming from an external actor is electrical power from the wall supply (see **wallPower** in *Figure 2.77*). Conversely, the resistance the system continuously applies to the pedal is an example of an output (see **RiderPedalResistance** in the same figure). These will be modeled as *flow properties* in the resulting interfaces:

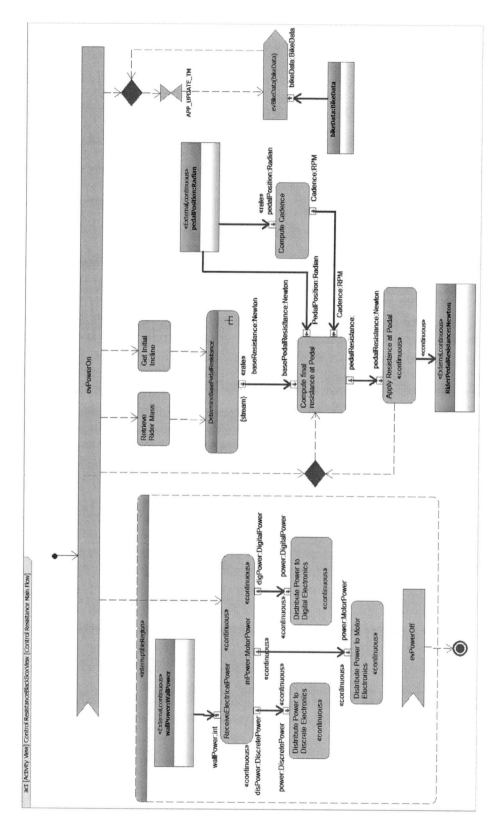

Figure 2.77 – Control Resistance activity flow for creating interfaces

Figure 2.78 shows the details for the **Determine Pedal Resistance** call behavior from the previous figure. In it, we see the base pedal resistance is computed using another call behavior, **Compute Bike Physics**. The **Determine Pedal Resistance** behavior never terminates (at least until the entire behavior terminates), so it uses a *«rate»* stereotype to indicate the data output on this activity's parameter streams. Remember that normal activity parameters require the activity to terminate before they can output a value:

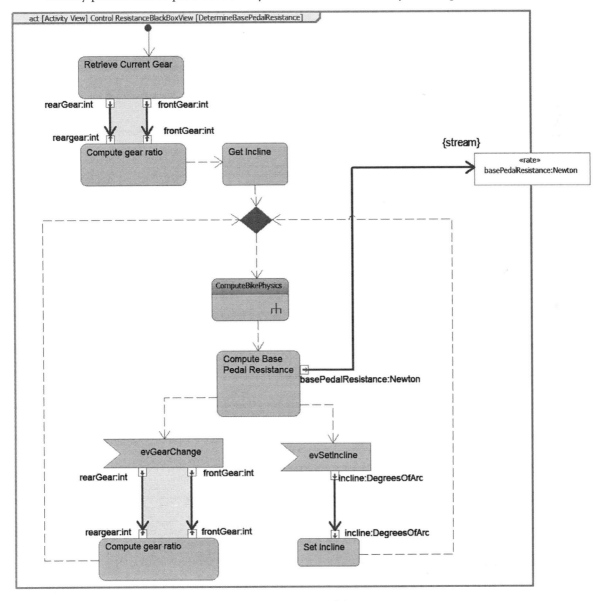

Figure 2.78 – Determine Base Pedal Resistance activity

Lastly, we have the **Compute Bike Physics** call behavior, shown in *Figure 2.79*. This simulates the physics of the bike using the rider mass, current incline, current speed, and the power applied by the rider to the pedal to compute the resistance to movement, and couples that with the combined bike and rider inertia to compute the simulated bike speed and acceleration:

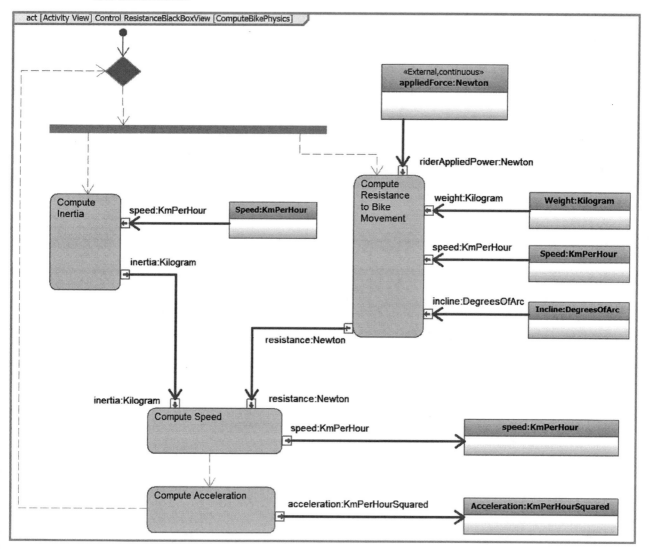

Figure 2.79 – Compute Bike Physics activity

Capture the use case scenarios

The interfaces can be produced directly from the activity model but it is often easier to produce it from a set of sequence diagrams derived from the activity model. Event receptions and flows on activities don't indicate the source, but this is clearly shown in the sequences. If you do create a set of sequence diagrams, it is adequate to produce the set of scenarios such that all inputs and outputs and internal flows are represented in at least one sequence diagram.

Figure 2.80 shows the first such scenario, which solely focuses on the delivery of power. It is also the only scenario shown that actually powers up and powers down the system. The power delivery is modeled as *«continuous»* flows to and inside the system:

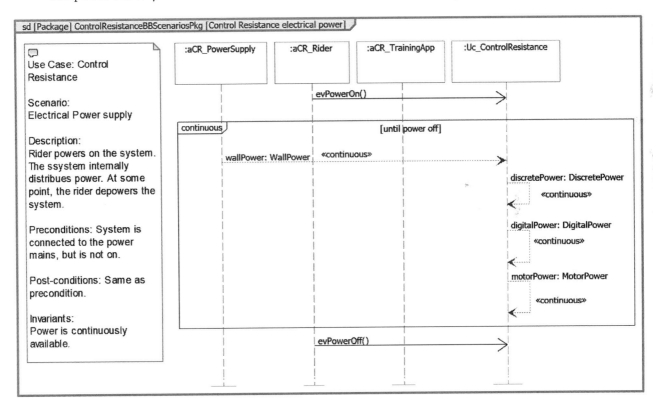

Figure 2.80 – Electrical Power scenario

The next three diagrams show the functional behavior modeled to follow the same structure as the activity model. *Figure 2.81* shows the high-level behavior. Note the use of «*continuous*» flows for the power the rider applies to the pedal (**appliedPower**), the resistance to movement supplied by the system (**pedalResistance**), and the position of the pedal (**pedalPosition**). The continuous *interaction occurrence* provides a scope for the continuous flows. The referenced interaction occurrence, **Determine Base Pedal Resistance**, references the sequence diagram shown in *Figure 2.82*:

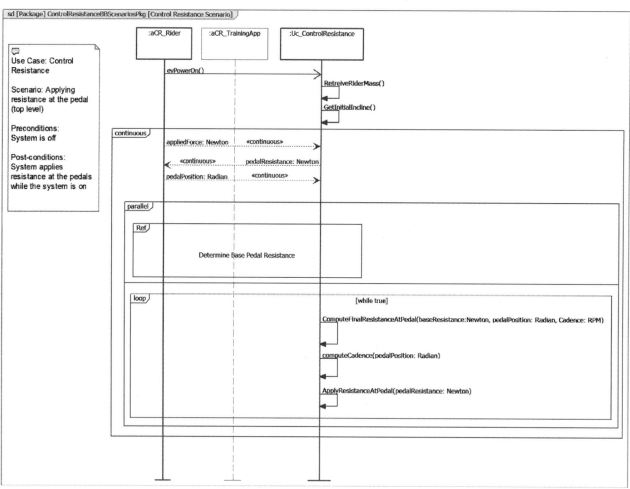

Figure 2.81 – Control Resistance scenario

Throughout the entire scenario shown in *Figure 2.82*, the continuous flows are active, so no scoping continuous interaction occurrence is required:

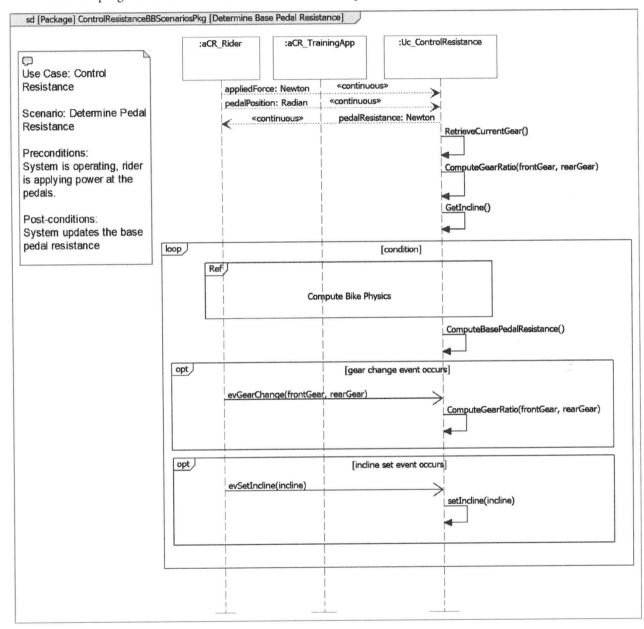

Figure 2.82 – Determine Base Pedal Resistance scenario

The presence of these flows isn't strictly required since they are active at the high-level scenario, but they are included here as a reminder. This scenario also includes a nested scenario. This one is the referenced **Compute Bike Physics**, scenario shown in *Figure 2.83*:

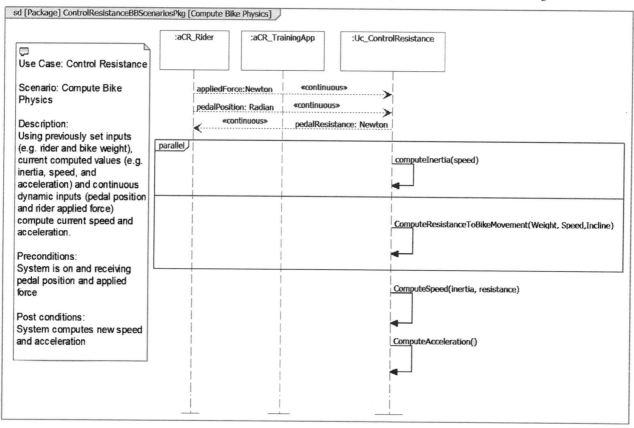

Figure 2.83 – Compute bike physics

Lastly, we must add the scenario for updating the **Training App** (*Figure 2.84*):

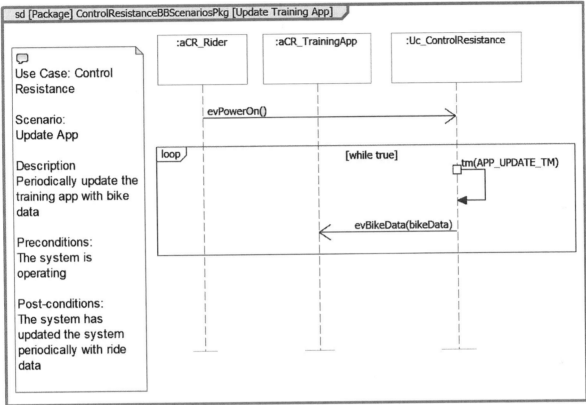

Figure 2.84 – Update Training App with ride data

Add message parameters

Rather than show all the stages of development of the scenarios, the previous step is shown already including the message parameters.

Add flows

Rather than show all the stages of development of the scenarios, the previous step is shown already including the continuous flows.

Create parameter and flow types

The details of how to create all the types is the subject of the next recipe, *Creating the logical data schema*. The reader is referred to that recipe for more information.

Create ports and interfaces

Now that we have the set of flows between the actors and the system and have characterized them, we can create the interfaces. In this example, we are using the SysML 1.3 standard approach of using *proxy ports* and *interface blocks*, rather than *standard ports*, *flow ports*, and standard *interfaces*. This is a bit more work than using the older approach, but is more modern and descriptive.

The IBD in *Figure 2.85* shows the execution context of the use case analysis for the **Control Resistance** use case. The instances of the **Uc_ControlResistance** use case block and the **aCR_PowerSource**, **aCR_Rider**, and **aCR_TrainingApp** actor blocks expose their proxy ports and are connected via SysML connectors. Note that, by convention, the unconjugated interface is referenced at the use case block end of the connector and the conjugated form is used at the actor end, as indicated by the tilde (~) in front of the interface block name.

At the top of the diagram are the (current empty) interface blocks that will be elaborated in this step. Later, during architecture development, these interface blocks will be added to the interfaces provided by the system and decomposed and allocated to the subsystems.

A note about naming conventions

The IBD shown here provides a sandbox for the purpose of analyzing the **Control Resistance** use case. To that end, a block representing the use case is created and given the name **Uc_ControlResistance**. For the actors, local blocks are created for the purpose of analysis and are given the names of a (for actor) followed by the initials of the use case (CR) followed by the name of the actor (with white space removed). So, these sandbox actor blocks are named **aCR_PowerSource**, **aCR_Ride**, and **aCR_TrainingApp**. The interfaces are all named i *<use case block name>_<actor block name>*, as in **iUc_ControlResistance_aCR_PowerSource**. This makes it easy to enforce naming consistency at the expense of sometimes creating lengthy names.

The creation of the elements is automated via the *Harmony SE Toolkit*, provided with the Rhapsody modeling tool:

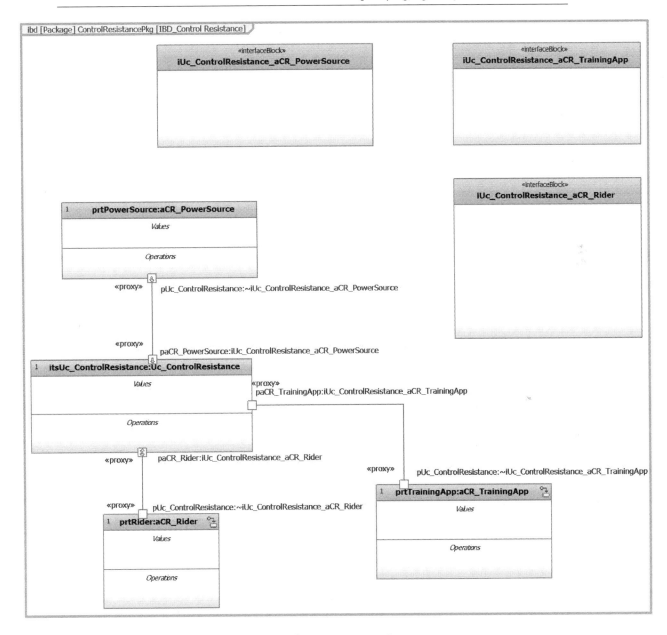

Figure 2.85 – Control Resistance execution context

Since we have the flows all shown in the sequence diagrams, it is a simple matter to add these elements to the interface blocks:

- For each message from the use case to an actor, add that event reception as *required* to the interface block defining that port.

- For each message from an actor to the use case, add that event reception as *provided* to the interface block defining that port.

- For each flow from the use case to an actor, add that flow as an *output* flow property to the interface block defining that port.

- For each flow from an actor to the use case, add that flow as an *input* flow property to the interface block defining that port.

Rhapsody does provide some assistance here in the Harmony SE Toolkit, although it is not difficult to do manually:

1. First, realize all the messages for the sequence diagrams; this creates event receptions on the target blocks.

2. Then apply the Harmony SE Toolkit helper called **Create Ports and Interfaces** to populate the interfaces.

You will still need to add the flows manually as flow properties.

The result is shown in *Figure 2.86*. Note that the event receptions are either *provided* (*prov*) or *required* (*reqd*) while the flow properties are either *in* or *out* (from the use case block perspective):

 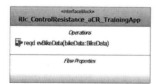 

Figure 2.86 – Created interface blocks

You should note that these are, of course, logical interfaces. As such, they reflect the intent and content of the messages, but not their physical realization. For example, bike data sent to the training app is modeled in the logical interface as an event, but the physical interface will actually be as a Bluetooth message. Wall power is modeled as a flow (its content will be described in the next recipe), but the actual interface involves the flow of electrons over a wire. The creation of physical interfaces from logical ones is discussed in *Chapter 4, Handoff to Downstream Engineering*.

Creating the logical data schema

A big part of the specification of systems is specifying the inputs and outputs of the system as well as what information a system must retain and manage. The inputs and outputs are data or flows and may be direct flows or may be carried via service requests or responses. Early in the systems engineering process, the information captured about these elements is logical. The definition of a logical schema is provided here, along with a set of related definitions.

The definitions are as follows:

- **Data Schema**: A data or type model of a specific problem domain that includes blocks, value properties, value types, dimensions, units, their relations, and other relevant aspects collectively known as *metadata*. This model includes a type model consisting of the set of value types, units, and dimensions, and a usage model showing the blocks and value properties that use the type model.

- **Logical Schema**: A data schema expressed independently from its ultimate implementation, storage, or transmission means.

- **Value Property**: A property model element that can hold values. Also known as a variable.

- **Value Type**: Specify value sets applied to value properties, message arguments, or other parameters that may carry values. Examples include **integer** (`int` in C++ action language), **real** (`double` in C++), **Boolean** (`bool` in C++), **character** (`char` in C++) and **String** (often `char*` in C++). These base types may have additional properties or constraints, specified as metadata.

- **Metadata**: Literally *data about data*, this term refers to ancillary properties or constraints on data, including the following:

  a. Extent – The set of values of an underlying base value type that are allowed. This can be specified as follows:

  - A subrange, as in 0 … 10

  - A low value and high value pair, as in *low value =-1, high value = 1*

  - An enumerated list of acceptable values

  - A specification of prohibited values that are excluded from the base type

  - The specification of a rule or constraint from which valid values can be determined

b. Precision – The degree exactness of specified values; this is often denoted as *number of significant digits*.

c. Accuracy – The degree of conformance to an actual value, often expressed as ±*<value>*, as in ± 0.25. Accuracy generally refers to an output or outcome.

d. Fidelity – The degree of exactness of a value. Fidelity is generally applied to an input value.

e. Latency – How long after a value change occurs that the value representation updated.

f. Availability – The percentage of the system life cycle that is actually accessible.

Note

These properties are sometimes not properties of the value type but of the value property specified by that value type. In any case, in SysML, these properties are often expressed in tags and metadata added to describe model elements.

Value types can have kinds of representations in the underlying action language, such as enumeration (enum in C++), a language specification (such as char* in C++), a structure (struct in C++), a typedef, or a union.

- **Dimension**: Specifies the *kind* of value (its dimensionality). Examples include *length*, *weight*, *pressure*, and *color*. Also known as **Quantity Kind** in SysML 1.3 and later.

- **Unit**: Specifies a standard against which values in a dimension may be directly compared. Examples include *meters*, *kilograms*, *kilopascals*, and *RGB* units. SysML provides a model library of SI Units that are directly available for use in models. However, it is not uncommon to define your own if needed.

  Other than schema, SysML directly represents the concepts in its language definition. Note that a value property can be specified in terms of a unit, a dimension, or a value type at the engineer's discretion.

- **Recommendation**: Each value property should be typed by a unit, unless it is unitless, in which case it should be typed by a defined value type.

Schematically, these definitions are shown in *Figure 2.87* in the data schema metamodel:

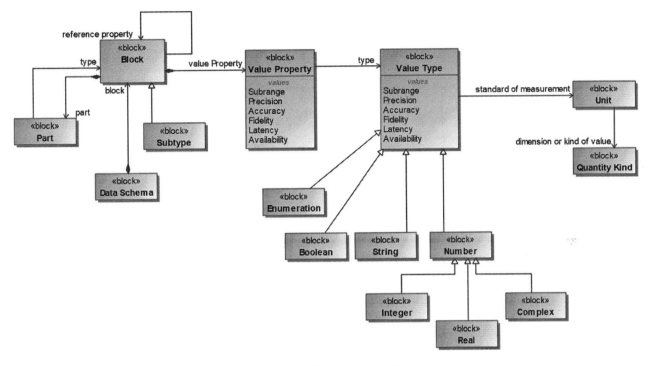

Figure 2.87 – Data schema metamodel

> **Note**
>
> Although this is called the *data schema*, it is really an information schema as it applies to elements that are not data per se, such as physical flows. In this book, we will use the common term *data schema* to apply to flows as well.

Beyond the underlying type model of the schema, described previously, the blocks and their value properties and the relationships between them constitute the remainder of the data schema. These relations are the standard SysML relations: association, aggregation, composition, generalization, and dependency.

A quick example

So, what does a diagram showing a logical data schema look like?

Typically, a data schema is visualized within a block definition diagram, and shows the data elements and relevant properties. Consider an aircraft navigation system that must account for *the craft's own* position, its velocity, acceleration, jerk, flight plans, attitude, and so on. See *Figure 2.88*:

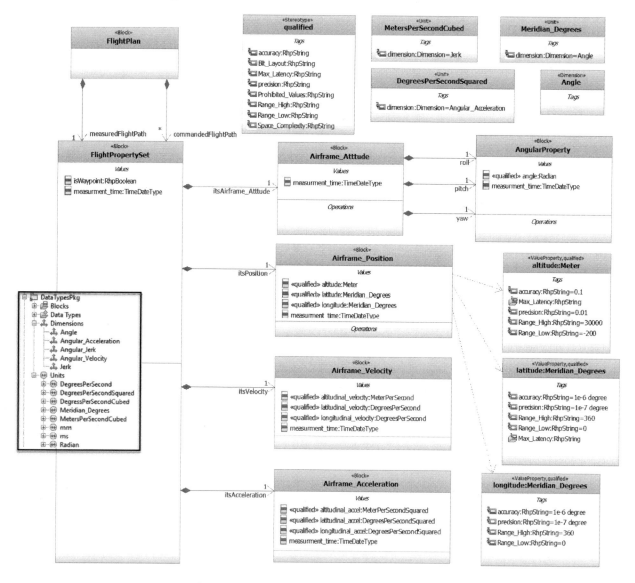

Figure 2.88 – Data schema for the Flight Property Set

You can see in the figure that the **Flight Property Set** contains **Airframe_Position**, **Airframe_Velocity**, **Airframe_Acceleration**, and so on. These composed blocks contain value properties that detail their value properties; in the case of **Airframe_Position**, these are **altitude**, **latitude**, and **longitude**. **Altitude** is expressed in **Meters** (defined in the Rhapsody SysML type library) while **latitude** and **longitude** are defined in terms of the unit **Meridian_Degrees**, which is not in the SysML model library (and so is defined in the model).

On the left of the diagram, you can see that the **Flight Plan** contains multiple **Flight Property Sets** identifying planned waypoints along the **commanded flight path**. These **Flight Property Sets** may be actual current information (denoted with the **measuredFlightPath** role end) or commanded (denoted with the **commandedFlightPath** role end). The latter forms a list of commanded flight property sets and so stores the set of commanded waypoints. On the left, the diagram shows a superimposed image of the Rhapsody model browser, showing the units and dimensions created to support this data schema.

In the diagram, you see the **«qualified»** stereotype, which specifies a number of relevant metadata properties of the information, such as **accuracy**, **bit_layout**, and **precision**. Several value properties, along with their values for these metadata tags, are shown in the diagram. We see, for example, that the **longitude** value property has a range of 0 to 360 **Meridian_Degrees**, with an accuracy of 10^{-6} degrees and a representation precision of 10^{-7} degrees.

Purpose

The purpose of the logical data schema is to understand the information received, stored, and transmitted by a system. In the context of this capture-of-system specification, it is to understand and characterize data and flows that cross the system boundary to conceptually solidify the interfaces a system provides or requires.

Inputs and preconditions

The precondition is that a use case and a set of associated actors have been identified or that structural elements (blocks) have been identified in an architecture or design.

Outputs and postconditions

The output is a set of units, dimensions, types (the type model), and the value properties that they specify, along with the relationships between the value types and blocks that own them (the usage model).

How to do it...

The workflow for this recipe is shown in *Figure 2.89*:

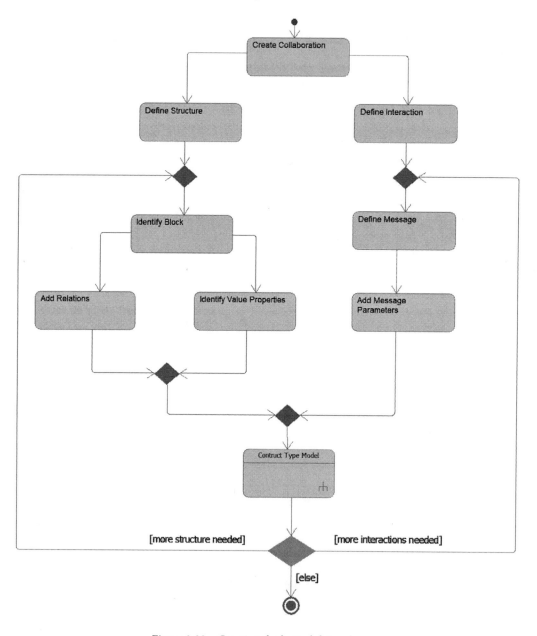

Figure 2.89 – Creating the logical data schema

The **Construct Type Model** call behavior is shown in *Figure 2.90*:

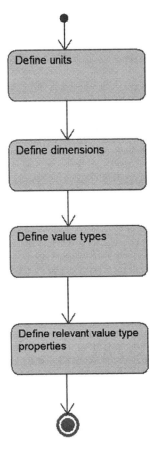

Figure 2.90 – Construct Type Model

Create a collaboration

This task creates the collaboration between elements. This provides the context in which the types may be considered. In the case of system specification, this purpose is served by defining the use case and its related actors, or by the execution context of block stand-ins for those elements. In a design context, it is generally some set of design elements that relate to some larger-scale purpose, such as showing an architectural aspect or realizing a use case.

Define the structure

This step adds blocks and other elements to the collaboration, detailed in the following *Identify the block*, *Add relations*, and *Identify value properties* sections.

Identify the block

These are the basic structural elements of the collaboration, although value properties may be created without an owning block.

Add relations

These relations link the structural elements together, allowing them to send messages to support the necessary interactions.

Identify value properties

This step identifies the data and flow property features of the blocks.

Define the interaction

The interaction consists of a set of message exchanges among elements in the collaboration. This is most often shown as sequence diagrams.

Define the messages

Messages are the primitive elements of interaction. These may be synchronous (such as function calls) or asynchronous (as in asynchronous event receptions). A single interaction typically contains a set of ordered messages.

Add message parameters

Most messages, whether synchronous or asynchronous, carry information in the form of parameters (sometimes called *arguments*). The types of these data must be specified in the data model.

Construct a type model

Once a datum is identified, it must be typed. This call behavior is detailed in the following steps.

Define the units

Most data relies on units for proper functioning, and too often units are only implied rather than explicitly specified. This step references existing units or creates the underlying unit and then uses it to type the relevant value properties. SysML defines a non-normative extension to include a model library of SI units. Rhapsody, the tool used here, has an incomplete realization of these units, so many common units, such as **radians**, are missing and must be added if desired. Fortunately, it is easy to do so.

Define the dimensions

Most units reply on a quantity kind (or *dimension*). For example, the unit **meter** has the dimension **length**. Most dimensions have many different units available. **Length**, for example, can be expressed in units of **cm, inches, feet, yards, meters, miles, kilometers**, and so on.

Define value types

The underlying value type is expressed in the action language for the model. This might be C, C++, Java, Ada, or any common programming or data language. The **Object Management Group** (**OMG**) also defined an abstract action language called **ALF** (short for **Action Language for Foundational** UML), which may be used for this purpose. See `https://www.omg.org/spec/ALF/About-ALF/` for more information. This book uses C++ as the action language, but there are equally valid alternatives.

Define the relevant value type properties

It is almost always inadequate to just specify the value type from the underlying action language. There are other properties of considerable interest. As described earlier in this section, they include extent, precision, latency, and availability. Other properties of interest may emerge that are domain-specific.

Example

We'll now see an example.

This example will use the **Measure Performance Metrics** use case. The *Model-based threat analysis* recipe used this use case to discuss modeling cybersecurity. We will use it to model the logical data schema. For the most part, the data of interest is the performance data itself, although the threat model identified some additional security-relevant data that can be modeled as well.

Create collaboration

The use case diagram in *Figure 2.67* provides the context for the data schema, but usually the corresponding IBD of the execution context is used. This diagram is shown in *Figure 2.91*:

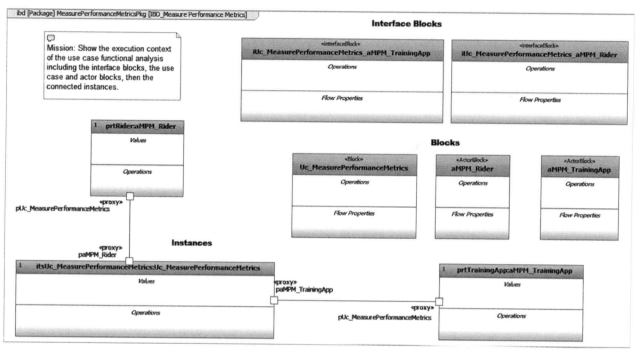

Figure 2.91 – Measure Performance Metrics execution context

Define the structure

This task is mostly done by defining the execution context, shown in *Figure 2.91*. In this case, the structure is pretty simple.

Identify the blocks

As a part of defining the structure, we identified the primary functional blocks in the previous figure. But now we need to begin thinking about the data elements as blocks and value types. *Figure 2.92* shows a first cut at the likely blocks. Note that we don't need to represent the data schema for the actors because *we don't care*. We are not designing the actors since they are, by definition, out of our scope of concern:

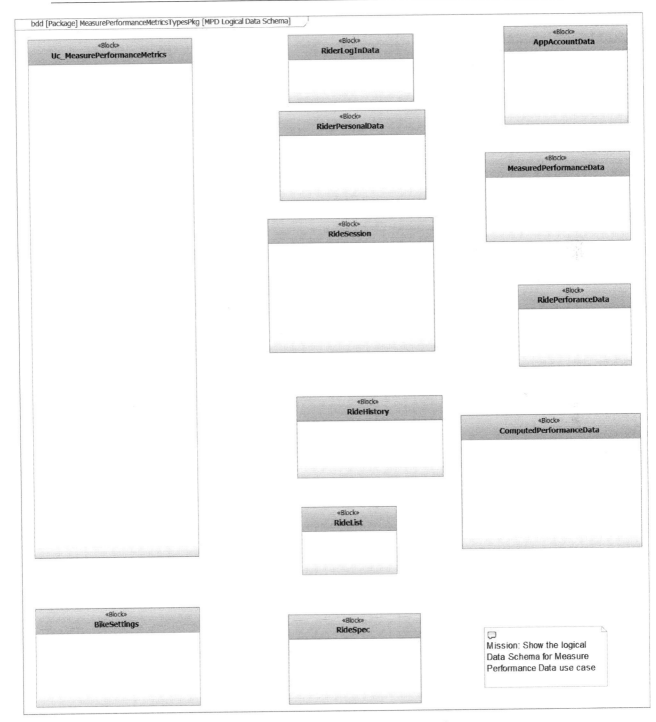

Figure 2.92 – Blocks for the Measure Performance Data schema

Add relations

The instances of the core functional blocks are shown in *Figure 2.91*. The relations of the data elements to the use case block are shown in *Figure 2.93*. This is the data that the use case block knows (owns) or uses:

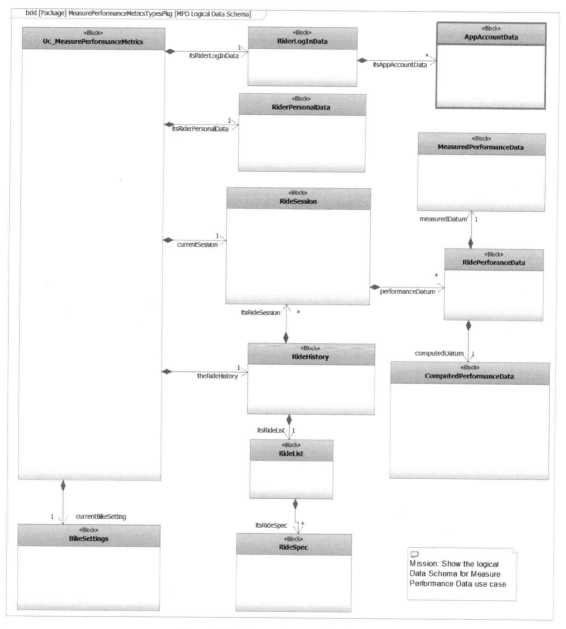

Figure 2.93 – Data schema with relations

Identify the value properties

The blocks provide owners of the actual data of interest, which is held in the value properties. *Figure 2.94* shows the blocks populated with value properties relevant to the use case:

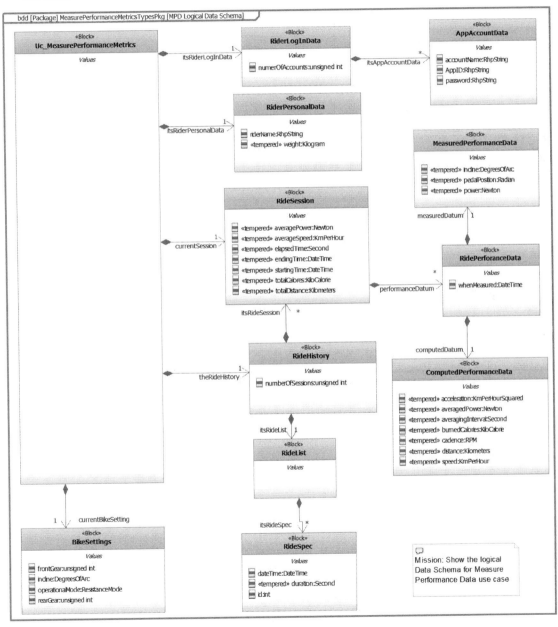

Figure 2.94 – Data schema value properties

Define interactions, define messages, and add message parameters

Another way to find data elements to structure is to look at the messaging; this is particularly relevant for use case and functional analysis since the data on which we focus during this analysis is the data that is sent or received. These three steps – *define interactions*, *define messages*, and *add message parameters* – are all discussed together to save space.

The first interaction we'll look at is for uploading real-time ride metrics during a ride. This is shown in *Figure 2.95*:

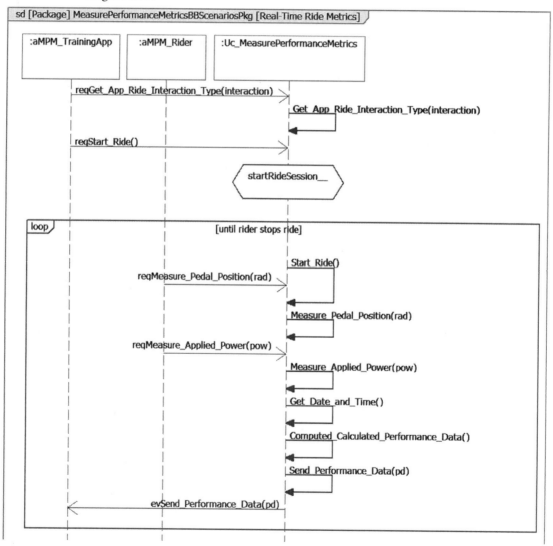

Figure 2.95 – Real-time ride metrics

The second interaction is for uploading an entire stored ride to the app. This is in *Figure 2.96*:

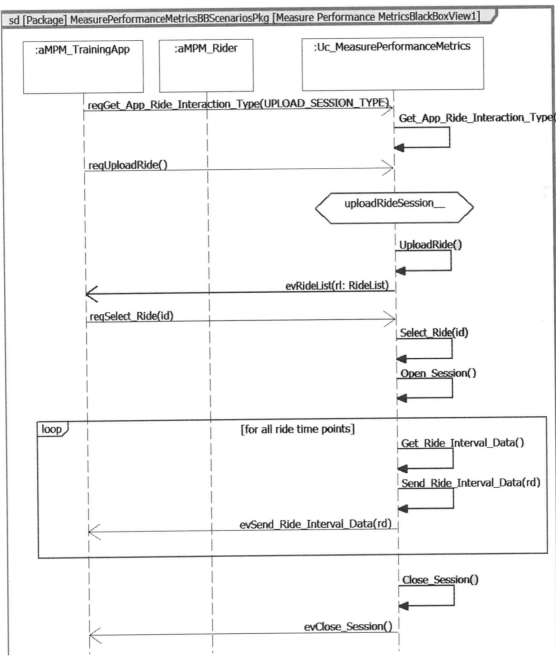

Figure 2.96 – Upload a saved ride

Note that these are just two of many scenarios for the use case, as they do not consider concerns such as dropped messages, reconnecting sessions, and other rainy-day situations. However, this is adequate for our needs.

Construct the type model

Figure 2.94 goes a long way toward the definition of the type model. The blocks define the structured data elements, but at the value property level, there is still work to be done. The underlying value types must be identified, their units and dimensions specified, and constraints placed on their extent and precision.

Define units

It is common for engineers to just reference base types – **int**, **real**, and so on – to type value properties, but this can lead to avoidable design errors. This is because value types may not be directly comparable, such as when **distanceA** and **distanceB** are both typed as **Real** but in one case is captured in **kilometers** and in the other in **miles**. Further, we cannot reason about the extent of a type (the permitted set of values) unless we also know the units. For this reason, we recommend – and will use here – unit definitions to disambiguate the values we're specifying.

The SI Units model library of the SysML specification is an optional compliance point for the standard. Rhapsody includes some SI units and dimensions but is far from complete. In this model, we will reference those that exist and create those that do not.

Figure 2.94 uses a number of special units for value properties and operation arguments, including the following:

- DegreesOfArc
- Radian
- Newton
- DateTime
- KmPerHour
- KmPerHourSquared
- Second
- KiloCalorie

- RPM

- Kilometer

- ResistanceMode

- APP_INTERACTION_TYPE

Two of these (**Newton** and **Second**) already exist in the Rhapsody SysML Profile SI Types model library and so may just be referenced. The others must be defined, although two of them – **ResistanceMode** and **APP_INTERACTION_TYPE** – will be specified as value types rather than units.

DegreesOfArc is a measure of angular displacement and is used for the cycling incline, while **Radian** is a unit of angular displacement used for pedal position. **RPM** is a measure of rotational velocity used for pedaling cadence. **DateTime** is a measure of when data was measured. **Kilometer** is a measure of linear distance (length), while **KmPerHour** is a measure of speed and **KmPerHourSquared** is a measure of acceleration. **KiloCalorie** is a measure of energy used to represent the rider's energy output. In our model, we will define all these as units. They will be defined in terms of their dimensions in the next section.

Define dimensions

Dimension is also known as *quantity kind* and refers to the kind of information held by a unit. For example, **kilometer**, **meter**, and **mile** all have the dimension of **distance** (or length).

As with the SI units, some of the dimensions are already defined in the Rhapsody SysML SI Types model library (**time**, **length**, **energy**) while others (**angular displacement** and **rotational velocity**) are not. We will reference the dimensions already defined and specify in our model the ones that are not.

In keeping with the approach used by the Rhapsody SysML SI Types model library, the dimensions themselves are defined with a typedef kind to the SysML **Real** type (which is, in turn, is a typedef of **RhpReal**). In models using the C++ action language, this will end up being a **double**. The advantage of this approach is the independence of the model from the underlying action language.

Figure 2.97 shows the units and dimensions defined for this logical data schema. Dimensions used from the SysML model library are referenced by the units but not otherwise shown on the diagram:

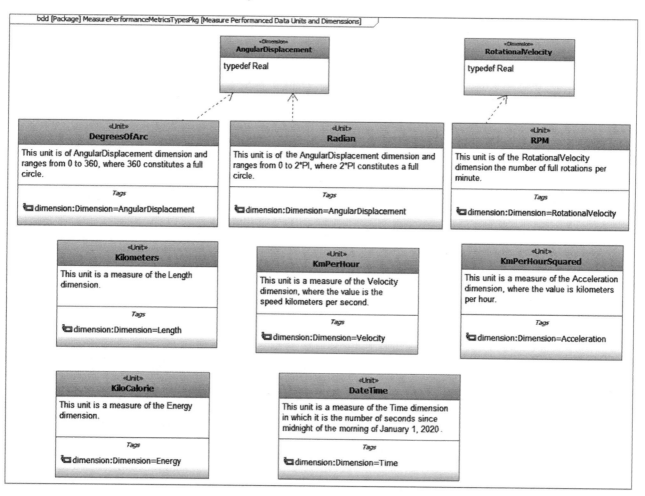

Figure 2.97 – Units and dimensions

Define value types

Apart from the blocks, units, and dimensions described in the previous sections, there are also a few value types in the model. In this particular case, there are two of interest, both of which are enumerations. *Figure 2.98* shows that **APP_INTERACTION_TYPE** may be either **REAL_TIME_INTERACTION**, used for loading performance data in real time during a cycling session, or **UPLOAD_INTERACTION**, used to upload a saved ride to the app:

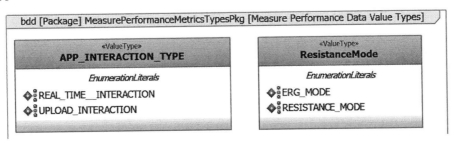

Figure 2.98 – Measure performance data value types

Another value type, **Resistance Mode**, can either be **ERG_MODE**, which in the system maintains a constant power output of the rider regardless of cadence by dynamically adjusting the resistance, and **RESISTANCE_MODE**, where the power varies as the **Rider** modifies their cadence, incline, or gearing.

Define relevant value type properties

The last thing we must do is specify relevant value type properties. In the logical data schema, this means specifying the extent and precision of the values. This can be done at the unit/value type level; in this case, the properties apply to all values of that unit or type. These properties can also be applied at the value level, in which case the scope of the specification is limited to the specific values but not to other values of the same unit or type.

The best way to specify these properties is to specify them as SysML tags within a stereotype, apply the stereotype to the relevant model elements, and then elaborate the specific values. To that end, we will create a *«tempered»* stereotype. This stereotype applies to attributes (value properties), arguments, types, action blocks (actions), object nodes, pins, and types in the SysML metamodel and so can apply to units as well.

The stereotype provides three ways to specify extent. The first is the **extent** tag, which is a string in which the engineer can specify a range or list of values, such as $[0.00 .. 0.99]$ or $0.1, 0.2, 0.4, 0.8, 1.0$. Alternatively, for a continuous range, the **lowValue** and **highValue** tags, both of type **Real**, can serve as well; in the previous example, you can set **lowValue** to 0.0 and **highValue** to 0.99. Lastly, you can provide a range or list of prohibited values in the **prohibitedValues** tag, such as $-1, 0$.

The stereotype also provides three means for specifying scale. The **scaleOfPrecision** tag, of type integer, allows you to define the number of significant digits for the value or type. You can further refine this by specifying **scaleOfFidelity** to indicate the significant digits when the value is used as an input and **scaleOfAccuracy** when the value is used as an output.

Another stereotype tag is **maxLatencyInSeconds**, a **Real** value that specifies the maximum age of a value. Other metadata can be added to the stereotype as needed for your system specification.

This level of detail of specification of quantities is important for downstream design. Requiring two digits of scale is very different than requiring six and drives the selection of hardware and algorithms. In this example, it makes the most sense to specify the necessary scale at the unit and type level, rather than at the specific value property level for the units that we are defining.

Those units are shown in *Figure 2.99*:

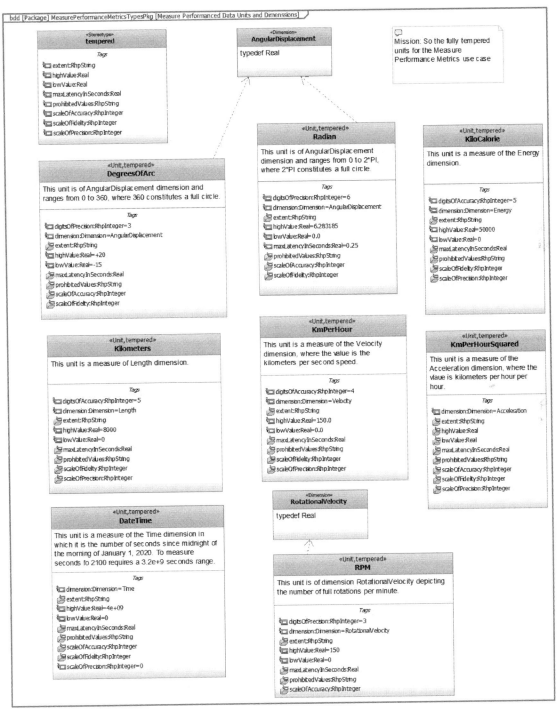

Figure 2.99 – Measure Performance Metrics tempered units

> **Note**
>
> **Precision** technically refers to the number of significant digits in a number, while **scale** is the number of significant digits to the right of the decimal point. The number **123.45** has a precision of **5**, but a scale of **2**. People usually speak of precision while meaning scale.

Lastly, we must specify the extent and scale for the values that are either unitless or use standard predefined units but are constrained within a subrange. *Figure 2.100* and *Figure 2.101* provide that detail:

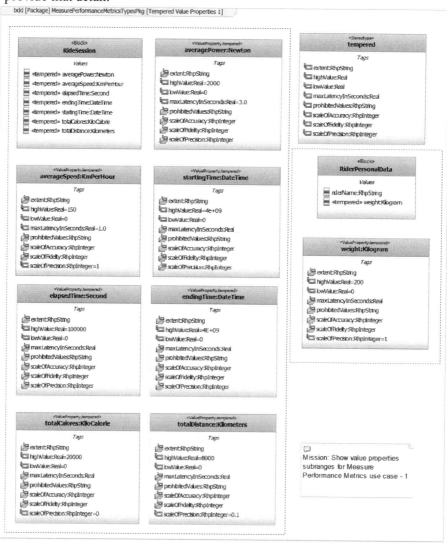

Figure 2.100 – Value subranges and scale – 1

Note that the figures show the relevant value properties for the blocks grouped with a rectangle with a dotted border. This rectangle has no semantics and is only used for visual grouping:

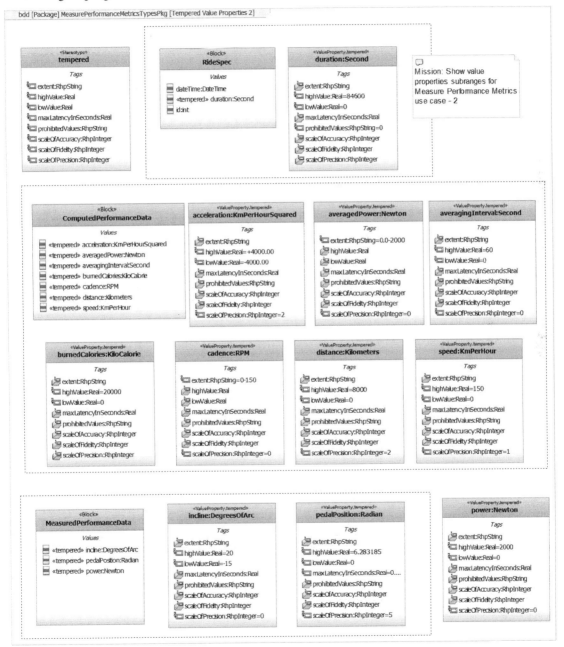

Figure 2.101 – Value subranges and scale – 2

And there you have it: a logical data schema for the values and flows specified as a part of the **Measure Performance Metrics** use case. These, along with data schema from other use cases, will be merged together into the architecture in the architecture design work phase.

3
Developing System Architectures

System analysis pays attention to the required properties of a system, such as its functionality, while system design focuses on how to implement a system that implements those needs effectively. There are many different designs that can realize the same functionality, and system engineers must select a design based on how well it optimizes crucial system properties. This degree of optimization is determined by examining the **measures of effectiveness** (**MoEs**) that have been applied to the design. Design is all about optimization, and architecture is no different. Architecture is where high-level design concerns that organize and orchestrate the overall structure and behavior of the system are integrated.

Design exists at (at least) three levels of abstraction. The highest level – the focus of this chapter – is **architectural design**. Architectural design helps us make choices that optimize the system's overall properties at a system-wide level. The next step down is known as **collaboration design**, which seeks to optimize collaborations of small design elements that collectively perform important system behaviors. Collaborative design is generally an order of magnitude smaller in scope than architectural design. Finally, **detailed design** individually optimizes those small design elements in terms of their structure or behavior.

In this chapter, we will cover the following recipes:

- Architectural trade studies
- Architectural merge
- Pattern-driven architecture
- Subsystem and pattern-driven architecture
- Component architecture
- Architectural allocation
- Creating subsystem interfaces from use case scenarios

Let's get started!

Five critical views of architecture

There are five critical views, as shown in the following diagram:

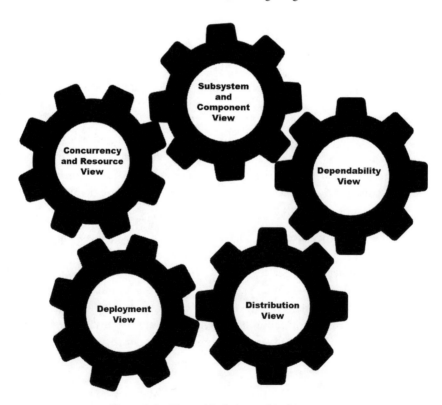

Figure 3.1 – Five critical views of architecture

Each view focuses on a different aspect of the largest-scale optimization concerns of the system:

- **Subsystem/Component Architecture** is about identifying subsystems, allocating responsibilities to the subsystems, and specifying their interfaces.

- **Distribution Architecture** chooses how distributed parts of the system interact, including middleware and communication protocols. This includes, but is not limited to, the network architecture.

- **Concurrency and Resource Architecture** details sets of concurrency regions (threads and processes), how semantic elements map into those concurrency regions, how they are scheduled, and how they effectively share and manage shared resources.

- **Dependability Architecture** refers to large-scale design decisions that govern the ability of stakeholders to depend on the system. This is subdivided into the following three pillars of dependability:

  A. **Safety Architecture**: The large-scale mechanisms by which the system ensures the risk of harm is acceptable

  B. **Security architecture**: The important design decisions that control how the system avoids, identifies, and manages attacks

  C. **Reliability Architecture**: The system-wide decisions that manage the availability of services

- **Deployment Architecture** allocates responsibilities to different engineering facets, such as software, electronics, and mechanical design concerns.

This chapter focuses on developing and verifying system architectures by covering some key recipes, including the following:

- Selecting architectural alternatives via trade studies
- Merging different use case analyses together into a system architecture
- Applying architectural design patterns
- Creating the subsystem and component architecture
- Allocating system properties to the subsystem architecture
- Defining system interfaces

In the next section, we'll look at some general architectural guidelines.

General architectural guidelines

As we learned in *Chapter 1*, *Basics of Agile System Modeling*, in *Figure 1.27*, a good architecture has the following properties:

- It is architected early.
- It evolves frequently.
- It is as simple as possible (but no simpler than that).
- It is based on patterns.
- It integrates into project planning via technical work items.
- It optimizes important system properties.
- It is written down (specifically, it is modeled).
- It is kept current.

The *Architecture 0* recipe in *Chapter 1*, *Basics of Agile System Modeling*, concentrated on creating an early model of the architecture so that more detailed engineering work had a structural context. Nevertheless, the expectation is that the architecture progresses as more development work is done, and as more functionality is added to the evolving system design.

This chapter provides some important recipes that cover defining architectures, whether this is done as a big design up-front or as an incremental agile process.

Architectural trade studies

Trade studies are specifically concerned with selecting an approach or technology that optimizes the important concerns that are specific to the system's development, the system's environment, or stakeholder needs. At a very fundamental level, trade studies are about making design choices that optimize important properties of the system at the expense of properties deemed less critical. To effectively perform trade studies, it is important to identify the things that can be optimized, the aspects subject to optimization, the measures of optimization, and a set of alternatives to be evaluated.

Purpose

The purpose of performing an architectural trade study is to select an optimal design solution from a set of alternatives.

Inputs and preconditions

The inputs for this recipe are as follows:

- Functionality of concern, scoped as a set of requirements and/or use cases
- Design options capable of achieving that functionality

Outputs and post conditions

The primary output of this recipe is the evaluation of alternatives, generally with a single technical selection identified as the recommended solution. This output is often formatted as a **decision analysis matrix**. This matrix is normally formatted like so:

Candidate Solutions	Solution Criteria										Weighted Total
	Power Consumption ($W_1 = 0.3$)		Recurring Cost ($W_2 = 0.2$)		Robustness ($W_3 = 0.15$)		Development Cost ($W_4 = 0.1$)		Security ($W_5 = 0.25$)		
	MoE	Score	MoE	Score	MoE	Score	MoE	Score	MoE	Score	
Gigabit Ethernet Bus	2	0.6	2.7	0.54	4	0.6	8	0.8	4	1.0	3.54
1553 Bus	3	0.9	4	0.8	10	1.5	1.5	0.15	6	1.5	4.85
CAN Bus	6	1.8	8	1.6	7	1.05	3	.3	1	0.25	5.0

Table 3.1– Example decision analysis matrix

As we can see, the middle columns show the optimization criteria; in this case, there are **Power Consumption, Recurring Cost, Robustness, Development Cost,** and **Security.** Each is shown with a relative **weight (W)**. This weighting factor reflects the relative importance of that criteria with respect to the others. It is common, as shown in this example, for the weights to be normalized so that they sum to **1.00**. It is also common to normalize the **MoE** values as well, although this was not done in this example.

Each of these columns is subdivided into two. The first is the **Measures of Effectiveness (MoE)** value for a particular solution, followed by the **MoE** value times the weighting factor for that criterion. This is the weighted **Score** value in the table for that criterion. Coming up with a good MoE is key to having a useful outcome for the trade study.

The last three rows in the example are different technical solutions that must be evaluated. In this case, the trade study compares **Gigabit Ethernet Bus, 1553 Avionics Bus,** and the **Control Area Network (CAN) Bus.**

The last column is the weight score for each of the solutions, which is simply the sum of the weighted scores for the solution that's been identified in that row. The matrix is set up so that the highest value here *wins* as it's determined to be the best overall solution based on the MoEs and their weights.

How to do it...

The following diagram shows the basic workflow for performing an architectural trade study:

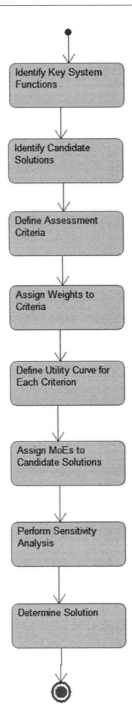

Figure 3.2 – Performing a trade study

This approach is useful when you have a relatively small set of alternatives (known as the **trade space**) in the evaluation. Other techniques are more appropriate when you have a very large trade space. Note that we will be using SysML parametric diagrams in a specific way to perform the trade study, and that these specific techniques will be reflected throughout this recipe.

Identifying key system functions

Key system functions are system functions that are important, architectural in scope, and subject to optimization in alternative ways. System functions that are not important architecturally or cannot be optimized in multiple ways don't need to be considered in this recipe. To be *subject to optimization in alternative ways* means the following:

- At least one criterion of optimization can be applied to this system function.

- There is more than one technical way to perform the system function.

An example of a system function would be to provide motive force for a robot arm. This could be optimized against different criteria, such as life cycle cost, reliability, responsiveness, accuracy, or weight.

Identifying candidate solutions

Candidate solutions are the technical means to achieve the system's functionality. In the case of providing motive force for a robot arm, technical means include pneumatics, hydraulics, and electric motors. All these solutions have benefits and costs that must be considered in terms of the system's context, related aspects of the system design, and stakeholder needs.

This step is often performed in two stages. First, you must identify all reasonable, potential technical solutions. Second, you must trim the list so that it only contains viable options for consideration. It is not uncommon for a number of potential solutions to be immediately dismissed because of technical maturity issues, availability, cost, or other feasibility reasons. At the end of this step, there is usually a "short list" of three to 10 potential solutions that must be evaluated.

In SysML, we will model the key system function as a block and add the assessment criteria (in the next step) as value properties. The different candidate solutions will be then modeled as instance specifications of this block, with different values assigned to the value properties.

Defining assessment criteria

The assessment criteria are the solution properties that the goodness of the solution will be assessed against.

There's a wide variety of potential evaluation criteria, including the following:

- Development cost

- Life cycle cost (also known as *recurring cost*)

- Requirements compliance

- Functionality, including range of performance and accuracy

- Performance (execution speed), including worst-case performance, average performance, predictability of performance, and consistency of performance

- Programmatic

- Technical risk (also known as *technical maturity*)

- Dependability, including reliability, system safety, security, maintainability, and availability

- Quality

- Human factors, including ease of use, ease of training to use, support for a standardized workflow, and the principle of *minimum surprise*

- Presence or use of hazardous materials

- Environmental factors and impact EMI, including chemical, biological, and thermal

- Power required

- Project risk, including budget risk, schedule risk, and technical risk (*the technology's maturity or availability*)

- Operational complexity

- Engineering support (tools and training)

- Verifiability

- Certifiability

- Engineering familiarity

To perform this step, a small, critical set of criteria must be selected, and then a metric must be identified for each to measure the goodness of the candidate solution with respect to that criterion.

In SysML, we will model these concerns as value properties of the block being used for the trade study.

Assigning weights to criteria

Not all assessment criteria are as important as others. To address this, each criterion is assigned a weight, which is a measure of its relative criticality. It is common to normalize these values so that the weights sum to a standard value, such as 1.00.

Defining a utility curve for each criterion

A **utility curve** for an assessment criterion defines the *goodness* of a raw measure. The computed utility value for a raw measurement is none other than the MoE for that criterion. It is common to normalize the utility curves so that all the return values are in a set range, say 0 to 10, where 0 denotes the worst case under consideration and 10 denotes the best case.

While any curve can be used, the most common approach is to use a linear curve (straight line). Creating a linear utility curve is simple; please refer to the following steps:

1. Among the selected potential solutions, identify the worst solution for this criterion and set its utility value to 0.

2. Identify the best solution for this criterion and set its utility value to 10.

3. Create a line between these two values. That is the utility curve.

The math for this is very straightforward. The equation for a line, when given two points (x1, y1) and (x2, y2), is as follows:

$$y = \frac{y2 - y1}{(x2 - x1)} x + b$$

We have special conditions such as (worst, 0) and (best, 10) on the linear curve. This simplifies the utility curve to the following:

$$moe = \frac{10}{best - worst} CandidateValue + b$$

And:

$$b = -\frac{10}{best - worst}worst$$

Here, we have the following:

- `best` is the value of the criterion for the best candidate solution.
- `worst` is the value of the criterion for the worst candidate solution.

For example, let's consider a system where our criterion is *throughput*, measured in messages processed per second. The worst candidate under consideration has a throughput of 17,000 messages/second, while the best candidate has a throughput of 100,000 messages/second. Applying our last two equations provides a solution for our moe, as shown here:

$$moe = \frac{Throughput}{8300} - 170/83$$

A third candidate solution with a throughput of 70,000 messages per second would then have a computed MoE score of 6.39, as computed from the preceding equation.

Assigning MoEs to each candidate solution

This step applies the constructed utility curves for each criterion to each of the potential solutions. The total weighted score for each candidate solution, known as its **weighted objective** function, is the sum of each of the outputs of the utility curve for each assessment criteria, times its weight:

$$Weighted \ Objective \ Function_k = \sum_j Utility_j(criterion \ value_k) * Weight_j$$

So, for each candidate solution, k, we compute its weighted objective function as the sum of the product of that solution's utility score for each criterion j times the weight of that criterion. This is easier to apply than it is to describe.

Performing sensitivity analysis

Sometimes, the MoEs for different solutions are close in value but the difference is not really significant. This can occur when there is measurement error, low measurement precision, or values are reached via consensus. In such cases, lack of precision in the values can affect the technical selection based on the trade study analysis. This issue can be examined through *sensitivity analysis*, which looks at the sensitivity that the resulting MoE has to small variations in the raw values. For example, consider the precision of the measurement of message throughput in the example provided earlier. Is the value exactly 70,000 or is it somewhere between 68,000 and 72,000? Would that difference affect our selection? Sensitivity analysis repeats this computation while making small variations to the value and checks if different solutions can be selected in those cases. If so, closer examination might be warranted.

Determining the solution

The recommended solution is simply the candidate solution with the highest value for its computed objective function.

Example

Let's apply this recipe to our system and consider how resistance is generated in the Pegasus smart bicycle trainer.

Identifying key system functions

The key system function for the example trade study is **produce resistance**.

Identifying candidate solutions

There are a number of ways to generate resistance on a smart bicycle trainer, and they all come with pros and cons. Let's take a look at some examples:

- **Wind turbine**: A bladed turbine that turns based on the power output. This is cheap and light, and resistance increases with speed but in a linear fashion. This is not closely related to the actual riding experience, where effort increases as a function of velocity cubed.

- **Electric motor with flywheel**: An electric motor generates resistance. It is expensive and potentially fairly heavy, but it can produce resistance in any algorithmically defined way.

- **Hydraulic with flywheel**: Moving fluid in an enclosed volume with a programmatically controlled aperture to generate resistance. This is the heaviest solution but it provides smooth resistance curves.

- **Electrohydraulic**: This combines the hydraulic approach with an electric motor to simulate inertia. This solution is available as a pre-packaged unit for easy installation.

Defining assessment criteria

There are many factors to consider when selecting a technology for generating resistance:

- **Accuracy of resistance**: This criterion is concerned with how closely and accurately resistance can be applied. This is very important to many serious cyclists. This is measured as a percentage of the commanded wattage versus the actual wattage. Since this is a measure of deviation from a commanded value, smaller values are better.

- **Reliability**: This is a measure of the availability of services, as determined by the **mean time between failure** (**MTBF**), measured in hours. Larger numbers are better because they indicate that the system is more reliable.

- **Mass**: The weight of the system increases the cost of shipping, and also makes it more difficult for a home user to move and set up the system. Smaller numbers are better for this metric.

- **Parts cost**: This is a measure of recurring cost or cost per shipped system. Smaller values are better.

- **Rider feel**: This is a subjective measure of how closely the simulated resistance matches a comparable situation on a road bike. This is particularly important in the lower power generation phase of the pedal stroke, as well as when you're simulating inertia over a longer timeframe for simulated climbing and descending. This is determined by conducting an experiment with experienced cyclists on hand-built mock-up prototypes over a range of fixed resistance settings and then averaging the results. The scale will be from 0 (horrible) to 100 (fantastic); larger numbers are better.

For our proposed **GenerateResistance_TradeStudy** block, these properties are modeled as value properties, as shown in the following screenshot. Note that we added units such as **US_dollars** and **MTBF_Hours** based on the *Creating the logical data schema* recipe of *Chapter 2, System Specification*. **Watt** and **Kilogram** are already provided as units in the Rhapsody SysML SI Units model library.

In the following screenshot, I added a stereotype named **«Criterion»** that defines tags that will hold the properties of interest; that is, the best and worst values for the criterion, as well as its weight (importance):

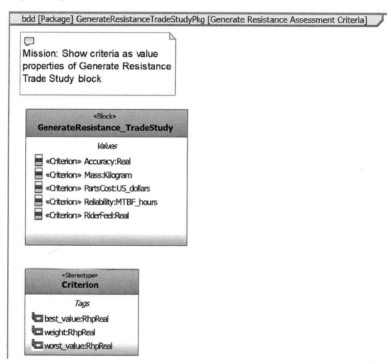

Figure 3.3 – Example block and value properties for a trade study

Assigning weights to criteria

In our example, we'll be using the following weights:

- Accuracy: 0.30 (very important)
- Mass: 0.05 (meh)
- Reliability: 0.15 (important)
- Parts Cost: 0.10 (kind of important)
- Rider Feel: 0.25 (pretty important)

These values, along with the best and worst values from the candidate solutions, are captured in the tags, as shown in the following screenshot:

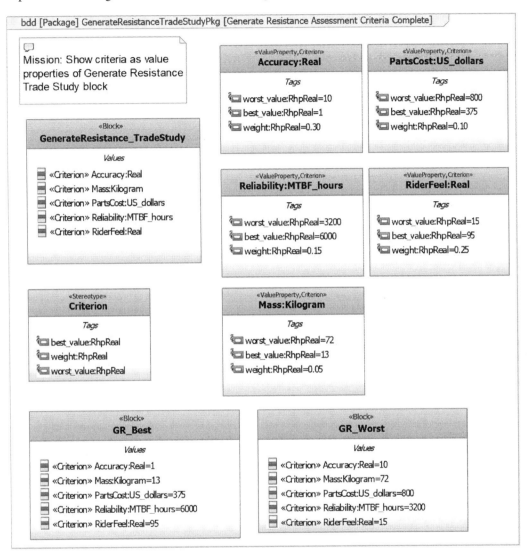

Figure 3.4 – Criteria properties captured in tags

These weights will be reflected in a parametric constraint block (see *Figure 3.5*) so that they can be used in later computations:

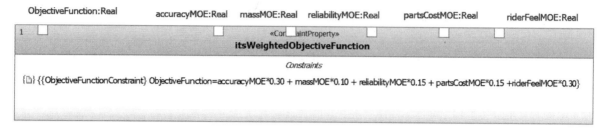

Figure 3.5 – Objective function as a constraint block

This constraint block will be used to generate the overall goodness score (known as the **objective function**) of the candidate solutions.

Defining the utility curve for each criterion

To determine the utility curves, we need to know the best and worst possible values for each of the criterial. *Figure 3.4* also shows two new blocks containing that data, taken from the potential solutions. **GR_Best** contains all the value properties of **GenerateResistance_ TradeStudy** but contains the best values for any of the considered solutions, as defined by the default value of the value property. For example, **GR_Best::Accuracy** has a default value of 1 because having a 1% error rate is the best possible outcome for any solution being considered; similarly, **GR_Best::Reliability** has a default value of 6,000 because that's the best for any solution under consideration. **GR_Worst** contains the worst-case values, **GR_Worst::Accuracy** contains the default value of 10 because having a 10% error rate is the worst case in the trade study, and **GR_Worst::Reliability = 3200** since this is the smallest MBTF for any proposed solution.

This information can also be shown in tabular format in Rhapsody (*Table 3.2*). It should be emphasized that these values are defined by the solutions we are considering in our trade study:

Name in pkg	Name in Blk	Name in vp	Weight	Worst Value	best Value
⊟ 🗀 GenerateResistanceTradeStudyPkg					
	🗋 GenerateResistance_TradeStudy	▦ Accuracy	📇 0.30	📇 10	📇 1
	🗋 GenerateResistance_TradeStudy	▦ Mass	📇 0.05	📇 72	📇 13
	🗋 GenerateResistance_TradeStudy	▦ PartsCost	📇 0.10	📇 800	📇 375
	🗋 GenerateResistance_TradeStudy	▦ Reliability	📇 0.15	📇 3200	📇 6000
	🗋 GenerateResistance_TradeStudy	▦ RiderFeel	📇 0.25	📇 15	📇 95

Table 3.2 – Criteria properties shown in a table

Now that we have our data, we can create our utility curves. In this example, we will use a linear curve (that is, a straight line) for each criterion utility curve. To compute these, we will define a **LinearUtilityCurve** constraint block that constructs a curve for us and incorporates various assumptions, including that the worst input should have a utility function value of 0 and the best input should have an output value of 10. This can be seen in the following screenshot:

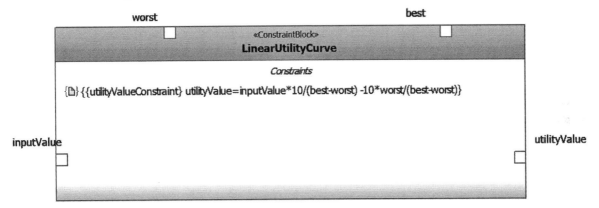

Figure 3.6 – Linear utility curve

In this constraint block, the `worst` and `best` inputs are used to construct the slope and intercept of the utility curve for that criterion; the `inputValue` constraint parameter is the value of that criterion for the selection under evaluation; the resulting `utilityValue` is the value of the utility curve for the input value. Since we have five criteria, we must create five constraint properties from this constraint block – one for each utility function.

Assigning MoEs to each candidate solution

In our example, this results in four instance specifications that contain the values that correspond to these MOEs. For this purpose, let's assume that the following table represents the raw measured or estimated values for the different criteria for the different solutions:

Solution/MoE	Accuracy (% error)	Mass (kg)	Reliability (MTBF hours)	Parts cost ($)	Rider Feel
Hydraulic	5	72	4,000	800	80
Electric	1	24	3,200	550	95
Electrohydraulic	2	69	3,500	760	92
Wind turbine	10	13	6,000	375	15

Table 3.3 – Example raw criteria values

We must then create a set of instance specifications that provide those specific values:

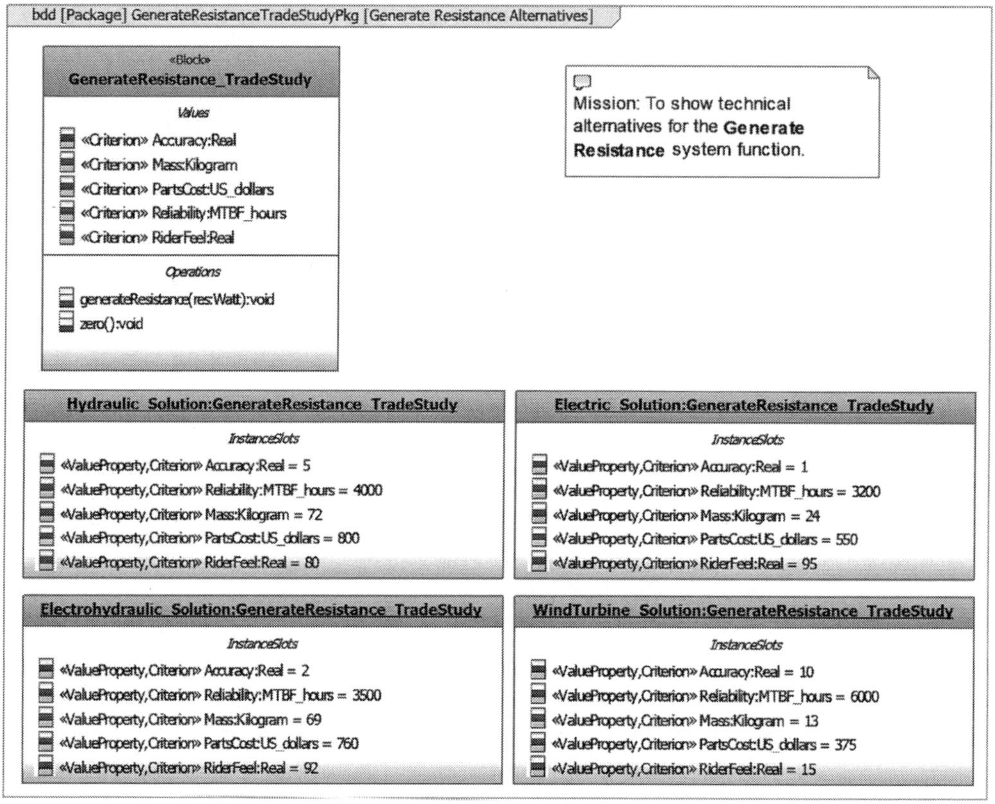

Figure 3.7 – Instance specifications for trade study

Once we've done this, we must elaborate on the parametric diagram by adding the **GeneralResistance_TradeStudy** block and connecting it to multiple instances of the **LinearUtilityCurve** constraint block. This results in the output shown in *Figure 3.8*. While *Figure 3.8* looks complex, it's really not, since it just repeats a simple pattern multiple times:

- The **GeneralResistance_TradeStudy** block is shown with value properties representing the criteria we're concerned about.

- In the middle, each criterion is represented by a **LinearUtilityCurve** constraint property, which is connected to its source value property and to the corresponding input in the **itsWeightedUtilityFunction** constraint property.

- Additionally, the relevant value properties for **GR_Best** and **GR_Worst** provide information that's relevant for constructing each utility curve.

- The final computed **ObjectiveFunction** value then gives us the overall weighted score for a selected solution:

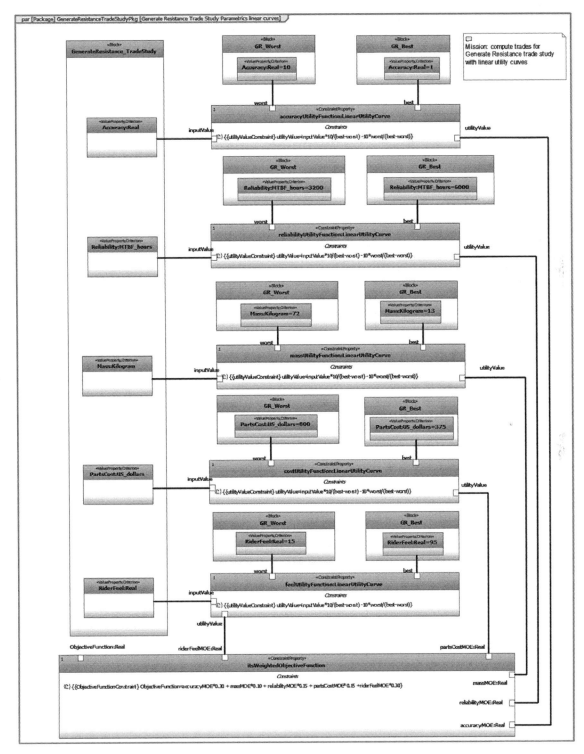

Figure 3.8 – Complete parametric diagram

To perform the required computations, simply compute the equation set for each instance specification. Rhapsody supports this computation with its **Parametric Constraint Evaluator (PCE)** profile. I won't go into setting up and configuring the PCE profile here, but running the evaluation on the four alternatives produces the three cases for the trade study, as shown in the following table:

Solution/MoE	Accuracy (% error)	Mass (kg)	Reliability (MTBF hours)	Parts cost ($)	Rider Feel	Objective Function
Hydraulic	5	72	4,000	800	80	4.533
Electric	1	24	3,200	550	95	7.696
Electrohydraulic	2	69	3,500	760	92	5.907
Wind turbine	10	13	6,000	375	15	4

Table 3.4 – Trade study results with objective functions

Performing sensitivity analysis

No sensitivity analysis needs to be performed here because the electric solution is a clear winner by a wide margin.

Determining the solution

In this case, the electric motor wins the trade study because it has the highest computed weighted objective function value.

Understanding architectural merging

The recipes in the previous chapter were all about system specifications (requirements). In those recipes, we created specifications in an agile way by using epics, use cases, and user stories as organizing elements. One of the key benefits of that approach is that different engineers can work on different functional aspects independently to construct viable specifications for the different aspects of system. A downside of this is that when it comes to creating an architecture, those efforts must be merged together since the system architecture must support all such specification models.

What to merge

During functional analysis, various system properties are identified. Of these, most should end up in the system architecture, including the following:

- System functions
- System data
- System interfaces

Issues with merging specifications into a single architecture

Merging specifications into an architecture sounds easy, right? Take all the features from all the use case analyses and copy them to the system block and you're done. In practice, it's not that easy. There are several cases for each feature that must be considered, as follows:

- The feature is unique to one use case.
- The feature occurs in exactly the same form in multiple use cases.
- The feature has different names in different use cases but is meant to be the same feature.
- The feature has the same name and form in different use cases but is intended to be a semantically different feature.
- The feature occurs in multiple use cases but in different forms:

  Case 1: Same name, different properties

  Case 2: Different name, different properties, but nevertheless still describes the same feature

Here, the term *property* refers to aspects such as structuring, argument or data type, argument order, feature name, type of service (event reception or operation), and metadata such as extent, units, timeliness, dependability, and precision.

As an aside, we should *copy* the features to the system block rather than *move* or *reference* them because we want to preserve the integrity of the use case analysis data. This allows us to come back later and revisit the use case models and modify them, if the stakeholder needs to change or evolve those requirements. This does mean that some additional work needs to be done to maintain consistency, but it can save significant time overall.

Cases 1 and 2 are trivially simple; just add the feature to the system block. The other cases require some thought. However, *trivial* might be an overstatement for interfaces since they reference the local sandbox proxies rather than the actual actors, so some cleanup is required to deal with that. This recipe will address that concern.

In a traditional V-life cycle, this merge takes place once, while in an agile approach, it takes place repeatedly, typically once per iteration. Our approach supports both traditional and agile life cycles.

Purpose

The purpose of this recipe is to help you incorporate system features that have been identified during functional analysis into our architectural model.

Inputs and preconditions

Our architectural merge can be performed with at least two use cases, including identifying and characterizing system functions, system data, and system interfaces relevant to our use cases.

Outputs and postconditions

A system block is identified. This contains the relevant system properties that were identified in the incorporated use cases.

How to do it...

While non-trivial, merging use case features into the architecture is quite straightforward (*Figure 3.9*). Please note that this can be done once, like we would do in a traditional V-life cycle, or iteratively, as we would do while following an agile approach:

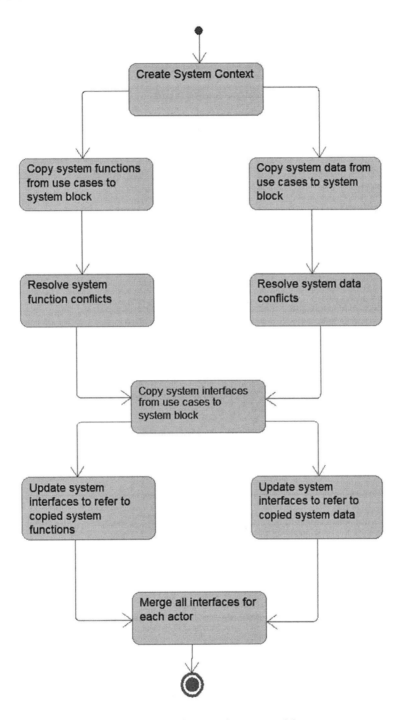

Figure 3.9 – Architectural merge workflow

Creating system context

The system context includes a block denoting the system of concern and its connection to the actors that it interacts with in its environment. This is normally visualized as a *context diagram*, a block definition diagram whose purpose is to show system context. We call this BDD the *system type context*. In addition, we want to see how the system block connects to the actors. This is shown as an internal block diagram and is referred to as the *system connected context*.

Copying system functions from use cases to the system block

During use case analysis, use case blocks are created and elaborated. The following are the primary reasons this is done:

- To create high-quality requirements related to the use case
- To identify the relevant actors for the use case
- To characterize the system features that are necessary to support the use case

The latter purpose includes identifying system data elements (represented as value properties and blocks, as detailed in the use case's logical data schema), system functions (represented as actions executed in operations and event receptions), and system behaviors (represented using activity, sequence, and/or state machines). This step copies the operations and event receptions from the use cases to the system block.

> **Note**
>
> Certain features may have been added to the use case block for purposes other than specification, such as to support simulation or to aid in debugging the use case's analysis. Such features should be clearly identified; the Rhapsody Harmony SE profile includes a «nonNormative» stereotype to mark such features for this purpose. Non-normative features don't need to be copied to the system block since they do not levy requirements or constraints based on the system's structure or behavior.

Resolving system function conflicts

As we mentioned earlier, it's likely that there will be at least some conflicts in the system due to different use cases. These can be different operations that are meant to be the same, or the same operation that's meant to do different things. These cases must be resolved. For the first case – different operations meant to be the same thing – a single operation should generally be created that meets all the needs that have been identified in the included use cases. This includes their inputs, outputs, and functionality. For the second case – the same operation that's meant to do different things – it is a matter of replicating the conflicting functions with different names to provide the set of required system behaviors. In both cases, the hard part is identifying which is which.

Copying system data from use cases to the system block

This step copies the data elements from the various use cases to the system block, including the value properties of the use case and the data schema that defines the data relationships. Remember, however, that if we just copy the operations, the input and output parameters of the functions will refer to the original model elements in the use case packages. As a part of this step, we must update the copied system functions so that they refer to our newly copied data elements. As we mentioned previously, non-normative value properties and data don't need to be copied to the architecture.

Resolving system data conflicts

The same kinds of conflicts that occur with copying the system functions can also occur with system data. This step identifies and resolves those conflicts.

Copying interfaces from use cases to the system block

As part of our use case analysis, the interfaces between the use case and the actors are defined. These need to be copied to the architecture as well.

Updating interfaces to refer to copied system functions

As with the copied functions and data, the interfaces will also refer to the elements that were originally referenced in the use case analysis packages. These references must be updated so that they point to the copied system features in the architecture while also taking into account that the conflicts have been resolved. In this case, the function names and parameters list will probably change.

Updating interfaces to refer to copied system data

The interfaces can refer to data either as flow properties or as parameters on the functions within the interface. This step resolves those references to the architectural copies of those data elements, and they are updated based on the *resolve conflicts* step.

Merging all the interfaces for each actor

Actors interact with multiple use cases. This means that different interfaces related to the same actor will be copied over from the use cases to the system architecture. Often, the set of interfaces from the use cases to the actor are merged into a single interface between the system and that actor. However, if an interface from the system to an actor is particularly complex, this might result in multiple interfaces supporting different kinds of services.

Example

In this example, we will use some of the use cases we analyzed in *Chapter 2, System Specification*:

- Control resistance
- Emulate basic gearing
- Emulate front and rear gearing
- Measure performance metrics

Creating the system type context

The system type context can be shown in a couple of ways. The following is one way of showing this:

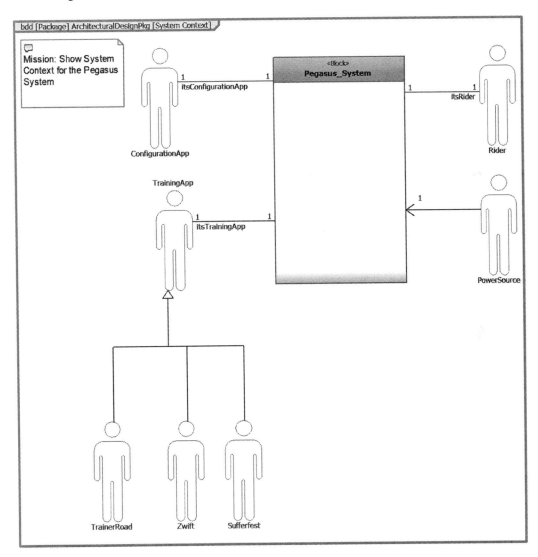

Figure 3.10 – System type context as a block definition diagram

Since I plan to use ports for actual connections, it can also be shown in an IBD, as shown in the following screenshot. This shows the system-connected context and focuses on how the system and the actors connect to each other:

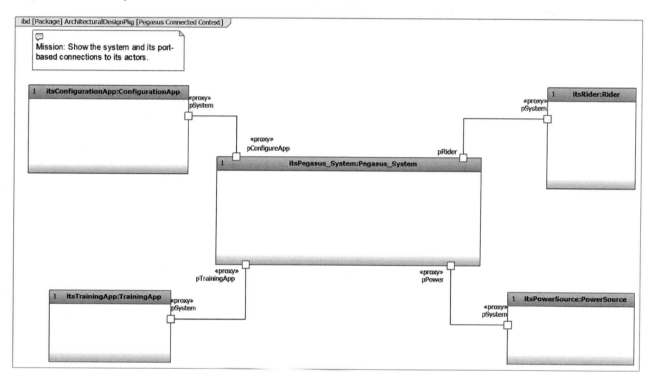

Figure 3.11 – System-connected context as an internal block diagram

Copying system functions from use cases to the system block

To illustrate this, the following screenshot shows a block definition diagram and all its included use cases (as *use case blocks*), along with their system functions and value properties and the **Pegasus_System** block we must update:

Figure 3.12 – Use case block features to copy

To actually perform the copy, we can use the Rhapsody tool Harmony SE toolkit, which provides an architectural merge feature (**SE Toolkit | Architectural Tools | Merge Functional Analysis**) that does this. It isn't difficult to do this manually, although it can be a bit time-consuming.

Resolving system function conflicts

As shown in the preceding screenshot, the system block must merge a large number of functions. For the most part, there is no conflict; either the system functions are unique, such as **Uc_MeasurePerformanceMetrics::Upload_Ride()**, or they are used in exactly the same way, such as **Uc_EmulateBasicGearing::applyResistance()** and **Uc_ControlResistance::applyResistance()**. Nevertheless, a detailed inspection uncovers a few cases that must be considered.

For example, consider **Uc_EmulateBasicGearing::changeGear(newGear: Real)** and its related functions, such as **checkGearing(gear: Real)**, and the **gearing(gear: Real)** events. These help emulate basic gearing. But how are those functions related to the specific front and rear gearing functions of our **Emulate front and rear gearing** use case, such as **selectGear(front: int, rear: int)**, **augmentFrontGear()**, **augmentRearGear()**, **augmentFrontGear()**, **decrementRearGear()**, and the **evCurrentGearing(front: int, rear: int)** event?

It could be that the **changeGear** function is called by the more specific functions that set the gearing for the front and rear chain rings, but does the training app need both the gearing (in gear inches) and the currently selected front and rear? Gearing is a function of not only the gear ratio between the front and rear chain rings but also the wheel size, which the training app may not know. If the training app uses the current front and rear as a display option for the rider, does it still need the gearing value? Probably not, since the system itself calculate metrics such as power, speed, and incline, not the training app. In this case, it is enough to send the **evCurrentGearing** event and not the *gearing* event to the training app, so the latter event can be removed from the **Pegasus_System** block and the merged system interfaces.

There's some subtlety in the various system functions and events. For example, the training app sends the event that triggers the **Uc_MeasurePerformanceMetrics::reqStartRide()** event's reception to indicate that it is ready to begin the ride and therefore ready to receive incoming data, while the **Uc_EmulateFrontandRearGearing::evBeginRiding()** event's reception is triggered by an event being sent from the rider, not the training app. This points out just how important it is for every important system property to have a meaningful description! It would be very easy to get these events confused.

Copying system data from use cases to the system block

In addition to showing the system functions to copy, *Figure 3.12* also shows the data, as value properties, to copy as well.

Resolving system data conflicts

Just like the system functions, the data copies over without any issue, but there are a few questions to resolve. **Uc_EmulateFrontandRearGearing::gearInches: RhpReal** is the gearing ratio, computed as a function of front and rear chain rings and wheel size. This is the same as **Uc_ControlResistance::gearRatio: Real**, so they can be merged into a single feature. We will use **gearRatio: Real** for the merged value property.

Copying interfaces from use cases to the system block

A number of interfaces were produced in the merged use case analyses. To start with, we will copy not only the interfaces themselves but also the events and any data types and schemas that were passed as arguments for those events.

The following screenshot shows the copied interfaces in three different browsers, each showing different kinds of elements. The browser on the left shows the interface blocks that were copied over and exposes their operations and flow properties. The middle browser shows (most of) the events that were copied over. Finally, the browser on the right shows the copied data elements:

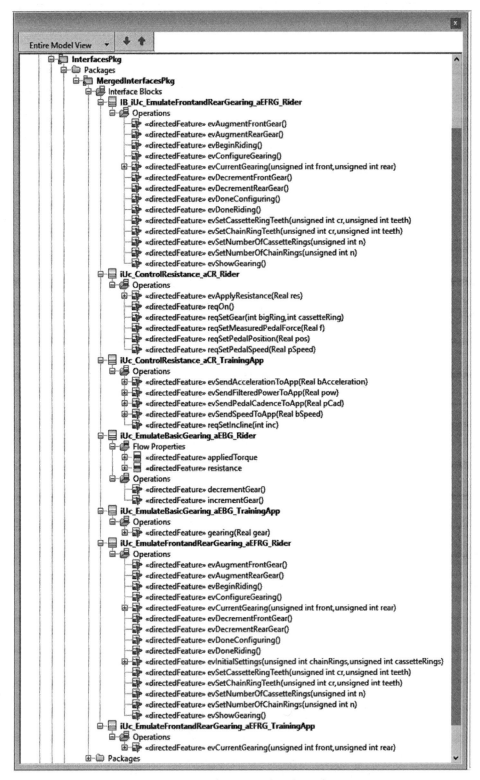

Figure 3.13 a – Interfaces copied to the architecture

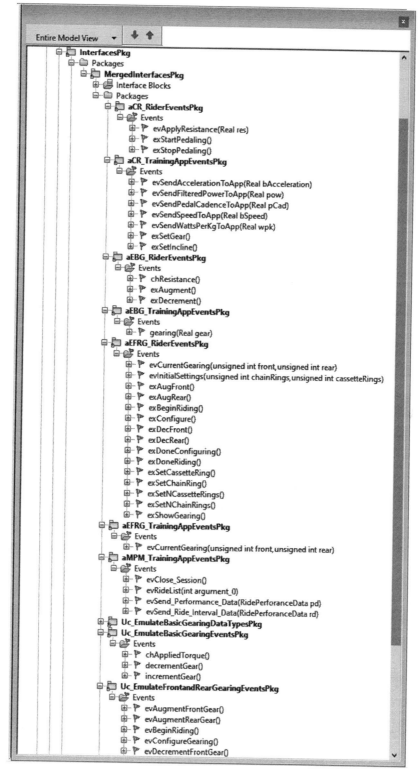

- InterfacesPkg
  - Packages
    - **MergedInterfacesPkg**
      - Interface Blocks
      - Packages
        - **aCR_RiderEventsPkg**
          - Events
            - evApplyResistance(Real res)
            - exStartPedaling()
            - exStopPedaling()
        - **aCR_TrainingAppEventsPkg**
          - Events
            - evSendAccelerationToApp(Real bAcceleration)
            - evSendFilteredPowerToApp(Real pow)
            - evSendPedalCadenceToApp(Real pCad)
            - evSendSpeedToApp(Real bSpeed)
            - evSendWattsPerKgToApp(Real wpk)
            - exSetGear()
            - exSetIncline()
        - **aEBG_RiderEventsPkg**
          - Events
            - chResistance()
            - exAugment()
            - exDecrement()
        - **aEBG_TrainingAppEventsPkg**
          - Events
            - gearing(Real gear)
        - **aEFRG_RiderEventsPkg**
          - Events
            - evCurrentGearing(unsigned int front, unsigned int rear)
            - evInitialSettings(unsigned int chainRings, unsigned int cassetteRings)
            - exAugFront()
            - exAugRear()
            - exBeginRiding()
            - exConfigure()
            - exDecFront()
            - exDecRear()
            - exDoneConfiguring()
            - exDoneRiding()
            - exSetCassetteRing()
            - exSetChainRing()
            - exSetNCassetteRings()
            - exSetNChainRings()
            - exShowGearing()
        - **aEFRG_TrainingAppEventsPkg**
          - Events
            - evCurrentGearing(unsigned int front, unsigned int rear)
        - **aMPM_TrainingAppEventsPkg**
          - Events
            - evClose_Session()
            - evRideList(int argument_0)
            - evSend_Performance_Data(RidePerforanceData pd)
            - evSend_Ride_Interval_Data(RidePerforanceData rd)
        - **Uc_EmulateBasicGearingDataTypesPkg**
        - **Uc_EmulateBasicGearingEventsPkg**
          - Events
            - chAppliedTorque()
            - decrementGear()
            - incrementGear()
        - **Uc_EmulateFrontandRearGearingEventsPkg**
          - Events
            - evAugmentFrontGear()
            - evAugmentRearGear()
            - evBeginRiding()
            - evConfigureGearing()
            - evDecrementFrontGear()

Figure 3.13 b – Interfaces copied to the architecture

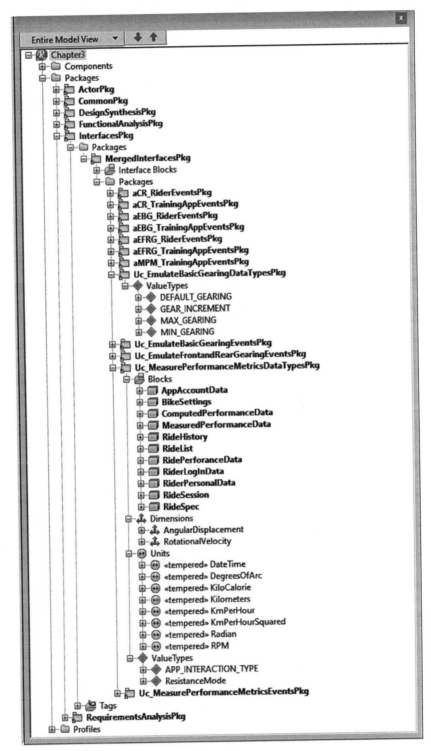

Figure 3.13 c – Interfaces copied to the architecture

Updating the interfaces so that they refer to copied system functions

The copied interfaces refer to the events back in the originating use case analysis packages. In our use case analyses, we followed the convention that all the services in these interfaces are modeled as event receptions, so we can limit our focus to ensure that the interface blocks refer to the event definitions in the architecture rather than their definition in their original source; that is, the use case analysis packages:

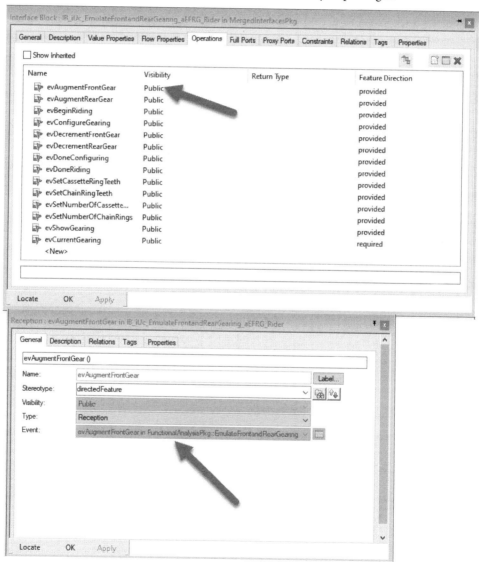

Figure 3.14 – Interface feature references to original event

In the preceding screenshot, the event receptions point to the original source, as shown by the detailed definition on the right (**evAugmentFrontGear** in **FunctionalAnalysisPkg::EmulateFrontandRearGearing**). We can update the copied interface event reception so that it refers to our copied event instead, as shown in the following screenshot. This must be done for all such event receptions:

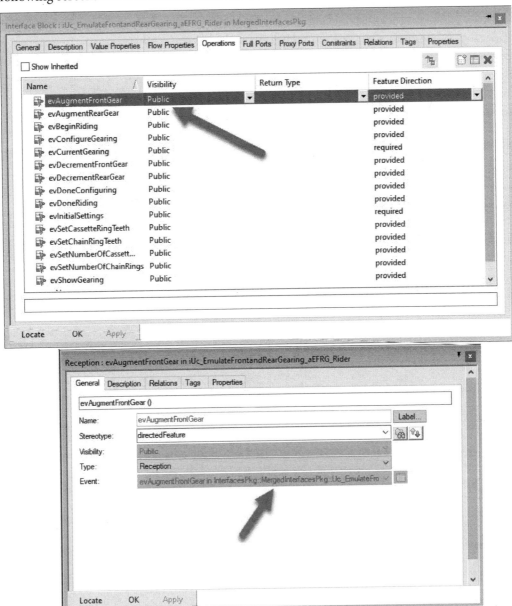

Figure 3.15 – Interface feature references to copied event

Updating interfaces to refer to copied system data

The system functions and event receptions of the **Pegasus_System** block must all refer to the copied data types, not the original data types. This is also true for any flow properties in the interface blocks.

In this particular case, no user-defined types are used in the interfaces, so the data references don't need to be changed.

Merging all interfaces for each actor

The last step in this recipe is to create the interfaces for the actors. In the previous chapter, we created interfaces not for the actors themselves but rather as blocks meant to serve as local stand-ins for those actors. The naming convention for these interfaces reflects that choice. For example, the **iUc_EmulateBasicGearing_aEBG_Rider** interface block is an interface between the **EmulateBasicGearing** use case and its local proxy for the **Rider** actor, **aEBG_Rider**. In this way, we can see which interfaces we can merge. All the interfaces that contain *a…Rider* should be merged into an **iRider** interface. A similar process is followed for the other actors. This is because the system architecture must merge all the interfaces referring to the same actor. In the end, we'll have an interface for each actor that specifies the interface between the system and the actor.

The following screenshot shows all the merged interfaces. However, two of the interfaces are empty: **iConfigureApp** and **iPowerSource**. That is because the use case analyses we performed didn't uncover any services or flows between the system and those actors. If they are really actors to the system, their interfaces will be uncovered as more use cases are elaborated or they will be discovered as system design progresses.

If they end up containing no content, then they can be removed from the architecture:

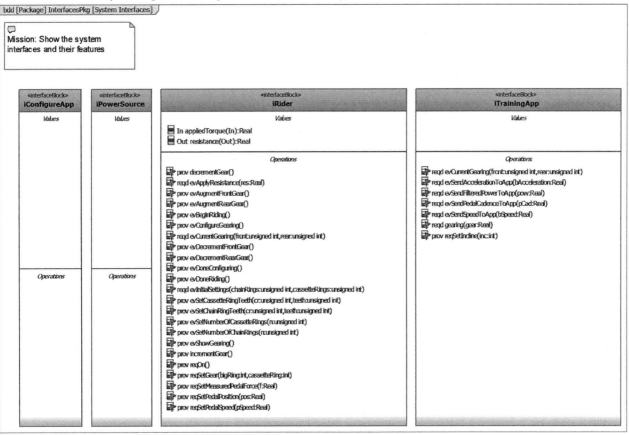

Figure 3.16 – Merged system interfaces

The pattern-driven architecture

A design pattern is a *generalized solution to commonly occurring problems.* Let's break this down.

First, a design pattern captures a design solution in a general way. That is, the aspects of the design that are unique to the specific problem being solved are abstracted away, leaving the generally necessary structures, roles, and behaviors as-is. The process of identifying the underlying conceptual solution is known as **pattern mining**. This discovered abstracted solution can now be reapplied to a different design context, a process known as **pattern instantiation**. Furthermore, while each design context has unique aspects, design patterns are appropriate for problems or concerns that reappear in many systems designs.

> **Note**
> Please refer to *Design Patterns for Embedded Systems in C*, by *Bruce Douglass, Ph.D. 2014*, for more information.

To help you work with design patterns, you should keep two fundamental truths in mind:

- Design is all about optimizing important properties at the expense of others (see the *Architectural trade studies* recipe).

- There are almost always many different solutions to a given design problem.

With many design solutions (patterns) able to address design concerns, how can we possibly choose? Simple – the best pattern is the one that solves the design problem in an optimal way, where **optimal** means that it maximizes the desired outcomes and minimizes the undesired ones. Typically, this means that the important **Quality of Service** (**QoS**) properties should be given a higher weight than those properties that are less important. A good solution, therefore, solves the problem at hand by providing desired benefits at a cost we are willing to pay. This is often determined via a trade study.

Dimensions of patterns

Patterns have four key aspects or dimensions:

- **Name**: The name allows us to reference the pattern independent of its application in any specific design.

- **Purpose**: The purpose of the pattern identifies the design problem the pattern addresses and the necessary design context preconditions necessary for its use.

- **Solution**: The solution details the structural elements, their collaboration roles, and their singular and collective behavior.

- **Consequences**: The pattern's consequences highlight the benefits and costs of using the pattern while focusing on the design properties that have been optimized and deoptimized through its use. This is arguably the most important dimension because it is how we will decide on which pattern to deploy from the set of relevant patterns.

Pattern roles

Structural roles are fulfilled by the structural elements (blocks) in system engineering. A *role* can be defined as the *use of an instance in a context*. Design patterns have two broad categories of roles. The first is as *glue*. Roles of this type serve to facilitate and manage how the design elements that the pattern is a part of are executed.

The second is as a *collaboration parameter*. Design patterns can be described as parameterized collaborations. These parameterized roles are placeholders that will be replaced by specific elements from your design; that is, some design elements will substitute these roles during pattern instantiation. Design elements that substitute pattern parameters are known as **pattern arguments**. Once the pattern has been instantiated, the glue roles will interact with the pattern arguments to provide an optimized design solution.

Patterns in an architectural context

Architecture is *design writ large*. Architectural design choices affect most, if not, all of the system, and the more detailed design elements must live within the confines of the architectural decisions. As we discussed in the *Architecture 0* recipe of *Chapter 1, Basics of Agile Systems Modeling*, we must focus on five key views of the architecture: the subsystem and component view, the concurrency and resource view, the distribution view, the dependability view, and the deployment view. Each of these views have their own rich sources for design patterns. A system architecture is a set of architectural structures that have been integrated with one or more patterns in each of these views.

This recipe will provide a workflow that will help you identify and integrate a design pattern in general. We will use this pattern in later recipes to address their more specific concerns.

> **Note**
>
> See *Real-Time Design Patterns by Bruce Douglass, Ph.D. 2003 or Pattern-Oriented Software Architecture Volume 1: A System of Patterns*, by Buschmann, Meunier, Rohnert, Sommerlad, and Stal (1996), for information.

Purpose

The purpose of design patterns is two-fold. First, design patterns capture good design solutions so that they can be reused, providing an engineering history of good design solutions. Secondly, they allow designers to reuse existing design solutions that have proven to be useful.

Inputs and preconditions

The fundamental precondition for using design patterns is that there is a design problem to be solved, and some design elements have been identified.

Outputs and postconditions

The primary output of applying a design patten is an optimized collaboration that solves the design solution in an optimal way.

How to do it...

The use of design patterns is conceptually simple, as shown in the following diagram:

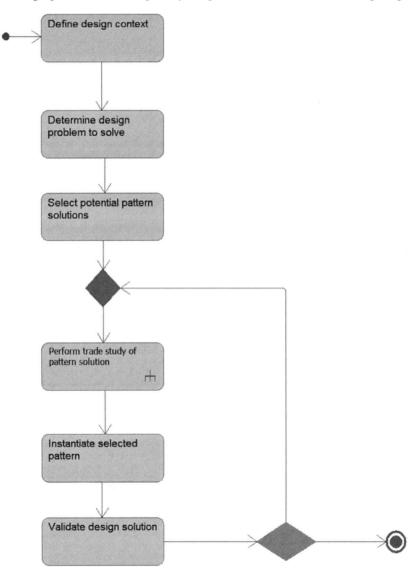

Figure 3.17 – Applying design patterns

This simple flow somewhat belies the difficulty of good design because a good design generally contains a number of interconnected patterns working together to optimize many aspects at once.

Defining the design context

This step is generally a matter of defining the essential elements of the design (sometimes known as the **analysis model**) without any optimization. This includes properties such as value properties, operations, state behavior, and relationships. A general guideline I use is that this design context is demonstrably functionally correct, as demonstrated through testing and execution, before optimization is attempted. Optimizing too soon (that is, before the design context has been verified) generally leads to bad outcomes.

Determining the design problem to solve

While developing the design context, it is common to uncover a design issue that impacts the quality of the services of the design, such as performance, reusability, safety, and security. These design issues are often solved by other designers in different ways.

Selecting potential pattern solutions

This step involves reviewing the pattern's literature for solutions that other designs have found to be effective. A set of patterns is selected from the potential solution candidates based on how they can be applied to the design issue at hand, how similar they are, and the aspects of the design that they can optimize.

Performing a trade study of the pattern's solution

Earlier in this chapter, we learned how to perform architectural trade studies. In some cases, a full-blown trade study may not be called for, but in general, this step selects an option from a set of alternatives, which is what a trade study does. You may have noticed that the icon we used in *Figure 3.17* for this step is a *call behavior*, which is a formal use of the previous recipe.

Instantiating the selected pattern

Once a pattern has been selected, it must be instantiated. This is largely a matter of creating the structural and behavioral elements of the pattern and making small changes to some of the existing design elements to make them proper arguments for the design pattern parameters (also known as **refactoring**).

Validating the solution design

Once the pattern has been instantiated, it must be examined for two things. First, before the pattern was instantiated, the design collaboration worked, albeit suboptimally (*step 1, Defining the design context*). We want to verify that we didn't break it so that it no longer works. Secondly, we applied the design pattern for a reason – we wanted to achieve some kind of optimization. We must verify that we achieved our optimization goals. If we have not, then a different pattern should be used instead or in addition to the current pattern. Patterns can be combined to provide cumulative effects in many cases.

Example

In this example, we will take a non-architectural design context. Later examples will apply this to the Pegasus architecture so that we can look at specific views of the architecture.

Defining the design context

In this example, we'll consider a part of the internal design that acquires measured ride data from the power and pedal position sensors:

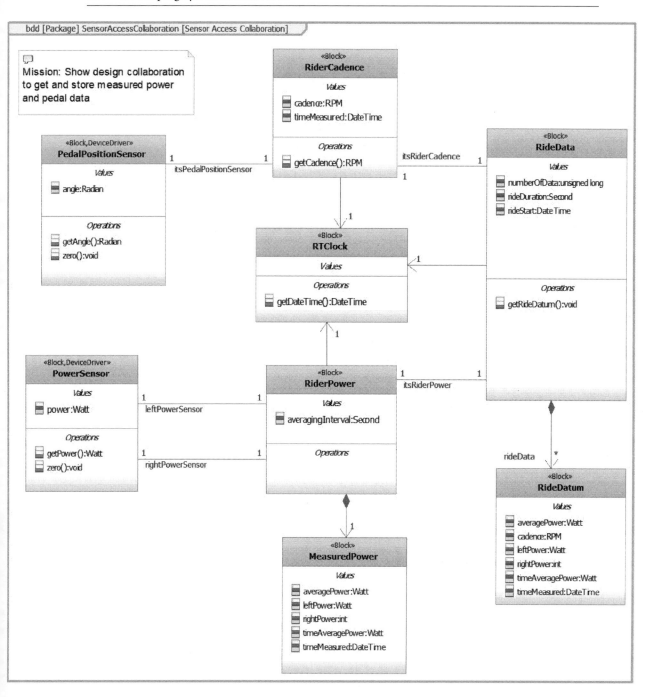

Figure 3.18 – Design collaboration (pre-pattern)

This design shows three device driver parts: two for the rider power (left- and right-hand side sensors) and one for the pedal position for determining pedal cadence.

The **RiderPower** block gathers data from the two **PowerSensor** instances and aggregates it, along with the current time, into a **MeasuredPower** block that includes the left and right power, the average of those two values, the time averaged average, and a time stamp. The **RiderCadence** block gets the pedal's position, which, using the real-time clock, can determine cadence. The **RideData** block then aggregates this data into an ordered collection, **RideDatum**, constituting the information about the ride. The actual design incorporates much more computed data, such as computed speed and distance, but we'll ignore that for now.

Determining the design problem to solve

At this stage, some design optimization questions may arise.

First, what's the best way to get the data from the sensors in a timely way? It must be sampled fast enough so that we don't miss any peak power and cadence spikes (riders love that kind of data), and the data from the two different sources must be synchronized in terms of when they were measured. On the other hand, sampling at too high a rate requires more data storage and could limit the lengths of the rides that can be recorded and stored.

Furthermore, note the existence of multiple clients for the real-time clock. Is having all the clients request the current time the best approach?

Selecting potential pattern solutions

Let's consider three design patterns that address how we can get data in a timely manner: the *Interrupt Pattern*, the *Opportunistic Polling Pattern*, and the *Periodic Polling Pattern*. The first creates an interrupt driver that notifies the clients when data becomes available. The second pattern requires the client to poll the data sources when it gets a chance. The last pattern is a modification of the second pattern, in which the client is notified, via a timer interrupt, when it should poll the data:

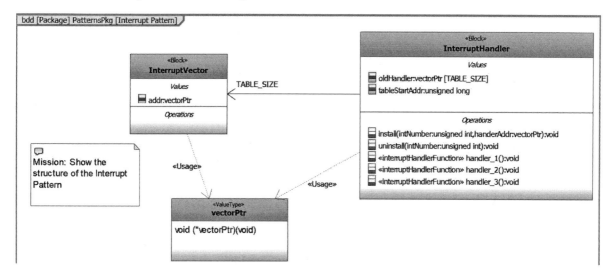

Figure 3.19 – Interrupt Pattern

> **Note**
>
> To find out more about the *Interrupt Pattern,* the *Opportunistic Polling Pattern*, and the *Periodic Polling Pattern*, please read *Design Patterns for Embedded Systems in C*, 2014, by Bruce Douglass.

The preceding diagram shows the *Interrupt Pattern*. Conceptually, it is very simple: an interrupt handler installs a set of interrupt handler functions by saving the old address in the interrupt vector table for the selected interrupt, and then puts the address of the desired interrupt handler in its place. Later, when that interrupt occurs, the CPU invokes the selected interrupt handler function. There are some subtleties of writing interrupt handlers, but that's the basic idea.

Take a look at the following diagram:

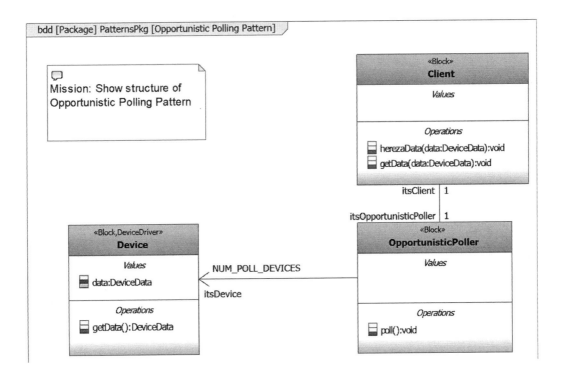

Figure 3.20 – Opportunistic Polling Pattern

The preceding diagram shows the *Opportunistic Polling Pattern*. It works by having a **Client**, on whatever criteria it decides to use, invoke the OpportunisticPoller::poll() function. OpportunisticPoller then gets data from all the devices it polls (defined by NUM_POLL_DEVICES) and returns it to the Client. Easy peasy! Now, let's take a look at the following diagram:

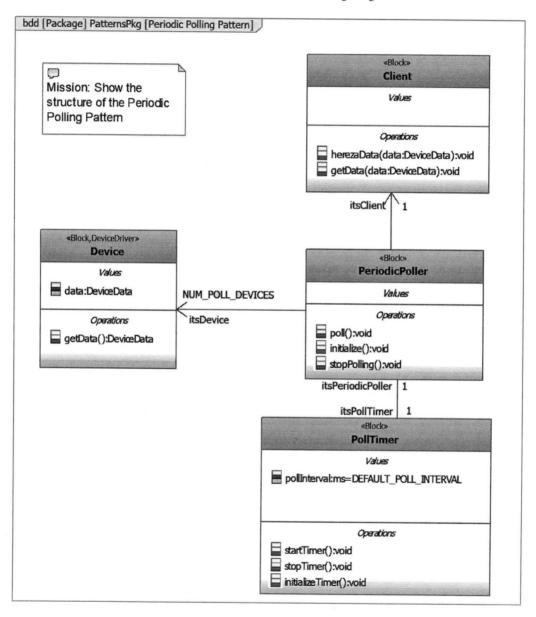

Figure 3.21 – Periodic Polling Pattern

The preceding diagram shows a specialized form of the previous pattern, called the *Periodic Polling Pattern*. In this pattern, polling is driven by a timer; `PeriodicPoller` initializes and sets up the timer, which then invokes it with the specified period (ms is being used here, but finer grained polling can be supported with the appropriate hardware resources).

The consequences of these patterns can be summarized as follows:

Pattern	Pros (Benefits)	Cons (Costs)
Interrupt	• Highly responsive to incoming data events	• Can lead to data corruption unless interrupts are disabled during interrupt processing • Can lead to data loss if the interrupt handler takes too long • Can lead to processing starvation if data arrival is too frequent
Opportunistic Polling	• Simple implementation • Efficient use of processor resources since data is acquired when the processor is otherwise idle	• No timeliness guarantees • Slow polling can lead to data loss • Less responsive to incoming data • Data can be corrupted if interrupts are not disabled during polling
Periodic Polling	• Relatively simple implementation • Period can be tuned for data arrival frequency	• Data can be lost if the polling period is too long • Processing starvation can occur if the frequency is too high • Handling timer interrupts must be done quickly as they can lead to data loss • Data can be corrupted if interrupts are not disabled during polling

Table 3.5 – Design patterns for timely data acquisition

Performing a trade study of the pattern's solution

I won't detail the process of performing the trade study, but instead provide a summary in *Table 3.6*. In this trade study, the *Periodic Polling Pattern* is selected:

Pattern	Criteria						Total Weighted Score
	Simplicity (W1 = 0.1)		Avoid Data Loss (W2 = 0.7)		Resource Efficiency (W3 = 0.2)		
	MoE	Score	MoE	Score	MoE	Score	
Interrupt	4	0.4	6	4.2	6	1.2	5.8
Opportunistic Polling	6	0.6	3	2.1	2	0.4	3.1
Periodic Polling	2	0.2	6	4..2	8	1.6	6

Table 3.6 – Results of the trade study

These results show that the *Periodic Polling Pattern* is the best fit for our design.

Instantiating the selected pattern

The next step is to instantiate the pattern. Conceptually, this is a matter of replacing the parameters of the pattern with design elements. In practice, this is often done by specializing the parameters so that the design classes now inherit the structure and behavior that must be integrated into the pattern. Additionally, a small amount of reorganization (known as *refactoring*) may be required, including removing or modifying the relationships in the pre-pattern collaboration.

The following diagram shows the instantiated design pattern. I've added colored shading to the pattern elements to highlight their use. The `RiderData` block subclasses the pattern's `PeriodicPoller` block; `RiderCadence` and `RiderPower` both subclass the `Device` block. I've also elected to show the inherited features in the updated design blocks (indicated with a caret, ^). Those inherited operations will be implemented in terms of the existing functions within those specialized blocks. Furthermore, the inherited data elements will not be used; the original data elements from the design elements will be used in their stead.

Also, note that the original relationships between `RideData` and `RiderCadence` and `RideData` and `RiderPower` have been deleted and subsumed by the single relationship from `RideData` to `Device`; this relationship applies to both `RiderCadence` and `RiderPower` since the latter two blocks are subtypes of `Device`. In this case, `NUM_POLL_DEVICES` is 2. As we mentioned previously, this change falls under the heading of refactoring:

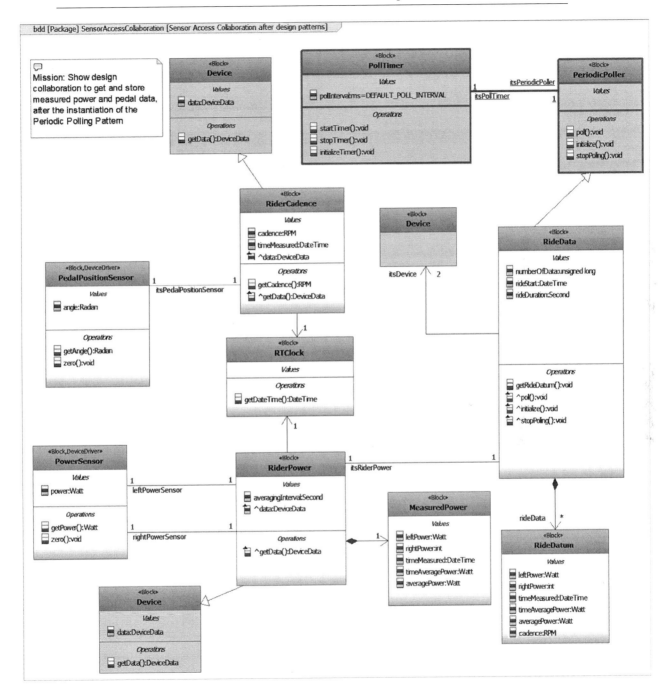

Figure 3.22 – Instantiated design pattern

Validating the solution design

At this point, we must reapply the test cases that were used to verify the collaboration previously and then ensure our objectives (as stated by the trade study criteria) have been addressed.

Subsystem and component architecture

The subsystem and component architecture view focuses on identifying and organizing system features into large-scale system elements – subsystems, their responsibilities, and their interfaces. In the *Understanding architectural merging* recipe, we learned how system features may be aggregated into a singular system block, as well as how to create merged interfaces and an associated logical data schema. In this recipe, we'll learn how to identify subsystems, allocate functionality to those subsystems, and create subsystem-level interfaces.

So, what's a subsystem?

We'll use the definition from *Agile Systems Engineering*, which is as follows:

"Subsystem: An integrated interdisciplinary collection of system components that together form the largest-scale pieces of a system. It is a key element in the Subsystem and Component Architecture of the system."

Note that this definition includes the notion of a subsystem being interdisciplinary. This means that you will not define a software subsystem, an electronics subsystem, and a mechanical subsystem, although in a particular subsystem, one engineering discipline may dominate the design. Instead, subsystems are focused on tightly coupled requirements and coherence, and are then implemented with a combination of engineering disciplines. The contribution from an engineering discipline to a subsystem is referred to as a *facet* to distinguish it from subsystems and components. Discipline-specific facets will be discussed in *Chapter 4, Handoff to Downstream Engineering*.

> **Note**
>
> You can find out more about subsystems in *Agile Systems Engineering* by Bruce Douglass, Ph.D., Morgan Kaufman Press, 2016.

Modeling a subsystem in SysML

In SysML, a subsystem is just a block, although it is common to add a *«Subsystem»* stereotype. It is common – although by no means required – to connect subsystems together by adding connectors between ports on the subsystems. In this book, we will use SysML proxy ports for that purpose.

More specifically, we will use proxy ports for dynamic connections; that is, connections that require us to exchange flows, such as control, energy, fluid, or data, whether discrete or continuous. For static connections, such as when mechanical pieces are bolted together, we will use associations between the blocks and connectors between the parts (instances).

Block definition diagrams will be used to show the subsystem's types and properties. This view is known as the system **composition architecture**. Internal block diagrams will show how the instances of the blocks are connected to create a running system. This latter view is sometimes known as the system connected **architecture**.

Choosing a subsystem architecture

It is important to remember that many subsystem architectures can achieve the same system-level functionality. Selecting a specific subsystem architecture is always an optimization decision.

Some of these optimization criteria are typically stated as *guidance* or *rules of thumb*, but they are really stating properties you'd like a good subsystem architecture to enhance. Some goals and principles when it comes to creating good subsystems are as follows:

- The goals of a subsystem and component architecture:

    a) Reuse proven subsystem architectural approaches (patterns).

    b) Support end-to-end performance needs easily.

    c) Minimize recurring system costs (cost per shipped system).

    d) Maximize ease of maintenance:

    e) Minimize cost of repair.

    f) Leverage team skills.

    g) Leverage existing technology and **intellectual property** (**IP**)

- Principles of subsystem and component architecture selection:

  a) Coherence: Subsystems should have coherent intent and content.

  b) Contractual interaction: The subsystem should provide a small number of well-defined interfaces and services.

  c) Encapsulation: Tightly coupled requirements and features should be in the same subsystem.

  d) Collaboration: Loosely coupled requirements and features should be in different subsystems.

  e) Integrated teams: A subsystem is typically developed by a well-integrated interdisciplinary team.

  f) Reusability: Good subsystems can be reused in other, similar systems without them requiring other contextual elements.

Purpose

The purpose of creating this architectural view is to identify the subsystems, their responsibilities, features, connections, and interfaces. This provides us with a large-scale view of the largest-scale pieces of the system that more detailed design work will fit in.

Inputs and preconditions

The inputs include a set of requirements that define the system's overall functionality. It is recommended that these requirements are organized into use cases, though other organization methods can be used. This input is a natural consequence of the recipes that were shown in *Chapter 2, System Specification*.

Additionally, a set of external actors – elements outside the system with which the system must interact – have been defined. This input is a natural consequence of the recipes shown in *Chapter 2, System Specification*.

Finally, an initial set of system functions, flows, and information have been identified through the requirements or use case analysis and merged into a system block via the *Understanding architectural merge* recipe or its equivalent.

Outputs and postconditions

At this stage, a set of subsystems have been identified, including their key system functions, data, and interfaces.

How to do it...

This recipe's workflow can be seen in the following diagram:

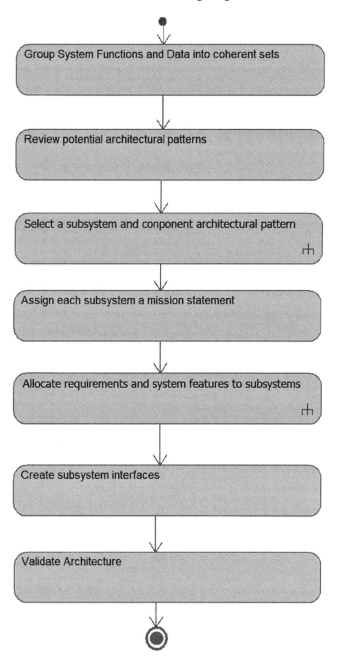

Figure 3.23 – Creating a subsystem and component architecture

Group system functions and data into coherent sets

This task groups system features together by commonality. This commonality can be different dimensions, such as a common flow source (sensors or system inputs), similar processing/transformation, similar use, reuse coherence (things that tend to be reused together), and dependability level (high security or high safety features tend to be grouped together).

These sets form the basis of how subsystems can be identified.

Reviewing potential architectural patterns

As we mentioned previously, there are many ways to organize subsystems. The book *Real-Time Design Patterns* identifies a number of popular subsystem patterns, such as the *Microkernel*, *Layered*, and *Hierarchical Control* patterns. Here, you should select one or more patterns rovide the desired system properties.

> **Note**
>
> You can find more information in *Real-Time Design Patterns* by *Bruce Douglass, Ph.D., Addison-Wesley Press, 2003.*

Selecting a subsystem and component architectural pattern

This step is actually a reference to the *Pattern-driven architecture* recipe. This recipe details how to quantitatively select from a set of alternative technical approaches.

Assigning each subsystem a mission statement

Once a set of subsystems has been identified, each should be given a description that identifies the criteria for deciding whether or not it should host or contribute to a system's capability.

Allocating requirements and system features to subsystems

This step allocates system functionality, flows, and data to the subsystems. This is sometimes a little tricky, which is why this will be implemented in the next recipe, *Architectural allocation.*

Creating subsystem interfaces

System functionality will be provided by a collaboration of subsystems, so those subsystems must communicate and coordinate. The subsystem's interfaces specify the services and flows that will be used to accomplish this. They often tie in with the system-actor interfaces at one end or the other, but not necessarily. These system interfaces can be created by following the *Specifying logical system interfaces* recipe in the previous chapter.

Validating the architecture

This step examines the resulting subsystem architecture to ensure that it can deliver the necessary system functionality, as well as to ensure that it achieves the optimization goals that were used to select the subsystem pattern.

Example

In this example, we'll create an architecture for the Pegasus system based on some of the use cases that were considered in previous recipes, such as **Emulate front and rear gearing**, **Control resistance**, **Measure performance metrics**, and **Manually Adjust Bike Fit**.

Group system functions and data into coherent sets

The functionality of the system can be grouped by their purpose and capability. A good way to do this is by looking at the system's use cases, as we did in *Chapter 2, System Specification*. Similar to how we treat requirements and system functions, either a use case can be directly allocated to a single subsystem OR it must be decomposed into subsystem-level use cases that can also be allocated. This decomposition is best represented with the «include» relationship. Any subsystem-level use cases created in this way will be tagged with the *«Subsystem»* stereotype.

First, let's consider a set of use cases (*Figure 3.24*). Note that while this set encompasses a wide range of system capabilities, it doesn't include all capabilities. We recommend that you do this incrementally; additional use cases – and even subsystems – can be added later as the need arises:

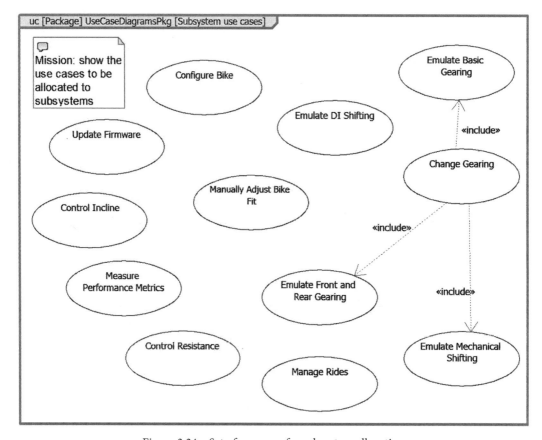

Figure 3.24 – Set of use cases for subsystem allocation

Some of these use cases are likely to be allocated to a single subsystem. For example, the **Manually Adjust Bike Fit** use case might be allocated to a single **Mechanical Frame**. Others are likely to use multiple subsystems; for example, the **Control Incline** use case might be decomposed into subsystem-level use cases that map functionality to the **User Input** and **Mechanical Frame** subsystems. The exact decomposition will, of course, depend on the set of subsystems that we decide to use.

Reviewing potential architectural patterns

There are many potential subsystem patterns we can choose from. From Buschmann et al., the *Model-View-Controller* and *Microkernel* architecture patterns seem potentially viable, although the former is more of a design collaboration-level pattern than an architectural design pattern. From the previously mentioned *Real-Time Design Patterns* book, the *Layered*, *Channel*, and *Hierarchical Control* patterns are also possibilities.

> **Note**
>
> Please refer to *A System of Patterns,* by *Buschmann, Meunier, Rohnert, Sommerlad, and Stal, Wiley Press (1996),* for more information.

Selecting a subsystem and component architectural pattern

Using the workflow from the *Pattern-driven architecture* recipe, we will select **Five-Layer Architecture Pattern** from **Real-Time Design Patterns** as our base pattern. We will modify it so that it uses subsystems rather than packages and replace **Abstract OS Layer** with **Abstract Common Services Layer** since it seems more relevant to our design:

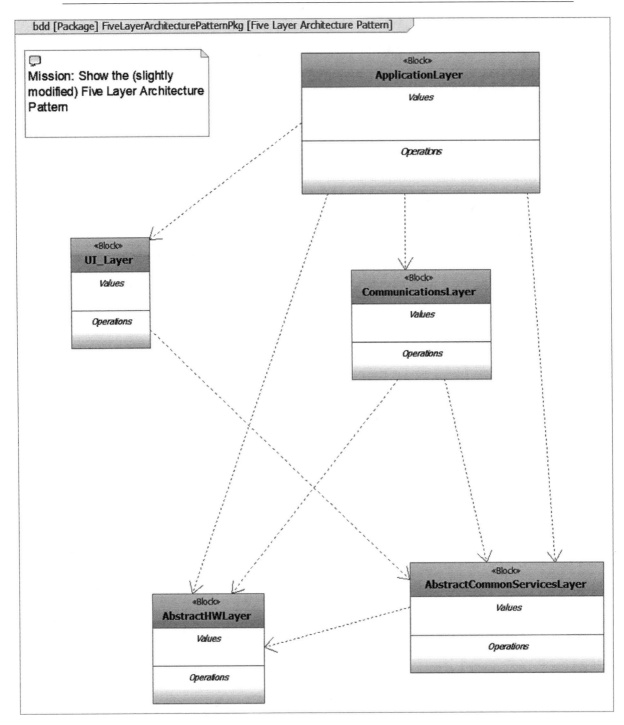

Figure 3.25 – Modified five-layer architecture pattern

Each block in the pattern may have multiple instantiations for peers (such as multiple application layer elements) or may have an internal sub-subsystem structure (which we will simply refer to as *subsystems*).

Each block in the pattern has its own purpose and scope.

Application layer

This layer contains features at the application level, so system features (data and services) such as **Ride and Rider** metrics and properties would reside in this layer.

UI layer

This layer contains elements for the system's user input. This includes selecting and displaying the current gear, for example. Most display features actually reside on the third-party training apps being used, so the system itself has a limited UI.

Communications layer

The system requires Bluetooth and ANT+ communications protocols, sessions to be set up, and so on. All those features reside largely in this layer.

Abstract common services layer

This layer contains common services such as data storage and data management, as well as electric power delivery.

Abstract HW layer

This layer focuses on electronic and mechanical aspects; frame adjustment, drive train, various sensors, and so on all reside here. This is likely to have peer instantiations and different substructures.

Now, let's look at the pattern's instantiation.

In the following diagram, we can see a set of six proposed subsystems, along with their high-level parts (identified as subsystems here).

Note that in Rhapsody, the «Subsystem» stereotype is already defined, but, curiously, the «System» stereotype is not. I added it to the **CommonPkg** package and specified that it can be applied to the `Class` metatype (`Block` is, of course, derived from `Class`) and then applied it to the `Pegasus_System` block:

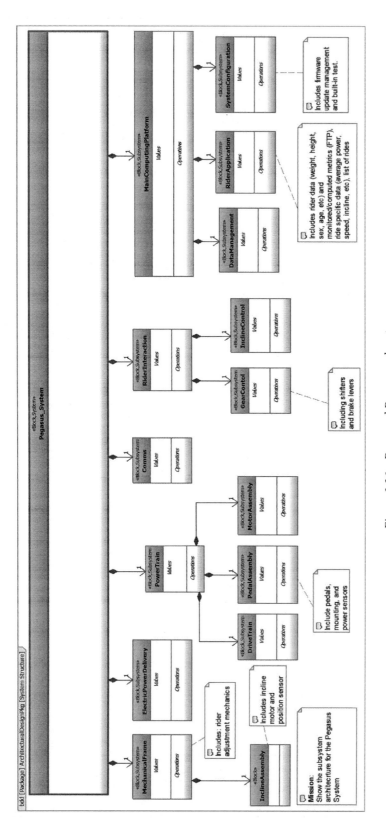

Figure 3.26 – Proposed Pegasus subsystems

We can also create a *connected architecture* view that shows how we expect the subsystems to connect to each other. This will evolve as we elaborate on the architecture and allocate functionality. The following diagram shows the connected architecture, but only the high-level subsystems:

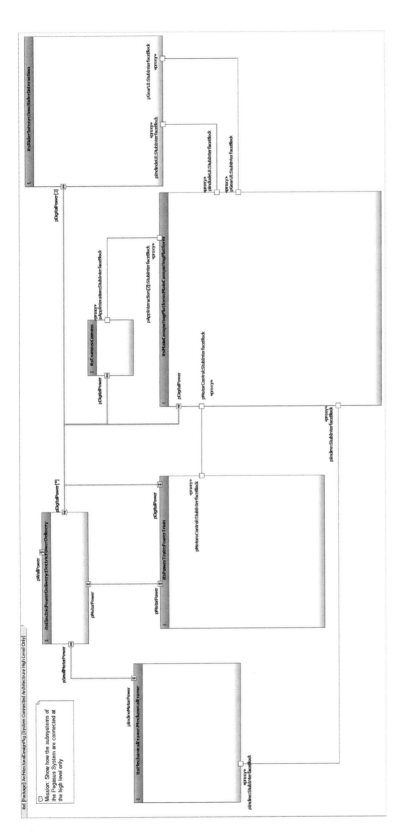

Figure 3.27 – High-level connected Pegasus architecture

The following diagram shows the same view but with the internal structure we've identified so far. In both cases, I used Rhapsody's **Display Options** feature to change the line color for the electrical power connections to highlight their presence. These connections are notional at this point and may change as we dive into the details of the architecture:

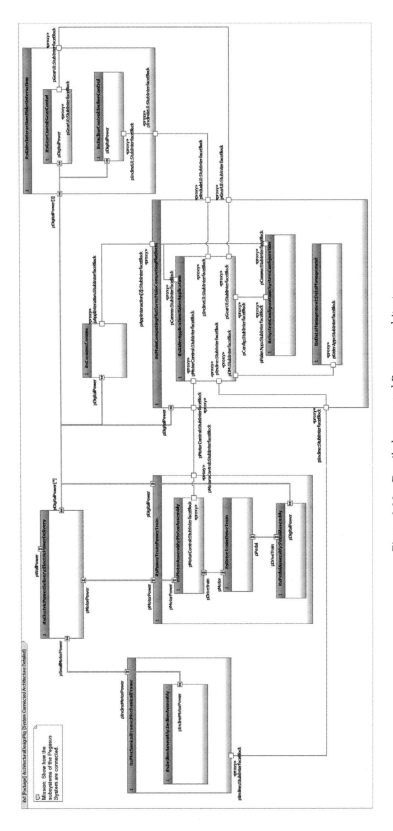

Figure 3.28 – Detailed connected Pegasus architecture

Assigning each subsystem a mission statement

The mission statement for each subsystem is added to the *Description* field of the subsystem block. The mission statements for the high-level subsystems are provided in the following table:

Subsystem	Mission Statement
Mechanical frame	This subsystem provides the physical system structure and rider adjustment features, all of which are assumed to be strictly mechanical in nature, as well as the inclination delivery/monitoring capability, which is planned to be motorized. This subsystem is envisioned to primarily consist of mechanical and electronic aspects.
Electric power delivery	This subsystem is responsible for receiving wall power and distributing managed electrical power to the other subsystems. This includes low amp power for digital electronics, moderate amp power for the motorized inclination capability, and high amp power for the rider power and its resistance. This subsystem design is envisioned to be dominated by electronics aspects.
Comms	This subsystem is responsible for all communications with external devices. At the time of writing, this includes low-power Bluetooth and ANT+ communications protocols. This includes the physical layer through the network layer of the OSI protocol stack. The initial concept for this subsystem includes one or more smart communications processors managing communications. This subsystem is envisioned to primarily consist of digital electronics and software.
Main computing platform	The main computing platform contains the primary computing electronics and software for the system. It manages rider-level applications, such as controlling and monitoring rides and sensor data, system configuration (including motor transfer function tuning and rider settings), and data management. This subsystem is envisioned to primarily contain software and digital electronics hardware.

Subsystem	Mission Statement
Rider interaction	This subsystem provides the primary user interface (except for pedals) for the system, including shift and brake levers, and displays the currently selected gear. This system is envisioned to include mechanical, electronic, and software aspects. This subsystem also provides controls for and displays the current incline.
Power train	This subsystem manages the pedal assembly, monitoring the rider's power and pedal cadence input, and creating resistance to pedaling under the direction of the Main Computing Platform subsystem. This system is envisioned to include mechanical, electronic, and software aspects.

Table 3.7 – Subsystem missions

Allocating requirements and system features to subsystems

This task is complex enough that it has its own dedicated recipe, *Architectural allocation*, which can be found later in this chapter. We'll elaborate on this example in that recipe.

Creating subsystem interfaces

This task is complex enough that it has its own recipe, *Creating subsystem interfaces from use case scenarios*, which can be found later in this chapter. We'll elaborate on this example in that recipe.

Architectural allocation

The recipes for functionally analyzing use cases have multiple outcomes. The primary outcome is a set of high-quality requirements. The second is identifying a number of system features – system functions, data, and flows. The third outcome is identifying interfaces necessary to support the behavior outlined in the use case. This recipe focuses on allocating the first two of these to the subsystem architecture.

Purpose

The purpose of this recipe is to detail the specification of the subsystems so that we can hand off those specifications to the interdisciplinary subsystem teams for detailed design and development.

Inputs and preconditions

A set of requirements and system features have been identified, and a subsystem architecture has been created so that each subsystem has a defined mission (scope and content).

Outputs and postconditions

The primary outcome of this recipe is a specification for each subsystem. This includes the following:

- System requirements allocated directly to the subsystem.
- Subsystem requirements derived from system requirements, which are then allocated to the subsystem.
- System features allocated directly to the subsystem.
- Subsystem features derived from system features, which are then allocated to the subsystem.

How to do it...

This recipe is deceptively simple. The tasks are straightforward, although difficult to completely automate. This task can take a while to perform because there are often many requirements and features to allocate. The basic is idea is that, given the selected subsystem structure, either allocate a feature directly or decompose that feature into subparts that can be allocated. The workflow for this is as follows:

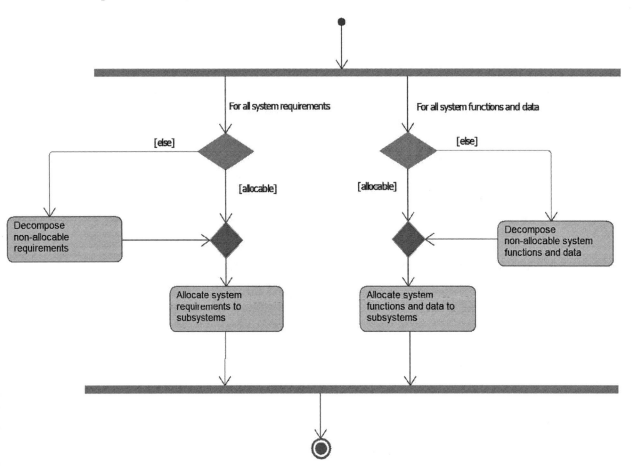

Figure 3.29 – Architectural allocation

Decomposing non-allocable requirements

Requirements can sometimes be directly allocated to a specific subsystem. In other cases, it is necessary to create *derived requirements* that take into account the original system requirements and the specifics of the selected subsystem architecture. In this latter case, you must create derived requirements that can be directly allocated to subsystems. Be sure to add <<deriveReqt>> relationships from the derived requirements back to their source system requirements.

Allocating system requirements

Here, we must allocate system requirements to the subsystems. In general, each requirement is allocated to a single subsystem so that, in the end, the requirements that have been allocated to each subsystem are clear. The set of allocated system requirements after this step are normally known as **subsystem requirements**.

Decomposing non-allocable system functions and data

Some system features – which refer to operations, event receptions, flows, and data – can be directly allocated to a single subsystem. In practice, many cannot. When this is the case, the feature must be decomposed into subsystem-level features that trace back to their system-level source feature but can be directly allocated to a single subsystem.

Allocating system functions and data

Here, we must allocate system features to subsystems. That is, each system function now becomes a subsystem function that's allocated to a single subsystem, or it is decomposed into a set of subsystem functions, each of which is also allocated. Similarly, system event receptions must be allocated to some subsystem and often, this results in new subsystem event receptions being added elsewhere in the architecture to support the subsystem collaboration required to fulfill the system functionality needs. System flows and data must also be allocated to subsystems.

Example

In real system development, this recipe can take a substantial amount of time. This is not due to the complexity of the task, but because of the large number of system requirements and features requiring allocation.

To keep this example manageable for the format of this book, we will focus on a subset of the requirements and system features that were identified in the use cases under consideration for this book:

req [Package] ComputeResistanceReqPkg [Allocation of Compute Resistance requirements]

Mission: Show requirements for allocation and identify requirements that must be decomposed into derived requirements for allocation.

«Requirement»
CR_requirement_15

The system shall send computed speed and acceleration to the connected training app, if any.

«Requirement»
CR_requirement_1

The system shall store the rider weight for the computation of pedal resistance.

«Requirement»
CR_requirement_4

The system shall compute pedal cadence.

«Requirement»
CR_requirement_7

The system shall provide time-filtering of power, supporting 0, 1-second, 3-second, and 5-second power averaging, settable by the rider.

«Requirement»
CR_requirement_10

The system shall store gear ratio from the gear setting.

«Requirement»
CR_requirement_2

The system shall store the current gear persistently so that the last gear is retained across power cycles and resets.

«Requirement»
CR_requirement_5

The system shall send pedal cadence to the associated training app, when connected.

«Requirement»
CR_requirement_8

The system shall send filtered power to the training app, if connected.

«Requirement»
CR_requirement_11

The system shall accept road incline from the connected training app.

«Requirement»
CR_requirement_3

The system shall monitor pedal position and speed.

«Requirement»
CR_requirement_6

The system shall measure force applied by the rider to the pedals.

«Requirement»
CR_requirement_9

The system shall accept simulated incline from the connected training app throughout a training session.

«Requirement»
CR_requirement_12

The system shall compute simulated drag based on computed rider inertia and simulated road incline.

«Requirement»
CR_requirement_13

The system shall compute simulated road speed based on computed inertia, incluven, current simulated speed and acceleration, and rider-applied force to the pedal.

«Requirement»
CR_requirement_21

The system shall update the training app with simulated bike speed at least 1.0 seconds

«Requirement»
CR_requirement_24

The system shall update the physics model frequently enough to provide the rider a smooth and road-line experience with respect to resistance.

«Requirement»
CR_requirement_25

The system shall send current watts per kilogram to the training app for the current power output at least every 1.0 seconds.

«Requirement»
CR_requirement_14

The system shall compute and apply resistance to pedal movement based on simulated inertia, speed, acceleration and rider power input.

«Requirement»
CR_requirement_22

The system shall update the training app with rider filtered power output at least 0.5 seconds

«Requirement»
CR_requirement_23

The system shall update the training app with pedal cadence at least 1.0 seconds.

«Requirement»
CR_requirement_0

The system shall respond to applied pedal torque with resistance calculated from the base level of resistance, current gearing and applied torque to simulate pedal resistance during road riding.

Figure 3.30 – Requirements selected for allocation

The preceding screenshot shows the set of requirements for a single use case; that is, **Compute Resistance**. For brevity, we will decompose and allocate a subset of these.

Decomposing non-allocable requirements

As we mentioned previously, some requirements must be decomposed into derived requirements before they are allocated. This is because these requirements are partially met by different subsystems. In this case, a set of derived requirements must be created that are collectively equivalent to the original requirement but are of appropriately narrow focus so that they can be directly allocated. This is modeled with the «deriveReqt» relationship, which goes *from* the derived requirement *to* the originating requirement:

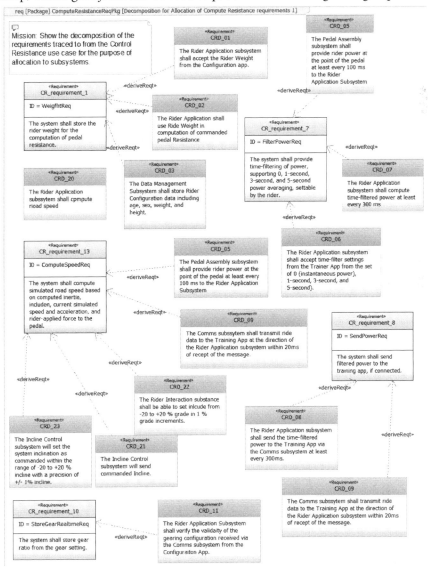

Figure 3.31 – Some derived requirements

The preceding screenshot shows some of the requirements that were created during the derivation process. I color-coded the original system requirements and the derived requirements as a visual aid. Again, note the directions of the relationships.

We can also see a number of the system requirements decomposed into subsystem requirements. For example, **CR_requirement_7** states *"The system shall provide time-filtering of power, supporting 0, 1-second, 3-second, and 5-second power averaging, settable by the rider."* This results in three derived requirements:

- **CRD_05**: The **Pedal Assembly** subsystem shall provide rider power at the point of the pedal at least every 100 ms to the **Rider Application** subsystem.

- **CRD_06**: The **Rider Application** subsystem shall accept time-filter settings from the **Trainer App** from as set of 0 (instantaneous power), 1-second, 3-second, and 5-second.

- **CRD_07**: The **Rider Application** subsystem shall compute time-filtered power at least every 300 ms.

It can be cumbersome to show numerous derived requirements. An alternative is to construct a table showing the originating and derived requirements. Such a matrix can be seen in the following screenshot:

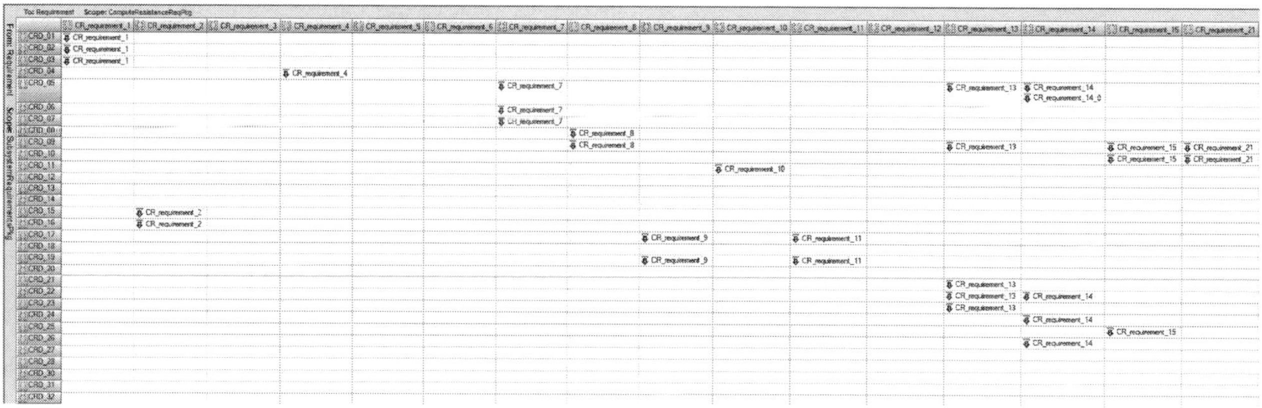

Figure 3.32 – Derived requirements matrix

As we create new subsystem requirements, we need a place to put them. In this example, we'll create a **SubsystemRequirementsPkg** under **RequirementsAnalysisPkg::RequirementsPkg** for this purpose. We may decide to create a package per subsystem within **SubsystemRequirementsPkg** later, if the number of derived requirements grows large enough to justify it.

Allocating system requirements

Allocation here means *assignment* in the sense that a subsystem is expected to implement its allocated requirements. This can be done diagrammatically, but in this case, we'll do this using an allocation matrix, as shown in the following screenshot. In this matrix, the allocation relationship goes *from* the subsystem *to* the requirement. The matrix itself is located in **DesignSynthesisPkg::ArchitecturalDesignPkg** in the model, but other locations are possible. The matrix layout used *Block* as the *from* element type, *Requirement* as the *to* element type, and *Allocation* as the *cell* element type.

The actual allocation is performed by walking through the requirements and creating an allocation relation from the subsystem to the requirement. The following diagram shows the system and its derived requirements, as well as their allocation for this subset:

From: Block Scope: ArchitecturalDesignPkg	Pegasus_System	PowerTrain	DriveTrain	PedalAssembly	MotorAssembly	Comms	RiderInteraction	GearControl	InclineControl	RiderApplication	DataManagement
CR_requirement_1	√ CR_requirement_1										
CR_requirement_2											
CR_requirement_3				√ CR_requirement_3							
CR_requirement_4				√ CR_requirement_4							
CR_requirement_5										√ CR_requirement_5	
CR_requirement_6				√ CR_requirement_6							
CR_requirement_7	√ CR_requirement_7										
CR_requirement_8	√ CR_requirement_8										
CR_requirement_9	√ CR_requirement_9										
CR_requirement_10										√ CR_requirement_10	
CR_requirement_11	√ CR_requirement_11										
CR_requirement_12											
CR_requirement_13	√ CR_requirement_13										
CR_requirement_14	√ CR_requirement_14										
CR_requirement_15	√ CR_requirement_15										
CR_requirement_21	√ CR_requirement_21										
CR_requirement_22	√ CR_requirement_22										
CR_requirement_23										√ CR_requirement_23	
CR_requirement_24	√ CR_requirement_24										
CR_requirement_25										√ CR_requirement_25	
CR_requirement_0	√ CR_requirement_0										
CRD_01											
CRD_02										√ CRD_02	
CRD_03											√ CRD_03
CRD_04				√ CRD_04							
CRD_05				√ CRD_05							
CRD_06										√ CRD_06	
CRD_07										√ CRD_07	
CRD_08										√ CRD_08	
CRD_09					√ CRD_09						
CRD_10										√ CRD_10	
CRD_11										√ CRD_11	
CRD_12											√ CRD_12
CRD_13											
CRD_14					√ CRD_14						
CRD_15										√ CRD_15	
CRD_16											√ CRD_16
CRD_17						√ CRD_17					
CRD_18						√ CRD_18					
CRD_19						√ CRD_19					
CRD_20										√ CRD_20	
CRD_21											
CRD_22									√ CRD_22		
CRD_23											
CRD_24					√ CRD_24						
CRD_25										√ CRD_25	
CRD_26			√ CRD_26								
CRD_27					√ CRD_27						
CRD_28										√ CRD_28	
CRD_30											
CRD_31								√ CRD_31			
CRD_32								√ CRD_32			

Figure 3.33 – Subsystem requirements allocation matrix (subset)

Note that the matrix uses the convention that system requirements that need to be decomposed are shown as allocated to **Pegasus_System**, while system requirements that are directly allocable are allocated directly to the subsystem. The requirements derived from these decomposed requirements are allocated to individual subsystems. Here, we can see that the system requirements are all named **CR_requirement_<#>**
(CR indicating the *Control resistance* use case), while the derived requirements are named **CRD_<#>**.

Also, note that, for the most part, the "high-level subsystems" – that is, those that contain subsystems themselves – don't have allocated requirements, although their internal parts do. This is not uncommon. Thus, the **Main Computing Platform**, **Power Train**, and **Rider Interaction** subsystems don't have requirements directly allocated to them, but each contains nested subsystems that do.

Finally, note that the matrix is sparsely populated. This is because it only shows requirements from a single use case. As use cases are added, this matrix will become much more densely populated.

As a Rhapsody-specific aside, the matrix is shown with the subsystems as the columns because I prefer to have matrices with more rows than columns for readability. This is done with the *Switch Rows and Columns* tool in the matrix toolbar.

Allocating system functions and data

For the system features, we'll use the features we allocated to the System object during the *Understanding architectural merge* recipe, earlier in this chapter. This set of system features can be seen in the following screenshot. Note that the **Pegasus_System** block is shown twice, with different features shown for readability reasons. The view on the left shows the flow and value properties, while the view on the right shows the operations and event receptions:

«Block,System»
Pegasus_System
Flow Properties
▣ prov appliedTorque(provided):Real
▣ Out resistance(Out):Real
Values
▣ gear:Real
▣ prov appliedTorque(provided):Real
▣ Out resistance(Out):Real
▣ nFrontChainRings:int
▣ nCassetteRings:int
▣ chainRing[3]:int
▣ cassette[12]:int
▣ selectedCassetteRing:int
▣ selectedChainRing:int

«Block,System»
Pegasus_System
Operations
▫ checkGearing(newGear:Real):RhpBoolean
▫ applyResistance():void
▫ computeResistance():void
▫ changeGear(newGear:Real):void
▸ decrementGear()
▸ incrementGear()
▸ chAppliedTorque()
▫ setDefaultsForChainRings(rings:int):void
▫ setDefaultsForCassetteRings(rings:int):void
▫ displayError(s:RhpString):void
▫ display1Num(s:RhpString,num:RhpReal):void
▫ display2Num(s1:RhpString,n1:RhpReal,s2:RhpString,n2:RhpReal):void
▫ selectGear(frontRing:int,rearRing:int):void
▫ augmentFrontGear():void
▫ augmentRearGear():void
▫ decrementFrontGear():void
▫ decrementRearGear():void
▫ numberOfChainRingsOK(n:int):RhpBoolean
▫ numberOfCassetteRingsOK(n:int):RhpBoolean
▫ chainRingTeethOK(teeth:int):RhpBoolean
▫ cassetteRingTeethOK(teeth:int):RhpBoolean
▫ setFrontChainRing(ring:int,teeth:int):void
▫ setCassetteRing(ring:int,teeth:int):void
▫ computeGearInches(front:int,rear:int):void
▫ displayGearing():void
▸ evConfigureGearing()
▸ evDoneConfiguring()
▸ evBeginRiding()
▸ evDoneRiding()
▸ evSetNumberOfChainRings(n:unsigned int)
▸ evSetNumberOfCassetteRings(n:unsigned int)
▸ evSetCassetteRingTeeth(cr:unsigned int,teeth:unsigned int)
▸ evAugmentFrontGear()
▸ evDecrementFrontGear()
▸ evAugmentRearGear()
▸ evDecrementRearGear()
▸ evSetChainRingTeeth(cr:unsigned int,teeth:unsigned int)
▸ evShowGearing()
▫ Get_App_Ride_Interaction_Type(interaction:APP_INTERACTION_TYPE):void
▫ Start_Ride():void
▫ Measure_Pedal_Position(rad:Radian):void
▫ Measure_Applied_Power(pow:Newton):void
▫ Get_Date_and_Time():void
▫ Compued_Calculated_Performance_Data():void
▫ Send_Performance_Data(pd:RidePerforanceData):void
▫ UploadRide():void
▫ Select_Ride(id:int):void
▫ Open_Session():void
▫ Get_Ride_Interval_Data():void
▫ Send_Ride_Interval_Data(rd:RidePerforanceData):void
▫ Close_Session():void
▫ Computed_Calculated_Performance_Data():void
▸ reqGet_App_Ride_Interaction_Type(interaction:APP_INTERACTION_TYPE)
▸ reqStart_Ride()
▸ reqMeasure_Pedal_Position(rad:Radian)
▸ reqMeasure_Applied_Power(pow:Newton)
▸ reqUploadRide()
▸ reqSelect_Ride(id:int)

Figure 3.34 – System features for allocation

The standard way of performing allocation, following an architectural merge, is to *move* the system feature to the appropriate subsystem. Any system features that remain after that initial pass are then decomposed and allocated (the last step in this recipe).

Rhapsody has a helper for this that comes with the Harmony SE Profile. Using this helper isn't necessary to perform the task, but it can be a great time saver. To use it, use the **File | Add Profile To Model** feature to add the profile to your model. Once the profile has been added, right-click the **Pegasus_System** block and select **SE-Toolkit | Allocation | Allocation Wizard**. You will see the following dialog:

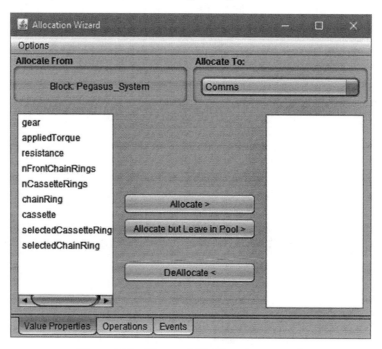

Figure 3.35 – Harmony SE Allocation Wizard

At the bottom of the dialog, you'll see tabs for value properties, operations, and event receptions. At the top-right, you'll see a drop-down list containing the different subsystems. To allocate, simply select the features you want to allocate, the desired subsystem, and click on the **Allocate** button. If you want to allocate a feature to more than one subsystem, you can use the **Allocate but Leave in Pool** button; this keeps the original feature in the system block so that it can be allocated again. For example, consider the **appliedTorque** value property. It is computed by the **Rider Application** subsystem but is actually applied by the **Motor Assembly**, transmitted by the **Drive Train**, and delivered to the **Rider** via the **Pedal Assembly**. Out of these subsystems, **Rider Application** and **Motor Assembly** seem like they should contain the value property. You should allocate operations to a subsystem when it performs that system function, while you should allocate event receptions to a subsystem when that subsystem receives and handles that event.

Important

It should be noted that the term *allocation* is used in a couple of ways. In SysML, it is a specific relationship between model elements. The Allocation Wizard uses this term instead of *ownership*.

As we mentioned earlier, this helper isn't required, but it does save us some time.

Sometimes, a system feature cannot be allocated – not because it must be decomposed, but because there is no appropriate subsystem. In this case, the missing subsystem must be added. It can also happen that, at the end of the entire recipe, there are subsystems to which no requirements or features have been allocated. This simply means that the subsystem isn't being used in the current iteration but might be used in future iterations. Generally speaking, at the end of the recipe, all the subsystems should have features allocated to them or they should serve other purposes (such as organizing and containing smaller subsystems).

The following screenshot shows the result of this step. Several of the subsystems have value properties, event receptions, and operations allocated to them:

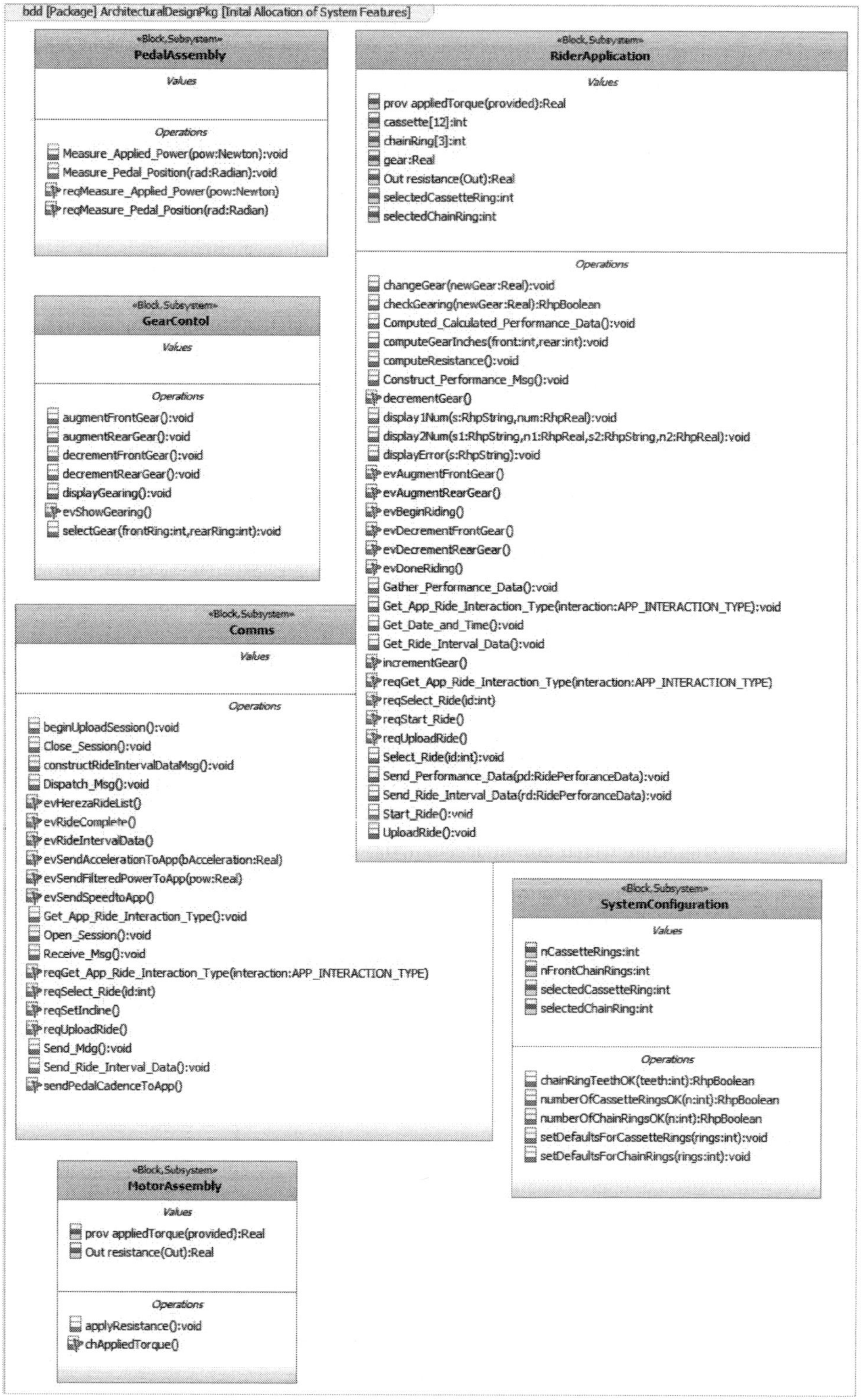

Figure 3.36 – Initial allocation of system features

Decomposing non-allocable system functions and data

Here, the only system feature that's not been directly allocated is the **Send_Performance_Data** operation. We'll decompose this service into the following:

- Gather_Performance_Data (allocate to the **Rider Application** subsystem)
- Construct_Performance_Data_Msg (allocate to the **Rider Application** subsystem)
- Send_Msg (allocate to the **Comms** subsystem)

While we're doing that, note that we also need the Receive_Msg and Dispatch_Msg system functions for the **Comms** subsystem.

To allocate these system features, we must leave the decomposed system feature in the System block and directly add the created features to the appropriate subsystem. Then, we must add the relationships from the original feature to the derived features. In this case, we'll use the «derive» relationship (as opposed to «deriveReqt» since these are system properties, not requirements). This can be seen in the following diagram:

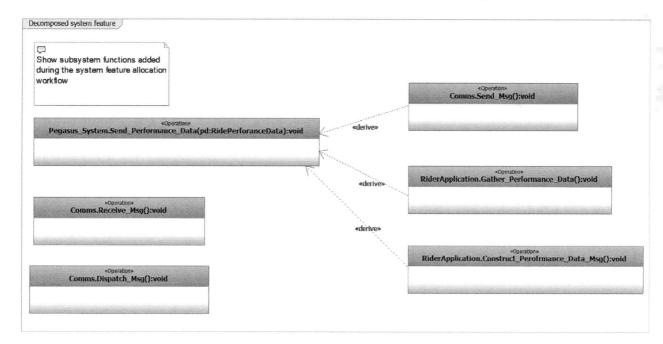

Figure 3.37 – Derived system features

Creating subsystem interfaces from use case scenarios

There are various ways subsystem interfaces can be created. For example, a common approach is to refine the black box activity diagrams from use case analysis into so-called **white box** activity diagrams, with swim lanes representing the different subsystems. When control flows cross into other swim lanes, the flow or service invocation is added to the relevant subsystem interface. Another common approach is to do the same thing but use the use case sequence diagrams rather than the activity diagrams. The advantage of these approaches is that they tie back to the use case analysis. It is also possible to create the interfaces *de novo* by allocating the system features to the subsystems.

This recipe focuses on sequence diagrams. One advantage of this approach is that we can leverage messages on sequence diagrams that have been created by executing the use case models that may not appear on the activity diagram. Furthermore, many engineers use these activity diagrams as a starting point, but the state machines become the normative specification of the use case; that is, the activity diagrams are not fully fleshed out, but the state machines are. In such cases, this approach is superior to basing the interface definitions on incomplete activity diagrams.

Purpose

The purpose of this recipe is to help you develop interfaces between the subsystems being used so that the subsystem teams can design with an understanding of the flows and services they must provide to – and require from – other subsystems. These interfaces are still *logical,* reference essential aspects and are largely technology independent. These interfaces will be refined into physical interfaces that explicitly expose technical details in the recipes that will be discussed in the next chapter.

Inputs and preconditions

The inputs include the identified set of subsystems to which system features have been allocated. In addition, each referenced use case has a set of black box sequence diagrams showing the interactions between the use cases and the actors.

Outputs and postconditions

The primary outcome of this recipe is the set of interfaces (as interface blocks) defining the logical flows and service invocations between the subsystems and between the system and the actors. A part of that definition will be the logical data schema for flows and service parameters.

How to do it...

This recipe is straightforward, although it can be a little tedious to perform by hand with many use case scenarios. Fortunately, Rhapsody Harmony SE Toolkit provides some automation once the white box scenarios are created. The following diagram shows the workflow for this. In any case, the end result is a set of subsystem interfaces that support the necessary interactions for the architecture to realize the use case's behaviors:

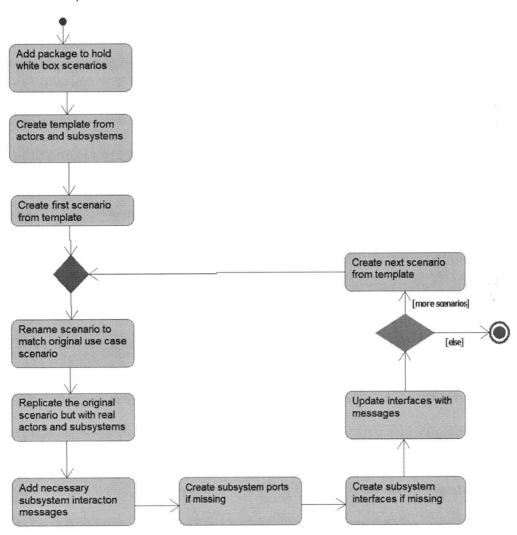

Figure 3.38 – Creating subsystem interfaces from use case scenarios

Adding packages to hold white box scenarios

If you followed the *Organizing Your Models* recipe in *Chapter 1*, *Basics of Agile Systems Modeling*, then the `FunctionalAnalysisPkg` package will contain a nested package for each use case that's been analyzed. This package is where the black box use case scenarios reside. These will serve as the starting point for this recipe, but they must be copied and modified. A new package should be created to hold these scenarios. Based on the organizational schema from *Chapter 1*, *Basics of Agile Systems Modeling*, this package will be in `DesignSynthesisPkg::ArchitecturalDesignPkg`. I normally name the new package something like `WBScenarios`. If there are many scenarios, I generally add subpackages, organized around the use cases, just to manage all the scenarios, but that is a design choice.

> **Note**
>
> We will use the term *scenario* synonymously with *sequence diagram* in this recipe since we have modeled each scenario of interest as a single sequence diagram in most cases.

Creating a template from actors and subsystems

A scenario template is empty, except for its lifelines, and provides a common structure to detail the subsystem scenarios. These use case scenarios often use actor blocks and a use case block. These are proxies for the actual actors and the system and are meant to make it easier for us to build executable use case models. This template will use the actual system actors and the actual subsystems because we are now elaborating on the system architecture. Using a common template simplifies how we create and compare different scenarios.

Creating a scenario from a template

Either copy the template in the browser or create an entirely new sequence diagram and copy in the lifelines from the template. We must do this for each scenario in every included use case. As a part of this step, you can add a «refine» relationship from the new architectural scenario back to the original use case scenario.

In Rhapsody, the easiest way to do this would be to create a new *matrix layout* in a common location (I create a `CommonPkg` for these kinds of elements) that has the **Sequence Diagram** as both the **From Element Type** and the **To Element Type** and the **Refinement** as the **Cell Element Type**. Then, in `WBScenariosPkg`, add a matrix view that uses this layout and sets **From Scope** to `ArchitecturalDesignPkg` and **To Scope** to `FunctionalAnalysisPkg`. Once you've done this, adding a refinement relationship is as easy as adding the new diagram in the architectural package, refreshing the matrix view, and then right-clicking the matrix to add the refinement.

Renaming the scenario so that it matches the original use case scenario

This is an optional step, but I find it useful to add _WB to the name of the original sequence diagram to ensure that it isn't confused with its original source.

Replicating the original scenario but with the real actors and subsystems

In this step, we will recreate the messages from the actor block to the use case and from the use case to the actor block in the new scenario. What will be different is that the actual actor will be used and the message for termination inside the system will be some specific subsystem rather than the use case or use case block.

Adding necessary subsystem interaction messages

This is a "magic step" in this recipe and requires the engineer to decide on how subsystem interaction should occur to realize the use case messages at the black box level. The engineer must take into account the requirements, data, and services that have been allocated to the subsystems and create messages to support an interaction that will use them to achieve the system-level objective.

Creating subsystem ports (if they're missing)

If there is at least one message between a subsystem and another, or between a subsystem and an actor, then the subsystem must have a port to support that message exchange. If the message is between a subsystem and an actor, it will require a port on the **System** block itself. In this case, the subsystem's port will connect to the system's port, and then, in turn, the system's port will connect to the actor's port.

> **Note**
>
> The preceding data is true for real interfaces that support actual messaging. When a *message* is displayed on-screen or received by the system due to the user pressing a button on the system, then that interaction is *virtual* and no real system interface needs to be created in the architecture. This is typical of user interfaces owned by the system.

Creating subsystem interfaces (if they're missing)

Once the white box sequence diagram has been updated, interfaces can be created wherever two subsystems exchange messages. This means that in the architecture, they will be connected with a connector, generally (but optionally) via ports typed by interfaces that support those messages. These interfaces will include any operations, event receptions, and flow properties that cross the system's boundary.

Updating interfaces with messages

In the previous step, we added interfaces whenever there was at least one message being exchanged between a pair of subsystems. In this step, we will add the messages as event receptions. We will stereotype them as «directedFeatures» in the interface blocks if we're using proxy ports.

This cycle is repeated for all functional analysis scenarios included in the architectural design.

Example

For this example, we will focus on the scenarios from two use cases: **Measure performance metrics** and **Control resistance**. These scenarios show the interactions between actor blocks (acting as proxies for the actual actors) and the selected use case.

Adding a package to hold white box scenarios

Start by adding a package named WBScenariosPkg under DesignSynthesisPkg::ArchitecturalDesignPkg:

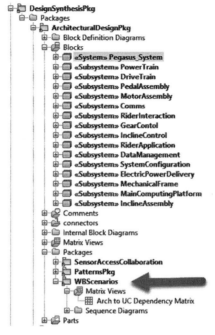

Figure 3.39 – Adding a new package

Creating a template from actors and subsystems

Next, create a template sequence diagram containing the actors (from `ActorsPkg`) and the subsystems (from `ArchitecturalDesignPkg`). In this example, we will only show the high-level subsystems, like so:

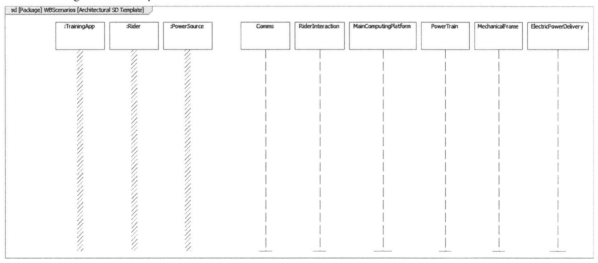

Figure 3.40 – Template sequence diagrams

Creating a scenario from a template

The first scenario is **Measure performance metrics black box view 1**, which was derived from the use case activity diagram. The original sequence diagram is as follows. We have provided this as a reference; we won't modify it, but we will replicate it in the upcoming steps:

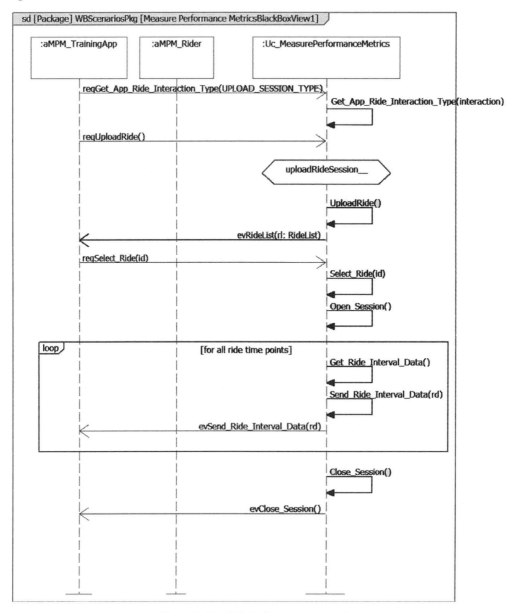

Figure 3.41 – Original use case scenario

In a browser, copy the template sequence diagram into a new tab, thus creating a new copy of the diagram shown in *Figure 3.40*.

Renaming the scenario

We will follow the naming convention of removing any black box references and adding _WB instead. Upon doing this, the name of this scenario will now be **Measure performance metrics 1_WB**.

Replicating the original scenario but with real actors and subsystems

The easiest way to work here is to open the new and original sequence diagrams so that they're next to each other, as shown in the following screenshot:

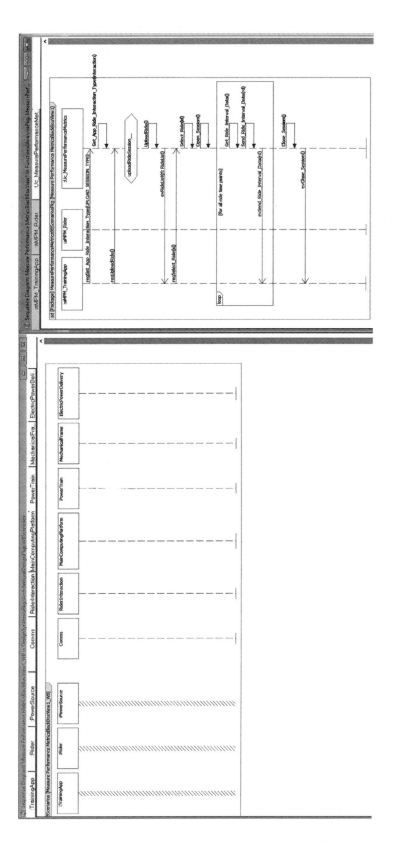

Figure 3.42 – Ready to replicate messages

This step is easy; using the original scenario as guidance, add *the same messages* to the new scenario. The slightly tricky part is deciding on which subsystem should be the sender or receiver lifeline. For this scenario, the lifeline that's receiving and sending the events to and from the **Training App** lifeline will be the **Comms** subsystem. Deciding on where the *messages to self* go is only a little harder. If the services are concerned with communications, for example, then they will be put on the **Comms** subsystem lifeline. In this case, all the other *messages to self* will be put on the **Main Computing Platform** lifeline.

The sequence diagram now looks like this:

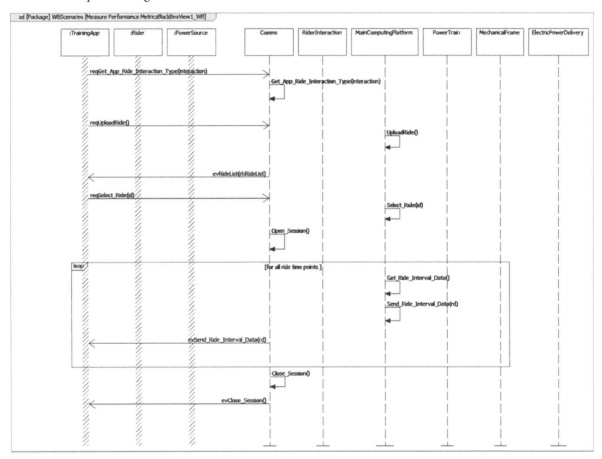

Figure 3.43 – Scenario replicated

Note that a "miracle occurs" between the **Comms** subsystem receiving a message and the **Main Computing Platform** doing something with it. That is because we are missing the messages between those subsystems; how we identify and elaborate on them will be the outcome of this recipe.

Adding the necessary subsystem interaction messages

As we go down the sequence, we need to add messages between the subsystems so that they can coordinate their actions and collectively interact with the actors. We may also discover discrepancies in the original interaction, such as missing messages to or from an actor or data that must be passed with an existing message. Since we are defining the actual logical messages within the architecture, we will address those defects here.

The result of this step is a white box sequence diagram that shows the interaction between the subsystems and other subsystems and the actors. Some of these messages will be realized by the operations that were allocated to the subsystem during the *Architectural allocation* recipe, earlier in this chapter. Others will be new.

> **Rhapsody hint**
>
> Right-click on the white space in the diagram and select **Auto Realize All Element** to add event receptions and operations that match the diagram.

The following screenshot shows the previous sequence diagram but with the messages between the subsystems to complete the architectural flow. If we repeat this for all the scenarios under consideration, we can use that to form the basis of the architectural interfaces:

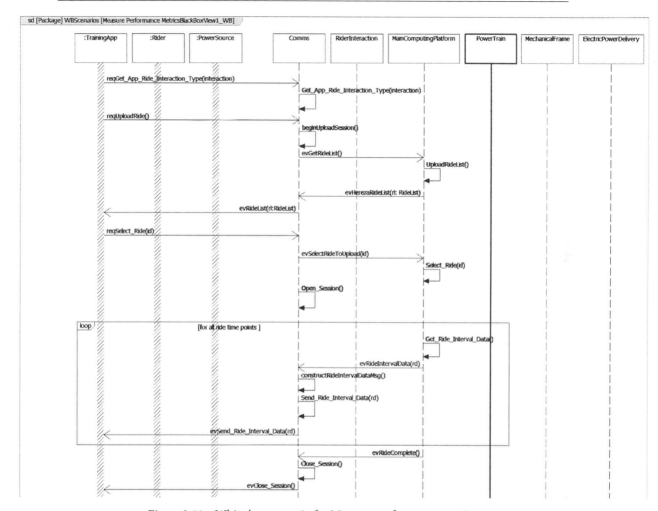

Figure 3.44 – White box scenario for Measure performance metrics

Repeating this elaboration process for the other three scenarios – **Control resistance**, **Process Pedal Inputs**, and **Execute Physical Model** – results in the following:

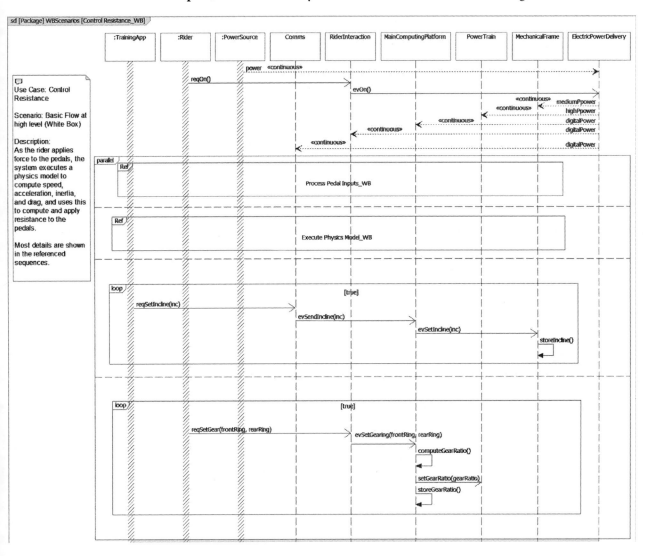

Figure 3.45 – White box scenario for Control resistance

The **Process Pedal Inputs** scenario:

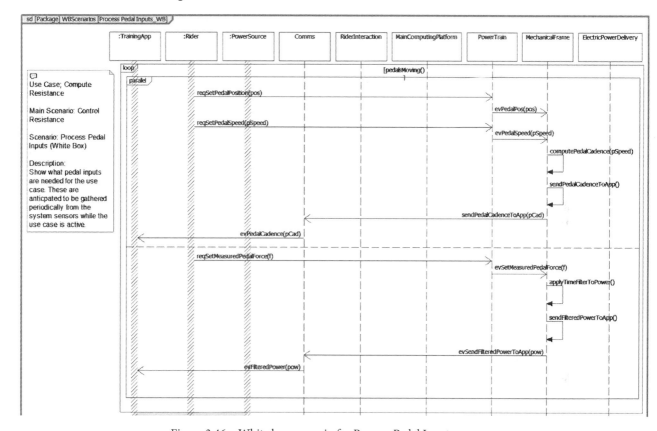

Figure 3.46 – White box scenario for Process Pedal Inputs

The **Execute Physical Model** scenario:

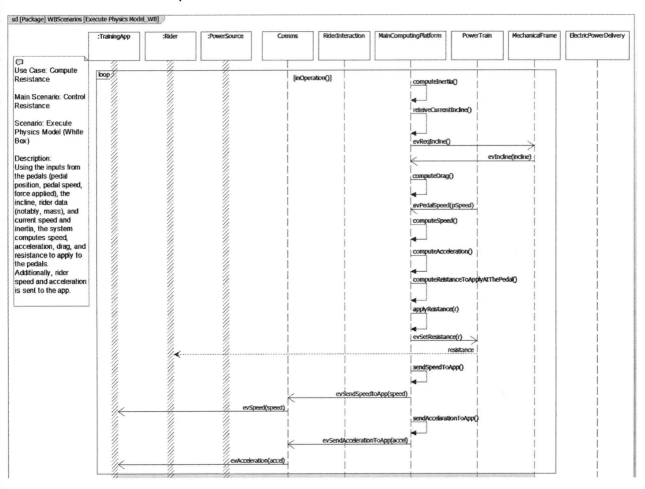

Figure 3.47 –White box scenario for Execute Physics Model

Creating subsystem ports (if they're missing)

Wherever at least one message exists between the elements in these white box scenarios, there must be a port pair that supports that message exchange. The ports that support these white box scenarios can be seen in *Figure 3.49*.

In this example, ports are named p, followed by the name of the target element to which they will connect. Therefore, the **Comms** port that will connect to the **Main Computing Platform** subsystem is named Comms.pMainComputingPlatform. The ports that are used to deliver power from the **Electric Power Delivery** subsystems are flow ports because they only deliver a singular flow without invoking services.

Creating subsystem interfaces (if they're missing)

While elaborating on our white box scenarios, we identified interactions between a number of subsystems and added port pairs to support its messaging capabilities.

Interface blocks are named i, followed by the name of the unconjugated user of the interface block, an underscore, and the name of the conjugated side of the connection. Let's say that the interface block is named iMainComputingPlatform_Comms; its name indicates that the MainComputingPlatform.pComms port uses the interface block in its normal form but that the Comms.pMainComputingPlatform port uses the interface block in conjugated form.

Updating interfaces with messages

This step adds the messages that were sent across the ports to the interface blocks. These messages are the messages on the white box sequence diagrams. Note that, by convention, we must use asynchronous messages between the subsystems and between the system and the actors to define these logical interfaces. Since these are proxy ports, SysML requires us to stereotype these messages in the interface blocks as «directedFeatures».

The following screenshot shows the interface blocks and their services, as identified in the scenarios we examined in this example:

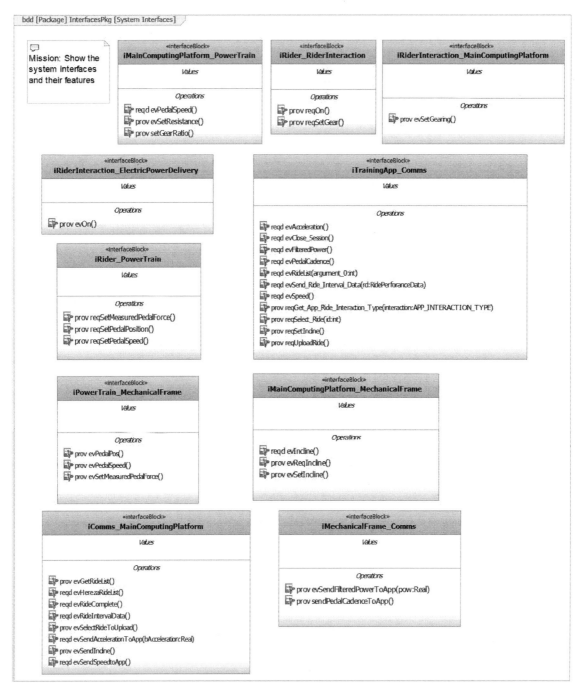

Figure 3.48 – Derived subsystem interface blocks

This ultimately results in an elaborated connected architecture, as shown here:

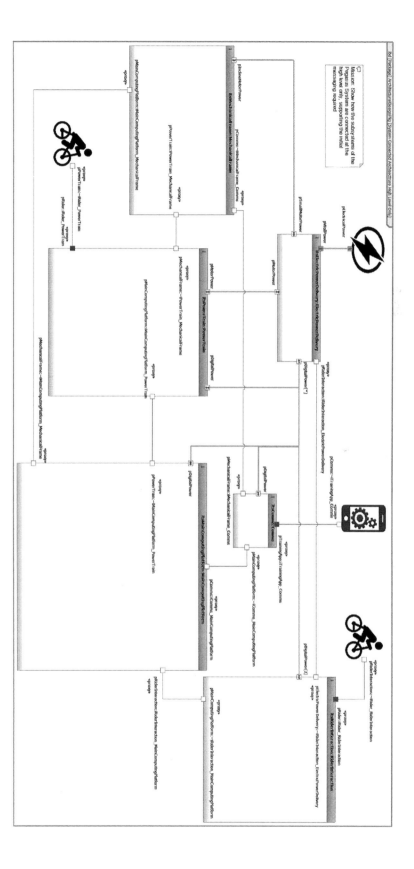

Figure 3.49 – Connected architecture with subsystem interfaces

This diagram has been customized a little bit. Here, we've added images for the actor instances and color-coded the ports to those actors to make them visually distinct from the subsystem-subsystem ports.

4
Handoff to Downstream Engineering

The purposes of the *Handoff to Downstream Engineering* recipes are as follows:

- To refine the system engineering data to a form that's usable by downstream engineers

- To create separate models to hold the prepared engineering data in a convenient organizational format (known as *model federation*)

- For each subsystem to work with downstream engineering teams to create a deployment architecture and allocate systems engineering data to that architecture

It is crucial to understand that the handoff is a *process* and not an *event*. There is a certain amount of work to do that is not entirely straightforward in order to achieve the preceding objectives. As with other activities in the Harmony MBSE process, this can be done once, but it is recommended to be implemented many times, in an iterative, incremental fashion. It isn't necessarily difficult work, but it is crucial work in terms of the project being successful.

The refinement of the systems engineering data is necessary because, to this point, we have been primarily focused on its conceptual nature and logical properties. What is needed by the downstream teams are the physical properties of the system, along with the allocated requirements, so that they may design and construct the physical subsystems.

The recipes covered in this chapter are as follows:

- Preparation for handoff
- Federating models for handoff
- Logical to physical interfaces
- Deployment architecture I – allocation to engineering facets
- Deployment architecture II – interdisciplinary interfaces

Activities regarding the handoff to downstream engineering

At a high level, creating the logical system architecture includes the identification of subsystems as types (blocks), connecting them up (the connected architecture), allocating requirements and system features to the subsystems, and specifying the logical interfaces between the architectural elements. Although the subsystems are "physical," the services and flows defined in the interfaces are almost entirely logical and do not have the physical realization detail required by the subsystem teams. One of the key activities in the handoff workflows will be to add this level of detail so that the resulting subsystem implementations created by different subsystem teams can physically connect to one another.

For this reason, the architectural specifications must now be elaborated to include physical realization detail. For example, a logical interface service between a RADAR and a targeting system might be modeled as an event, **evGetRadarTrack(rt: RadarTrack)**, in which the message is modeled as an asynchronous event and the data is modeled as the logical information required regarding the radar track. This allows us to construct an executing, computable model of the logical properties of the interaction between the **targeting** and **RADAR** subsystems. However, this logical service might actually be implemented as a 1553 bus message with a specific bit format, so it is crucial that both subsystems agree on its structure and physical properties for the correct implementation of both subsystems. The actual format of the message, including the format of the data held within the message, must be specified to enable these two different development teams to work together. That is a primary task of the *Handoff to Downstream Engineering* process step.

Other relevant tasks include establishing a single source of truth for the physical interface and shared physical data schema in terms of a referenced specification model, the large-scale decomposition of the subsystems into engineering facets, the allocation of requirements to those facets, and the specification of interdisciplinary interfaces. A *facet*, you may recall, is the term used for the design contribution from a single engineering discipline, such as software, electronics, mechanics, and hydraulics.

The recipes in this chapter are devoted to these activities.

Starting point for the examples

In this chapter, we will focus on the requirements and allocations from a number of use case analyses and architectural work done earlier in the book. Specifically, we'll focus on requirements from the **Compute Resistance**, **Emulate Front and Rear Gearing**, and **Emulate DI Shifting** use cases. Because not all subsystems are affected by these requirements, we will focus this incremental handoff on the following subsystems: **Comms**, **Rider Interaction**, **Mechanical Frame**, **Main Computing Platform**, and **Power Train**. The other subsystems will ultimately be elaborated upon and added to the system in future iterations. For brevity, we will not consider the subsystems nested within those subsystems, but focus solely on the high-level subsystems.

The relevant system architecture is shown in the internal block diagram of *Figure 4.1*. It uses Rhapsody features to depict actors using icons, and ports connecting to those actors are colored for the purpose of highlighting external interfaces:

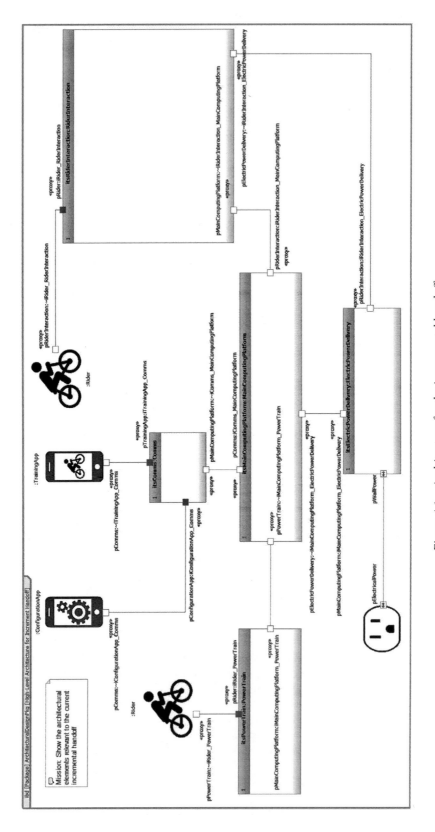

Figure 4.1 – Architecture for the incremental handoff

System requirements have either been allocated or derived and allocated. *Table 4.1* lists the set of requirements with their specification text:

Name	Specification
CR_requirement_0	The system shall respond to applied pedal torque with resistance calculated from the base level of resistance, current gearing, and applied torque to simulate pedal resistance during road riding.
CR_requirement_1	The system shall store the rider weight for the computation of pedal resistance.
CR_requirement_10	The system shall store the gear ratio from the gear setting.
CR_requirement_11	The system shall accept the road incline from the connected training app.
CR_requirement_12	The system shall compute the simulated drag based on the computed rider inertia and the simulated road incline.
CR_requirement_13	The system shall compute the simulated road speed based on the computed inertia, including the current simulated speed and acceleration, and the rider-applied force to the pedal.
CR_requirement_14	The system shall compute and apply resistance to the pedal movement based on the simulated inertia, speed, acceleration, and rider power input.
CR_requirement_15	The system shall send the computed speed and acceleration to the connected training app, if any.
CR_requirement_2	The system shall store the current gear persistently so that the last gear is retained across power cycles and resets.
CR_requirement_21	The system shall update the training app with simulated bike speeds at least every 1.0 seconds.
CR_requirement_22	The system shall update the training app with rider-filtered power output at least every 0.5 seconds
CR_requirement_23	The system shall update the training app with pedal cadence at least every 1.0 seconds.
CR_requirement_24	The system shall update the physics model frequently enough to provide the rider with a smooth and road-line experience with respect to resistance.
CR_requirement_25	The system shall send current watts per kilogram to the training app for the current power output at least every 1.0 seconds.
CR_requirement_3	The system shall monitor pedal position and speed.
CR_requirement_4	The system shall compute the pedal cadence.

Name	Specification
CR_requirement_5	The system shall send the pedal cadence to the associated training app, when connected.
CR_requirement_6	The system shall measure the force applied by the rider to the pedals.
CR_requirement_7	The system shall provide time filtering of the power, supporting 0, 1-second, 3-second, and 5-second power averaging, settable by the rider.
CR_requirement_8	The system shall send filtered power to the training app, if connected.
CR_requirement_9	The system shall accept a simulated incline from the connected training app throughout a training session.
CRD_01	The Rider Application subsystem shall accept the Rider Weight value from the Configuration app.
CRD_02	The Rider Application shall use the Rider Weight value in computation of the commanded pedal resistance.
CRD_03	The Data Management subsystem shall store Rider Configuration data, including age, sex, weight, and height.
CRD_04	The Pedal Assembly subsystem shall provide pedal cadence to the Rider Application subsystem.
CRD_05	The Pedal Assembly subsystem shall provide rider power at the point of the pedal at least every 100 ms to the Rider Application subsystem.
CRD_06	The Rider Application subsystem shall accept time-filter settings from the Trainer app from the set of 0 (instantaneous power), supporting 1-second, 3-second, and 5-second.
CRD_07	The Rider Application subsystem shall compute time-filtered power at least every 300 ms.
CRD_08	The Rider Application subsystem shall send the time-filtered power to the Training app via the Comms subsystem at least every 300 ms.
CRD_09	The Comms subsystem shall transmit ride data to the Training app at the direction of the Rider Application subsystem within 20 ms of receipt of the message.
CRD_10	The Rider Application subsystem shall send simulated road speed to the Training app via the Comms subsystem at least every 1,000 ms.

Name	Specification
CRD_11	The Rider Application subsystem shall verify the validity of the gearing configuration received via the Comms subsystem from the Configuration app.
CRD_12	The Data Management subsystem shall be able to store the gearing configuration.
CRD_13	The System configuration shall store the gearing configuration via the Data management system.
CRD_14	The Rider Application subsystem shall compute the resistance commanded to the Motor Assembly subsystem.
CRD_15	The Rider Application system shall store the current gear.
CRD_16	The Data Management subsystem shall store all its data persistently so that it is retained across power resets.
CRD_17	The Comms subsystem shall accept messages from the Trainer app.
CRD_18	The Comms subsystem shall accept messages from the Configuration app.
CRD_19	The Comms subsystem shall accept the set incline from the Training app and send it to the Rider Application subsystem.
CRD_20	The Rider Application subsystem shall compute the road speed.
CRD_21	The Incline Control subsystem shall send the commanded incline.
CRD_22	The Rider Interaction substance shall be able to set from -20 to +20% grade in 1% grade increments.
CRD_23	The Incline Control subsystem shall set the system inclination as commanded within the range of -20 to +20% incline with a precision of +/-1% incline.
CRD_24	The Motor Assembly subsystem shall create resistance under the command of the Rider Application subsystem in the range of 0 to 2,000 W.
CRD_25	The Rider Application subsystem shall compute the simulated acceleration.
CRD_26	The Drive Train subsystem shall transmit power from the motor to the pedal assembly.
CRD_27	The Motor Assembly subsystem shall change to the commanded power output in < 100 ms.

Name	Specification
CRD_28	The Rider Application subsystem shall compute and command the motor to set the power output at least every 100 ms during a ride.
CRD_30	The Mechanical Frame shall be able to accept 2,000 W of rider power for an extended period without noticeable frame deformation.
CRD_31	The Rider shall be able to select from the available front gearing.
CRD_32	The Rider shall be able to select from the available rear gearing.
DID01	The Rider Interaction subsystem shall provide an UP and DOWN button for shifting.
DID02	The Main Computing Platform subsystem shall respond to an upshift by going to the next highest gear ratio permitted with the current gear configuration.
DID03	The Main Computing Platform subsystem shall respond to a downshift and upshift by going to the next lowest gear ratio permitted with the current gear configuration.
DID04	The Main Computing Platform shall manage DI shifting when enabled.
DID05	The Main Computing Platform shall enter DI shifting mode when commanded by a message received via the Comms subsystem from the Configuration app.
DID06	The Comms subsystem shall receive shifting messages from the Configuration app and pass their data on to the Main Computing Platform for processing.
DID07	The Main Computing Platform shall enter Mechanical Shifting Mode when commanded by a message received via the Comms subsystem from the Configuration app.
DID08	The Rider Interaction subsystem shall provide both mechanical shifters and DI buttons for shifting that provide identical inputs to the Main Computing Platform.
DID09	The Rider Interaction subsystem shall only have either the mechanical shifters or the DI buttons active at any one time, as commanded by the Main Computing Platform.
DID10	The Main Computing Platform shall store the shifting selection across software and power resets and software updates.

Name	Specification
DID11	The Main Computing Platform shall initialize the Rider Interaction subsystem with shifting mode during startup.
DID12	The Comm subsystem shall receive and delegate to the Main Computing Platform messages from the Configuration app for gearing model selection.
DIQoSReq01	In DI Mode, shifts shall be executed in less than 400 ms or 1/4 pedal stroke, whichever is longer in time.
DIQosReq02	The DI Shifting button shall perform reliably for at least 100,000 presses.
DIQoSReq03	In DI Shifting mode, gear shifts may be taken regardless of the current power load being applied to the gears, from 0 W to the maximum load allowed.
DIReg01	In DI Shifting mode, if the UP button is pressed and the system is already in the highest possible gear, then the system shall audibly beep and keep the current gearing.
DIReg02	The system shall provide shifting with a DI Shifting mode that enables the DI shifting buttons and disables the shifting levers.
DIReg03	In DI Shifting mode, the UP button shall shift into the next highest possible gearing from the selected gear set, as measured in gear inches.
DIReg04	In DI Shifting mode, the UP button shall shift into the next highest possible gearing from the selected gear set, as measured in gear inches.
DIReg05	In DI Shifting mode, if the DOWN button is pressed and the system is already in the lowest possible gear, then the system shall audibly beep and keep the current gearing.
DIReg06	In DI Shifting mode, when an upshift requires changing the chain ring, the system shall progress to the next largest gearing, as measured by gear inches.
DIReg07	In DI Shifting mode, when a downshift requires changing the chain ring, the system shall progress to the next smallest gearing, as measured by gear inches.
DIReq10	The system shall enter DI Shifting mode by selecting that option in the Configuration app.
DIReq11	Once DI Shifting mode is selected, this selection shall persist across resets, power resets, and software updates.

Name	Specification
DIReq12	Mechanical shifting shall be the default on initial startup or after a factory settings reset.
DIReq13	The system shall leave DI Shifting mode when the user selects the Mechanical Shifting option in the Configuration app.
efarg01	The system shall notify the rider of the current number of chain rings and cassette rings on startup.
efarg02	The system shall accept a rider command to enter a mode to configure the gearing.
efarg03	The system shall accept a rider command to set up from 1 to 3 front chain rings, inclusive.
efarg04	The default number of chain rings shall be two.
efarg05	The rider shall be able to decrement the cassette ring from a higher (smaller number of teeth) to the next lower (larger number of teeth) gear until the largest cassette ring is reached.
efarg06	The system shall accept a rider command to set up from 10 to 12 cassette rings, inclusive.
efarg07	The default number of cassette rings shall be 12.
efarg08	The system shall accept a rider command to set any chain ring to have from 20 to 70 teeth.
efarg09	The system shall accept a rider command to set up any cassette ring to have from 10 to 50 teeth.
efarg10	The default number of teeth for 1 chain ring shall be 48.
efarg11	The default number of teeth for 2 chain rings shall be 34 and 53.
efarg12	The system shall inform the rider of the new gearing when the gear is changed.
efarg13	The default number of teeth for 3 chain rings shall be 28, 40, and 56.
efarg14	The system shall inform the training app of the new gearing when the gear is changed.
efarg15	The default number of teeth for 10 cassette rings shall be 11, 12, 14, 16, 18, 20, 22, 25, 28, and 32.
efarg16	The default number of teeth for 11 cassette rings shall be 11, 12, 13, 14, 15, 16, 17, 19, 21, 23, and 25.

Name	Specification
efarg17	The default number of teeth for 12 cassette rings shall be 11, 13, 15, 17, 19, 21, 24, 28, 32, 36, 42, and 50.
efarg18	The rider shall be able to command the system to leave configuration mode.
efarg19	The default starting gear shall be chain ring 1 and cassette ring 1 when starting a ride.
efarg20	The rider shall be able to augment the front chain ring from a lower to the next higher gear until the largest chain ring is reached.
efarg21	The rider shall be able to decrement the front chain ring from a higher to the next lower gear until the smallest chain ring is reached.
efarg22	The rider shall be able to augment the cassette ring from a lower (larger number of teeth) to the next higher (smaller number of teeth) gear until the smallest cassette ring is reached.
efarg23	The system shall send the current gearing to the training app when the current gearing changes.
efarg24	The system shall respond to a rider-initiated increase in gear by applying the new level of gearing provided that it does not exceed the maximum gearing of the gearing configuration.
efarg25	The system shall respond to a ride-initiated decrease in gear by applying the new level of gearing provided that it does not exceed the minimum gearing of the gearing configuration.
efarg26	The system shall display the currently selected gear.
efarg27	The system shall default to the minimum gear during initialization.
EFD01	The Main Computing Platform shall notify the Rider Interaction subsystem of the current simulated front and rear gear selection.
EFD02	The Comms system shall receive commands to set up gearing from the Configuration app and delegate to the Main Computing Platform.
EFD03	The Main Computing Platform shall process and store the front and rear gearing configurations received via the Comms subsystem from the Configuration app.

Name	Specification
EFD04	The Rider Interaction subsystem shall display the currently selected front and rear gear, as commanded by the Main Computing Platform.
EFD05	The Rider shall be able to shift to the next highest or next lowest gear.
EFD06	The Main Computing Platform shall allow upshifting or downshifting until either the highest or lowest gear is reached.
PowerReq01	The Electrical Power Delivery subsystem shall accept input power from 100 to 240 V at 50-60 Hz with a maximum current draw of 2.5 amps.
PowerReq02	The Electrical Power Delivery subsystem shall supply digital current to power computing devices.
PowerReq03	The Rider Interaction subsystem shall provide a switch to power the system on and off.
PowerReq04	Upon receiving a power off message from the Rider Interaction subsystem, the Main Computing Platform shall store system and rider configurations and then send a message to the Electrical Power Delivery subsystem to remove power.
PowerReq05	The Electrical Power Delivery subsystem shall supply adequate power to create rider resistance to the Power Train subsystem.
PowerReq06	The Electrical Power Delivery subsystem shall provide adequate power for changing the system inclination to the Mechanical Frame subsystem.

Table 4.1 – Subsystem requirements

Next we have *Table 4.2*, which shows how they are allocated to subsystems:

Requirements	Power Train	Comms	Rider Interaction	Electric Power Delivery	Mechanical Frame	Main Computing Platform
CR_requirement_0						CR_requirement_0
CR_requirement_1						CR_requirement_1
CR_requirement_10						CR_requirement_10
CR_requirement_11		CR_requirement_11				CR_requirement_11
CR_requirement_12						CR_requirement_12
CR_requirement_13						CR_requirement_13
CR_requirement_14						CR_requirement_14
CR_requirement_15		CR_requirement_15				CR_requirement_15
CR_requirement_2						CR_requirement_2
CR_requirement_21		CR_requirement_21				CR_requirement_21
CR_requirement_22		CR_requirement_22				CR_requirement_22
CR_requirement_23		CR_requirement_23				CR_requirement_23
CR_requirement_24	CR_requirement_24					CR_requirement_24
CR_requirement_25		CR_requirement_25				CR_requirement_25

Requirements	Power Train	Comms	Rider Interaction	Electric Power Delivery	Mechanical Frame	Main Computing Platform
CR_require-ment_3	CR_require-ment_3					CR_require-ment_3
CR_require-ment_4						CR_require-ment_4
CR_require-ment_5		CR_require-ment_5				CR_require-ment_5
CR_require-ment_6	CR_require-ment_6					
CR_require-ment_7						CR_require-ment_7
CR_require-ment_8		CR_require-ment_8				CR_require-ment_8
CR_require-ment_9		CR_require-ment_9				CR_require-ment_9
CRD_01						CRD_01
CRD_02						CRD_02
CRD_03						CRD_03
CRD_04	CRD_04					
CRD_05	CRD_05					
CRD_06						CRD_06
CRD_07						CRD_07
CRD_08		CRD_08				CRD_08
CRD_09		CRD_09				
CRD_10		CRD_10				CRD_10
CRD_11		CRD_11				CRD_11
CRD_12						CRD_12

Requirements	Power Train	Comms	Rider Interaction	Electric Power Delivery	Mechanical Frame	Main Computing Platform
CRD_13						CRD_13
CRD_14	CRD_14					CRD_14
CRD_15						CRD_15
CRD_16						CRD_16
CRD_17		CRD_17				
CRD_18		CRD_18				
CRD_19		CRD_19				CRD_19
CRD_20						CRD_20
CRD_21					CRD_21	
CRD_22						CRD_22
CRD_23					CRD_23	
CRD_24	CRD_24					CRD_24
CRD_25						CRD_25
CRD_26	CRD_26					
CRD_27	CRD_27					
CRD_28	CRD_28					CRD_28
CRD_30					CRD_30	
CRD_31			CRD_31			
CRD_32			CRD_32			
DID01			DID01			
DID02						DID02
DID03						DID03
DID04						DID04

Requirements	Power Train	Comms	Rider Interaction	Electric Power Delivery	Mechanical Frame	Main Computing Platform
DID05						DID05
DID06						DID06
DID07						DID07
DID08			DID08			
DID09			DID09			
DID10						DID10
DID11						DID11
DID12		DID12				
DIQoSReq01			DIQoSReq01			
DIQosReq02			DIQosReq02			
DIQoSReq03						DIQoSReq03
DIReg01						DIReg01
DIReg02			DIReg02			
DIReg03			DIReg03			
DIReg04			DIReg04			
DIReg05						DIReg05
DIReg06						DIReg06
DIReg07						DIReg07
DIReq10		DIReq10	DIReq10			DIReq10
DIReq11						DIReq11
DIReq12						DIReq12
DIReq13		DIReq13	DIReq13			DIReq13
efarg01			efarg01			

Requirements	Power Train	Comms	Rider Interaction	Electric Power Delivery	Mechanical Frame	Main Computing Platform
efarg02		efarg02				efarg02
efarg03						efarg03
efarg04						efarg04
efarg05			efarg05			
efarg06						efarg06
efarg07						efarg07
efarg08						efarg08
efarg09						efarg09
efarg10						efarg10
efarg11						efarg11
efarg12			efarg12			
efarg13						efarg13
efarg14						efarg14
efarg15						efarg15
efarg16						efarg16
efarg17						efarg17
efarg18		efarg18				efarg18
efarg19						efarg19
efarg20						efarg20
efarg21						efarg21
efarg22						efarg22
efarg23						efarg23
efarg24						efarg24

Requirements	Power Train	Comms	Rider Interaction	Electric Power Delivery	Mechanical Frame	Main Computing Platform
efarg25						efarg25
efarg26			efarg26			
efarg27						efarg27
EFD01			EFD01			EFD01
EFD02		EFD02				
EFD03						EFD03
EFD04			EFD04			
EFD05			EFD05			
EFD06						EFD06
PowerReq01				Power-Req01		
PowerReq02				Power-Req02		
PowerReq03			PowerReq03			
PowerReq04			PowerReq04			PowerReq04
PowerReq05	PowerReq05			Power-Req05		
PowerReq06				Power-Req06	Power-Req06	

Table 4.2 – Requirements – subsystem allocation matrix

Based on the white box scenarios, the interface blocks for the ports have been elaborated, as shown in the block definition diagram in *Figure 4.2*. Most of these interfaces will result in physical interface specifications, but note that the interfaces to the **Rider** actor are *virtual* in the sense that the system must provide sensors and hardware with which the **Rider** actor will interact. These include the pedals (for application of movement and force), the physical on/off switch, the display (for currently selected gearing), and the shift levers and buttons.

The *virtual* interfaces are highlighted in a special color as a visual reminder:

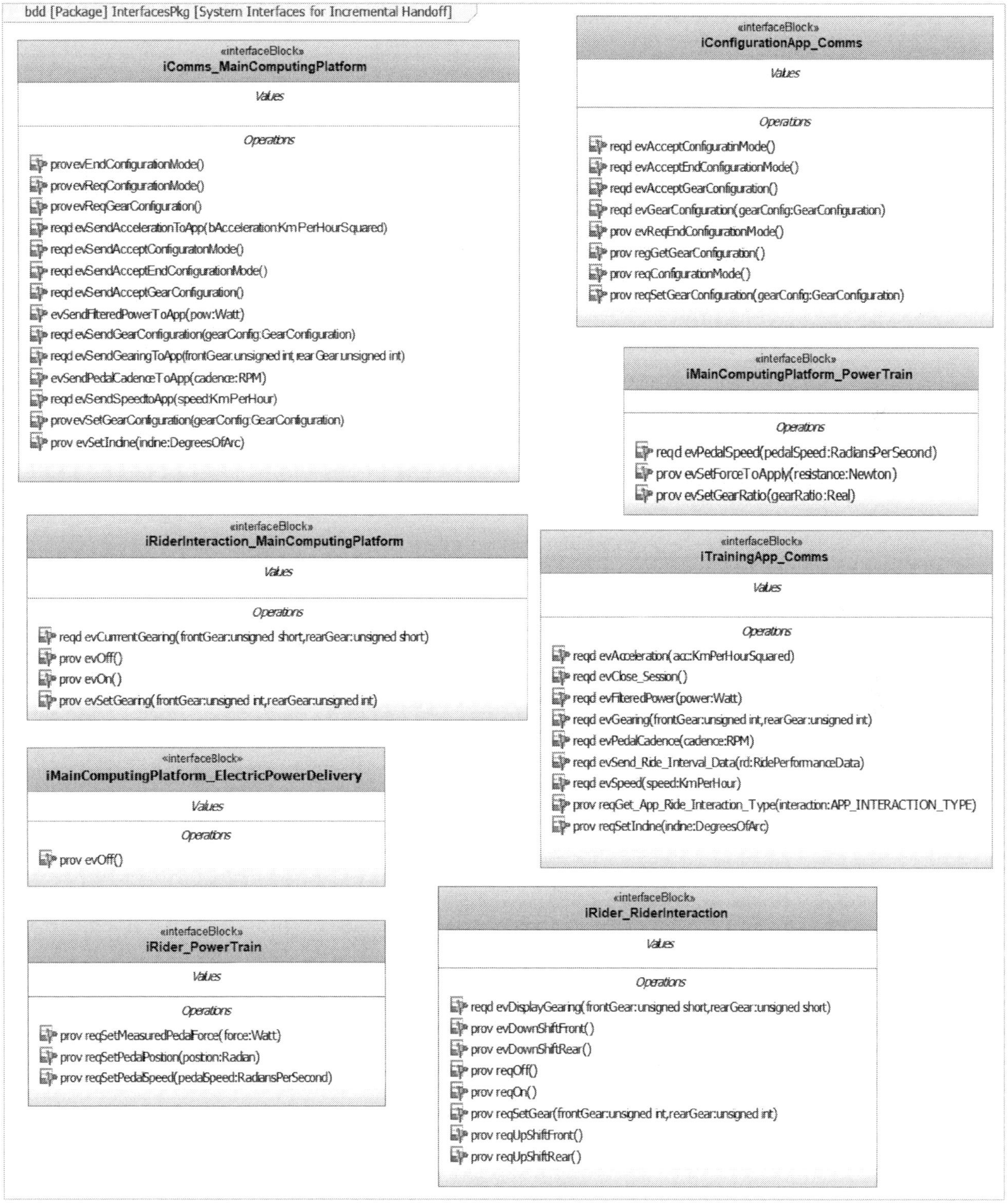

Figure 4.2 – Subsystem interface blocks for incremental handoff

The logical data schema for data passed in the services has been partially elaborated. The information is collected in the **InterfacesPkg::LogicalDataSchemaPkg** subpackage. *Figure 4.3* shows the scalar value types, units, and dimensions. Named constants are shown with the values that define them, although internally they are defined as *Language Kind*, with a specification in the form #define %s <value>. The diagram also shows the «tempered» stereotype, which is used to specify important value type metadata such as extent (allowable range of values), lowest and highest values, latency, explicitly prohibited values, and the scale of precision, accuracy, and fidelity. *Figure 4.4* shows the logical data schema that uses those types to represent the information within the architecture. I want to emphasize again that this is not the entire, final architecture; rather, is it is the architecture for a particular iteration. The final, complete architecture will contain many more elements than this.

> **Note**
>
> While *precision* is the number of significant digits in a number, *scale* is the number of significant digits to the right of the decimal point. We use *accuracy* to refer to the precision of an output, and *fidelity* to refer to the precision of an input.

The following figure shows various scalar value types, dimensions, and units:

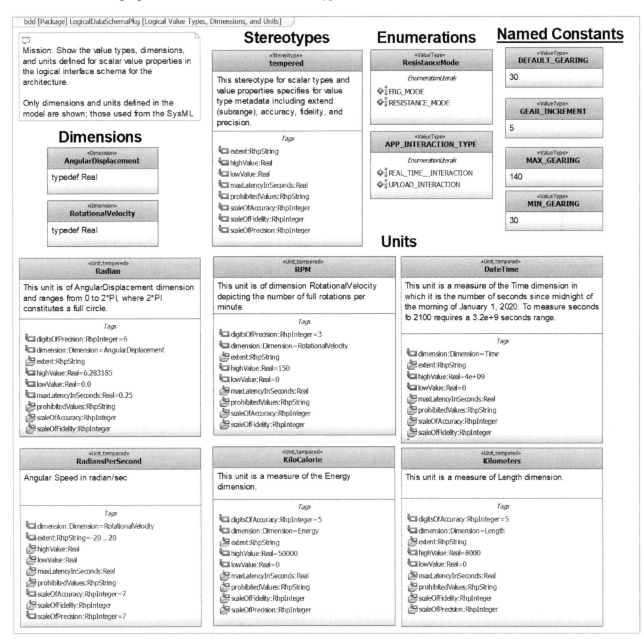

Figure 4.3 – Scalar value types, units, and dimensions

The next figure shows logical data schema and block data types:

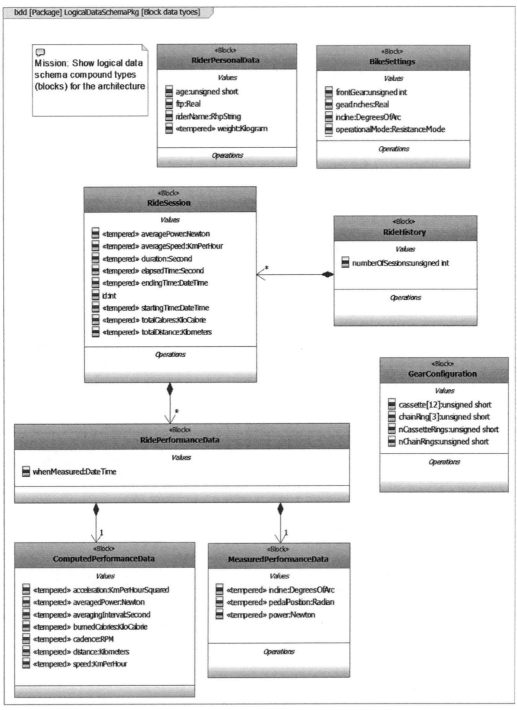

Figure 4.4 – Blocks and logical data schema

Preparation for handoff

Once the system's model has all the data necessary for the downstream engineering teams to work, it is necessary to manipulate it for the transition from systems engineering. This recipe prepares the model for this transition process to begin

Purpose

The purpose of this recipe is to facilitate the handoff from systems engineering to downstream engineering. This will consist of a review of the handoff specifications for adequacy and organizing the information to facilitate the handoff activities. Ideally, each subsystem team needs to access system model information in specific and well-defined locations and they only see information that is necessary in order for them to perform their work.

Inputs and preconditions

The precondition for this recipe is that the architecture is defined well enough to be handed off to subsystem teams for design and development. This means that the following preconditions are necessary:

1. The system requirements for the handoff are stable and fit for purpose. This doesn't necessarily mean that the requirements are complete, however. If an iterative development process is followed, the requirements need only be complete for the purpose of this increment.

2. The subsystem architecture is defined, including how subsystems connect to other subsystems and the system actors. As in the previous point, not all subsystems need to be specified, nor must the included subsystems be fully specified in a given iteration for an incremental engineering process. It is enough that the subsystem architecture is specified well enough to meet the development needs for the current iteration.

3. The subsystem requirements have been derived from the system requirements and allocated to the subsystems.

4. The logical subsystem interfaces are defined so that the subsystems can collectively meet the system needs. This includes not only the logical specification of the services, but also the logical data schema for the information those services carry. In addition, flows not directly related to services must also be logically defined as part of the subsystem interfaces.

Outputs and postconditions

The resulting condition of the model is that it is organized well to facilitate the handoff workflows. Subsystem requirements and structures are accessible from external models with minimal interaction between the system and subsystem models.

How to do it...

Figure 4.5 shows the workflow for preparing for the handoff. While straightforward, doing a good job here means that subsequent work associated with the handoff will be much easier:

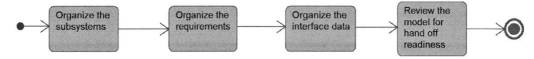

Figure 4.5 – Preparing for handoff

Organizing the subsystems

The next recipe, *Federating models for handoff*, will create a model for each subsystem. Each subsystem should reach into the system model as efficiently as possible to retrieve its – and only its – specification details. This is not intended to hide information about other subsystems, but is instead meant to simplify the process for retrieving specification information that it needs. We must organize each subsystem into its own package so that the subsystem team can add this package to their model to serve as their starting architectural specification.

Organizing the requirements

At this point, all the requirements relevant to the current handoff should be allocated to the subsystems. This means that the subsystems have relations identifying the requirements they must meet. These may be either *«allocate»* or *«satisfy»* relations, owned by the subsystem blocks and targeting the appropriate subsystems. This step involves locating the requirements so that they can be usably accessed by the downstream engineers and provided in summary views (tables and matrices). The package holding the requirements, which might be organized into subpackages, will be referenced by the individual subsystem models during and after the handoff.

Organizing the interface data

One of the things put into the **Shared Model** (in recipes later in this chapter) is the physical interface specifications and the physical data schema for the data used within those interfaces. The logical interfaces and related schema must be organized within the systems engineering model so that they can easily be referenced by the **Shared Model**. This means putting the interfaces, interface blocks, and data definition elements, such as blocks, value types, dimensions, and units, in a package so that the **Shared Model** can easily reference it.

Reviewing the model for handoff readiness

After all the information is readied, it should be reviewed for completeness, correctness, and appropriateness for the downstream handoff workflow to occur. Participants in the review should include not only the systems engineers creating the information, but also the subsystem engineers responsible for accepting it.

To review the readiness of the systems model for handoff, we look at the parts of the model that participate in the process:

- Subsystems:

    a. Are the subsystems each nested within their own package?

    b. Does each subsystem have ports defined with correct interfaces or interface blocks and with the proper conjugation?

    c. Is the set of all subsystems complete with respect to the purpose of the handoff (for example, does it support the functionality required of this specific iteration)?

    d. Does each subsystem package have a reference to the requirements allocated to it?

- Requirements:

    a. Are the requirements all located within a single package (with possible subpackages) for reference?

    b. Are all requirements relevant to this handoff either directly allocated to subsystems or decomposed and their derived requirements allocated?

- Interfaces:

    a. Is all the interface data located within a single package (which may have subpackages)?

    b. Are all the interfaces or interface blocks detailed with the flow properties, operations, and event receptions?

    c. Is the directionality of each interface feature set properly?

    d. Are the properties of the services (operations and event receptions) complete, including data passed via those services?

    e. Is the logical interface data schema fully, properly, and consistently defined for blocks, value types, dimensions, and units?

Example

The starting point for the example in this recipe is the detail shown at the front of this chapter. In this recipe, we will organize and refactor this information to facilitate the other handoff activities.

Organizing the subsystems

Here, we will create a package within **Design Synthesis Pkg::Architectural Design Pkg** for each subsystem and relocate the subsystem block into that package. This will support later import into the subsystem model. These packages will be nested within **Design Synthesis Pkg::Architectural Design Pkg**. See *Figure 4.6*:

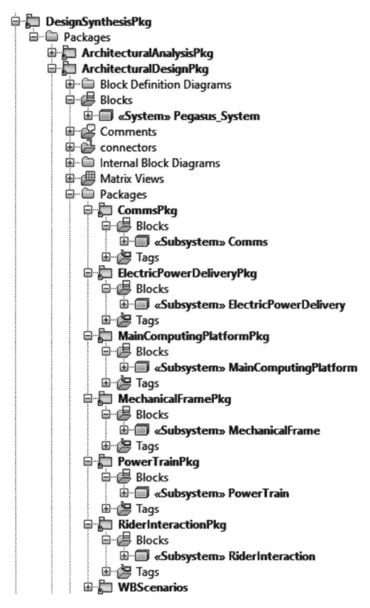

Figure 4.6 – Subsystem organization in the system model

Organizing the requirements

The requirements are held within **Requirements Analysis Pkg:: Requirements Pkg**. While it is possible to redistribute the requirements into a package per subsystem based on those relations, it isn't always practical to do so. Minimally, two summary views are needed. First, a table of the requirements showing the name and specification text of all requirements must be provided. This should be placed in **Requirements Analysis Pkg::Requirements Pkg** so that the subsystem teams can access it easily (such as *Table 4.1*), and use it to determine their requirements. Secondly, matrix views showing the allocation relations between the subsystems and the allocated requirements are required (such as *Table 4.2*). Since the subsystems are the owners of the *«allocate»* relations, it makes sense for these matrices to be in **Design Synthesis Pkg::Architectural Design Pkg**. The overall matrix can be put there in that package directly. *Figure 4.7* shows the package organization of the requirements in the model:

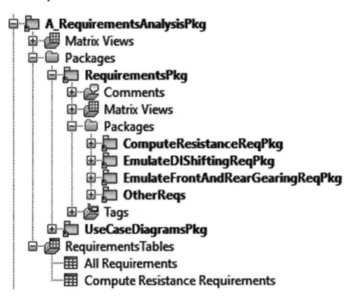

Figure 4.7 – Requirements organization

In addition, each subsystem package contains an allocation matrix just showing the requirements allocated to that specific subsystem. *Figure 4.8* shows the example of the **Comms** subsystem. The Rhapsody *Toggle empty rows and columns* feature is used to just show the requirements allocated to the **Comms** subsystem:

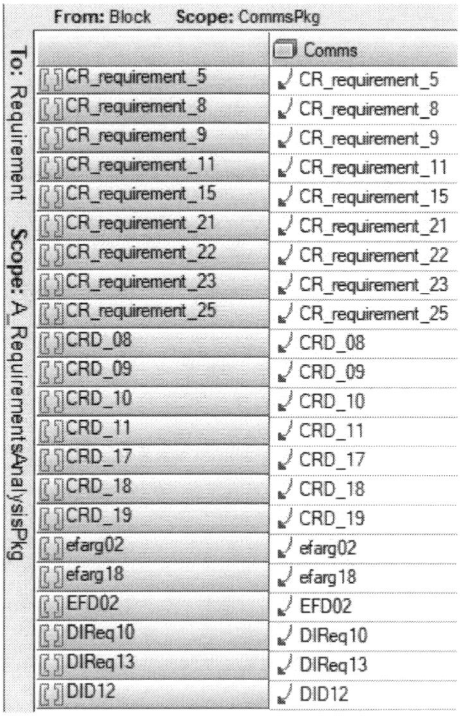

From: Block	Scope: CommsPkg
To: Requirement	Comms
CR_requirement_5	CR_requirement_5
CR_requirement_8	CR_requirement_8
CR_requirement_9	CR_requirement_9
CR_requirement_11	CR_requirement_11
CR_requirement_15	CR_requirement_15
CR_requirement_21	CR_requirement_21
CR_requirement_22	CR_requirement_22
CR_requirement_23	CR_requirement_23
CR_requirement_25	CR_requirement_25
CRD_08	CRD_08
CRD_09	CRD_09
CRD_10	CRD_10
CRD_11	CRD_11
CRD_17	CRD_17
CRD_18	CRD_18
CRD_19	CRD_19
efarg02	efarg02
efarg18	efarg18
EFD02	EFD02
DIReq10	DIReq10
DIReq13	DIReq13
DID12	DID12

Figure 4.8 – Comms subsystem allocated requirements

Organizing the interface data

In the canonical model organization used in the example, the logical interfaces are located in the systems engineering model **InterfacesPkg**. These may be either *interfaces* or *interface blocks* depending on whether standard or proxy ports are used. In addition, the package contains the specifications of the logical data passed via those interfaces, whether that data is expressed as service-independent flow properties or arguments of services. All this information should be organized for reference by the **Shared Model**, defined in the next recipe. The **Shared Model** will define physical interfaces and associated data schemas that represent the logical interfaces and data schema in the systems model. Those physical interfaces will then be made available to the subsystem teams via the model federation defined in the next recipe.

The information for this example is already shown in *Figure 4.2* to *Figure 4.4*. The organization of the interface data is shown in *Figure 4.9*. Although the screenshot only shows the services for a single interface block, note that we have followed the convention of using event receptions for all logical service specifications in the systems engineering model.

These will be changed into a physical schema in later recipes in this chapter:

Figure 4.9 – Organization of the interface data

Reviewing the model for handoff readiness

In this example, the model is set up and ready for handoff.

Federating models for handoff

The systems engineering model is, at least abstractly, a single model. In practice, large systems engineering models may be split up into multiple projects (roughly, but not precisely, "models"), but that is done for convenience. Logically, it is a singular coherent model with the systems engineering data.

Downstream engineering is different in that many separate, independent models will be created. These models will interact with each other in specific and well-defined ways. A set of such independent, yet connected models is called a *federation*, and the process of creating the models and their linkages is called *model federation*.

One of the key ideas in model federation is the notion of a *single source of truth*. This concept means that while there may be multiple sources for engineering data, each specific datum is owned in a single, well-defined location known as the datum's *authoritative source*. When a value is needed, the authoritative source for that data is referenced.

This means that, for the most part, data is not *copied* from model to model, which can lead to questions such as "The value reported for this datum is different if I look at different sources, so which is correct?" Instead, data is *referenced*.

In the Rhapsody tool, model federations are constructed with the **File | Add to Model** feature. This feature can add data, usually packages with their contained elements, to other models. The default behavior of this feature is to add a reference to the original model elements (although this can be changed to a copy if needed). If you want to modify the referenced model elements, you must edit the original source model, as it cannot be changed in the referencing model. When the data in a referenced model is changed, that change is reflected in the referencing model (although only after reloading the reference). Thus, the single source of truth is preserved.

While many models might be federated, including CAD models, PID control models, environment simulation models, and implementation models, we will focus on a core set of models in the recipe. The models in our federation will be as follows:

- Systems engineering model: This is the model we've been working in so far.

- Shared model: This model contains elements used by more than one subsystem model. Our focus here will be the system and subsystem physical interfaces, including the physical data schema for information passed in those interfaces.

- Subsystem model [*]: A separate model per subsystem is created to hold its detailed design and implementation.

Purpose

The purpose of this recipe is to provide workspaces to support both the handoff process itself and the downstream engineering work to follow.

Inputs and preconditions

The starting point for this recipe is the systems engineering model with engineering data necessary to perform the handoff to downstream engineering, including the set of identified subsystems. This information is expected to be organized to facilitate the referencing of requirements, architectural elements, and interface data for the linking together of the models in the federation.

Outputs and postconditions

At the end of the recipe, a set of models are constructed with limited and well-defined points of interaction. Each model is created with a standard canonical model organization supportive of its purpose.

How to do it...

The steps involved in the recipe are shown in *Figure 4.10*:

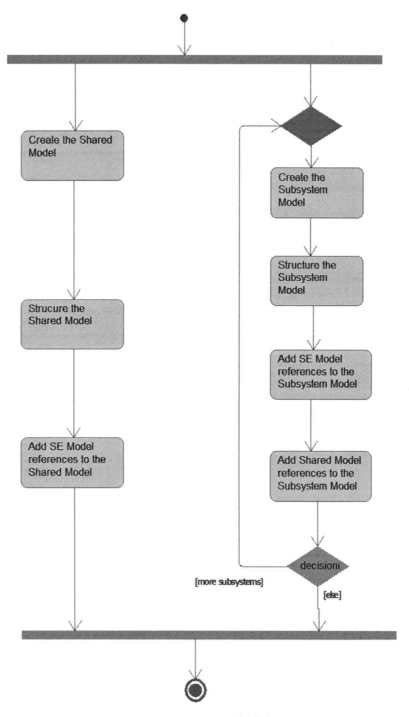

Figure 4.10 – Creating a model federation

Creating the shared model

Create a new model, named the **Shared model**. This is normally located in a folder tree underneath the folder containing the systems engineering model, but this might not necessarily be the case.

Structuring the shared model

This model has a recommended initial structure containing the **Physical Interfaces** package, which will be referenced by the **subsystem models**. This package will hold the specification of the interfaces and has two nested packages, one for the physical data schema and the other for the stereotypes-related data schema for use by the subsystems. The stereotypes are commonly used to specify metadata to indicate subranges, extent, and precision, and this information is important for the subsystem teams to use that data successfully. The subsystems need a common definition for interfaces and they get it by referencing this package.

It should be noted that it is common to add an addition, **DomainsPkg**, later in the downstream engineering process to hold design elements common to multiple subsystems, but the identification of such elements is beyond the scope of the handoff activity.

Adding SE model references to the shared model

There are a small number of SE model packages that must be referenced in the Shared model. Notably, these include the following:

- The `requirements` package
- The `interfaces` package
- The `common` package

The first two are discussed in some detail in the previous recipe. The **Common Stereotypes** package includes stereotypes and other reusable elements that may be necessary to properly interpret the elements in the referenced packages.

In Rhapsody, adding these references is done with the **File | Add to Model** feature. If you select the menu item, the **Add To Model** dialog will open (*Figure 4.11*):

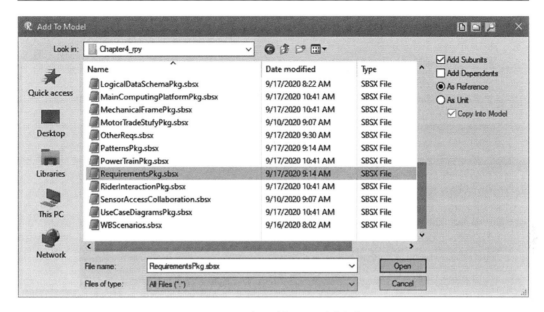

Figure 4.11 – The Add To Model dialog

The files with the `.sbs` or `.sbsx` extensions are packages. Normally, and in this case, we will add a package. The other settings allow adding as a reference (the default) or as a unit (separate copy), and whether to include nested subunits (yes) and dependencies (no).

Creating the subsystem model

It is assumed that each subsystem is a well-defined, mostly independent entity and will generally be developed by a separate interdisciplinary engineering team. For this reason, each subsystem will be further developed in its own model. In this step, a separate model is created for the subsystem.

This step is repeated for each subsystem.

Structuring the subsystem model

A standard canonical structure is created for the subsystem. It consists of two packages, of particular importance although it is expected that the subsystem team will elaborate on the package structure during the design and implementation of that subsystem. These packages are as follows:

- **The subsystem spec package**: This package is intended to hold any requirements and requirements analysis elements the team finds necessary. Further recipes will discuss the creation of refined requirements for the included engineering disciplines and their facets.

- **The deployment package**: This package contains what is known as the *deployment architecture* for the subsystem. This is a creation of engineering discipline-specific facets, which are contributions to the subsystem design from a single engineering discipline. The responsibilities and connections of these facets define the deployment architecture.

This step is repeated for each subsystem.

Adding SE model references to the subsystem model

Each subsystem model has two important references in the SE model:

- **The subsystem package**: In the previous recipe, each subsystem was located in its own package, along with its properties and a matrix identifying the requirements it must meet. The package has the original name of the subsystem package in the **SE model**.

- **The Requirements Pkg package**: This is a reference to the entire set of requirements, but the matrix in the subsystem package identifies which of those requirements are relevant to the design of the subsystem.

While in almost all cases, it is preferable to add these other model packages to the subsystem model by reference, it is common to add the subsystem package *by value* (copy). The reason is that in an iterative development process, systems engineering will continue to modify the SE model for the next iteration while the downstream engineering teams are elaborating on the subsystem design for the current iteration. As such, the subsystem teams don't want to see new updates to their specification model until the next iteration. By adding the subsystem spec package by copy, it can be updated at a time of the subsystem team's choosing and **SE model** updates won't be reflected in the subsystem model until the subsystem model explicitly updates the reference. Any relations from other subsystem model elements to the elements in the subsystem spec package will be automatically updated because the reloaded elements will retain the same **GUID** (**Globally Unique Identifier** or **Universally Unique Identifier**). This is a 128-bit integer number used to identify resources. However, any changes made to the copied elements will be lost.

Insulation from changes made by systems engineers can also be handled by a configuration management tool that manages baselined versions of the referenced models, so there are multiple potential solutions to this issue.

This step is repeated for each subsystem.

Adding shared model references to the subsystem model

The relevant package to reference in the shared model is **Physical Interfaces Pkg**. This will contain the interface definitions and related data used by the subsystems, including the physical data schema.

This step is repeated for each subsystem.

Example

In this example, we will be creating a shared model and a subsystem model for the **Comms**, **Electrical Power Delivery**, **Main Computing Platform**, **Mechanical Frame**, **Power Train**, and **Rider Interaction** subsystems.

Creating the shared model

We will put all these models, including the shared model, in a folder located in the folder containing the **SE model**. This folder is named `Subsystem Models`, and contains a nested folder, `SharedModel`.

Structuring the shared model

It is straightforward to add **Physical Interfaces Pkg** and its nested packages.

Adding SE model references to the shared model

It is similarly straightforward to add the references back to the common requirements and logical interfaces packages in the systems engineering model. Once this step is complete, the initial structure is as shown in *Figure 4.12*:

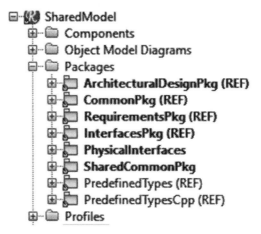

Figure 4.12 – Initial structure of the shared model

Creating the subsystem model

For every subsystem, we will create a separate subsystem model. If we are practicing incremental or agile development, the handoff recipes will be performed multiple times during the project. In this case, it isn't necessary for all of the subsystems to be involved in every increment of the system, so subsystem models only need be created for the subsystems that participate in the current iteration.

In this example, those subsystems are **Comms**, **Electric Power Delivery**, **Main Computing Platform**, **Mechanical Frame**, **Power Train**, and **Rider Interaction**.

Structuring the subsystem model

Although the subsystem models may evolve differently depending on the needs and engineering disciplines involved, they all start life with a common structure. This structure consists of the **Subsystem Spec** and **Deployment** packages. If software engineering is involved in subsystem development, then additional packages to support software development are added as well. While not strictly a part of the handoff activity *per se*, I've added a typical initial structure for software development in the **Main Computing Platform** model, shown in *Figure 4.13*.

Adding SE model references to the subsystem model

Each subsystem model must reference its specification from the SE model. In the previous recipe, we organized the SE model to simplify this step, so that a single reference is all that is needed for that. In our example SE model, the names of these subsystem packages are simply the names of the subsystem followed by the suffix Pkg. For example, the package containing the **Main Computing Platform** subsystem is **Main Computing Platform Pkg**.

In addition, each subsystem model must reference the **Requirements Pkg** package so that it can easily locate the requirements it must satisfy.

Adding shared model references to the subsystem model

Finally, each subsystem needs to reference the common physical interface specifications held in the **Shared** model.

When the recipe is complete, the set of models will look like *Figure 4.13*. The screenshot also shows the contents of three of the models at a high level – the **Electric Power Delivery**, **Main Computing Platform**, and **Shared** models. Some packages are marked as **read-only** (**RO**) because only the project set to be the *active project* may be edited. Other packages are marked as **reference** (**REF**), which indicates that with that model, this package references content in another model, and may not be edited in the referencing model:

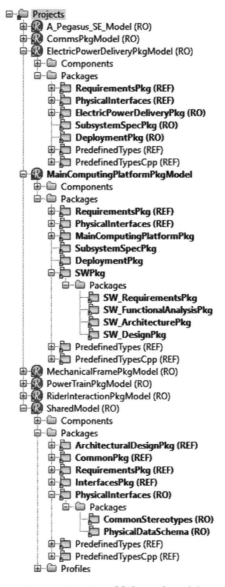

Figure 4.13 – Set of federated models

Logical to physical interfaces

The previous chapters developed interfaces from the functional analysis (*Chapter 2, System Specification*) and the architecture (*Chapter 3, Developing System Architectures*). These are all logical interfaces that are defined by a set of logical services or flows. These logical interfaces characterize their logical properties – extent, precision, timeless, and so on – as metadata on those features. In this book, all services in the logical interface are represented as events that may optionally carry information. In this recipe, that information is elaborated on in a physical data schema, refining their physical properties.

The subsystem teams require physical interface specifications, since they are designing and implementing physical systems that will connect in the real world. We must refine the logical interfaces to include their implementation details, including the physical realization of the data, so that the subsystems can be properly designed and can be guaranteed to properly connect and collaborate in actual use.

For example, a logical service specifying a command to enter configuration mode such as **evSetMode(CONFIGURATION_MODE)** might be established between an actor, such as the **Configuration** app, and the system. The physical interface might be implemented as a Bluetooth message carrying the commanded mode in a specific bit format. The bit format for the message that sends the command is the physical realization of the logical service.

Purpose

The purpose of this recipe is to create physical interfaces and physical data schemas and store them in the **Shared Model** so that subsystem teams have a single source of truth regarding the definition of actor, system, and subsystem interfaces.

Note that any interfaces defined *within* a subsystem are beyond the scope of this recipe and for the **Shared Model**. This recipe only addresses interfaces between subsystems, the system and the actors, or between the subsystems and the actors.

Inputs and preconditions

The inputs for the recipe include the logical interfaces and the logical data schema. Preconditions include the construction of the **Shared Model**, complete with references to the logical interfaces and data schema in the **SE model**.

Outputs and postconditions

The outputs from this recipe include both the physical interface specifications and the physical data schema organized for easy import into the subsystem models.

How to do it...

The workflow for the recipe is shown in *Figure 4.14*:

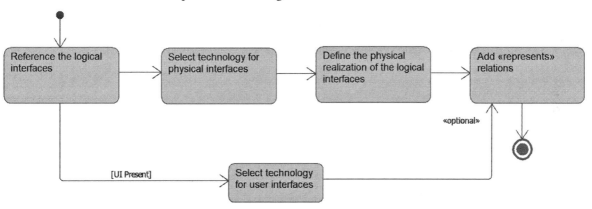

Figure 4.14 – Defining physical interfaces

Referencing the logical interfaces

The physical interfaces we create must satisfy the needs of the already-defined logical interfaces. To start this recipe, we must review and understand the logical interfaces.

Selecting the technology for physical interfaces

Different technological solutions are available for implementation of physical interfaces. Even for something like a mechanical power transfer interface, different solutions are possible, such as friction, gearing, and direct drive. For electronic interfaces, voltage, wattage, amperage, and phase must be specified. However, software interfaces, or combined electro-software interfaces, are where most of the interface complexity of modern systems resides.

In the previous recipes, we specified logical interface using a combination of flow properties (mostly for mechanical and electronic interfaces) and events (for discrete and software interfaces). This frees us from early concerns regarding technical details while allowing us to specify the intent and logical content of interfaces. Once we are ready to direct the downstream subsystem teams, this missing detail must be added.

Flow properties with mechanical or electronic realization may be implemented as energy or matter flows, or, if informational in nature, perhaps using a software middleware such as a **Data Distribution Service (DDS)**. Events are often implemented as direct software interfaces or as messages using a communication protocol. The latter case is an electro-software interface, but the electronics aspect is dictated by a standard in the physical layer of the protocol definition and while the software messages are constrained by the defined upper layers of the protocol stack. This is assuming that your realization uses a pre-defined communications standard. If you define your own, then you get the joy of specifying those details for your system.

In many cases, the selection of interface technology will be driven by external systems that already exist. In such cases, you must often select from technology solutions that those external systems already provide. In other cases, the selection will involve the performance of trade studies (refer to the *Architectural trade studies* recipe from the previous chapter) to determine the best technical solutions.

Selecting the technology for user interfaces

User interfaces (UIs) are a special case for interface definition. Logical interfaces defining UIs are *virtual* in the sense that our system will not be sending flows or services directly to the human user. Instead, a UI provides sensors and actuators manipulated or used by the human users to provide the information specified in the logical interfaces. These sensors and actuators are part of the system design. Inputs from users in a UI may be via touchscreens, keyboards, buttons, motion sensors, or other such devices. Outputs are perceivable by one or more human sensors, typically vision, hearing, or touch. The definition of the interactions required of the UI are often defined by a human factors group that does interaction workflow analysis to determine how users should best interact with the system. The physical UI specification details the externally accessible interactions, although not necessarily the internal technical detail. For example, the human factors group may determine that selection buttons should be used for inputs and small displays for output, but the subsystem design team may be charged with the responsibility of selecting the specific kinds of buttons (membrane versus tactile) and displays (LED, LCD, plasma, or CRT).

Although this may change in the future if we add chips to our brains. Something to look forward to.

Defining the physical realization of the logical interfaces

Once the technology of the physical interfaces is decided, the use of the technology for the interfaces must be defined. This is straightforward for most mechanical and electronic interfaces, but many choices might exist for software. For example, TCP/IP might be a selected technology choice to support an interface. The electronic interfaces are well defined in the physical layer specification. However, the software messages at the application layer of the protocol are defined in terms of datagrams. The interfaces must define the internal structuring of information within the datagram structure.

> **Note**
>
> See `https://en.wikipedia.org/wiki/Transmission_Control_Protocol` for a description of TCP.

The basic approach here is to define the message packet or datagram internal data structure, including the message identifier and data fields, so that the different subsystems sending or receiving the messages can properly create or interpret the messages. Be sure to add a dependency relation from the physical packet or datagram structure to the logical service being realized. I create a dependency stereotype named «*represents*» for this purpose. The relations can best be visualized in matrix form.

Adding «represents» relations

It is a good idea to add navigable links from the physical interfaces back to their logical counterparts. This can be done as a «*trace*» or «*refine*» relation, but I prefer to add a stereotype just for this purpose named «*represents*». I believe this adds clarity whenever you have model elements representing the same thing at different levels of abstraction. The important thing is that from the logical interface, I can identify how it is physically realized and, from the physical realization, I can locate its logical specification.

Example

In this example, we will focus on the logical interfaces shown in *Figure 4.2*. We will define the physical interfaces and physical ports.

Referencing the logical interfaces

In the last recipe, we added the **Interfaces Pkg** package from the **SE model** by reference. This means that we can open up and view the content, but cannot change it in the **Shared Model**. The model reference allows us to create navigable relations from our physical schema to its logical counterpart.

Selecting the technology for physical interfaces

The interfaces in *Figure 4.2* have no flow properties, so we must only concern ourselves with the event receptions of the interfaces. Specifically, **Configuration App** and **Training App** communicate with the system via the **Bluetooth Low Energy** (**BLE**) wireless protocol. The system must also interact with its own sensors via either BLE or ANT+ protocols for heart rate and pedal data, but we are considering those interfaces to be internal to the subsystems themselves, and so they will not be detailed here. The BLE interfaces within our current scope of concern are limited to the **Comms** subsystem and **Configuration App** and **Training App.**

For internal subsystem interfaces, different technologies are possible, including RS-232, RS-485, **Control Area Network** (**CAN**) bus, and Ethernet. Once candidate solutions are identified, a trade study (not shown here) would be conducted and the best solution selected.

In this example, we select the CAN bus protocol. This technology will be used to connect all subsystems that are software services, such as the interfaces among the **Comm**, **Main Computing Platform**, **Rider Interaction**, and **Power Train** subsystems. The interactions for the **Electric Power Delivery** subsystem will be electronic digital signals. *Table 4.3* summarizes the technology choices:

Interface	Participants	Purpose	Technology
App Interface	Comm subsystem Training app Configuration app	Send rider data to Training app for display and analysis. Support system configuration by the Configuration app.	Bluetooth Low Energy (BLE)
Pedal Interface	Rider Power Train subsystem	Reliably connect to rider's shoes via cleats for determination of power from the Rider from which position and cadence can be computed.	Look™ compatible clipless pedal fit Standard pedal spindle Pedal-based power meter
Internal Bus	Comms subsystem Rider Interaction subsystem Power Train subsystem Main Computing Platform subsystem Mechanical Frame subsystem	Send commands and data between subsystems for internal interaction and collaboration, including sending information to the Comms subsystem for sending to the apps and sending information received from the apps that is received by the Comms subsystem to other subsystems.	CAN bus
Power Enable	Power subsystem Rider Interaction subsystem Main Computing Platform subsystem	Signal the power system to turn power on and off.	Digital voltage 0-5 V DC
Electrical Power	Electric Power Source Electrical Power Delivery subsystem	Electrical power provided from the external power source to the system.	100-240 V, 5A, 50-60 Hz AC

Interface	Participants	Purpose	Technology
Electrical Power Distribution	Electric Power Delivery subsystem and • High Power: Power Train subsystem • Medium Power: Mechanical Frame subsystem • Digital Power: Rider Interaction subsystem, Main Computing Platform subsystem, Comms subsystem, Power Train subsystem	Electrical power is transformed and delivered to subsystems in one of three ways: • High power for the motor to generate resistance to pedaling for the rider • Medium power for the Mechanical Frame subsystem to raise or lower the incline • Digital Power provided to the components using digital power	To be defined by the Electric Power Delivery subsystem team working with the other subsystem teams

Table 4.3 – Interface technologies

Of these technologies, the BLE and CAN bus will require the most attention.

Selecting the technology for UIs

There are a number of points of human interaction of this system that are not within the scope of this particular example handoff, including the mechanical points for fit adjustments, the seat, and the handle bars. In this particular example, we focus on the rider interface via the pedals, the gear shifters, the power button, and the gearing display. The rider metrics and ride performance are all displayed by the **Training app**, while the **Configuration app** provides the UI for setting up gearing and other configuration values.

The Pegasus features a simple on-bike display for currently selected gearing and current incline, mocked up in *Figure 4.15*. It is intended to be at the front of the bike, under the handlebars, but in easy view of the **rider**. It sports the power button, which backlights when pressed, a gearing display, and the currently selected incline. The gearing display will display the index of the gear selected, not the number of teeth in the gear:

Figure 4.15 – On-bike display

To support Shimano and **Digital Indexed** (**DI**) shifting emulation, each handlebar includes a brake lever that can be pressed inward to shift up or down for the bike (left side for the chain ring, right side for the rear cassette). In addition, the inside of the shifter has one button for shifting (left side for up, right side for down) to emulate **DI** shifting.

Defining the physical realization of the logical interfaces

Let's focus on the messaging protocols as they will implement the bulk of the services. Bluetooth and its variant BLE are well-defined standards. It is anticipated that we will purpose a BLE protocol stack so we only need be concerned with the structuring of the messages at the application layer, that is, structuring the data within the **Payload** field of the **Data Channel PDU** (*Figure 4.16*):

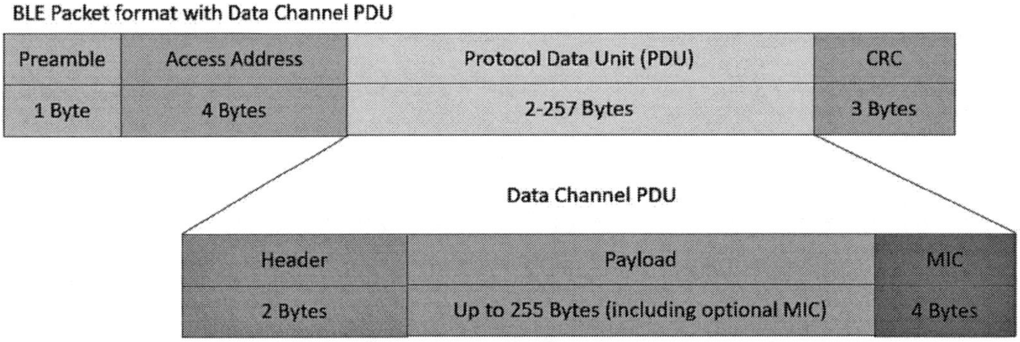

BLE Packet format with Data Channel PDU

Preamble	Access Address	Protocol Data Unit (PDU)	CRC
1 Byte	4 Bytes	2-257 Bytes	3 Bytes

Data Channel PDU

Header	Payload	MIC
2 Bytes	Up to 255 Bytes (including optional MIC)	4 Bytes

Figure 4.16 – BLE packet format

See https://www.bluetooth.org/docman/handlers/downloaddoc.ashx?doc_id=478726.

Similarly, for internal bus communication, the CAN bus protocol is well developed with commercial chipsets and protocol stacks available. The CAN bus is optimized for simple data messages and comes in two forms, one providing an 11-bit header and another a 29-bit header. The header defines the message identifier. Because the CAN bus is a bit-dominant protocol, the header also defines the message priority in the case of message transmission collisions. We will use the 29-bit header format, so we needn't worry about running out of message identifiers. In either case, the data field may contain up to 8 bytes of data, so that if an application message exceeds that limit, it must be decomposed into multiple CAN bus messages and reassembled at the receiver end. The basic structure of CAN bus messages is shown in *Figure 4.17*:

CAN Message format including Extended Frame

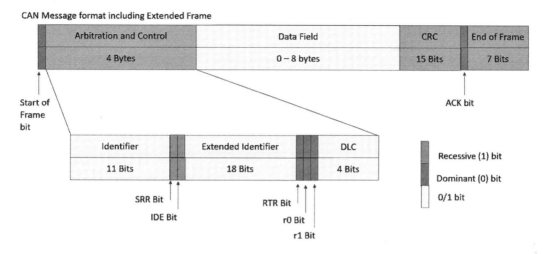

Figure 4.17 – CAN bus message format

For CAN bus messages, we'll use an enumeration for the message identifier and define the structure of the data field for interpretation by the system elements.

The CAN Bus standard, ISO 11898-1, is available for purchase at `https://www.iso.org/standard/63648.html`.

The basic approach taken is to create base classes for the BLE and CAN bus messages. Each will have an ID field that is an enumeration of the message identifiers; it will be the first field in the **Bluetooth Low Power Protocol Data Unit** (**BLE PDU**). That is, the BLE messages that have no data payload will only contain the message ID field in the BLE message Data PDU. The CAN bus messages will be slightly different; the ID field in the message type will be extracted and put into the 29-bit identifier field. Data-less messages will have no data in the CAN bus data fields, but will at least have the message identifier.

We won't show all the views of all the data elements, but *Figure 4.18* shows the types for the BLE packets and physical data types:

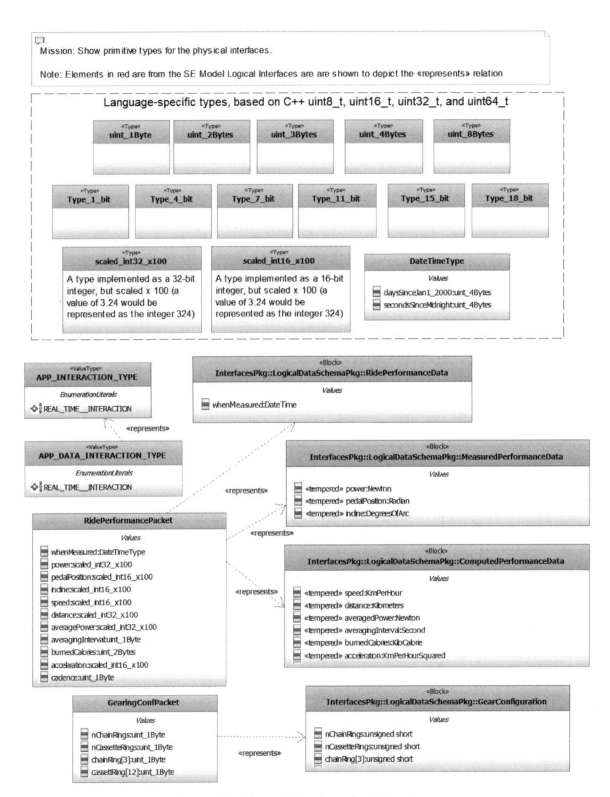

Figure 4.18 – Physical data schema for BLE messages

This diagram merits a bit of discussion. First, this data schema denotes the physical schema for bits-over-the-air; this is not necessarily how the subsystem stores the data internally for their own use. Secondly, note that the diagram denotes the use of some C++ language-specific types, such as **unit8_t** as the basis for the corresponding transmission type, **uint_1Byte**. The language-specific types could be used directly and given the **UseAsExternal** (Rhapsody-specific) property to load them in from the C++ library file, **stdint.h**, if desired. Next, note the types **scaled_int32x100** and **scaled_int16x100**. These take floating-point values and represent them as scaled integers; in the former case, multiplying the value by 100 and storing it as a 32-bit signed integer, and in the latter case, multiplying the value by 100 and storing it in a 16-bit signed integer. The practice of using scaled integers is very common in embedded systems and cuts down on bandwidth when lots of data has to be passed around. Lastly, note how the physical data schema classes (remember classes are the UML equivalent to SysML blocks) have *«represents»* relations back to elements in the logical data schema (color coded to show them more distinctly).

Figure 4.19 shows how these data elements are used to construct BLE packets. The logical data interface blocks for the **Training app** and **Configuration app** are shown in the upper part of the diagram (again, with special coloring), along with their services. Each service must be represented by one of the defined packet structures. The structure of the **BLE Packet** class has a **pdu** attribute, of the type **PDU_Base**. **PDU_Base** contains a 2-byte **header**, which indicates the message size, as well as a **msg_type** attribute of the **APP_MESSAGE_ID_TYPE** type, which is an enumeration of all possible messages. Messages without data, such as **evClose_Session**, can be sent with a BLE packet with a **pdu** attribute of the type **PDU_Base**.

For messages that carry data, **PDU_Base** is subclassed to add appropriate data fields to support the different messages, so that **BLE Packet** can be constructed with an appropriate subtype of **PDU_Base** to carry the message data.

For example, to send the logical message **evReqSetGearConfiguration**, **BLE Packet** would use the **PDU_Gearing** subclass of **PDU_Base**:

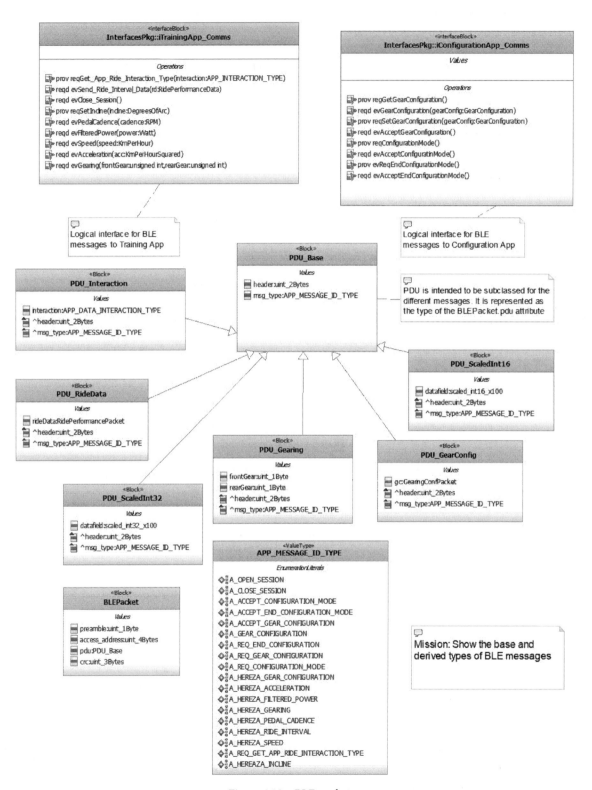

Figure 4.19 – BLE packets

While messages between the system and the apps use Bluetooth, messages between subsystems use an internal CAN bus. The CAN bus physical schema is different in that it must be detailed to the bit level, since there are packet fields of 1, 4, 7, 11, and 18 bits in addition to elements of one or more bytes length. We'll let the software engineers define the bit level of manipulation of the fields and just indicate, by explicit typing, those fields that have special bit lengths where necessary. *Figure 4.20* shows the structure of the CAN bus messages that correspond to the services:

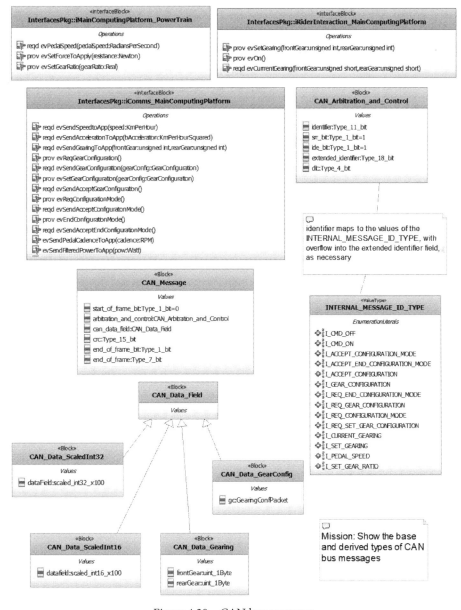

Figure 4.20 – CAN bus messages

Adding «represents» relations

We must add the *«represents»* relations so that it is clear which Bluetooth or CAN bus messages are used to represent which logical services in the **SE model** interface blocks. The Harmony SE profile of the Rhapsody tool has a helpful wizard for adding dependencies (our *«represents»* relation is a stereotype of dependency). If you want to use this wizard in the **Shared model**, then use the **File | Add Profile** model to add the `HarmonySE.sbs` profile file. Then select a source element in the browser, right-click, select **SE Toolkit | Add Dependencies | From Selected**, and a dialog will pop up and help you with the creation of these relations.

These relations are best visualized in a matrix. We will define a matrix layout that uses the following settings:

- *From* element types: Block, Class
- *To* element types: Operations, Receptions
- Cell element types: Represents

Then we can use that matrix layout to create a matrix view with the **Physical Interfaces Pkg** package set to `From Scope`, and the **Interfaces Pkg** package referenced from the **SE model** set to `To Scope`.

When you're all done, you should have a matrix of the relations from the messaging classes to the event receptions in the **SE model** interface blocks, as in *Figure 4.21* (although I used the Rhapsody *Switch Rows and Columns* feature to improve the readability of the display):

Figure 4.21 – Message mapping to logical services

Deployment architecture I – allocation to engineering facets

The *Federating models for handoff* recipe created a set of models, a **Shared Model** and a separate model per subsystem. The current recipe creates what is called the *deployment architecture* and allocates subsystem features and requirements to different engineering disciplines. Once that is done, the software, electronic, and mechanical design can begin, post-handoff.

Deployment architecture

Chapter 3, Developing System Architectures, began with a discussion of the *Five Critical Views of Architecture.* One of these, the *deployment architecture,* is the focus of this and the next recipes. The deployment architecture is based on the notion of *facets.* A facet is the contribution to a design that comes from a single engineering discipline (*Figure 4.22*). A typical subsystem integrates a number of different facets, the output from engineering in disciplines including the following:

- Electronics: Power, motor, analog, digital
- Mechanics: Thermodynamics, materials, structural mechanics, pneumatics, hydraulics, aerodynamics, hydrodynamics
- Optics
- Acoustics
- Chemical engineering
- Software: Control, web/cloud, communications, AI, data management

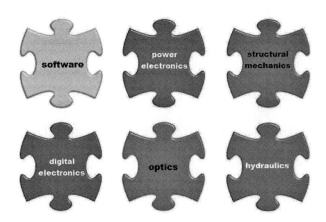

Figure 4.22 – Some engineering facets

These disciplines may result in facets at a high level of abstraction, such as an electronics facet, or may result in more detailed facets, such as power, motor, and digital electronics, depending on the needs and complexity of the subsystem.

A subsystem team generally comprises multiple engineers of each discipline working both independently on their aspect of the design and collaboratively to produce an integrated, functioning subsystem.

Creating a deployment architecture involves identifying and characterizing the facets and their responsibilities in the scope of the subsystem design. This means that the system features – subsystem functions, information, services, and requirements – must be allocated to the facets. This makes it clear to the subsystem discipline-specific engineers what they need to design and how it contributes to overall subsystem functionality.

The deployment architecture definition is best led by a systems engineer, but includes input and contributions of the discipline-specific engineers that must carry it forward. This is often called an **interdisciplinary product team (IPT)**. Historically, a common cause of project failure is when a single engineering discipline is responsible for the creation of the deployment architecture and allocation of responsibilities. Practice clearly demonstrates that an IPT is a better way.

The system engineering role in the deployment architecture is crucial because systems engineers seek to optimize the system as a whole against a set of product-level constraints. Nevertheless, it is a mistake for systems engineers to create and allocate responsibilities without consulting the downstream engineers responsible for the detailed design and implementation. It is also a (common) mistake to let one discipline make the deployment decisions without adequate input from the others. I've seen this on many projects, where the electronics designers dictate the deployment architecture and end up with a horrid software design because they didn't adequately consider the needs of the software team. It is best for the engineers to collaborate on the deployment decisions, and, in my experience, this results in a superior overall design.

Purpose

The purpose of this recipe is to create the deployment architecture and allocate subsystem features and requirements to enable creation of the electronic, mechanical, and software designs.

Inputs and preconditions

The preconditions are that the subsystem architecture has been defined, subsystems have been identified, and system features and requirements have been allocated to the subsystems.

Inputs include the subsystem requirements and system features, notably system data, system services, and system functions, that have been allocated to the subsystem.

Outputs and postconditions

The outputs of this recipe are the defined deployment architecture, identified subsystem facets, and allocation of system features to those facets.

The output is the updated subsystem model with those elements identified and allocated.

How to do it...

Figure 4.23 shows the recipe workflow. This recipe is similar to the *Architectural allocation* recipe in *Chapter 3, Developing System Architectures*, except that it focuses on the facets within a subsystem rather than on the subsystems themselves. This recipe is best lead by a systems engineer but performed by an IPT to optimize the deployment architecture:

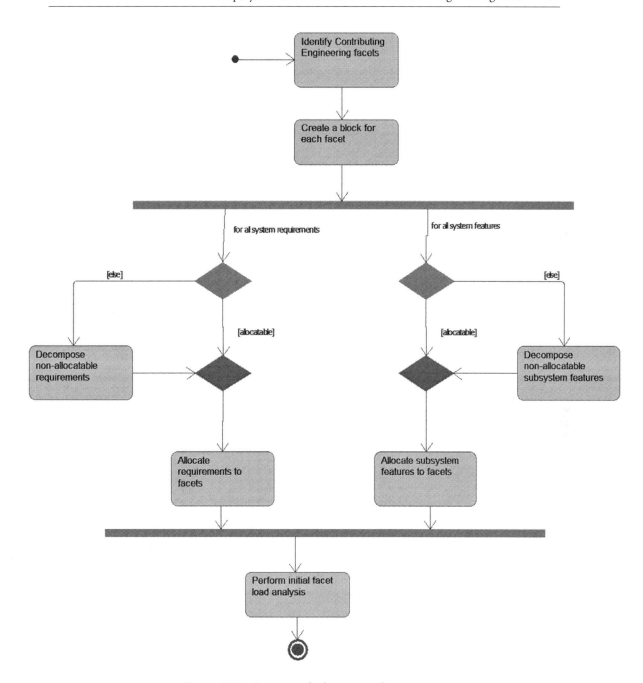

Figure 4.23 – Creating a deployment architecture

Identifying contributing engineering facets

The first step in the recipe is to identify the engineering disciplines involved. Some subsystems might be mechanical only, electrical-mechanical, software-electronic, or virtually any other combination. Any involved engineering discipline must be represented so that its facet contribution can be adequately characterized. For an embedded system, a software-centric subsystem typically also includes electronic computing infrastructure (a digital electronic facet) to provide hardware services to support the functionality. The capacities of the electronics facet, including memory size, CPU throughput, and so on, are left to a negotiation among the coordinating engineering disciplines. This topic is discussed in a bit more detail in the next recipe, *Deployment architecture II – interdisciplinary interfaces*.

Creating a block for each facet

In the deployment model, we will create a block for each facet. We will not, in general, decompose the facet to identify its internal structure. That is a job for the discipline-specific engineers who have highly developed skills in their respective subject matters. It is enough, generally, to create a separate block for each facet. Each facet block will serve as a container or collector of specification information about that facet for the downstream engineering work.

Decomposing non-allocatable requirements

Requirements can sometimes be directly allocated to a specific facet. In other cases, it is necessary to create *derived requirements*, which take into account the original subsystem requirements and the specifics of the subsystem deployment architecture. In this latter case, create derived requirements that can be directly allocated to subsystems. Be sure to add «*deriveReqt*» relations from the derived requirements back to their source subsytem requirements. These derived requirements can be stored in either the subsystem model, the system model, or in a requirements management tool, such as IBM DOORS™.

Allocating requirements to facets

Allocate system requirements to the identified facets. In general, each requirement is allocated to a single facet, so at the end, the requirements within the subsystem are clearly and unambiguously allocated to facets. The set of allocated subsystem requirements after this step is normally known as *software*, *electronic*, or *mechanical requirements*. It is crucial that the engineers of the involved disciplines are a part of the allocation process.

Decomposing non-allocatable subsystem features

Some subsystem features, which refer to operations, event receptions, flows, and data, can be directly allocated to a single facet. In practice, most cannot. When this is the case, the feature must be decomposed into engineering-specific-level features that trace back to their subsystem-level source feature, but that can be directly allocated to a single facet.

Allocating subsystem features to facets

Allocate subsystem features to facets. That is, each subsystem function now becomes a service allocated to a single facet OR it is decomposed to a set of services, each of which is so allocated. Subsystem flows and data must also be allocated to facets.

Performing initial facet load analysis

This step seeks to broadly characterize the size, capacity, and other summary quantitative properties of the facets. The term *load* means different things in different disciplines. For mechanical facets, it might refer to weight or shear strength. For digital electronics, it might refer to CPU throughput and memory size. For power electronics, it might mean maximum available current. For software, it might mean volume (roughly, "lines of code"), nonvolatile storage needs, volatile memory needs, or computational complexity. The important properties will also differ depending on the nature of the system. Helicopters, for example, are notoriously weight sensitive, while automobiles are notoriously component price-sensitive (meaning they want to use the smallest CPUS and the least memory possible). These system characteristics will drive the need for quantification of different system properties.

These properties will be estimates of the final product qualities, but will be used to drive engineering decisions. Digital electronics engineers will need to design or select CPU and memory hardware, and they need a rough guess of the requirements by the software to do so. It is far too common that a lack of understanding leads to the design of underpowered computing hardware, resulting in decreased software (and therefore, system) performance. Is a 16-bit processor adequate or does the system need a pair of them or a 32-bit CPU? Is 100 KB of memory adequate or does the system need 10 MB? Given these rough estimates, downstream design refines and implements these properties.

Estimating the required capacity of the computing environment is difficult to do well and a detailed discussion is beyond the scope of this book. However, it makes sense to provide an introduction to the topic and illustrate how it might be applied in this example. Let's consider memory sizing first.

Embedded systems memory comes in several different kinds, each of which must be accessible by the software (in other words, part of the software "memory map"). Without considering the underlying technology, the kinds of memory required by embedded software are as follows:

- Non-reprogrammable non-volatile memory: This kind of memory provides storage for code that can never be changed after manufacturing. It provides boot loading code and at least lower-level operating system code.

- Programmable non-volatile memory: This kind of memory provides storage for software object code and data that is to be retained across power resets. This can be updated and rewritten by program execution or via **Over-The-Air** (**OTA**) updates.

- Programmable read-write memory for software object code execution: Because of the relatively slow access times for non-volatile memory, it is not uncommon to copy software object code into normal RAM for execution. Normally, the contents of this memory are lost during power resets.

- Programmable read-write memory for software data (heap, stack, and global storage): This memory provides volatile storage for variables and software data during execution. Generally, the contents of this memory are lost during power resets.

- Electronic registers ("pseudo-memory"): This isn't really memory, *per se*, as it refers to hardware read-only, write-only, and read-write registers used to interface between the software and the digital electronics.

- Interrupt vector table: This isn't a different kind of memory as it may be implemented in any of the preceding means, but must be part of the memory map.

A typical approach is to estimate the need for each of the preceding kinds of memory and then construct a memory map assigning blocks of addresses to the kinds of memory. It is common to then add a percentage beyond the estimated need to provide room to grow in the future.

CPU capacity can be measured in many ways. CPU capacity estimating can be performed by comparing the computation expectations of a new system based on throughput measurements of existing systems. An alternative is to base it on experimentation: write a "representative" portion of the software, run it on the proposed hardware platform, measure the execution time, bandwidth, or throughput, and then scale it to your estimated software size. You can even do "cycle counting" by determining the CPU cycles needed to perform critical functionality on a given CPU, and then compute the CPU speed as a cycle rate fast enough to deliver the necessary functionality within the timeliness requirements. Of course, there are many other considerations that go into a CPU decision, including cost, availability, longevity, and development support infrastructure.

Example

We will limit our example to a single subsystem identified in the last chapter – the **Power Train** subsystem.

Identifying contributing engineering facets

The **Power Train** subsystem is envisioned to have mechanical, electronic, and software aspects.

Creating a block for each facet

Figure 4.24 shows the blocks representing these facets, while *Figure 4.25* shows how they connect. Note the *«software»*, *«electronics»*, and *«mechanical»* stereotypes added to the facet blocks. I defined these stereotypes in the **Shared Model::Physical Interfaces::Common Stereotypes** package so that they are available to all subsystems. This is an example of the use of stereotypes to indicate a special kind of modeling element.

Also note the connection points for those facets. There are two pairs of ports between the **Software** and **Electronics** blocks, one for communications (it is anticipated that the electronics will provide an interface to the CAN bus) and one for interaction with the electronics of the power train. This separation is not a constraint on either the software or electronics design, but indicates that these connections between the facets are really independent of one another.

There is both a port pair and an association between the **Electronic** and **Mechanical** blocks on the BDD and a corresponding connector between their instances on the IBD. This is a personal choice as to how I like to separate *dynamic* and *static* connections between these facets by modeling them with ports and direct associations, respectively. By *dynamic*, I am referring to connections that convey information or flows during system operation. By *static*, I am referring to connections that do not, such as the physical attachments of electronic components to the mechanical power train with bolts or screws:

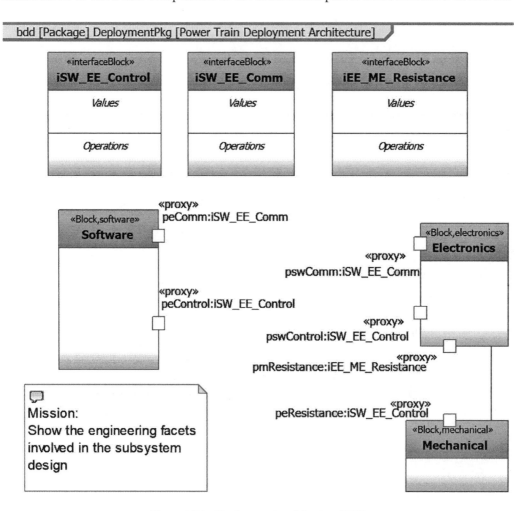

Figure 4.24 – Deployment architecture BDD

The following figure displays the connected deployment architecture:

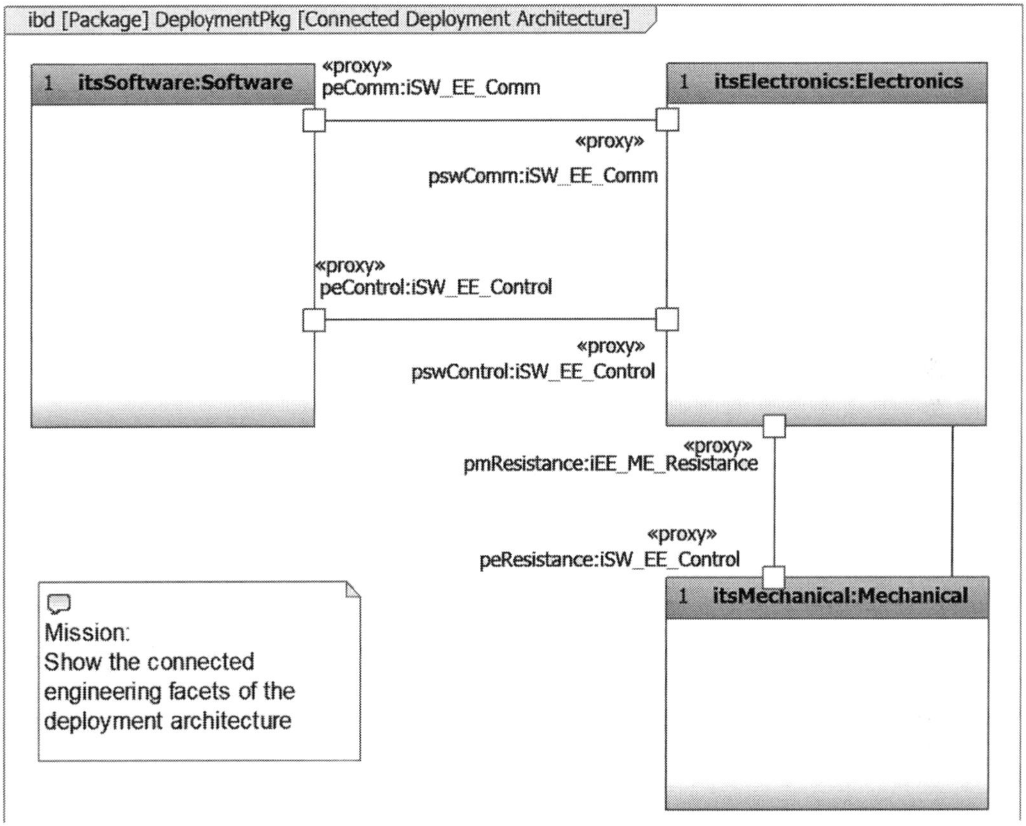

Figure 4.25 – Connected deployment architecture IBD

Decomposing non-allocatable requirements

These facets provide responsible elements to which requirements may be allocated. As mentioned, many requirements must be decomposed into derived requirements prior to allocation.

One issue is where to place such requirements. If you are using a third-party requirements management tool such as DOORS, then clearly, this tool should hold those requirements. If you are instead managing the requirements directly in your model, then there are a couple of options: the **Requirements** package in the **SE model** or in the subsystem model. I personally prefer the latter, but valid arguments can be made for the former. In this case, I will create a **Subsystem Requirements** package inside **Subsystem Spec Pkg** to hold these requirements and *«deriveReqt»* relations to the base requirements that they own.

Before we can decompose requirements for this subsystem, we need to highlight which are the relevant requirements, in other words, the ones to which the **Power Train** subsystem has an *«allocate»* relation. **Power Train Pkg**, imported from the **SE model**, has these relations, and **Requirements Pkg**, also loaded from the **SE model**, has the requirements. The appropriate requirement may be easily identified either by looking at the **Power Train** block itself in the model browser or by building a matrix (in this case, using the *Harmony SE Profile* **Subsystem Requirements Allocation Matrix Layout**, with *Switch Rows and Columns* and *Toggle Empty Rows and Columns* selected to hide requirements not allocated to this subsystem). This is shown in *Figure 4.26*:

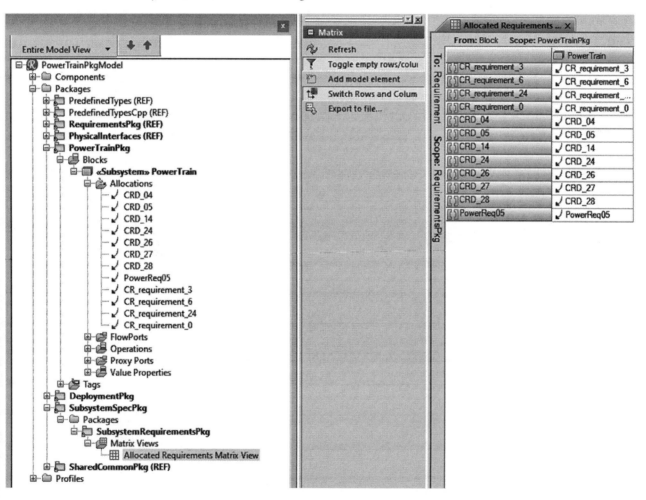

Figure 4.26 – Finding requirements allocated to the subsystem

Having identified the relevant requirements, it is a simple matter to build a requirements diagram exposing just those requirements in the **Subsystem Requirements** package (*Figure 4.27*):

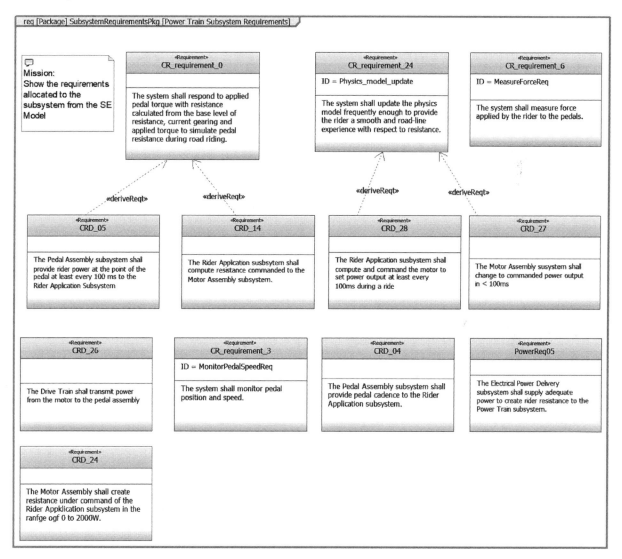

Figure 4.27 – Requirements allocated to the power train subsystem

Working in diagrams, adding derived requirements is straightforward. For example, look at *Figure 4.28*. In this diagram, which works with a subset of the subsystem requirements, we see the facet requirements with «deriveReqt» relations. I've also added the facet stereotypes to clarify the kind of requirement being stated:

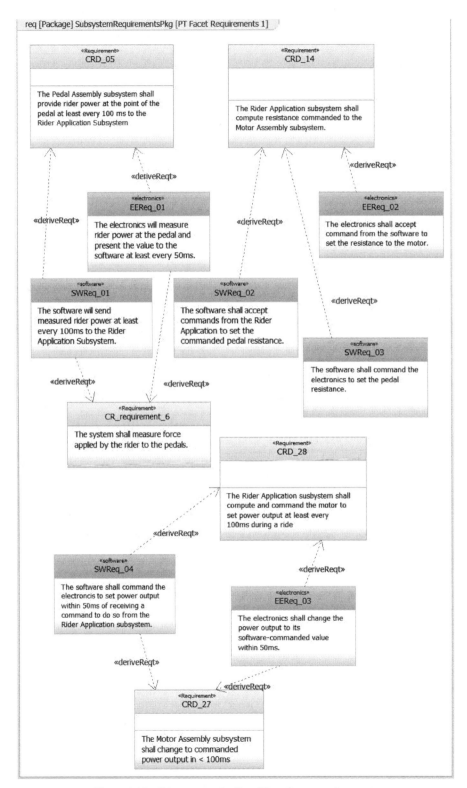

Figure 4.28 – Diagrammatically adding facet requirements

The other subsystem requirements are decomposed in other requirements diagrams. The derived requirements are summarized in *Table 4.4*:

Requirement Name	Specification	Derived From
EEReq_01	The electronics shall measure rider power at the pedal and present the value to the software at least every 50 ms.	CRD_05, CR_requirement_6
EEReq_02	The electronics shall accept commands from the software to set the resistance to the motor.	CRD_14
EEReq_03	The electronics shall change the power output to its software-commanded value within 50 ms.	CRD_28, CRD_27
EEReq_04	The electronics shall measure pedal position within 1 degree of accuracy.	CR_requirement_3
EEReq_05	The motor shall produce resistance to be applied to the pedal.	CRD_26
EEReq_06	The electronics shall measure pedal position at least every 10 ms.	CR_requirement_3
EEReq_07	The electronics shall provide measured pedal position to the software at least every 10 ms.	CR_requirement_3
EEReq_08	The electronics shall accept commands from the software to set the resistance to the rider resulting in power to the pedals in the range of 0 to 2,000 W.	CRD_24
EEReq_09	The electronics shall produce resistance resulting in the command power with an accuracy of at least +/-1 W.	CRD_24
EEReq_10	The electronics shall update the resistance at the pedal to the commanded value within 10 ms.	CRD_24

Requirement Name	Specification	Derived From
MEReq_01	The mechanical drive train shall transmit the motor resistance to the pedal without rider-perceivable loss.	CRD_26
MEReq_02	The mechanical drive train shall deliver resistance to the pedal with power loss of < 0.2 W.	CRD_24
SWReq_01	The software shall send measured rider power at least every 100 ms to the Rider Application subsystem.	CRD_05, CR_requirement_6
SWReq_02	The software shall accept commands from the Rider Application to set the commanded pedal resistance.	CRD_14
SWReq_03	The software shall command the electronics to set the pedal resistance.	CRD_14
SWReq_04	The software shall command the electronics to set power output within 50 ms of receiving a command to do so from the Rider Application subsystem.	CRD_28, CRD_27
SWReq_05	The software shall read the measured pedal position from the electronics at least every 10 ms.	CR_requirement_3
SWReq_06	The software shall compute pedal cadence and pedal speed from pedal position changes at least every 20 ms.	CR_requirement_3
SWReq_07	The software shall convey pedal position and pedal cadence at least every 50 ms to the Rider Interaction subsystem.	CRD_04
SWReq_08	The software shall receive resistance commands from the Rider Application subsystem and convey them to the electronics within 10 ms.	CRD_24

Requirement Name	**Specification**	**Derived From**
SWReq_09	The software shall reject commanded resistance resulting in power outputs that fall outside the range of 0-2,000 W and return an error message to the Rider Application subsystem.	CRD_24
SWReq_10	The software shall convey commanded resistance to the electronics within 50 ms of receipt from the Rider Application subsystem.	CRD_24

Table 4.4 – Derived facet requirements table

Allocating requirements to facets

The next step in the recipe is to allocate the requirements to the facets. *Figure 4.29* shows the allocation mapping. Note that only a single subsystem requirement, **PowerReq5**, was directly allocated to a facet. All the other requirements allocated to the subsystem were decomposed and the resulting derived requirements were allocated. This is typical:

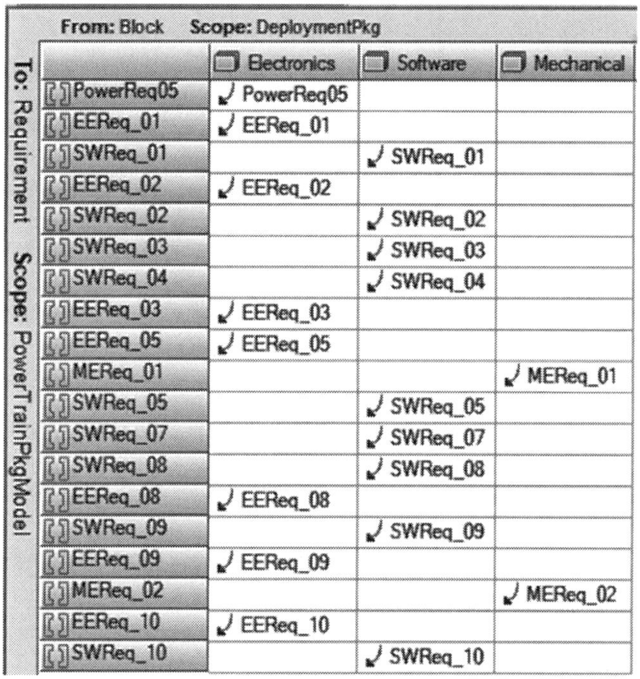

From: Block Scope: DeploymentPkg

To: Requirement Scope: PowerTrainPkgModel

	Electronics	Software	Mechanical
PowerReq05	PowerReq05		
EEReq_01	EEReq_01		
SWReq_01		SWReq_01	
EEReq_02	EEReq_02		
SWReq_02		SWReq_02	
SWReq_03		SWReq_03	
SWReq_04		SWReq_04	
EEReq_03	EEReq_03		
EEReq_05	EEReq_05		
MEReq_01			MEReq_01
SWReq_05		SWReq_05	
SWReq_07		SWReq_07	
SWReq_08		SWReq_08	
EEReq_08	EEReq_08		
SWReq_09		SWReq_09	
EEReq_09	EEReq_09		
MEReq_02			MEReq_02
EEReq_10	EEReq_10		
SWReq_10		SWReq_10	

Figure 4.29 – Matrix of facet and subsystem requirements

Decomposing non-allocatable subsystem features

Figure 4.30 shows the subsystem block features to allocate. On the right side of the diagram is the logical **Power Train** subsystem block from the **SE model**, while on the left is the physical version. There are a number of differences:

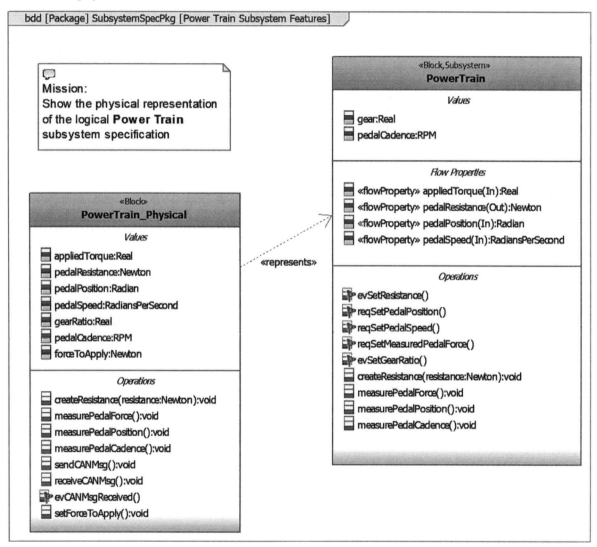

Figure 4.30 – Subsystem block features to allocate

First, note that the physical version contains no flow properties because all the flow properties for this specific block represent things that the subsystem's internal sensors will measure. Secondly, the gearing and computation of gear ratio is really managed by the **Main Computing Platform** subsystem and all this subsystem cares about is the **gear ratio** itself. Third, all of the event receptions, specifying the logical services available across the interface, are summarized by a single event – **evCanMsgReceived()** – and two operations – **sendCANMsg()** and **receiveCANMsg()**.

All of the value properties in the **Power Train_Physical** block must be decomposed into elements in the electronics and software facets. For example, let's suppose that **appliedTorque** is measured by the hardware in a range of 0 to 10,000 in a 16-bit hardware register. The software must convert that value to a scaled integer value (**scaled_int32_x100**) that represents applied force in watts (range 0 to 2,000) for sending in a CAN message. We want the software in the **Power Train** subsystem to encapsulate and hide the motor implementation from other subsystems to ensure robust, maintainable design in the future. This means that the information is represented in both the software and the electronic facets. The expectation is that the software will be responsible for scaling, manipulation, and communication of these values with the **Main Computing Platform subsystem**, while the electronics will be responsible for setting or monitoring device raw data and presenting it to the software.

Figure 4.31 and *Figure 4.32* show the derived value properties and operations, respectively. I added a **«deriveFeature»** stereotype for the dependency between the derived features and its base feature in the **Power Train_Physical** block:

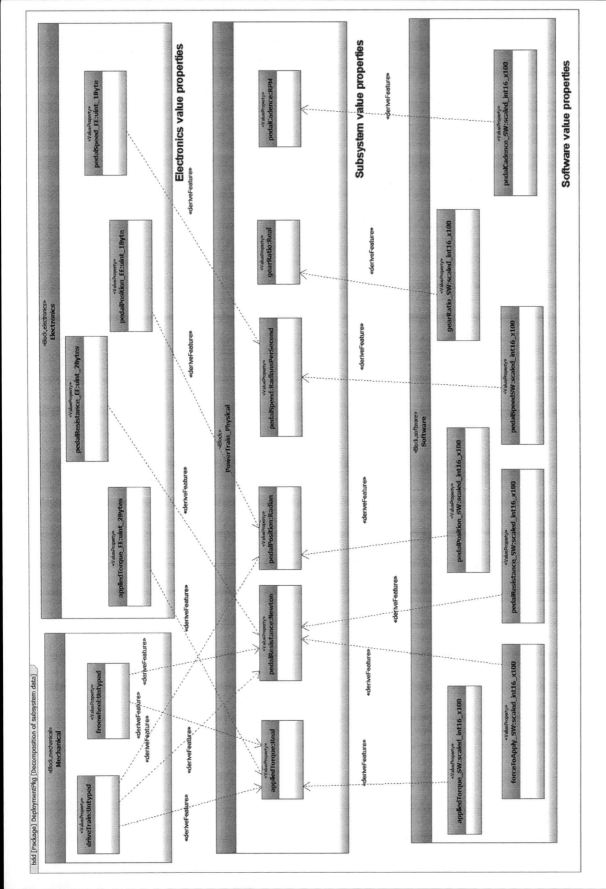

Figure 4.31 – Derived facet value properties

The **Pedal cadence** subsystem value property is only represented in the software because the software will compute it from the **Pedal speed** value property, which is provided by the electronics. Similarly, the **gear ratio** is used by the software to determine how much resistance should be applied to the pedal given the **Pedal cadence** and desired **Pedal resistance** values:

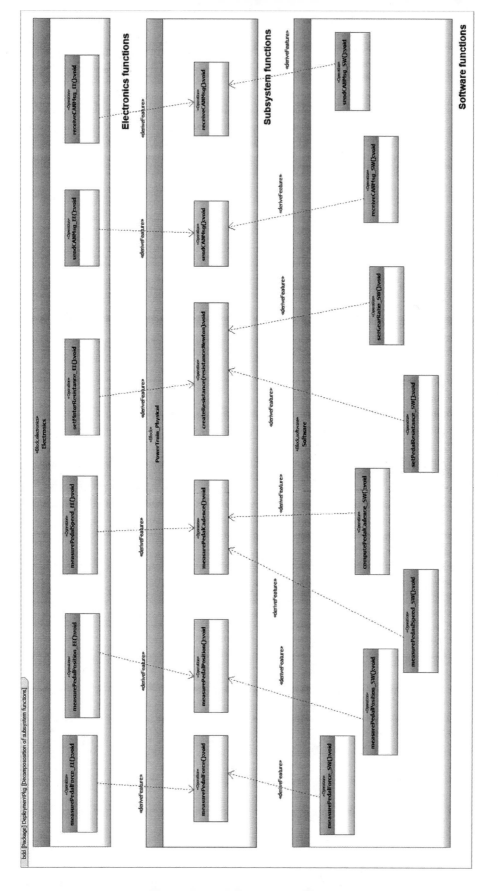

Figure 4.32 – Derived facet functions

The allocation of subsystem data and functions is not meant to overly constrain the design of the facets; they are simply internal features that the design of these features must support, rather than the actual design of that feature. Facets should feel free to design those features in whatever means makes the most sense to them. The primary reason for the allocation of the system features to facets is to be clear of the data and functionality that the facet design is expected to deliver.

Allocating subsystem features to facets

In this example, the identification of the derived facet features was performed concomitantly with their allocation, as shown in the previous two diagrams.

Performing initial facet load analysis

The final step in the recipe is to determine facet capacity. In this example, the primary concerns are the power of the motor and the computational capacity and memory size of the digital electronics. The motor power is specified in the requirements; the system is expected to deliver up to 2,000 W of power via resistance to the rider pedal motion.

In this case, we determine that a 32-bit STM32F2 ARM processor running at 120 MHz with 1 MB ROM and 1 MB RAM is the best fit for our needs and expected future expansion.

Deployment architecture II – interdisciplinary interfaces

One of the most common points of failure in the development of embedded systems is inadequately nailing down the interdisciplinary interfaces, especially the electronics-software interfaces. These interfaces inform related disciplines about common expectations regarding the structure and behavior of those interfaces. Left to their own devices (so to speak), software engineers will develop interfaces that are easy for software implementation, while electronics engineers will develop interfaces that simplify the electronic design. Interdisciplinary interfaces are best developed cooperatively with all the contributing engineering disciplines present.

In my experience, it is best to develop these interfaces early to set expectations and freeze these interfaces under configuration management. This is important even if some of the details may change later. When it becomes obvious during the development of a facet that an interface needs to be modified, then thaw the interface from configuration management, discuss things with all the stakeholders of that interface, agree upon an appropriate revision, and refreeze it in the **Configuration Management** (**CM**) tool. Failure to define the interfaces early will inevitably lead to significant downstream rework and often to suboptimal designs and implementations. It is an annoyingly common problem.

Purpose

The purpose of this recipe is to detail the interactions between the engineering facets in a system or subsystem design.

Inputs and preconditions

The context of the deployment architecture (typically a subsystem) must be specified in terms of its external interfaces and its responsibilities (requirements). Additionally, the contributions of the engineering facets to the design of the context (in other words, the requirements allocated to the facets) must be understood.

Outputs and postconditions

When the recipe is completed, the interfaces among the disciplines are adequately specified to enable the design of the facets involved.

How to do it...

Figure 4.33 shows the workflow for the recipe. The flow is pretty simple, but some of the actions identified in the workflow may require significant thought and effort:

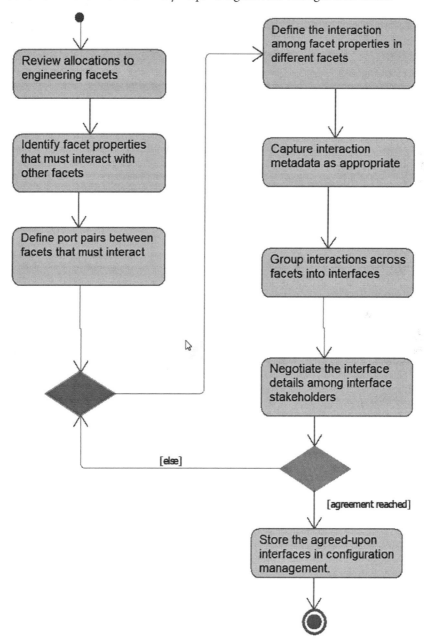

Figure 4.33 – Defining interdisciplinary interfaces

Reviewing allocations to engineering facets

The previous recipe allocated requirements, values, and functions to the different engineering disciplines. Having a clear understanding of the contributions that must be provided by the engineering facets is a crucial step to creating good interdisciplinary interfaces.

Identifying facet properties that must interact with other facets

Interfaces are all about defining the interactions between collaborating elements. In this case, we want to focus on the coordination of elements in different engineering facets. The previous recipe decomposed subsystem features into features within different engineering disciplines. The task here is to relate the properties in collaborating facets. For example, an electronic sensor may provide a value to the software for manipulation and use, so the device driver (in the software facet) must interact with the actual sensor (in the electronics facet). This interaction will result in a service or flow connection of some kind.

Defining port pairs between facets that must interact

Once we have identified the fact that properties in two facets must interact, we define a port pair between the facets to convey the values or service invocations that will be added to the interface.

Defining the interaction among facet properties in different facets

The exact nature of the interaction between the facets must be captured in the interfaces. For example, the software sensor device driver may write to a hardware register to signal the sensor to read a value, wait at least 1 ms, read the sensed value from another hardware register, and then scale the value to what the software needs to manipulate. This interaction and use must be clear in the interface specification.

Capturing interaction metadata as appropriate

Metadata is data about data. In this case, we use metadata to capture the aspects of an interface that may not be obvious or easy to model in other ways. For example, the previous paragraph provided a simple example of the interaction of a software device driver with an electronic sensor. Relevant metadata would be the memory map address of the hardware registers, and the bit mapping of the values in the registers. For example, in the *sensor control register*, writing a 1 to bit 0 might activate the sensor, while writing a 0 bit to the same register has no effect; the value from bits 1-5 might provide a read-only error code should the electronics fail. The fact that the software must wait for 1 ms after activating the sensor before reading the value must be captured in the interface as metadata if the software and electronics are to work together properly.

Grouping interactions across facets into interfaces

All the interactions between the facets must be captured in interfaces. These interfaces must capture relevant information about the interfaces, including how they are accessed by the respective facets. This is most obvious with respect to electronics-software interfaces. The two most common technical means for interfacing between software and electronics are memory-mapped registers and hardware-generated software interrupts.

Negotiating the interface details among interface stakeholders

The two things to keep in mind in this step are that the engineering disciplines must be free to develop their facets using their hard-won engineering skills without being overly encumbered by expectations from other engineering disciplines. In other words, the systems or software engineers shouldn't dictate design of the electronics, and the systems or electronics engineers shouldn't dictate software design. Nevertheless, the interfaces do specify the overlap between the disciplines. All stakeholders should agree on the specifications of the interfaces. This includes the systems engineers, who have a stake in overall system optimization, and the involved engineering disciplines.

Storing the agreed-upon interfaces in configuration management

There should always be a "known target" for the interfaces between facets even if that interface changes in the future. Yes, changing interfaces downstream will entail some amount of rework, but in practice it is much less rework than if agreements aren't there in the first place. The worst outcomes occur when the disciplines continue without a shared understanding of those interfaces. Storing the interfaces under configuration management establishes a baseline and a source of truth from which the engineering disciplines can draw. Should future work uncover some inadequacy of the interfaces, the interfaces can be renegotiated and configuration-managed baselines updated.

Example

This example will continue from the last recipe with the definition of the **Power Train** subsystem interfaces. The example in the previous section detailed the allocated requirements and subsystem features in the disciplines of mechanical and electronic engineering and software.

Reviewing allocations to engineering facets

Read the example from the previous section to review the requirements, values, and function allocation.

Identifying facet properties that must interact with other facets

To avoid over-specification of the facet designs, let's limit our concerns to the subsystem features that are decomposed into elements mapped in different facets. In the previous example, we added dependencies from the decomposed facet-specific features to the subsystem block features. *Figure 4.34* shows the mapping of facet features to subsystem block features:

To: Operation, ValueProperty / Scope: SubsystemSpecPkg	createResistance	measurePedalForce	measurePedalPosition	measurePedalCadence	sendCANMsg	receiveCANMsg	appliedTorque	pedalResistance	pedalPosition	pedalSpeed	gearRatio	pedalCadence
measurePedalForce_EE		measurePedalForce										
measurePedalPosition_EE			measurePedalPosition									
setMotorResistance_EE	createResistance											
measurePedalResistance_EE												
measurePedalSpeed_EE				measurePedalCadence								
sendCANMsg_EE					sendCANMsg							
receiveCANMsg_EE						receiveCANMsg						
measurePedalForce_SW		measurePedalForce										
measurePedalPosition_SW			measurePedalPosition									
measurePedalSpeed_SW				measurePedalCadence								
computePedalCadence_SW				measurePedalCadence								
sendCANMsg_SW					sendCANMsg							
receiveCANMsg_SW						receiveCANMsg						
setGearRatio_SW	createResistance											
setPedalResistance_SW	createResistance											
appliedTorque_EE							appliedTorque					
pedalResistance_EE								pedalResistance				
pedalPosition_EE									pedalPosition			
pedalSpeed_EE										pedalSpeed		
CANSendBuffer												
CANReceiveBuffer												
appliedTorque_SW							appliedTorque	pedalResistance	pedalPosition	pedalSpeed		pedalCadence
forceToApply_SW							appliedTorque		pedalPosition			
pedalPosition_SW								pedalResistance	pedalPosition			
pedalSpeed_SW										pedalSpeed		
gearRatio_SW											gearRatio	
pedalRatio_SW												pedalCadence
pedalResistance_SW								pedalResistance				
drive_METrain							appliedTorque					
freewheel_ME												

Figure 4.34 – Features decomposed to facets

Defining port pairs between facets that must interact

We previously defined the port and added empty interfaces to define them. See *Figure 4.25*.

Defining the interaction among facet properties in different facets

This is the interesting part of the recipe: define exactly how the facets will interact. Because we are using SysML proxy ports, we will capture these as interface blocks, as shown in *Figure 4.35*:

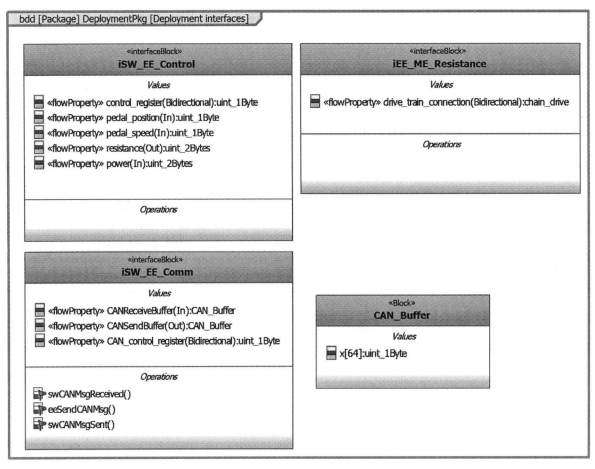

Figure 4.35 – Deployment interfaces

The software-electronic interfaces are mostly composed of hardware registers, represented as flow properties. Both the **iSW_EE_Control** and **iSW_EE_Comm** interface blocks have control and data registers. The software triggers hardware actions or reads status information with these control registers. The data registers provide raw data from the software to the hardware, or from the hardware to the software. The **iSW_EE_Comm** interface block also has two 64-byte blocks, one for sending a CAN bus message and the other for receiving one. The event receptions indicate interrupts generated by the hardware under different conditions. Also, the **iEE_ME_Resistance** electronics-mechanical interface block contains a drive train connection value property defined by the special value type **chain_drive**.

Let's now consider how the software-electronic interfaces will work, starting with the **iSW_EE_Control** interface block. In the real world, this would be the outcome of a discussion between software, electronic, and systems engineers.

The control register in this case will have control or error indication responsibility, each of which requires a single bit:

- Bit 0 will be a software write-only bit that informs the hardware to start monitoring the pedal and providing resistance. When a 1 is written to this bit, the hardware will start applying the force as specified in the resistance hardware register and also start measuring pedal position, pedal speed, and power. The electronics will write those values to the corresponding hardware registers. When a 0 is written to this bit, the electronics stop providing resistance to the pedals and stop measuring pedal and power data. The hardware must assure the software that the updates to any register are all completed within a single CPU cycle to prevent race conditions.

- Bit 1 of the control register is read-only by the software and is used to indicate an error condition in the delivery of power via the motor: a 0 value indicates no error, while a 1 indicates that an error has occurred.

- Bit 2 of the control register is read-only by the software and indicates an error in the pedal position or pedal speed measurement (0 is no error, while 1 indicates an error).

- Bit 3 is an indicator of an error reading power delivered by the rider (0 is no error, 1 indicates an error).

- Bits 4-7 are unused.

The other registers indicate either measured values from the electronics (read-only by the software) or commanded resistance from the software (write-only by the software). The electronics will have its own scale of these values using either 8 bits (such as for the pedal speed and position) or 16 bits (for resistance and power). The direction of the flow properties is from the software perspective (following our previous convention that the first field in the interface block name indicates the unconjugated side of the interface). However, the range of values represented is not scaled by how the user would interpret the values, but rather by the hardware capability. The software is expected to scale the values to units that are meaningful elsewhere.

The electronics measure pedal position as an 8-bit value from 0 (right crank vertical) to 255 (almost vertical). Pedal speed is an 8-bit value ranging from 0 (no movement) to 255 (maximum measured speed of the hardware). Resistance is written to the register by the software as a 16-bit value from 0 (no resistance) up to 65,535 (maximum resistance). Likewise, power is a hardware-measured value from 0 (no power) to 65,535 (maximum measured power). The exact scaling factors will be specified by the hardware at a later date.

The **iSW_EE_Comm** interface is a bit more interesting. The core flow properties are **CAN Receive Buffer** and **CAN Send Buffer**. Each of these is a 64-byte wide, byte-addressable memory register that holds CAN bus messages. The expected interaction flow looks as follows.

To send a message, the following occurs:

1. The software checks bit 0 of the CAN control register. If it's a 0, then data may be written to the CAN send buffer. If not, the software must wait.

2. The software then writes the CAN bus message it wants to send to the CAN send buffer.

3. The software then writes a 1 to bit 0 of the **CAN control register**.

4. The hardware sets the read value of this bit to 1.

5. The hardware bangs the bits out on the CAN bus.

6. When the hardware has sent the message, the hardware sets the software read value of bit 0 of the **control register** to 0.

7. The hardware generates an interrupt 2 to the software to indicate that the CAN send buffer is now available.

8. The software may install an interrupt service routine to interrupt 2 (**swCANMsgSend**) to send the next message, if desired.

To receive a message, the following occurs:

1. The hardware begins receiving the CAN bus message filling in the 64-byte wide **CAN Receive Buffer**.

2. When the message has been received and stored, the hardware generates interrupt 3 (**swCANMsgReceived**) and sets the read value of bit 1 of the control register to 1 to indicate that a message is available.

3. The software is expected to either poll bit 1 of the control register or install an interrupt service routine to read the message.

4. Once the software has read the message, it is expected to write a 0 value to bit 1. The hardware ignores this value, but it serves as a flag to the software.

Capturing interaction metadata as appropriate

The proper way to interpret the bits of the flow properties and the ordering and timing of actions to properly interact over the interface constitutes the metadata of interest. To this end, I created a set of stereotypes for this purpose and put them into a **handoff profile** (*Table 4.5*). Most of these stereotypes have tags to represent metadata of interest about the element, but some stereotypes are simply used to identify a "special kind of thing." There is some redundancy in the stereotype tags to allow a degree of flexibility in modeling the necessary information:

Stereotype	Applicable to	Tag	Description
bitmapped	Argument, Attribute/Value Property, Call Operation, Class/Block, Event, Flow/Flow Property/ Item Flow, Object/Part, Operation, Reception, Triggered Operation	bit_0	Interpretation and use, incl. Read, Write, or Read/Write
		bit_1	Interpretation and use, incl. Read, Write, or Read/Write
		bit_2	Interpretation and use, incl. Read, Write, or Read/Write
		bit_3	Interpretation and use, incl. Read, Write, or Read/Write
		bit_4	Interpretation and use, incl. Read, Write, or Read/Write
		bit_5	Interpretation and use, incl. Read, Write, or Read/Write
		bit_6	Interpretation and use, incl. Read, Write, or Read/Write
		bit_7	Interpretation and use, incl. Read, Write, or Read/Write
		bit_8	Interpretation and use, incl. Read, Write, or Read/Write
		bit_9	Interpretation and use, incl. Read, Write, or Read/Write

Stereotype	Applicable to	Tag	Description
		`bit_10`	Interpretation and use, incl. Read, Write, or Read/Write
		`bit_11`	Interpretation and use, incl. Read, Write, or Read/Write
		`bit_12`	Interpretation and use, incl. Read, Write, or Read/Write
		`bit_13`	Interpretation and use, incl. Read, Write, or Read/Write
		`bit_14`	Interpretation and use, incl. Read, Write, or Read/Write
		`bit_15`	Interpretation and use, incl. Read, Write, or Read/Write
		`Number_ Of_Bits`	Which bits are valid
		`Start_Ad- dress`	Memory map starting address
		`Tim- ing_Con- straints`	Timing and delays in use
		`Usage`	Description of the use of the register overall

Stereotype	Applicable to	Tag	Description
bytema-pped	Argument, Attribute/Value Property, Call Operation, Class/Block, Event, Flow/Flow Property/ Item Flow, Object/Part, Operation, Reception, Triggered Operation	Endianism	Big or little endian
		Format	How to interpret the collection bytes
		Number_ Of_Bytes	How many bytes are included in the value
		Start_Ad-dress	Memory map starting address
		Starting_ Byte_Num-ber	Index into a larger array, if necessary
		Tim-ing_Con-straints	Timing and delays in use
		Units	If appropriate, units represented by the value
		Usage	Description of the use of the register overall
inter-rupt-mapped	Call Operation, Event, Operation, Reception	Byte_ Width	Byte width of arguments (if any)
		Data_Ad-dress	Location of arguments (if any)
		Data_ Field_ Type	Format/interpretation of arguments (if any)
		Inter-rupt_num-ber	Interrupt vector #
		Usage	What the interrupt indicates

Stereotype	Applicable to	Tag	Description
`memory-mapped`	Argument, Attribute/Value Property, Call Operation, Class/Block, Event, Flow/Flow Property/ Item Flow, Object/Part, Operation, Reception, Triggered Operation	`Bitmap`	Internal format of the memory-mapped item
		`Numer_Of_Bytes`	Size (in bytes) of the memory-mapped item
		`Range_High`	High end of range (if continuous)
		`Range_low`	Low end of range (if continuous)
		`Start_Ad-dress`	Location of first element in the memory map
		`Tim-ing_Con-straints`	Timeliness constraints on use
		`Usage`	Description of the use of the element
`digital-Voltage`	Attribute/Value Property, Class/Block, Reception, Operation, Event, Object/Part	`Usage`	How to interpret different voltage levels
`ee_hy_in-terface`	Attribute/Value property, Argument, Call Operation, Class/Block, Object/Part, Operation, Reception, Triggered Operation	`<none>`	Indicates this interface is between electronics and hydraulics

Stereotype	Applicable to	Tag	Description
ee_me_interface	Attribute/Value property, Argument, Call Operation, Class/Block, Object/Part, Operation, Reception, Triggered Operation	<none>	Indicates this interface is between electronics and mechanical parts
electro-hydraulic	Attribute/Value Property, Class/Block, Object/Part, Operation, Reception	<none>	Indicates this element is composed of integrated electronics and hydraulics
electronics	Attribute/Value Property, Class/Block, Object/Part, Operation, Reception	<none>	Indicates this element is implemented in electronics
hydraulic	Attribute/Value Property, Class/Block, Object/Part, Operation, Reception	<none>	Indicates this element is implemented in hydraulics
mechanics	Attribute/Value Property, Class/Block, Object/Part, Operation, Reception	<none>	Indicates this element is implemented in mechanics

Stereotype	Applicable to	Tag	Description
`physical-Realiza-tion`	Dependency	`<none>`	Relates a logical element (target) to its physical realization (source)
`software`	Attribute/Value Property, Class/Block, Object/Part, Operation, Reception	`<none>`	Indicates this element is implemented in software
`staticMe-chanical`	Association, Link/Connector	`<none>`	Indicates that this relation signifies a mechanical linkage that does not convey a flow (for example, a static connection, such as bolting something together)
`sw_ee_in-terface`	Attribute/Value property, Argument, Call Operation, Class/Block, Object/Part, Operation, Reception, Triggered Operation	`<none>`	Indicates this is an interface between software and electronic elements
`voltagem-apped`	Attribute/Value Property, Flow/Flow Property/ Item Flow	`<none>`	Indicates this element represents values via voltage levels

Table 4.5 – Some useful handoff stereotypes

We will use these stereotypes to model relevant metadata for the interfaces in our model. The flow properties and event receptions in the interface blocks in *Figure 4.35* are elaborated and filled out in *Table 4.6*:

Interface	Feature	Feature Type	Tag	Value
iEE_ME_ Resistance	`drive_train_con-nection`	FlowProperty	`Direc-tion`	Bidirectional.
iSW_EE_ Comm	`CAN_control_reg-ister`	FlowProperty	`bit_0`	SW Read: 0 = data may be written to send to buffer; 1 = buffer is in use. SW Write: 0 = no effect, 1 = signal for electronics to send message.
iSW_EE_ Comm	`CAN_control_reg-ister`	FlowProperty	`bit_1`	SW Read 0 = no new message, 1=new message in CAN receive buffer. SW Write: 0 = value saved to display on next read (otherwise ignored by electronics).
iSW_EE_ Comm	`CAN_control_reg-ister`	FlowProperty	`Direc-tion`	Bidirectional.
iSW_EE_ Comm	`CAN_control_reg-ister`	FlowProperty	`Start_ Address`	A000: A0020.
iSW_EE_ Comm	`CAN_control_reg-ister`	FlowProperty	`Usage`	Controls/indicates status of CAN message flow.

Interface	Feature	Feature Type	Tag	Value
iSW_EE_Comm	CANReceiveBuffer	FlowProperty	Direc-tion	In
iSW_EE_Comm	CANReceiveBuffer	FlowProperty	Format	Defined by the CAN Bus standard
iSW_EE_Comm	CANReceiveBuffer	FlowProperty	Start_Address	A000: 0100
iSW_EE_Comm	CANReceiveBuffer	FlowProperty	Start-ing_Byte_Number	0
iSW_EE_Comm	CANReceiveBuffer	FlowProperty	Usage	Electronics writes the values to the buffer and notifies the SW when the complete message is stored
iSW_EE_Comm	CANSendBuffer	FlowProperty	Direc-tion	Out
iSW_EE_Comm	CANSendBuffer	FlowProperty	Format	Defined by the CAN Bus standard
iSW_EE_Comm	CANSendBuffer	FlowProperty	Start_Address	A000: 1200
iSW_EE_Comm	CANSendBuffer	FlowProperty	Usage	SW writes the CAN message to be sent and then noti-fies the electronics to send the mes-sage via the CAN Control Register. Electronics notifies the software when the send is com-plete.

Interface	Feature	Feature Type	Tag	Value
iSW_EE_Comm	swCANMsgReceived	Reception	Interrupt_number	3
iSW_EE_Comm	swCANMsgReceived	Reception	Usage	Electronics generates this interrupt to indicate that a message has been received and is available in the CAN receive buffer.
iSW_EE_Comm	swCANMsgSent	Reception	Interrupt_number	2
iSW_EE_Comm	swCANMsgSent	Reception	Usage	Electronics generates interrupt #2 to indicate that the commanded CAN message has been sent
iSW_EE_Control	control_register	FlowProperty	bit_0	SW WO (Write Only). 0 = do not provide resistance, 1 = provide resistance
iSW_EE_Control	control_register	FlowProperty	bit_1	SW RO (Read Only). 0 = no error in resistance, 1 = error
iSW_EE_Control	control_register	FlowProperty	bit_2	SW RO (Read Only). 0 = no pedal position error, 1 = pedal position error

Interface	Feature	Feature Type	Tag	Value
iSW_EE_ Control	`control_register`	FlowProperty	`bit_3`	SW RO (Read Only). 0 = no rider power measurement error, 1 = rider power measurement error
iSW_EE_ Control	`control_register`	FlowProperty	`Direc-tion`	Bidirectional
iSW_EE_ Control	`control_register`	FlowProperty	`Number_ Of_Bits`	4
iSW_EE_ Control	`control_register`	FlowProperty	`Start_ Address`	0xA000 0001
iSW_EE_ Control	`control_register`	FlowProperty	`Tim-ing_Con-straints`	None
iSW_EE_ Control	`control_register`	FlowProperty	`Usage`	Bit 0 enables/ disables power measurement and delivery. Other bits provide error indicators.
iSW_EE_ Control	`pedal_position`	FlowProperty	`Direc-tion`	In
iSW_EE_ Control	`pedal_position`	FlowProperty	`Numer_ Of_Bytes`	1
iSW_EE_ Control	`pedal_position`	FlowProperty	`Start_ Address`	A000: 0002
iSW_EE_ Control	`pedal_position`	FlowProperty	`Start-ing_ Byte_ Number`	0

Interface	Feature	Feature Type	Tag	Value
iSW_EE_ Control	pedal_position	FlowProperty	Units	Each value corresponds to 1/256 of a circle
iSW_EE_ Control	pedal_position	FlowProperty	Usage	SW RO (Read Only). Read the value to get the pedal position
iSW_EE_ Control	pedal_speed	FlowProperty	Direc- tion	In
iSW_EE_ Control	pedal_speed	FlowProperty	Numer_ Of_Bytes	1
iSW_EE_ Control	pedal_speed	FlowProperty	Start_ Address	A000 0004
iSW_EE_ Control	pedal_speed	FlowProperty	Units	Each value corresponds to 1/1,608 radians/min. (Maximum of 256 revs/ min.)
iSW_EE_ Control	pedal_speed	FlowProperty	Usage	SW RO (Read Only). Read this value to get the current velocity of the pedals
iSW_EE_ Control	power	FlowProperty	Direc- tion	In
iSW_EE_ Control	power	FlowProperty	Units	0 = no resistance, 0xFFFF = max. power (0.046 W per step)

Interface	Feature	Feature Type	Tag	Value
iSW_EE_Control	`power`	FlowProperty	`Usage`	SW RO (Read Only). Read the value of the power applied to the pedal by the rider
iSW_EE_Control	`resistance`	FlowProperty	`Direc-tion`	Out
iSW_EE_Control	`resistance`	FlowProperty	`Format`	16-bit value
iSW_EE_Control	`resistance`	FlowProperty	`Number_Of_Bytes`	2
iSW_EE_Control	`resistance`	FlowProperty	`Start_Address`	A000: 0006
iSW_EE_Control	`resistance`	FlowProperty	`Start-ing_Byte_Number`	0
iSW_EE_Control	`resistance`	FlowProperty	`Units`	0 = no resistance, 0xFFFF = max. resistance (18.3 N per step)
iSW_EE_Control	`resistance`	FlowProperty	`Usage`	SW WO (Write Only). Specify the resistance to be applied by the rider to the pedal

Table 4.6 – Power train deployment interface metadata

Grouping interactions across facets into interfaces

We have already incrementally added the interface block features directly into the interface blocks, so this step has already been done!

Negotiating the interface details among interface stakeholders

Now that we have defined the interface blocks and their features (flow properties and event receptions) and characterized them with metadata, the stakeholders can meet to review and negotiate the interface details. The stakeholders in this case include representatives from systems, software, electronics, and mechanical engineering. The interface will define a kind of contract that all parties agree to honor.

Storing the agreed-upon interfaces in configuration management

The defined interfaces can now be baselined in configuration management. All parties agree to uphold those interfaces. Should downstream work demonstrate inadequacies or identify a problem with the interface, the relevant stakeholders can meet again, renegotiate the interface definition, and get back to engineering.

5
Demonstration of Meeting Needs: Verification and Validation

This chapter is all about demonstrating that the system meets the needs of the stakeholders. There are a number of aspects to this, such as providing important information necessary for certification and system maintenance (for example, traceability), showing stakeholders what's in the work product(s) (walk-throughs and simulations), supporting analysis (simulation and analysis), demonstrating that the design satisfies the requirements (verification), and showing that the system meets the needs of the stakeholders (validation). This is not done just at the end but frequently or even continuously throughout the systems development process.

The recipes in this chapter are as follows:

- Model simulation
- Model-based testing
- Computable constraint modeling
- Traceability
- Effective reviews and walk-throughs
- Test-driven modeling

George Box famously said that *all models are wrong, but some are useful*. Although he was speaking of statistical models, the same can be said for MBSE models. In the systems world, models are approximations of real systems and contain subsets of their properties.

First, all models are abstractions in that they focus on details of the system of relevance but completely ignore all other aspects. Therefore, the models are *wrong* because they don't include *all aspects* of the system, just the ones we find of interest.

Second, all models are abstractions in that they represent information at different levels of detail. When we model fluid flow in a water treatment system, we don't model the interactions at the molecular level. Rather, we model fluid dynamics and not the interaction of electric fields of atoms bound together into molecules, let alone getting into quantum physics. Therefore, the models are *wrong*, because they don't model the electrodynamics of the particles and the interaction of the quantum fields of the elementary particles.

Third, all models are abstractions; they represent the information at a level of precision that we think is adequate for the need. If we model the movement of an aircraft rudder control surface, we may very well decide that position, represented by 3 significant digits and with an accuracy of $\pm$ 0.5 degrees, meets our needs. Therefore, our models are wrong because we don't model to 6 significant figures and ±0.0005 degrees of accuracy, or 9 significant digits.

Note

You can read about George Box here:

Box, G. E. P. (1976), *"Science and Statistics"* (http://www-sop.inria.fr/members/Ian.Jermyn/philosophy/writings/Boxonmaths.pdf), *Journal of the American Statistical Association* (https://en.wikipedia.org/wiki/Journal_of_the_American_Statistical_Association), 71 (356): 791799

You get the idea. Models are not exact replicas of reality. They are simplified characterizations that represent the aspects in a (hopefully) useful conceptual framework with (also hopefully) enough precision to meet the need.

So, questions arise when considering a model:

1. Is the model *right*?

2. What does *right* mean?

3. How do we *know*?

We will try to provide some practical answers to these questions in this chapter. The answers will vary a bit depending on the kind of model being examined.

Let's address the second question first: what does *right* mean? If we agree with the premise that all good models have a well-defined scope and purpose, then *right* surely means that it addresses that scope with the necessary precision and correctness to meet its purpose. If we look at a stakeholder requirements model, then the requirements it contains would clearly, unambiguously, and completely state the needs of the stakeholders with respect to the system being specified. If we develop an architecture, then the architectural structures it defines meet the system requirements and the needs of the stakeholder (or will, once it's developed) in an "optimal" way. If we develop a set of interfaces, then we describe all the important and relevant interactions (with all applicable details) of that system with its actors.

If we use that answer for question #2, then the answer to the first question pertains to the veracity of the statement that the model at hand meets its scope and purpose. Subsequently, the answer to the third question is that we generate evidence that confirms that the answer to question #1 is poitive.

Verification and validation

Most engineers will agree with the general statement that verification means the *demonstration that a system meets its requirements* while validation means the *demonstration that the system meets the need.* In my consulting work, I take this slightly further (*Figure 5.1*):

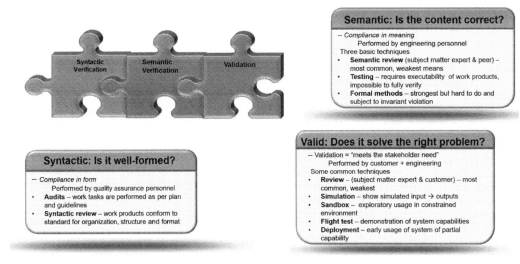

Figure 5.1 – Verification and validation core concepts

In my mind, there are two kinds of verification: syntactic and semantic. *Syntactic verification* is also known as *compliance in form*, because it seeks to demonstrate that the model is well-formed, not necessarily that it makes sense. This means that the model complies with the project modeling standards guidelines. These guidelines typically define how the model should be organized, what information it should contain, the naming conventions that are used, the action language used for primitive actions, and so on. Every project should have a modeling guidelines standard in place and it is against such a standard that the syntactic well-formedness of a model may be verified.

Semantic verification is about demonstrating that the content is correct; for this reason, it is also known as *compliance in meaning*. It is possible to have well-formed sentences that are either incorrect at best or nonsense at worst. There is even a law of Douglass about this:

> *Any language rich enough to say something useful is also expressive enough to state utter nonsense.*
>
> - *Law of Douglass, #60*

The reason this is important becomes clear when we look at the techniques of semantic verification (see *Figure 5.1*): semantic review, testing, and formal (mathematical) analysis.

If we have vague or imprecise models, we only have the first technique for ascertaining correctness: 'Let's look at it'. To be clear, a review is valuable and can provide insights into subtle issues or problems with a model, however, it is the weakest form of verification. The problem is largely one of vigilance. In my experience, humans are pretty good at finding issues for only a few hours at most before their ability to find problems degrades. You've probably had the experience of starting a review meeting with lots of energy but by the time the afternoon rolls around, you're thinking "kill me now." Reviews definitely add value to the verification process but they are insufficient. There's a reason we don't say "we can trust the 1 million lines of code for the nuclear reactor because Joe looked at it really hard."

> **Note**
>
> See `https://www.bruce-douglass.com/papers` for downloadable examples of MBSE and MDD guidelines. For the current state of the **Laws of Douglass**, see `https://www.bruce-douglass.com/geekosphere`.

The second technique for performing verification is to test it. Testing basically means that we identify a set of test cases – a set of inputs with specific values, a sequence, and timing and well-defined expected outputs or outcomes – and then apply them to the system of interest to see if it performs as expected. This approach is more expensive than just looking at the system, but yields far superior results in terms of demonstration of correctness and identifying differences between what you want and what you have. Testing fundamentally requires *executability* and this is crucial in the MBSE domain. If we want to apply testing to our model – *and we should* – then it means that our model must be specified using a language that is inherently precise, must use a method that supports executability, and must use a tool environment that supports execution. One issue with testing is that it isn't possible to fully test a system; there are always an essentially infinite set of combinations of inputs, values, sequences, and timings. You can get arbitrarily close to complete coverage at increasing levels of cost and effort, but you can never close the gap completely.

The third technique for verification is applying formal methods. This requires rendering the system in a mathematically precise language, such as Z or predicate logic, and then applying the rules of formal mathematics to demonstrate universals about the system. This is arguably the strongest form of verification but it suffers from two problems: It is incredibly hard to do, in general – PhDs and lots of effort are required; and secondly, the approach is sensitive to invariant violations. That means that the analysis must make some assumptions, such as *the power is always available* or *the user doesn't do this stupid thing* and if you violate those assumptions, you can't trust the results of the analysis. You can always incorporate any specific assumption into your analysis, but that just means there are other assumptions being made. Gödel was right.

> **Note**
>
> Kurt Gödel, 1931, "Über formal unentscheidbare Sätze der Principia Mathematica und verwandter Systeme, I", Monatshefte für Mathematik und Physik, v. 38 n. 1, pp. 173–198.

In my experience, the best approach for semantic verification is a combination of all three approaches – review, test, and analyze.

Verification is not the same as *validation*. To begin with, *valid* means that the model reflects or meets the true needs of the stakeholders, even if those needs differ from what is stated in the system requirements. If meeting the system requirements is demonstrated through *verification*, then meeting the stakeholders' needs is demonstrated through *validation*. For the most part, this is historically done with the creation of stakeholder requirements, and by then reviewing the work products that describe the system. There are a couple of problems with that.

First, there is an *air gap* between the stakeholder requirements and meeting the stakeholder needs. Many a system has failed because, while it met the requirements, the system didn't meet the true needs. This is primarily why Agile methods stress continuous customer involvement in the development process. If it can be discovered early that the requirements are not a true representation of the customer's needs, then the development can be redirected and the requirements can be amended.

In traditional methods, customer involvement is limited to reviews of work products. In government programs, a **System Requirements Review (SRR)**, **Preliminary Design Review (PDR)**, and **Critical Design Review (CDR)** are common milestones to ensure the program is "on track." These are almost always appraisals of many, many pages of descriptions, with all of the problems inherent in reviews previously mentioned. However, if you build executable models, then that execution – even if it is a simulated environment – can demonstrate how the system will operate in the stakeholder's operational context and provide better information about system validity.

In this chapter, I will use the terms *computable* and *executable* when referring to well-formed models. When I say *computable model*, I mean a model that performs a computation, such as *F=ma*. In that equation, given two values, the system can compute the third, regardless of which two values are given. An *executable* model is a computable model in which the computation has a specific direction. These are not always the same; it is impossible to unscramble that egg or unexplode that bomb – these are inherently irreversible processes.

This chapter contains recipes that provide approaches to demonstrate the correctness of your models. We'll talk about simulation when it comes to creating models, developing computational models for analysis, performing reviews, and creating system test cases for the system test cases.

Model simulation

When we test an aircraft design, one way is to build the aircraft and see if it falls out of the sky. In this section, I'm not referring to testing the final resulting system. Rather, I mean verifying the model of the system before detailed design, implementation, and manufacturing. SysML has some expressive views for representing and capturing structure and behavior and the Rhapsody SysML tool has some powerful features to execute and debug models as well as visualize and control that execution. There are other tools with similar capabilities. Notably, the Cameo Magic Draw Simulation Toolkit provides execution means almost as powerful as Rhapsody.

The Rhapsody modeling tool performs simulation by generating software source code from the model in well-defined ways and automatically compiling and executing that code. Rhapsody can instrument this code to interact with Rhapsody itself so that the tool can visualize the model execution graphically and provide control of the execution. The Cameo Magic Draw Simulation Toolkit does a simulation of the model semantics. In my experience, creating executable models in Magic Draw requires significantly more work than in Rhapsody, but not impossibly so. I have come across a number of limitations and a few out-right defects in the Cameo Simuation Toolkit, but for the most part, it is a powerful and useful way to understand and verify Cameo Magic Draw models. This means that SysML models can be simulated, executed, and verified in a relatively straightforward fashion, even by non-programmers.

Simulation can be applied to any model that has behavioral aspects. I commonly construct executable requirements models, something discussed in *Chapter 2, System Specification*. I do this one use case at a time so that each use case has its own executable model stored in its own package. Architectural models can be executed as well to demonstrate their compliance with the use case models or to verify architectural specifications. Any SysML model or model subset can be executed as long as it can be specified using well-defined activity or state semantics.

Purpose

The purpose of model simulation is to explore, understand, or verify the behavior of a set of elements defined within the model. This simulation can be used to evaluate the correctness of a model, to explore what-if cases, or to understand how elements collaborate within a context.

Inputs and preconditions

The model is defined with a purpose and scope, and the purpose and intent for simulation has been identified.

Outputs and postconditions

The results of the simulation are the computation results of running the simulation. These can be captured in values stored in the model, as captured diagrams (such as animated sequence diagrams), or as outputs and outcomes produced by the simulation.

How to do it...

Figure 5.2 shows the workflow for performing a general-purpose model-based simulation. Given the powerful modeling environment, it is generally straightforward to do, provided that you adhere to the tooling constraints:

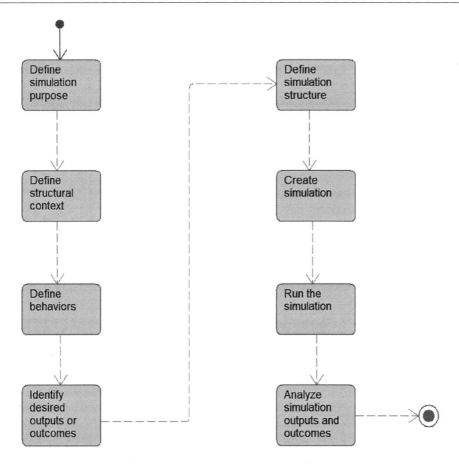

Figure 5.2 – Model simulation workflow

It is common to have many different simulations, to achieve different purposes and results, within a systems model. In Rhapsody, each simulation can be thought of as a *component* in the sense of a generated and compiled executable; it is common to have many such components within a single MBSE model.

Define simulation purpose

It is imperative that you understand *why* you're performing model simulation in order to get a useful outcome. I like to phrase this as *what does success smell like?* in order to ensure that you're going after the kind of results that will address your concerns. It matters because the simulations you create will vary depending upon what you want to achieve.

Common purposes of model simulation include the following:

- Ensure the completeness and correctness of a set of requirements traced to a use case.
- Demonstrate the adequacy of a set of interfaces.
- Explore behavioral options for some part of a design model.
- Prove compliance of an architecture with a set of requirements.
- Reveal emergent behaviors and properties of a complex design.
- Verify a system specification.
- Validate a system architecture.
- Explore the consequences of various input value, timing, and sequence variations ("what-if" analyses).

Define structural context

The structural context for the model identifies the structural elements that will exhibit behavior – or be used by structural elements that do – during the simulation. This includes blocks, use cases, and actors, along with their structural properties, such as value and flow properties, ports, and the relations among the structural elements.

Define behaviors

At a high-level, behavioral specifications such as activity and state models provide the behavior of the system context as a whole or of the individual structural elements. At a detailed level, operations and activities specify primitive behavioral elements, often expressed in an action language, such as C, C++, Java, or Ada.

It should be noted that the SysML views that contribute directly to the simulation and code generation are the activity and state diagrams, and any action language code snippets put into the action and operation definitions. Sequence diagrams, being only partially constructive, do not specify behavior; rather, they depict specific examples of it.

Identify desired outputs or outcomes

In line with the identification of the simulation purpose, it is important to specify what kind of output or outcome is desired. This might be a set of output interactions demonstrating correctness, captured as a set of automatically generated sequences (so-called **animated sequence diagrams**). Or it might be the demonstration that an output computation is correct under different conditions. It might even be "see what happens when I do *this*." Clarity in expectation yields satisfaction in outcomes.

Define simulation structure

The simulation structure refers to the elements used to create the simulation as well as the simulation configuration or compiler options to be used.. In Rhapsody, this manifests as the set of packages and elements to be included in the GMR (short for **Generate-Make-Run**) process. This might also include external model libraries, compiled code libraries, or even manually developed source code files, depending on the need.

Rhapsody has its own notion of a *component*. It is an executable constructed from a set of source elements. Each component may in turn have a number of *configurations*. Each configuration can specify different execution target environments including what instances you want to create at the start ("initial instances"), external files to include in the executable, the level of instrumentation, the target operating system, and compiler selection and options. For systems model simulation, it is most common to set the instrumentation mode to **Animation** and the target operating system to be the same as the modeling environment (generally Windows). The **Animation** setting means that Rhapsody will add code into the generated application to communicate back to the Rhapsody tool during simulation so that Rhapsody can visualize the execution for you using diagram animation.

It should be noted that Rhapsody supports code generation for a large number of target real-time operating systems, but their use is generally out of scope for system simulation. Targeting RTOSes is common for software design and implementation modeling, however.

Create simulation

Creating the simulation is easily done by clicking on the GMR button (or the **Simulate** button, depending on the edition in use) in Rhapsody. This runs the model compiler (generating the code), runs the source code compiler, and then runs the resulting executable. There are more options than this, but this use is the most common. Of course, it's easy only when you've done it right. If the model or primitive actions are ill-formed, you'll have to track down and repair the defects before your simulation will run.

Run the simulation

Once created, the executable can be run as many times and under as many different circumstances as you desire.

Analyze simulation outputs and outcomes

The point of running a simulation is to create some output or outcome. Once this is done, it can be examined to see what conclusions can be drawn. Are the requirements complete? Were the interfaces adequate? Did the architecture perform as expected? What behavior emerged under the examined conditions?

Example

The Pegasus model offers many opportunities to perform valuable simulations. In this case, we'll simulate one of the use cases from *Chapter 2, System Specification*. The use case was used as an example to illustrate the *Functional analysis with scenarios* recipe.

The mechanisms for defining simulations are tool-specific. The example here is simulated in Rhapsody. If you're using a different SysML tool, then the exact means of defining and executing your model will be different.

Define simulation purpose

The purpose of this simulation is to identify mistakes that are gaps in the requirements represented by the use case.

Define structural context

The execution context for the simulation is shown in *Figure 2.8*. This internal block diagram shows the connected instances of the **prtTrainingApp::aEBG_TrainingApp** and **prtRider::aEBG_Rider** actor blocks and the instance of the **itsUc_EmulatedBasicGearing:Uc::EmulateBasicGearing** use case block.

This model uses the canonical model organization structure identified in the *Organizing your models* recipe from *Chapter 1, Basics of Agile Systems Modeling* (see *Figure 1.35*). In line with this recipe, the detailed organization of the model is shown in *Figure 5.3*:

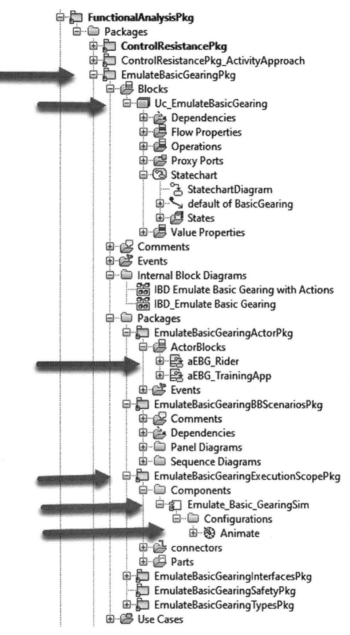

Figure 5.3 – Organization of simulation elements

The **FunctionalAnalysisPkg** package contains a package per use case for every use case being analyzed. In our case, the first arrow in the figure indicates the **EmulateBasicGearingPkg** package for the analysis of the use case in this example. The next two arrows point to the primary structural elements: the use case block and the actor blocks. The latter is held in a nested package named **EmulateBasicGearingActorPkg**.

Define behaviors

The use case block state machine is shown in *Figure 2.9*. This state machine specifies the behavior of the system while executing that use case. The state machine represents a concise and executable restatement of the requirements and is not a specification of the design of the system. *Figure 2.11* and *Figure 2.12* show the state machines for the actor blocks. Elaborating the behavior of the actors for the purpose of supporting simulation is known as *instrumenting the actors*. Actor instrumentation is non-normative (since the actors are external to our system and we're not designing them) and is only done to facilitate simulation.

Identify desired outputs or outcomes

The desired outcome is to either identify missing requirements by applying different test cases to the execution or to demonstrate that the requirements, as represented by the model, are adequate. To do this, we will generate animated sequence diagrams of different situations, examine the captured sequences, and validate with the customer that it meets their needs. We will also want to monitor the output values to ensure that the **Rider** inputs are processed properly and the correct information is sent to the **Training app**. Note that this is a low-fidelity simulation and doesn't emulate all the physics necessary to convert input **Rider** torque and cadence into output resistance and to take into account **Rider** weight, wind resistance, current speed, and incline. While that would be an interesting simulation, that is not our purpose here.

We want to ensure that the **Rider** can downshift and upshift within the gearing limits and this results in changing the internal gearing and the training app is notified. Further, as the **Rider** applies input power, the output torque should change; a bigger gear with the same input power should result in larger output torque. These relations are built into the model; applied torque and resistance are modeled as *flow properties*, while upshift and downshift are simulated with *increment gear* and *decrement gear* events. Further, the gearing (as measured in *gear inches*) should be limited to between a minimum of 30 and a maximum of 140, while a gear shift changes the gearing by a constant 5 gear inches, up or down.

For this simulation, the conditions we would evaluate include the following:

- The gearing is properly increased as we upshift.

- The gearing no longer increases if we try to upshift past the maximum gearing.

- The gearing is properly decreased as we downshift.

- The gearing no longer decreases if we try to downshift past the minimum gearing.

- For a given level of input force, the output resistance is increased as we upshift (although the correctness of the output resistance is not a concern here).

- For a given level of input force, the output resistance is decreased as we downshift (although the correctness of the output resistance is not a concern here).

Define simulation structure

Another nested package, named `EmulateBasicGearingExecutionScopePkg`, contains three things of interest with regard to the simulation structure. First, it contains the single component `Emulate_Basic_GearingSim`. This component specifies the scope of the model to include in the simulation. In this case, we have organized our model so that only `EmulateBasicGearingPkg` is needed (see *Figure 5.4*):

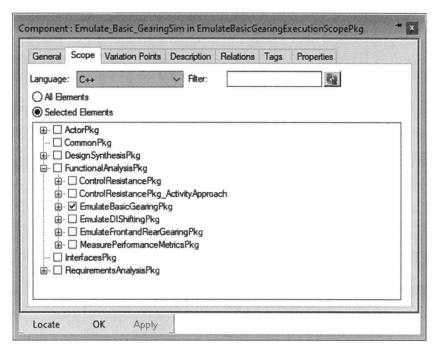

Figure 5.4 – Component settings

In Rhapsody, a component may have multiple configurations. That way, the same component can be used to generate executables that run in different environments, such as the host development environment and the target embedded platform environment, or with different levels of animation support. *Figure 5.5* shows the important settings for the **Animate** configuration: the **Instrumentation** level is set to **Animation**, the compiler is set to **Cygwin** C++ on the host development environment, and the default compiler switches are used:

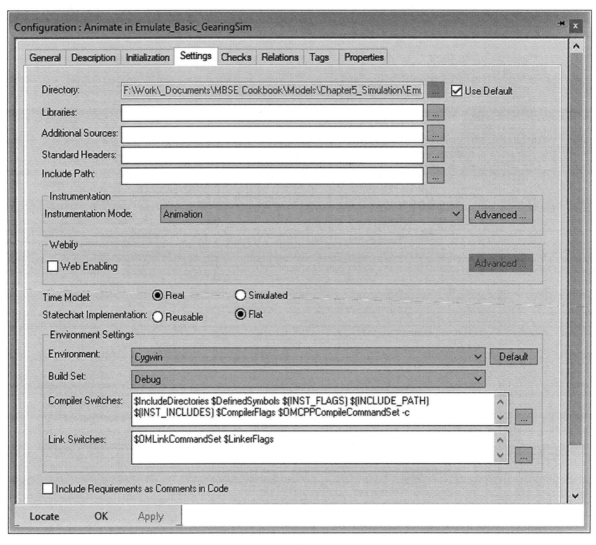

Figure 5.5 – Configuration settings

The other thing that this package contains is the *parts* or instances defined on the IBD (*Figure 2.8*).

Although not a part of the simulation structure *per se*, *Figure 2.13* shows a simple panel diagram used to visualize and input values and to enter events during the execution. Panel diagrams are not the only means Rhapsody provides to do this, but they are convenient.

Create simulation

Creating the simulation is a simple matter of clicking the **Generate/Make/Run (GMR)** button or using the menu option **Code | Generate** (which generates the code for the simulation), followed by **Code | Build** (which compiles and builds it). If the model checker, compiler, or linker discovers a problem, it will halt with an error message, and you'll have to go fix the issue and retry.

Run the simulation

After successful construction of the executable, you can run it. If you used the **GMR** button, it will run automatically. With Rhapsody, the executable starts in a *paused* state, waiting for you to click on the **Go** or **Go Idle** buttons in the **Execution Toolbar**. If you click the **Go** button, the application will start and open the control panel we added for the visualization and control of the simulation.

Because we want a record of the interaction of the structural elements during the execution, we'll start up an *animated sequence diagram* (**Tools > Animated Sequence Diagram**) to start with. We'll use one of the original sequence diagrams as a starting template, as they already have the lifelines of interest in place.

The Rhapsody tool at this point looks like *Figure 5.6* with the panel diagram (upper left), animated state machine view of the use case (lower left), and animated sequence diagram (right) shown:

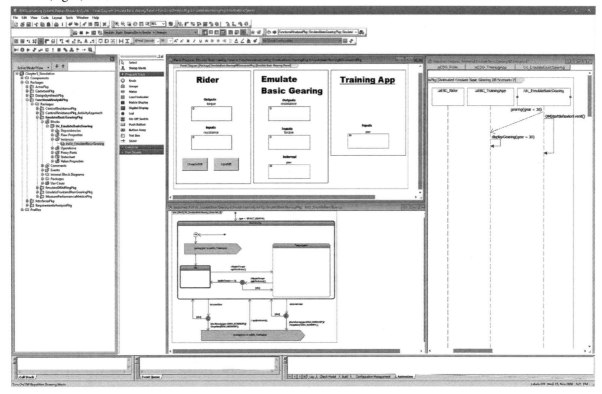

Figure 5.6 – Starting the simulation

Analyze simulation outputs and outcomes

We capture the inputs and outputs using a number of simulation runs. In the first such run, we initialize the running simulation to output a resistance of 100 and the rider to provide a power value of 200. Then we augment the gearing and see that it increases. Further, the training app is updated with the gearing as it changes. We see that in the animated sequence diagram in *Figure 5.7*:

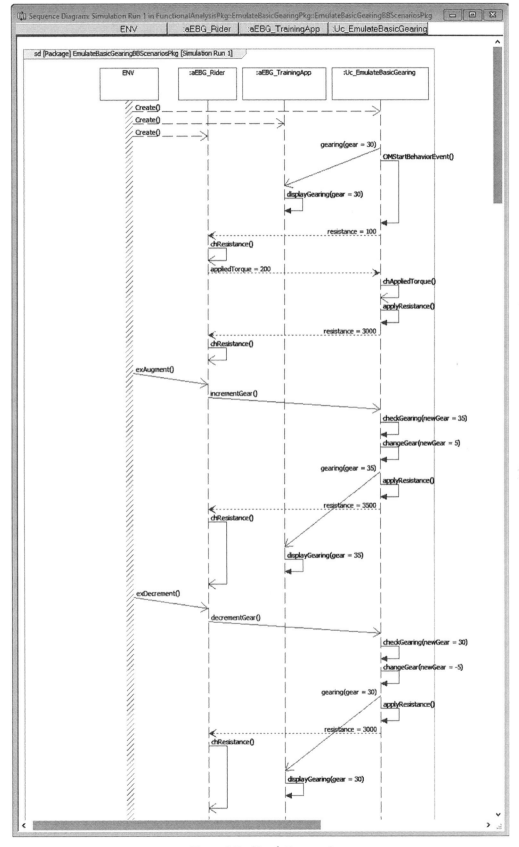

Figure 5.7 – Simulation run 1

Since the system starts in the lowest gear, the next simulation run should demonstrate that an attempt to downshift below the minimum gearing should result in no change. That's what we see in *Figure 5.8*; notice the coloring of the animated state machine shows the [else] path was taken and the gearing was not decremented. This is also to be seen in the gear value for the **Emulate Basic Gearing** panel (highlighted with arrows):

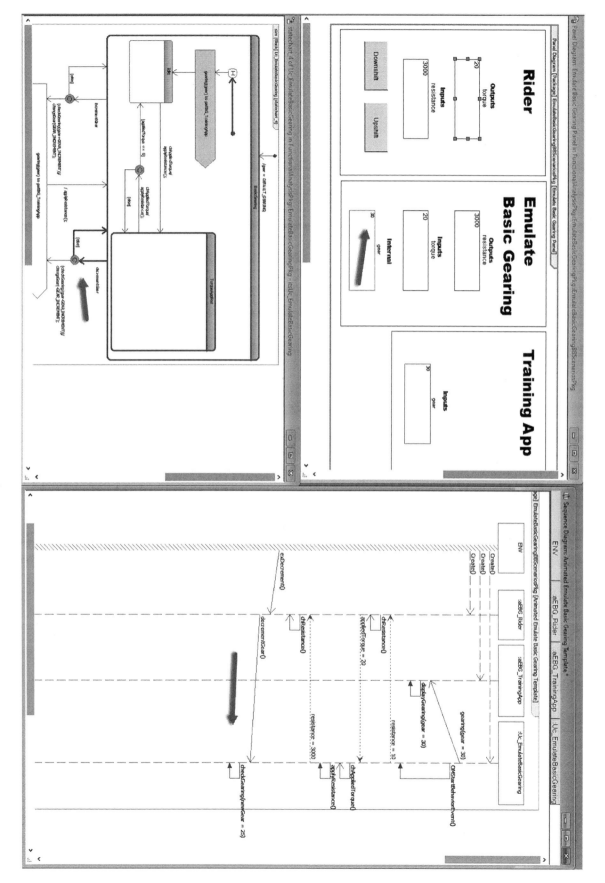

Figure 5.8 – Simulation run 2

In the last run shown here, we set the gearing to 135 and then augment it twice to try to exceed the maximum gearing of 140 gear inches. We should see the resistance value go up with the first upshift, and then not change with the second. This is in fact what we see in *Figure 5.9*.

I've marked relevant points in the figure. At point A, I set the current value of the gearing to 135 gear inches. At point B, the gearing is correctly augmented to 140, the maximum gearing. At point C, the state machine checks whether the current gearing can be augmented and finds that it cannot, so it rejects the request:

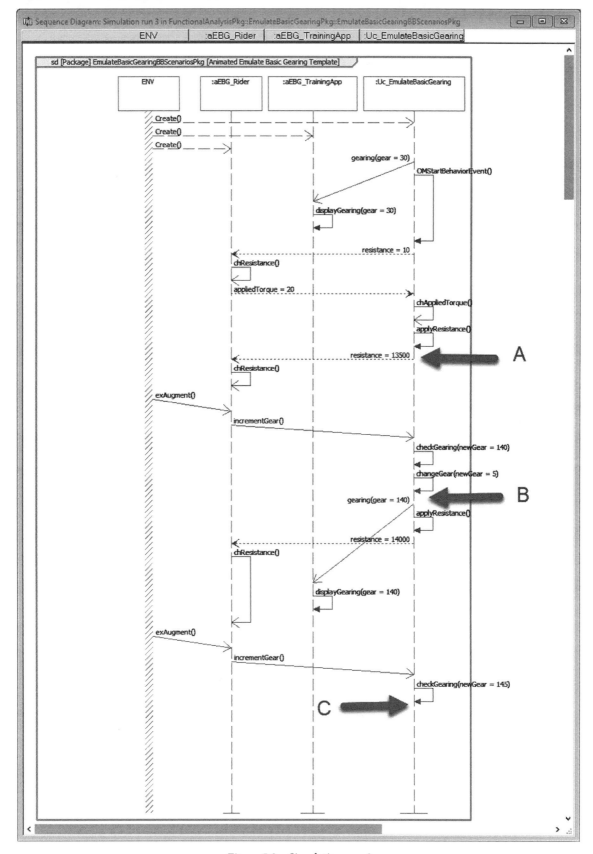

Figure 5.9 – Simulation run 3

We have achieved the desired outcome of the simulation by demonstrating that the requirements model correctly shifts up and down, stays within gearing limits, properly updates the output resistance as the gearing is changed, and the **Training App** is properly notified of the current gearing when it changes.

Model-based testing

If you agree that modeling brings value to engineering, then **model-based testing** (**MBT**) brings similar value to verification. To be clear, MBT doesn't limit itself to the testing of models. Rather, MBT is about using models to capture, manage, and apply test cases to a system, whether or not that system is model-based. In essence, MBT allows you to do the following:

- Define a test architecture, including a test context, test configuration, test components, the **System Under Test** (**SUT**), arbiter, and scheduler.

- Define test cases, using sequence diagrams (most commonly), activity diagrams, state machines, and code.

- Define test objectives.

Bringing the power of a model to bear the problems developing test architectures, defining test cases, and then performing the testing is compelling. This is especially true when applying it with a tool like Rhapsody, which provides such strong simulation and execution facilities.

While MBT can be informally applied, it does have a standard, the *UML Testing Profile*. The profile defines a standard way to model test concepts in UML (and therefore in SysML). *Figure 5.10* shows the basic meta-architecture of the profile. While it doesn't exactly represent what's in the profile, I believe it explains it a little better:

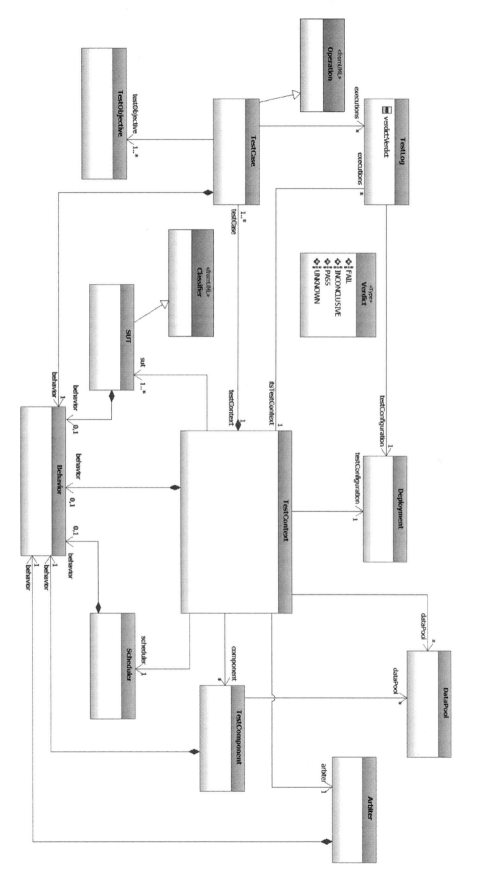

Figure 5.10 – UML Testing Profile meta-architecture

I don't want to spend too much time on the details of the profile definition; interested people can check out the standard itself or books on the topic such as *Model-Driven Testing* by Baker, et al. However, I do want to highlight some aspects.

First, note that a **Test Case** is a stereotype of UML's metaclass **operation**, and **Test Case** owns a **Behavior**. A Behavior may be represented in any standard form, including sequence, activity, or state diagrams. That means we can define a Test Case using the standard SysML behavioral representations.

The **Test Context** includes a set of **Test Cases**, and also a set (one or more) of SUTs. The SUT is a kind of **classifier**, from the UML metamodel; classifiers can be **blocks**, **use cases**, and **actors** (among other things, of course), which can be used in a context as singular design elements, composite elements such as subsystems, systems, or even an entire system context. SUTs themselves can, of course, have behavior. The **Test Log** records the executions of **Test Cases**, each of which includes a **Verdict**, an enumerated type.

> **Note**
>
> Refer to the following for further reading about model-based testing:
>
> ```
> https://www.omg.org/spec/UTP2/2.0/PDF
> ```
>
> ```
> https://www.amazon.com/Model-Driven-Testing-Using-
> UML-Profile/dp/3540725628/ref=sr_1_1?dchild
> =1&keywords=uml+testing+profile&qid=1606409327
> &sr=8-1
> ```

You can model these things directly in your model and build up your own Test Context, Test Cases, and so on. Rhapsody has the `TestConductor` add-on, which fully implements the *UML Testing Profile* standard, along with automation to assist in the development and execution of test cases. The Test Conductor tool is available from IBM but is developed by BTC Embedded Systems – a great bunch of people I've known for a long time. The tool is qualified under a number of standards, such as *DO-178C* (avionics) and *ISO-26262* (automotive). We won't use their tool in this recipe so you can see how to apply model-based testing in a general SysML tool, but if you're using Rhapsody, I encourage you to check out Test Conductor.

Purpose

The purpose of model-based testing is to verify the semantic correctness of a system under test by applying a set of test cases. This purpose includes the definition of the test architecture, the specification of the test cases, the generation of the outcomes, and the analysis of the verdict – all in a model-based fashion.

Inputs and preconditions

The preconditions include both a set of requirements and a system that purports to meet those requirements. The system may be a model of the system – such as a requirements or design model – or it may be the final delivered system.

Outputs and postconditions

The primary output of the recipe is a test log of a set of test executions, complete with pass/fail verdicts of success.

> **Note**
>
> Refer to this link for more details about BTC Embedded Systems, `https://www.btc-es.de/en`.

How to do it...

A model-based test flow (*Figure 5.11*) is pretty much the same as a normal test flow but the implementation steps are a bit different:

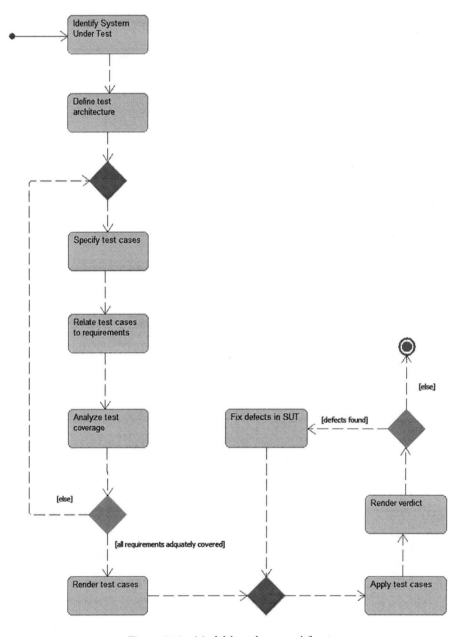

Figure 5.11 – Model-based test workflow

Identify SUT

The SUT is the system or system subset that we want to verify. This can be a use case functional analysis model, an architecture, a design, or an actual manufactured system. If it is a design, the SUT can include a single design element or a coherent set of collaborating design elements.

Define test architecture

The test architecture includes, at a minimum, the instance of the SUT and test components substituting for elements in the actual environment (test stubs). The test architecture can also include a test context (test manager), scheduler, and arbiter (to determine verdicts). These other test elements can be done manually by the tester but they can also be automated. The Rhapsody test conductor automagically creates executable architectural elements to fulfill these roles.

Specify test cases

Before we start to render the test cases themselves, we must specify the test cases. The test cases include the events the test architecture will introduce and include the values of data they will carry, their sequence and timing, and the expected output or outcome.

Relate test cases to requirements

I am a huge fan of *requirements-based testing*. I believe that all tests should ultimately try to verify the system against one or more requirements. This step in the recipe identifies one or more test cases for each requirement of the SUT. At the end, there should be no requirements that are not to be verified by at least one test case, and there should be no test cases for which there are no requirements.

Analyze test coverage

Test coverage is a deep topic that is well beyond the scope of this book. However, we will at least mention that coverage is important. Test coverage may be thought of in terms of the coverage of the specification (need) and coverage of the design (implementation). In terms of the coverage of the specification, we can think in terms of the coverage of the inputs (sources and events types, values, value fidelity, sequences, and timings) and outputs (targets and event types, values, sequences, accuracy, and timings).

Design coverage is different. Mostly, it is evaluated in terms of path coverage. This is best developed in safety-critical software testing standards such as DO-178 that talk about the following three levels of coverage:

- **Statement coverage**: Every statement should be executed in at least one test case.

- **Decision coverage**: Statement coverage plus each decision point branch should be taken

- **Modified condition/decision coverage (MC/DC)**.

In MC/DC, we have the following:

- Each entry and exit point is invoked.

- Each decision takes into account every possible outcome.

- Each condition in a decision is evaluated against every possible outcome.

- Each condition in a decision is independently evaluated as to how it affects the decision outcome.

> **Note**
>
> Refer to `https://my.rtca.org/NC__Product?id=a1B36000001IcmwEAC` or see `https://en.wikipedia.org/wiki/DO-178C` for a discussion on the DO-178C standard.

The point of the step is to ensure the adequacy of the testing given the set of requirements and the structure of the design.

Render test cases

In model-based testing, we have a number of options for test specification. The most common is to use sequence diagrams; since they are partially constructive, they are naturally suited to specify alternative interaction flows. The second most common approach is to specify multiple test paths using activity diagrams. The third is to specify the test cases with a state machine, a personal favorite. You can always write scripts (code) for the test cases, but as that isn't very model-based, we won't consider it here.

Apply test cases

The stage (test architecture) is set and the dialog (the test cases) has been written. Now comes the performance (test execution). In this step, the test cases are applied against the SUT in the context of the text architecture. The outcome of each test case is recorded in the **Test Log** along with a pass or fail verdict.

Render verdict

The overall verdict is a roll-up of the verdicts of the individual test cases. In general, an SUT is considered to pass the testing only when it passes *all* of the test cases.

Fix defects in SUT

If some test cases fail, that means that the SUT didn't generate the expected output or outcome. This can be either because the SUT, the test case, or the test architecture is in error. Before moving on, the defect should be fixed and the tests rerun. In some cases, it may be permissible to continue if non-critical tests fail. When I run Agile projects, the basic rule is that critical defects must be addressed before the iteration can be accepted, but non-critical defects are put into the backlog for a future iteration and the iteration can progress.

Example

In this example, we'll look at the portion of the architectural design of the Pegasus system that accepts inputs from the **Rider** to change gears and make sure that the gears are properly changed within the **Main Computing Platform**. To simplify the example, we won't look at the impact changing gears has on the delivered resistance.

Identify SUT

The system under design includes a few subsystems and some internal design elements. We are limiting ourselves to only design the part of the system related to the rider control of the gearing within those design elements. To show the element under test will take a few diagrams, so bear with me:

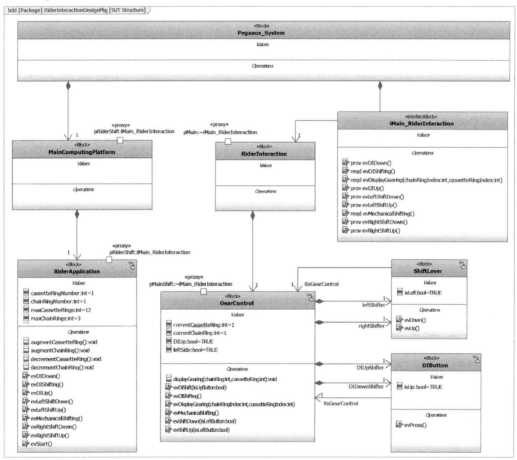

Figure 5.12 – SUT blocks

Figure 5.12 shows the blocks that together constitute the SUT: The **RiderInteraction** subsystem, which internally contains left and right **Shift Levers** and up and down **Digital Indexed (DI)** shift buttons. (**DI Button**) is one key part. The other key part is the **MainComputingPlatform**, which contains the **Rider Application**, which manages the gears. This diagram shows the blocks and their relevant properties.

This diagram doesn't depict the runtime connected structure well, so another diagram, *Figure 5.13*, shows how the instances connect:

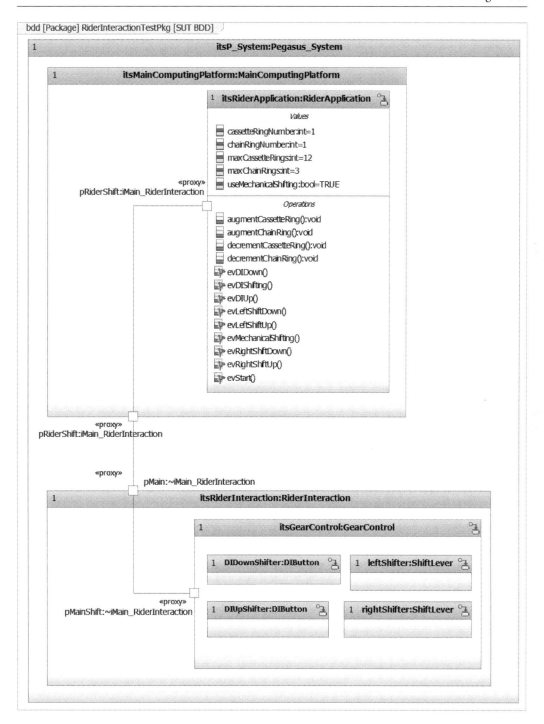

Figure 5.13 – Connected parts in the SUT

All of these blocks have state machines that specify their behavior. The **DI button** has the simplest state machine, as can be seen in *Figure 5.14*. As the Rider presses the **DI** button, it sends an **evDIShift** event to the **Gearing Control** instance. The event carries a *Boolean* parameter that specifies that it is the up (TRUE) or down (FALSE) button. The Gearing Control block initializes one of the **DI** buttons to be the up button and the other to be the down button:

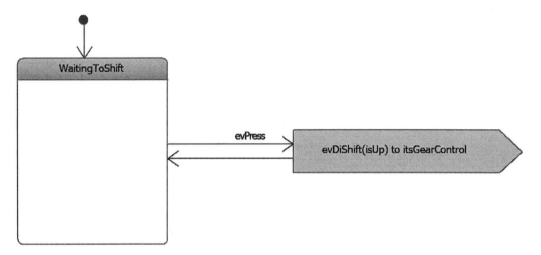

Figure 5.14 – DI button state machine

The **Shift Lever** state machine is only a little more complicated (*Figure 5.15*). The left **Shift Lever** controls the big chain ring and can either augment or decrement it; the right **Shift Lever** controls the cassette ring gear but works similarly. The state machine shows that either shift lever can send the **evShiftUp** or **eveShiftDown** event. As with the **evDIShift** event, these events also carry a parameter that identifies which lever (left (TRUE) or **right (FALSE)**) is sending the event:

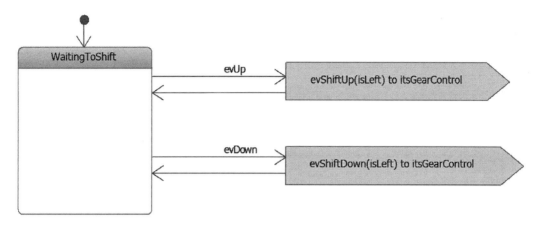

Figure 5.15 – Shift Lever state machine

The **Gear Control** state machine is more complex, as you can see in *Figure 5.16*. It receives events from the left and right **Shift Levers** and the up and down **DI** Buttons. It must use the passed parameters to determine which events to send on to the **RiderApplication**. It does this by assigning a value property to be the passed parameter (either **leftSide** or **DIUp**, depending on which event), and then uses that event in a guard. The SCS_x states are so called because **SCS** stands for **State Closure Step** to force the assignment of the passed parameter to the value property to take place prior to the evaluation of the guards.

The lower AND-state handles the display of the current gearing confirmed by the Rider Application; this is sent by the **Rider Application** after it adjusts to the selected gears.

Also notice the initialization actions on the transition from the **Initializing** to the **Controlling Gears** state; this specifies the handedness of the **Shift Levers** and the **DI** buttons. It also sets the links properly from those elements back to the instance of the **Gear Control** block:

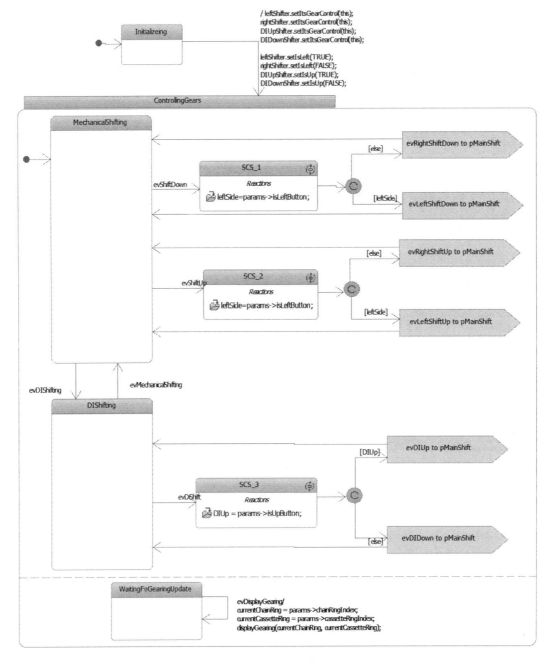

Figure 5.16 – Gear Control state machine

The last state machine, shown in *Figure 5.17*, is for the **Rider Application**, which is owned by the **Main Computing Platform** subsystem. This state machine supports both mechanical shifting and DI shifting. It works by receiving the events from the **Gear Control** block and augments/decrements the gearing based on the values:

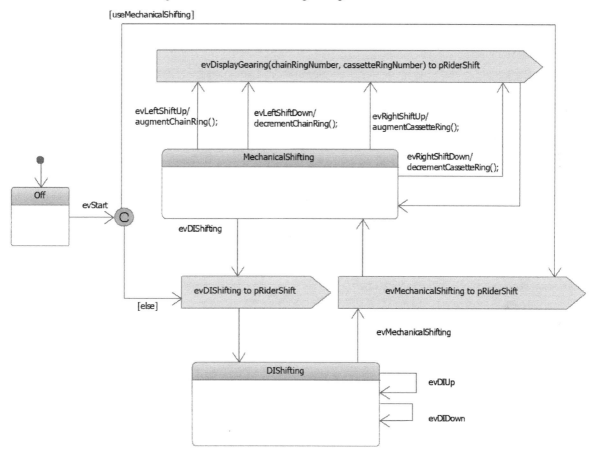

Figure 5.17 – Rider Application state machine for gearing

The gear adjustments are made by operations that ensure that the gearing remains within the set limits (1 to **maxChainRings** and 1 to **maxCassetteRings**). See *Figure 5.18:*

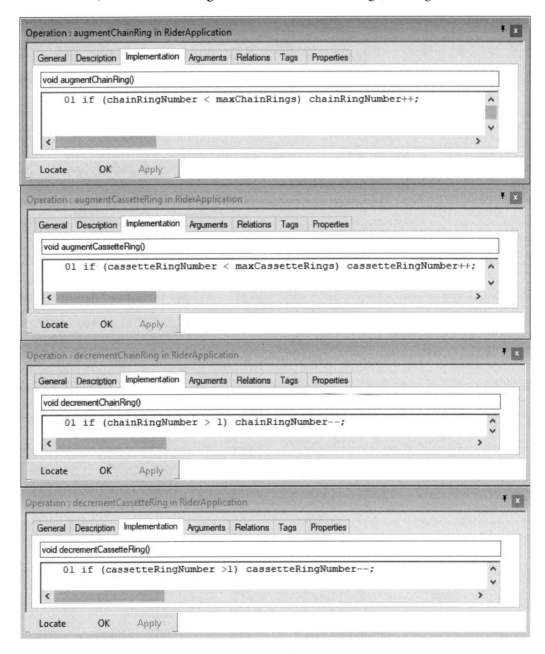

Figure 5.18 – Functions for setting gearing

So, there's our system under test. Is it right? How can you tell? Without testing, it would be easy for simple mistakes to creep in.

Define test architecture

The test architecture includes the development of the test fixtures or stubs we will use to perform the test. The test fixtures must provide the ability to repeatably set up the initial starting conditions for our tests, introduce the events with the proper values, sequences, and timings, and observe the results and outcomes.

We could create some blocks to do this in an automatic fashion. I personally use the stereotypes «testbuddy» and «testarchitecture» for such created elements:

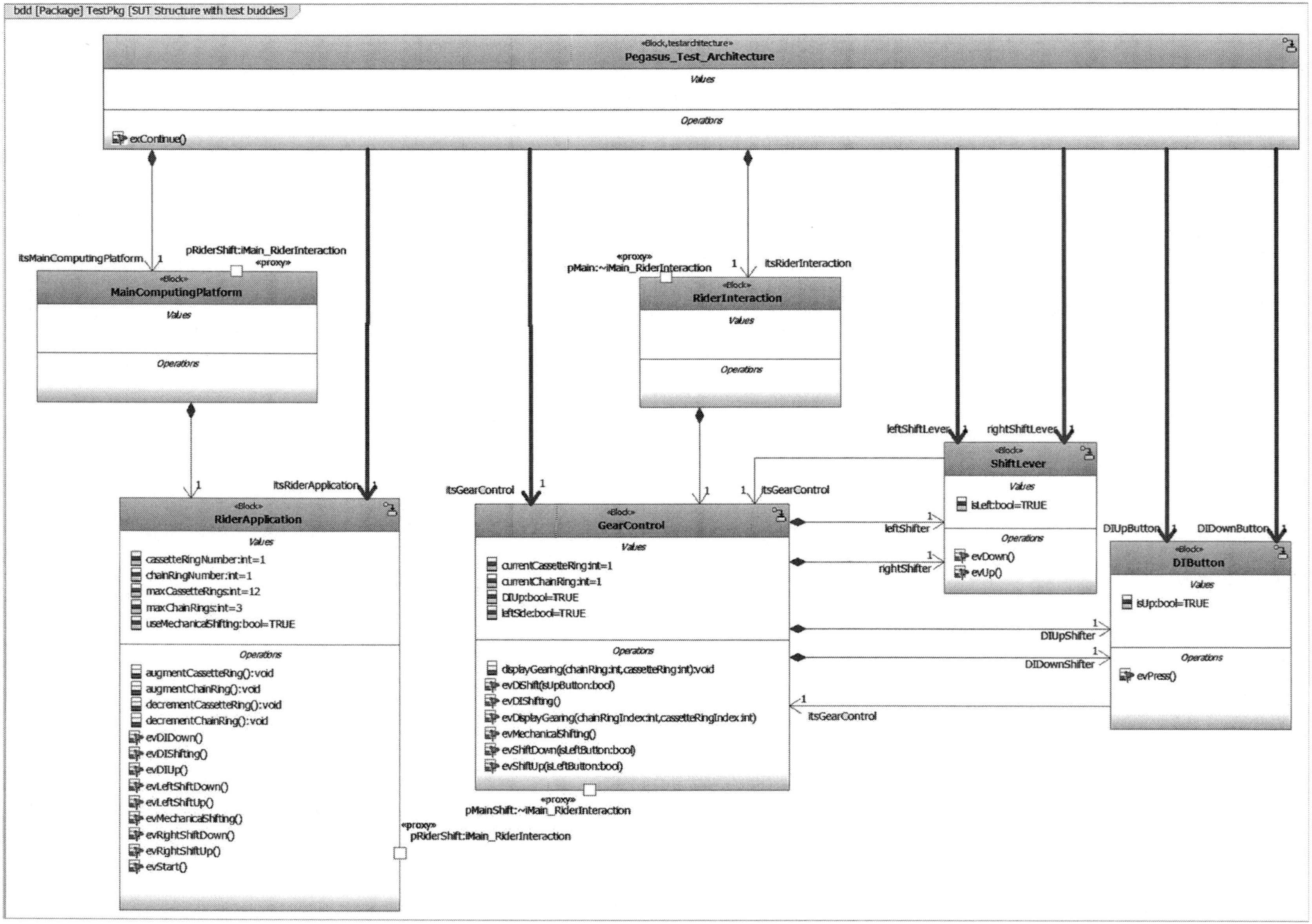

Figure 5.19 – Pegasus test architecture

Figure 5.19 shows The **Pegasus_System** block has been replaced with **Pegasus_Test_ Architecture** (stereotyped **«testarchitecture»**) The **Pegasus_Test_Architecture** block will use a state machine to drive the test cases (which will be captured as animated test scenarios). To do this effectively, I've added additional directed associations directly to the elements in the SUT. The test elements, including the relations, have been highlighted in green to make them visually distinct in *Figure 5.19*.

It is, of course, important to not modify the elements of the SUT for the purpose of the test, as much as possible. In this case, no modifications of the SUT to facilitate testing are necessary. Sometimes you may want to add **«friend»** relations from the elements of the SUT to the test components to make it easier to perform the tests.

Of course, we want to show the connected SUT and test architecture. This is done in *Figure 5.20*:

> **Note**
> As the testing maxim goes, "Test what you do; do what you test."

Figure 5.20 – Connected test architecture

A third alternative is to load the Test Conductor profile and have the profile automation create the test architecture automagically.

Specify test cases

Let's think about the test cases we want (*Table 5.1*). This table describes the test cases we want to apply:

Test Case	Preconditions	Expected Outcomes	Description
Test case 1	Initial starting conditions. Mechanical shifting, chain ring 1, cassette ring 1	Chain ring selection moves up to desired chain ring	Augment the front chain ring from 1 to **maxChainRings** (3)
Test case 2	Mechanical shifting, chain ring 1	Remain in chain ring 1	Decrement chain ring out of range low
Test case 3	Chain ring 3	Remains in chain ring 3	Augment chain ring out of range high
Test case 4	Initial starting conditions. Mechanical shifting, chain ring 1, cassette ring 1	Cassette ring selection moves up to desired cassette ring	Augment the front cassette ring from 1 to **maxCassetteRings** (12)
Test case 5	Mechanical shifting, cassette ring 1	Remain in cassette ring 1	Decrement cassette ring out of range low
Test case 6	Mechanical shifting, cassette ring 12	Remains in cassette ring 12	Augment cassette ring out of range high
Test case 7	Mechanical shifting	Switch to DI shifting	Move to DI shifting
Test case 8	DI Shifting	Switch to mechanical shifting	Move to mechanical shifting
Test case 9	DI shifting, chain ring 1, cassette ring 2	Augments to cassette ring 3, then 4, then 5	With DI shifting, press UP three times to see that shifting works
Test case 10	DI shifting in chain ring 2, cassette 1	Decrements to appropriate chain and cassette rings	Decrements to next lowest gear inches, augmenting chain ring, and going to appropriate cassette ring

Table 5.1 – Test case descriptions

To fully test with even the limited functionality we're looking at, more test cases are needed, but we'll leave those as exercises for the reader. This should certainly be enough to give the reader a flavor of model-based testing.

Relate test cases to requirements

To look at how the tests address the requirements, I created «verify» relations from each of the «testcase_reception» events to the set of requirements it purported to verify. I then created a table (with the context pattern "{pkg}Package*,{blk} Block,{rec}Reception,{ver}Verification:") that shows the block, event receptions, the name of the requirement it verifies, and the requirement text. Obviously, more test cases are needed, but *Figure 5.21* shows the starting point for test case elaboration:

Block	Event Reception test case	Requirement	Specification
	exContinue		
Pegasus_Test_Architecture	exStart		
Pegasus_Test_Architecture	exTest1	DID11	The Main Computing Platform shall initialize the Rider Interaction subsystem with shifting mode during startup.
Pegasus_Test_Architecture	exTest1	DID08	The Rider Interaction subsystem shall provide both mechanical shifters and DI buttons for shifting which provide identical inputs to the Main Computing Platform.
Pegasus_Test_Architecture	exTest1	EFD04	The Rider Interaction Subsystem shall display the currently selected front and rear gear, as commanded by the Main Computing Platform.
Pegasus_Test_Architecture	exTest1	efarg27	The system shall default to the minimum gear during initialization.
Pegasus_Test_Architecture	exTest1	efarg20	The rider shall be able to augment the front chain ring from a lower to the next higher gear until the largest chain ring is reached.
Pegasus_Test_Architecture	exTest1	efarg19	The default starting gear shall be chain ring 1 and cassette ring 1 when starting a ride.
Pegasus_Test_Architecture	exTest1	efarg12	The system shall inform the rider of the new gearing when the gear is changed.
Pegasus_Test_Architecture	exTest1	EFD05	The Rider shall be able to shift to the next highest or next lowest gear.
Pegasus_Test_Architecture	exTest1	efarg26	The system shall display the current selected gear.
Pegasus_Test_Architecture	exTest10	DIReg05	In DI Shifting mode, if the DOWN button is pressed and the system is already in the lowest possible gear, then the system shall audibly beep and keep the current gearing.
Pegasus_Test_Architecture	exTest10	DIReg07	In DI Shifting mode, when a downshift requires changing the chain ring, the system shall progress to the next smallest gearing, as measured by gear inches
Pegasus_Test_Architecture	exTest2	efarg21	The rider shall be able to decrement the front chain ring from a higher to the next lower gear until the smallest chain ring is reached.
Pegasus_Test_Architecture	exTest2	efarg05	The rider shall be able to decrement the cassette ring from a higher (smaller number of teeth) to the next lower (larger number of teeth) gear until the largest cassette ring is reached.
Pegasus_Test_Architecture	exTest3	efarg20	The rider shall be able to augment the front chain ring from a lower to the next higher gear until the largest chain ring is reached.
Pegasus_Test_Architecture	exTest3	efarg22	The rider shall be able to augment the cassette ring from a lower (larger number of teeth) to the next higher (smaller number of teeth) gear until the smallest cassette ring is reached.
Pegasus_Test_Architecture	exTest4	efarg20	The rider shall be able to augment the front chain ring from a lower to the next higher gear until the largest chain ring is reached.
Pegasus_Test_Architecture	exTest4	efarg22	The rider shall be able to augment the cassette ring from a lower (larger number of teeth) to the next higher (smaller number of teeth) gear until the smallest cassette ring is reached.
Pegasus_Test_Architecture	exTest5	efarg05	The rider shall be able to decrement the cassette ring from a higher (smaller number of teeth) to the next lower (larger number of teeth) gear until the largest cassette ring is reached.
Pegasus_Test_Architecture	exTest5	efarg21	The rider shall be able to decrement the front chain ring from a higher to the next lower gear until the smallest chain ring is reached.
Pegasus_Test_Architecture	exTest6	efarg20	The rider shall be able to augment the front chain ring from a lower to the next higher gear until the largest chain ring is reached.
Pegasus_Test_Architecture	exTest6	efarg22	The rider shall be able to augment the cassette ring from a lower (larger number of teeth) to the next higher (smaller number of teeth) gear until the smallest cassette ring is reached.
Pegasus_Test_Architecture	exTest7	DIReg02	The system shall provide shifting with a DI Shifting mode that enables the DI shifting buttons and disables the shifting levers.
Pegasus_Test_Architecture	exTest7	DID04	The Main Computing Platform shall manage DI shifting, when enabled.
Pegasus_Test_Architecture	exTest7	DID05	The Main Computing Platform shall enter DI shifting mode when commanded by a message received via the Configuration App.
Pegasus_Test_Architecture	exTest7	DIReq10	The system shall enter DI Shifting Mode by selecting that option in the Configuration App.
Pegasus_Test_Architecture	exTest8	DIReq13	The system shall leave DI Shifting mode when the user selects the Mechanical Shifting option in the Configuration App.
Pegasus_Test_Architecture	exTest9	DID05	The Main Computing Platform shall enter DI shifting mode when commanded by a message received via the Comm Subsystem from the Configuration App.
Pegasus_Test_Architecture	exTest9	DID04	The Main Computing Platform shall manage DI shifting, when enabled.
Pegasus_Test_Architecture	exTest9	DID02	The Main Computing Platform subsystem shall respond to an upshift by going to the next highest gear ratio permitted with the current gear configuration.
Pegasus_Test_Architecture	exTest9	DIReg04	In DI Shifting mode, the UP button shall shift into the next highest possible gearing from the selected gear set, as measured in gear inches.
Pegasus_Test_Architecture	exTest9	DIReg06	In DI Shifting mode, when an upshift requires changing the chain ring, the system shall progress to the next largest gearing, as measured by gear inches.
Pegasus_Test_Architecture	exTest9	DID01	The Rider Interaction subsystem shall provide an UP and DOWN button for shifting.
Pegasus_Test_Architecture	exTest9	DIReg03	In DI Shifting mode, the UP button shall shift into the next highest possible gearing from the selected gear set, as measured in gear inches.

Figure 5.21 – Test case verification requirements table

Analyze test coverage

For our purposes here, we will examine coverage in terms of both the requirements and path coverage in the SysML behavioral models; that is, our test cases should execute every transition in each state machine and every control flow in every activity diagram.

As far as requirements coverage, there is a test case for the requirements in *Figure 5.21*, but many more requirements are not covered. We must also consider the degree of completion of the coverage of requirements that are covered. The control of the chain ring in mechanical shifting mode is pretty complete: we have test cases to ensure that in the middle of the range, augment and decrement work properly, that you can't augment beyond the limit, and that you can't decrement below the minimum. However, what about DI mode? There are a couple of test cases but we should consider cases where augmentation forces a change in the chain ring as well as the cassette ring, where gear decrement forces a reduction in the chain ring, and cases where they can be handled completely by changing the cassette ring only. In addition, we need cases to ensure that the calculations are right for different gearing configurations and that we can't augment or decrement beyond available gearing.

To consider design coverage, you can color the transitions after execution during the execution of tests. As more tests are completed, fewer of the transitions in the design element state behaviors should remain uncolored. This requires manual effort during testing unless you're using a powerful tool such as Test Conductor, which can compute this coverage automatically as tests are run.

Render test cases

We will implement these case cases with state behavior in the **Pegasus_Test_Architecture** block. Because SysML: «testcase» formally applies only to operations, I've added «testcase_reception» to apply to event receptions that realize the test cases in the **Pegasus_Test_Architecture** state machine. The basic structure of this test state machine is shown in *Figure 5.22*. Each test is initiated with an exTest<#> event, configures for the test case preconditions, and then waits for the tester to insert the **exStart** event to run the test. It is assumed that the tester will create an animated state machine or monitor system behavior to record the test execution. The test states are intended to be elaborated as sub-machines; that is, these states will have nested state behaviors shown on other diagrams that perform the detailed test behavior. Also note the initialization of the test relations on the initial transition:

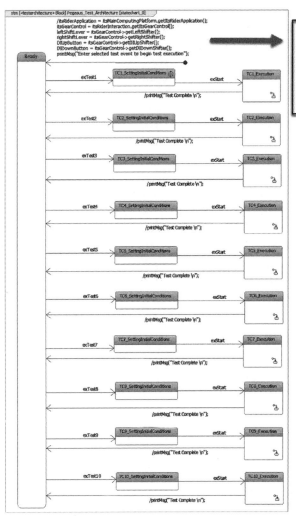

/itsRiderApplication = itsMainComputingPlatform.getItsRiderApplication();
itsGearControl = itsRiderInteraction.getItsGearControl();
leftShiftLever = itsGearControl->getLeftShifter();
rightShiftLever = itsGearControl->getRightShifter();
DIUpButton = itsGearControl->getDIUpShifter();
DIDownButton = itsGearControl->getDIDownShifter();
printMsg("Enter selected test event to begin test execution");

Figure 5.22 – Test Architecture state machine

To assist in the execution of the test cases, I also created a panel diagram that allows me to set and view values and insert internal events, as well as to insert the events to drive the test case executions:

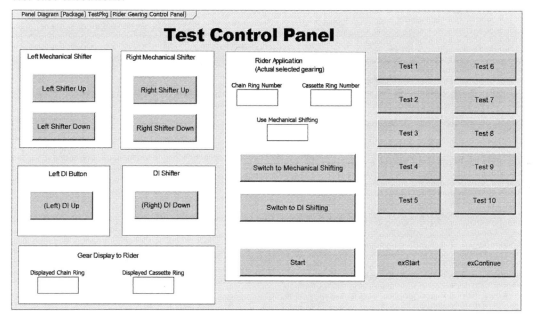

Figure 5.23 – Test panel diagram

Let's render just four of these test cases: 1, 2, 7, and 9.

Render test case 1: Augment the front chain ring from 1 to **maxChainRings (3)**.

Adding the state behavior for this test case is pretty simple. The initialization just needs to do the following:

- Set the shifting mode to mechanical shifting.
- Set the selected chain ring to the first (1).

The test execution behavior is pretty simple. First, send the **evStart** event to the **Rider Application**, and then the system just needs to send the left **Shift Lever** the **Left DI Up** event two times and verify after each that both the set chain ring and the displayed chain ring are correct. *Figure 5.24* shows the details of the state **TC1_Execution** submachine state:

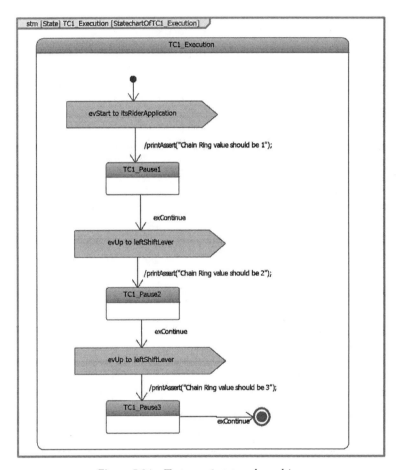

Figure 5.24 – Test case 1 state submachine

The `printAssert` statements identify a condition for the tester to check for correctness. In this case, the tester needs to check the value of the chain rings, and this value is also used in the messages. Its correctness is easy to verify with only the sequence diagram generated from the test execution. This may not always be true, but it is in test case 1. The use of the **exContinue** event gives the tester a chance to verify the asserted condition before moving on. The panel diagram allows the tester to easily enter the events and verify the values as well.

Render test case 3: Augment the chain ring out of the range high

In this test case, the setup for the test sets up for mechanical shifting and sets the selected chain ring to 3. It tries to augment the chain ring (which is already at its maximum); it should remain at the value 3. The test case state machine is shown in *Figure 5.25*:

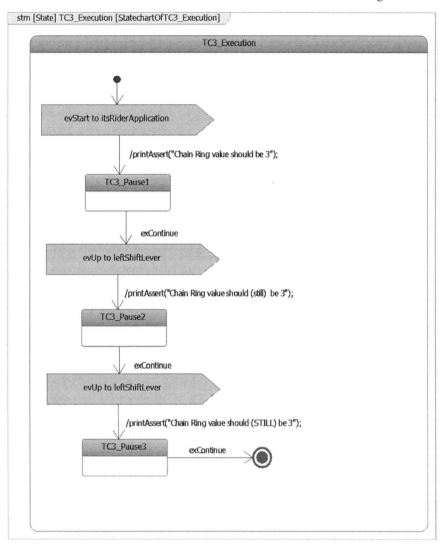

Figure 5.25 – Test case 3 state submachine

Render test case 7: Move to DI shifting

This is an easy test case. All we have to do is to run the system and then check that the system is set to use DI shifting; this is best done by manually examining the value of the `useMechanicalShifting` value property (it should be **FALSE**) and by looking at the animated state machine of the **Rider Application** and **Gear Control** instances. The state submachine for test case 7 is shown in *Figure 5.26*:

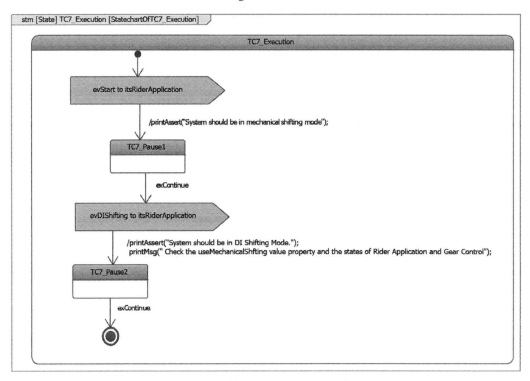

Figure 5.26 – Test case 7 state submachine

Render test case 9: With DI shifting, press UP three times to see that shifting works.

For the last test case, we'll enter DI mode then shift **UP** three times to ensure that shifting works. The gearing is initialized to chain ring 1 and cassette ring 2 with DI shifting enabled. The test presses the DI **Up Button** three times and we expect to see it augment the gearing to 1:3, 1:4, and finally 1:5:

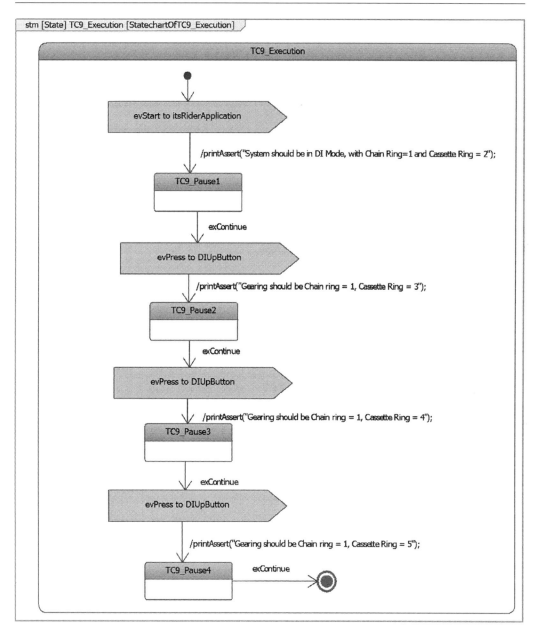

Figure 5.27 – Test 9 state submachine

Apply test cases

Now, let's run the test cases and look at the outcomes. Since I think you learn more from test failures than successes, prepare to see some failures.

Run test case 1

Figure 5.28 is the animated sequence diagram generated from executing test case 1:

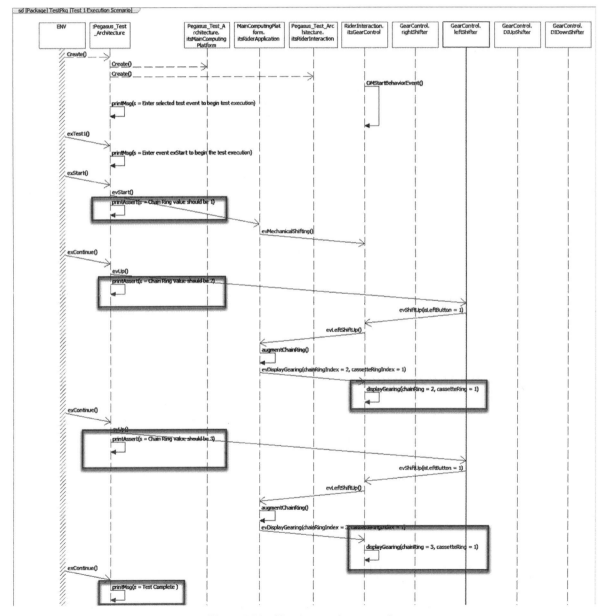

Figure 5.28 – Test 1 execution scenario

In the captured test scenario, we highlighted the `printAsset` statements and we can see the setting and display of the gearing. This test passes.

Run test case 3

Figure 5.29 shows the test run. In fact, we see that the selected chain ring augments to 4, rather than being capped at 3, so the test fails:

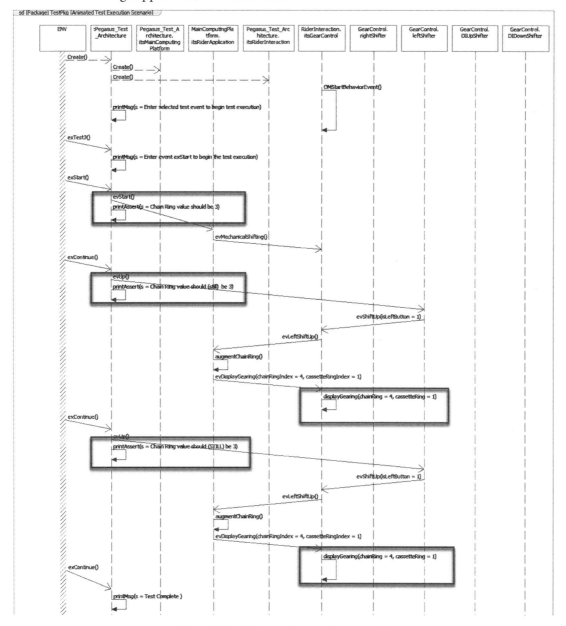

Figure 5.29 – Test case 3 execution scenario

Run test case 7

Test case 7 fails, because while the proper states are entered in the **Rider Application** and **Gear Control** state machines, the useMechanicalShifting value property wasn't properly set (1 indicates the value is **TRUE** but we expect it to be **FALSE**). This outcome is shown in the highlighted sections of *Figure 5.30*:

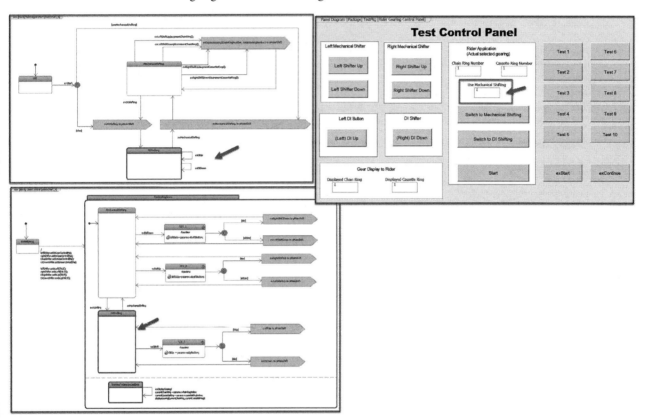

Figure 5.30 – Test case 7 outcomes

Run test case 9

Test case 9 also fails. While we can initialize the system just fine and the events we send to the **DI Up** button instance do get sent properly, the **Rider Application** fails to update the gearing internally and also fails to update the **Gear Control** display of the current gearing. This can be seen in the test scenario (*Figure 5.31*):

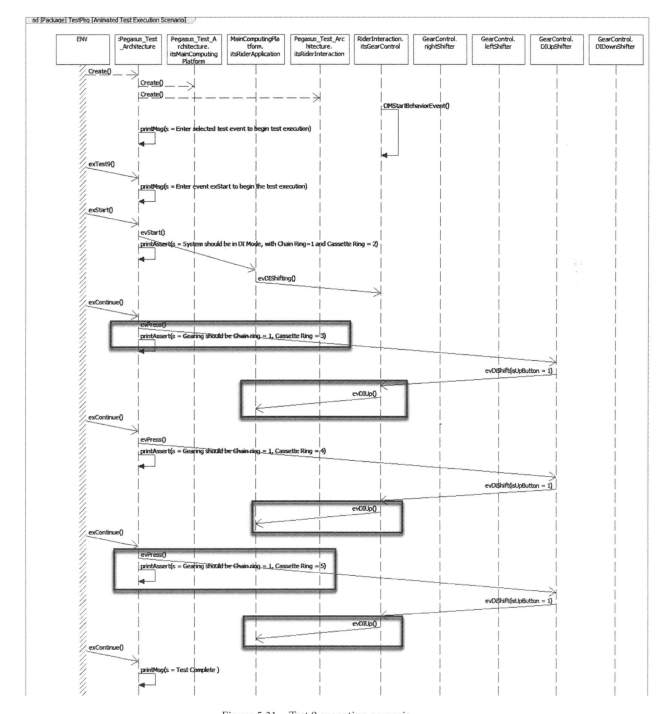

Figure 5.31 – Test 9 execution scenario

This can also be seen by looking at the actual values of the gearing in the panel diagram (*Figure 5.32*):

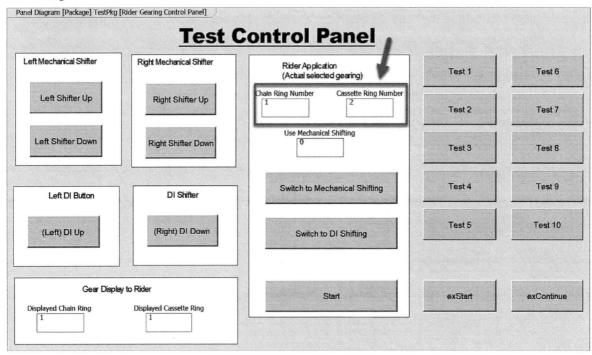

Figure 5.32 – Test 9 panel diagram at end of test

Render verdict

As not all tests succeeded, the test suite, as a whole, fails. This means that the design must be repaired and the tests rerun.

Fix defects in SUT

The defects are all fairly easy to fix. For test 3, the issue is in the implementation of the **Rider Application** operation **augmentChainRing**. The current implementation is as follows:

```
if (chainRingNumber <= maxChainRings) chainRingNumber++;
```

But it should be as follows:

```
if (chainRingNumber < maxChainRings) chainRingNumber++;
```

Test 7 failed because the **Rider Application** value property `useMechanicalShifting` wasn't properly updated. It's a simple matter to add an action to the transition triggered by `evDIShifting` to add the transition action:

```
evDIShifting/ useMechanicalShifting = false;
```

And similarly, to add the transition action to `evMechanicalShifting`:

```
evMechanicalShifting/ useMechanicalShifting = true;
```

The fix for test 9 is a bit more involved. If you look at the state machine for **Rider Application**, you can see that as the gears are changed, transition actions are invoked to actually update the gearing; and then an **evDisplayGearing** event is sent to **itsGearControl** to display the values. This functionality must be added to the **DIShifting** state. New operations are needed because in DI shifting mode, the system will decide when it can just adjust the cassette ring and when it must adjust the chain ring as well.

Computable constraint modeling

Mathematics isn't just fun, it's also another means by which you can verify aspects of systems. For example, in the *Architectural trade studies* recipe in *Chapter 3, Developing System Architectures*, we created a mathematical model to evaluate design alternatives as a set of equations, converting raw properties – including measurement accuracy, mass, reliability, parts costs, and rider feel – into a computed "goodness" metrics for the purpose of comparison. Using trade studies is a way to verify that good design choices were made. We did this using SysML constraints and parametrics diagrams to render the problem and "do the math."

Math can address many problems that come up in engineering, and SysML parametric diagrams provide a good way to cast, compute, and render such problems and their solutions. An archetypal example is computing the total weight of a system. This can be done by simply summing up the weights of all its constituent parts. However, far more interesting problems can be addressed.

Because math is the language of quantities, it is very general, so it is a challenge to come up with a workflow that encompasses the wide range of addressable problems. But we are not alone. Thinkers such as Polya and Wickelgren have come up with means by which we can apply mathematics to general kinds of problems. As we did with trade studies, we can systematically capture an approach that employs mathematics and SysML to provide a means to mathematically analyze and verify system aspects.

> **Note**
>
> You can refer to the following to read about solving problems:
>
> *Polya, G. How to Solve It: A new aspect of mathematical methods (Princeton University Press, 1945)* or recent rereleases such as those available on `Amazon.com`
>
> *Wickelgren, W. How to Solve Problems: Elements of a theory of problems and problem solving (W. H. Freeman and Co, 1974)*

Purpose

The purpose is to solve a range of problems that can be cast a set of equations relating to values of interest. We will call problems of this type **mathematically-addressable problems (MAPs)**.

Inputs and preconditions

The input to the recipe is a MAP that needs to be solved, such as the emergent properties of a system being developed.

Outputs and postconditions

The output of the recipe is the answer to the problem; typically, a quantified characterization of the emergent property (also known as *the answer*).

How to do it...

Figure 5.33 shows the steps involved:

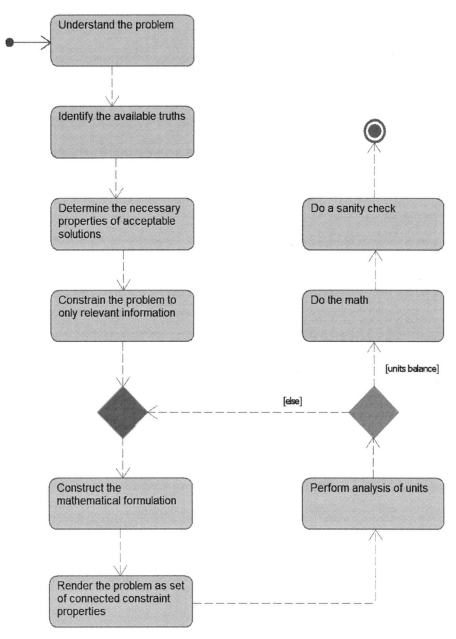

Figure 5.33 – Computational constraint modeling workflow

Understand the problem

The first step in this recipe is to understand the problem at hand. In MBSE, that generally means the following:

- Identifying the structural elements (blocks, value properties, and so on)
- Discovering how they connect
- Understanding how the elements behave both individually and collectively
- Reviewing the qualities of services of those behaviors (such as worst-case performance)
- Looking at other quantifiable properties of interest for the system or its elements

Identify the available truths

This step is about finding potentially relevant values and constraints. This might be universals – such as the value of the gravitational constant on the surface of the earth is 9.81 m/s^2 or that the value of π to 9 digits is 3.14159265. It might be constraints – such as the limit on the range of patient weights (0.5 kg to 300 kg). It might be quantifiable relations – such as F = ma.

Determine the necessary properties of acceptable solutions

This is the step where the problem gets interesting. I personally cast this as *what does the solution smell like?* I want to understand what kind of thing I expect to see when a solution is revealed. Is it going to be the ratio of engine torque to engine mass? Is it the likelihood of a fault manifesting as an accident in my safety-critical system? What is the nature of the result for which I am looking? Many times, this isn't known or even obvious at the outset of the effort but is critical in identifying how to solve the problem.

Constrain the problem to only relevant information

Once we understand the problem, the set of potentially useful information, and the nature of the solution, we can often limit the input information to a smaller set of truly relevant data. By not having to consider extraneous information, we simplify the problem to be solved.

Construct the mathematical formulation

In this step, we develop the equations that represent the information and their relations in a formal, mathematical way. Remember, *math is fun*.

Note
Yes, I'm a nerd.

Render the problem as a set of connected constraint properties

The equations will be modeled as a set of *constraints* owned by SysML *constraint blocks*. The input and output values of those equations are modeled as *constraint parameters*. Then the equations are linked together into computation sets as *constraint properties* on a parametric diagram.

Perform analysis of units

In complex series of computations, it is easy to miss subtle problems that could be easily identified if you just ensure that the units match. Perhaps you end up trying to add inches to meters or add values of force and power. Keeping track of units and ensuring the units balance is a way to avoid such mistakes.

Do the math

Rhapsody provides the **Parametric Constraint Evaluation** profile (**PCE profile**) to "do the math." It works by connecting Rhapsody to a third-party math engine, such as MATLAB or Maxima, passing the work off to the math engine to perform the calculations, and then receiving the results back.

Do a sanity check

A sanity check is a quick verification of the result by examining its reasonableness. One quick way that I often employ is to use "approximate computation." For example, if you say that 1723/904 is 1.906, I might do a sanity check by noting that 1800/900 is 2, so the actual value should be a little less than 2.0. If you tell me that a medical ventilator should deliver 150 L/min, I might perform a sanity check by noting that an average breath is about 500 ml (at rest) at an average rate of around 10 breaths/min, so I would expect a medical ventilator to deliver something close to 5 L/min, far shy of what you suggested.

More elaborate checks can be done. For a critical value, you might compute it using an entirely different set of equations, or you might perform *backward computation* whereby you attempt to start with the end result and reverse the computations and see if you end up with the starting values.

Example

The *Architectural trade studies* recipe example from *Chapter 3, Developing System Architectures*, showed one use for computable constraint models. Let's look at another.

In this example, I want to verify a resulting computation performed by the Pegasus system regarding simulated miles traveled as a function of gearing and cadence. We will build up and evaluate a SysML parameter model for this purpose.

Understand the problem

The potentially relevant properties of the **Bike** and **Rider** include the following:

- Chain ring gear, in number of teeth
- Cassette ring gear, in number of teeth
- Wheel circumference, in inches
- Cadence of the rider, in pedal revolutions per minute
- Power produced by the rider, in watts
- Weight of the rider and bike, in kilograms
- Wind resistance of the rider, in Newtons
- Incline of the road, in % grade
- How long the rider rides, in hours

The desired outcome is to know how far the simulated bike travels during the ride.

Identify the available truths

There are some constraints on the values these properties can achieve:

- Chain ring gears are limited to 28 to 60 teeth.

- Cassette ring gears are limited to 10 to 40 teeth.

- Wheel circumference for a normal road racing bike is 82.6 inches (2,098 mm).

- Reasonable rider pedal cadence is between 40 and 120 RPM.

- Maximum output power for elite humans is about 2000 W, with 150-400 W sustainable for an hour or more (depending on the awesomeness of the person).

- The UCI limits the weight of road racing bikes to no less than 15 lbs (6.8 kg) but 17-20 lbs is more typical.

- Rider weight is generally between 100 and 300 lbs (45.3 kg to 136 kg).

- Wind resistance is a function of drag coefficient, cross-sectional area, and speed.

- Road inclines can vary from -20 to +20% grade with an approximately normal distribution around 0%.

- Ride lengths of interest are from between 0.5 and 8 hours.

> **Note**
>
> You can read mote about speed here:
>
> `https://ridefar.info/bike/cycling-speed/air-resistance-cyclist/`
>
> A notable exception to the grades of the road inclines is the 32% climb in the *Savageman Triathlon* Westernport Wall: `https://kineticmultisports.com/races/savageman/`. They don't call it *Wussieman*.

Determine the necessary properties of acceptable solutions

What we expect is a distance in miles as determined by a ride of a certain length of time in specific gearing with other parameters being set as needed.

Constrain the problem to only relevant information

A little thought on the matter reveals that many of the properties outlined are not really relevant to the specific computation. Assuming no wheel slippage on the road, the only properties necessary to determine distance are the following:

- Chain ring gear
- Cassette ring gear
- Pedal cadence
- Wheel circumference
- Ride time

If the other properties vary, they will manifest as changing one or more of these values. For example, if wind resistance changes due to a headwind, then the rider will either pedal more slowly, change gear, or ride for a longer time to cover the same distance.

Construct the mathematical formulation

There are a number of equations we must construct, with several of them solely for converting units:

- *Gear ratio = chain ring teeth / cassette ring teeth*
- *Gear inches = gear ratio * wheel circumference*
- *Gear miles = gear inches / 12 / 5280*
- *Revolutions per hour = revolutions per minute * 60*
- *Speed in MPH = revolutions per hour * gear miles*
- *Distance = speed * duration*

Render the problem as a set of connected constraint properties

These equations are rendered as constraint blocks, as you can see in *Figure 5.34*. The inputs and outputs are shown as the constraint parameters, shown as included boxes along the edge of the constraint blocks. **frontGear** and **rearGear** are modeled as *integers*, but all other gears are represented as *reals*:

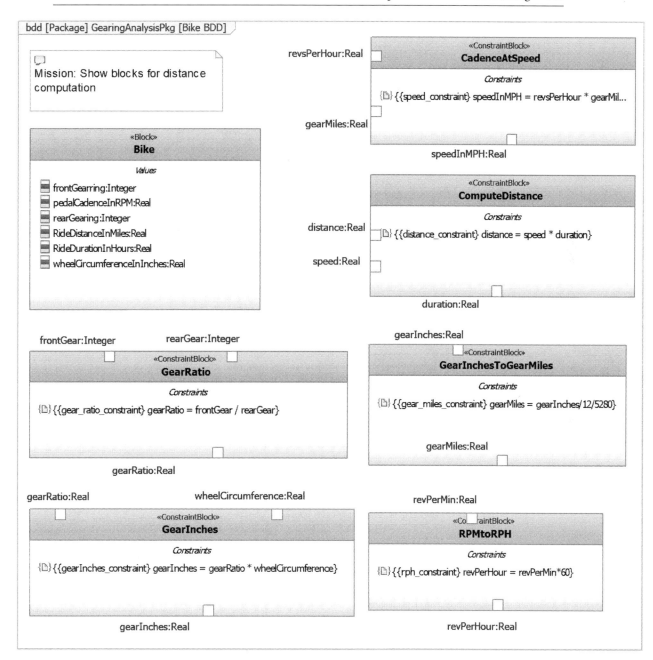

Figure 5.34 – Bike gear constraint blocks

A parametric diagram is a specialized form of an internal block diagram. The instances of the constraint blocks, known as constraint properties, are shown in *Figure 5.35*:

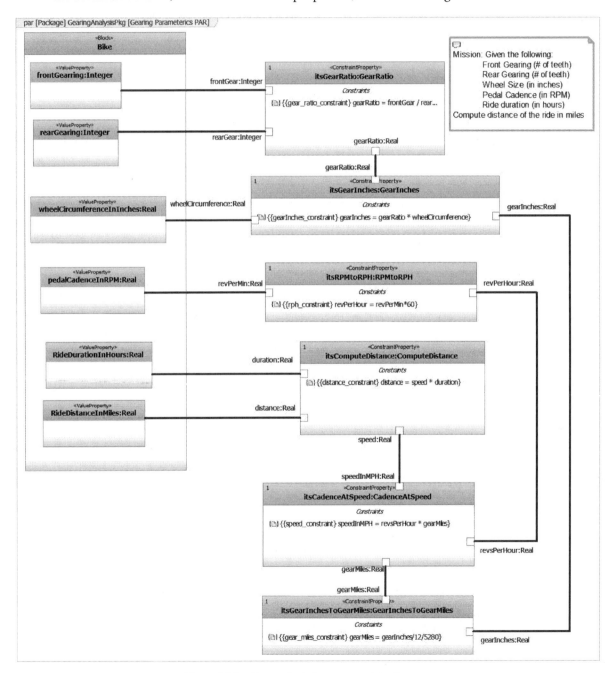

Figure 5.35 – Gear calculation parametric diagram

Note the binding connectors relate the constraint parameters together as well as relating the constraint parameters to the value properties of the **Bike** block. This will become important later in the recipe when we want to evaluate different cases.

Perform analysis of units

This problem is computationally simple but is easy to screw up because of the different units involved. Wheel circumference is measured in inches; pedal cadence in RPM. However, we ultimately want to end up with the distance in miles.

We can recast the equations as units to ensure that we got the conversions right:

- *Gear ratio = chain ring teeth / cassette ring teeth*

  Where *Real = teeth / teeth (note: the ratio is unitless)*

- *Gear inches = gear ratio * wheel circumference*

  Where *Inches / revolution = real * inches / revolution*

- *Gear miles = gear inches / 12 / 5280*

  Where

  miles / revolution = inches / revolution / (inches/foot) / (feet/mile)

    = feet / revolution / (feet / mile)

    = miles / revolution

- *Revolutions per hour = revolutions per minute * 60*

  Where *RPH = revolutions/min * (minute / hour)*

    = revolutions / hour

- *Speed in MPH = revolutions per hour * gear miles*

  Where *MPH = (revolutions / hour) * (miles / revolution)*

    = miles / hour

- *Distance = speed * duration*

  Where *Miles = miles / hour * hour*

    = miles

The units balance, so it seems that the equations are well-formed.

Do the math

Before we do the math, it will be useful to review SysML *instance specifications* a bit, as they are not covered in much detail in most SysML tutorials. An instance specification is the specification of an instance defined by a block. Instance specifications have *slots* that hold specific values related to the value properties of the block. That means we can assign specific values to the slots corresponding to value properties. In practice, we can assign a partial set of the slots values and use the parametric diagram to compute the rest. We can then save the resulting elaborated instance specification as an evaluation case, much like we might have multiple parts instantiating a block. This concept is illustrated in *Figure 5.36*:

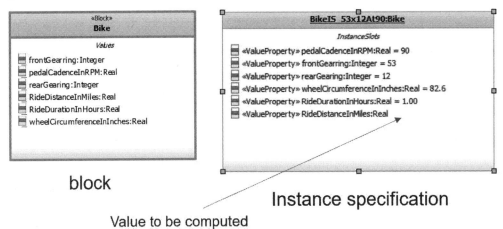

Figure 5.36 – Blocks and instance specifications

To perform the math, we'll define a set of instance specifications for the cases that we want to compute. In this example, we'll look at four cases (*Figure 5.37*):

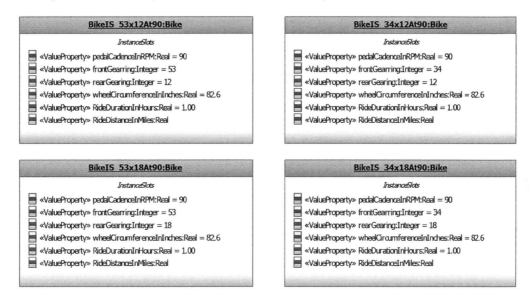

Figure 5.37 – Evaluation cases

Each of these cases is an instance specification typed by the **Bike** block. Note that there are no spaces in the name; underscores are used (this is a standard Rhapsody limitation on naming).

I won't go into the use of the profile to connect to the external math engine, although in this case, I used Maxima, which can be downloaded and used for free.

> **Note**
>
> For further information, on the Maxima too refer to `http://maxima.sourceforge.net/`.

To actually perform the in Rhapsody calculations is easy – if you know how (although it isn't well explained in the Rhapsody documentation). Simply put, to evaluate the parametric diagram once you've connected to the Maxima tool, do the following:

1. Create a constraint view in the package with the parametric diagram.

2. Right-click the constraint view to add a reference to the parametric diagram: **Add New | Constraint Evaluation | Reference to Parametric Diagram**.

3. Right-click the constraint view to add a reference to the instance specifications of interest (*Figure 5.37*).

4. Repeat these steps for each instance specification you want to evaluate.

Now, you can perform the computations. In Rhapsody, right-click the **constraint** view and select **Open Constraint View** at the bottom of the right-click menu. This will open up the evaluation window. *Figure 5.38* shows the same dialog, (upper) before the computation is performed and (lower) after clicking the **Evaluate** button to compute the resulting **Ride Distance In Miles**:

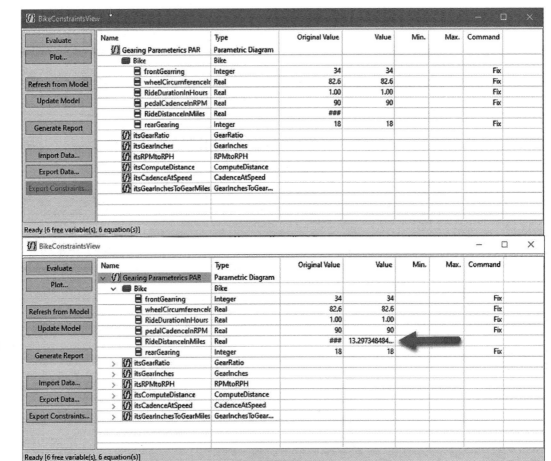

Figure 5.38 – Evaluation dialog

I updated the computed properties and then constructed a table of the values (*Figure 5.39*):

Name	Classifier	Value
⊟ 🔢 BikeIS_34x12At90	🖥 Bike	🔢 GearingAnalysisPkg.BikeIS_34x12At90
🔲 pedalCadenceInRPM		90
🔲 frontGearring		34
🔲 rearGearing		12
🔲 wheelCircumferenceInInches		82.6
🔲 RideDurationInHours		1.00
🔲 RideDistanceInMiles		19.946
⊟ 🔢 BikeIS_34x18At90	🖥 Bike	🔢 GearingAnalysisPkg.BikeIS_34x18At90
🔲 pedalCadenceInRPM		90
🔲 frontGearring		34
🔲 rearGearing		18
🔲 wheelCircumferenceInInches		82.6
🔲 RideDurationInHours		1.00
🔲 RideDistanceInMiles		13.2973
⊟ 🔢 BikeIS_53x12At90	🖥 Bike	🔢 GearingAnalysisPkg.BikeIS_53x12At90
🔲 pedalCadenceInRPM		90
🔲 frontGearring		53
🔲 rearGearing		12
🔲 wheelCircumferenceInInches		82.6
🔲 RideDurationInHours		1.00
🔲 RideDistanceInMiles		31.0923
⊟ 🔢 BikeIS_53x18At90	🖥 Bike	🔢 GearingAnalysisPkg.BikeIS_53x18At90
🔲 pedalCadenceInRPM		90
🔲 frontGearring		53
🔲 rearGearing		18
🔲 wheelCircumferenceInInches		82.6
🔲 RideDurationInHours		1.00
🔲 RideDistanceInMiles		20.7282

Figure 5.39 – Table of computed outcomes

Do a sanity check

Are these values reasonable? As an experienced cyclist, I typically ride at around 90 RPM and in a 53x18 gear, I would expect to go at about 20 miles, so the computed result for that case seems right. As I switch to a small 12-cog cassette, I would expect to go about 50% further, so the 31 miles at 53x12 seems about right. In a smaller front chain ring of 34 with a small cog (12), I'd expect to go about as far as in the 53x18 gear, so that seems reasonable as well.

Traceability

Traceability in a model means that it is possible to navigate among related elements, even if those elements are of different kinds or located in different packages. This is an important part of model verification because it enables you to ensure the consistency of information that may be represented in fundamentally different ways or in different parts of the model; for example:

- Are the requirements properly represented in the use case functional analysis?
- Do the design elements properly satisfy the requirements?
- Is the design consistent with the architectural principles?
- Do the physical interfaces properly realize the logical interface definitions?

The value of traceability goes well beyond model verification. The primary reasons for providing traceability are to support the following:

1. Impact analysis: determine the impact of change, such as the following:

- If I change this requirement or this design element, what are the elements that will be affected and must also be modified?
- If I change this model element, what will the cost be and what effort is required?

2. Completeness assessment: how done am I?

- Have I completed all the necessary aspects of the model to achieve its objectives, such as with a requirement, safety goal, or design specification?
- Do I have an adequate set of test cases to verify the requirements?

3. Design justification: why is this here?

- Safety standards require that all design elements exist to meet requirements. This allows the evaluation of compliance with that objective.

4. Consistency: are these things the same or do they work together? For example:

- Are the requirements consistent with the safety concept?
- Does the use case activity diagram properly define the requirements?
- Does the implementation meet the design?

5. Compliance

- Does the model, or elements therein, comply with internal and external standards?

6. Reviews

- In a review or inspection of some model aspect, is the set of information correct, complete, consistent, and well-formed?

By way of a very simple example, *Figure 5.40* schematically shows how you use a trace matrix. The rows in the figure are the requirements and the columns are different design elements. Requirement **R2** has no trace relation to a design element, indicating that is in an unimplemented requirement. Conversely, design element **D3** doesn't realize any requirements, so it has no justification:

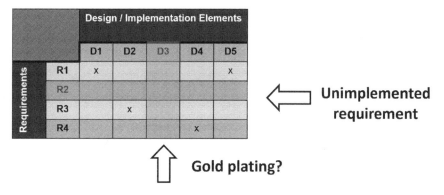

Figure 5.40 – Traceability

Some definitions

Traceability means that a navigable relation exists between all related project data without regard to the data location in the model, its representation means, or its format.

Forward traceability means it is possible to navigate from data created earlier in the project to related data produced later. Common examples would be to trace from a requirement to a design, from a design to implementation code, or from a requirement to related test cases.

Backward traceability means it is possible to navigate from data created later in the project to related data produced earlier in the process. Common examples would be to trace from a design element to the requirements it satisfies, from a use case to the requirements that it refines, from code back to its design, or from a test case to the requirements it verifies.

Trace ownership refers to the ownership of the trace relation, as these relations are directional. This relation is *almost always* in the backward direction. For example, a design element owns the `satisfy` relation to the requirement. Forward traceability is supported by tools via automation and queries by looking at the backward trace links to identify their owners. This is counter-intuitive to many people. A requirement *in principle* shouldn't know how it is implemented, but a design *in principle* needs to know what requirements it is satisfying. Therefore the «`satisfy`» relation is owned by the design element and not the requirement.

Trace matrices are tabular relations of the relations between sets of elements. Rhapsody supports the creation of matrix layouts that define the kinds of elements for the rows and columns and the kind of relation depicted. Matrix views can then select the layout to visualize and the locations in the model from which to select elements for the rows and columns. Multiple kinds of relations can be visualized in the same matrix, but in general, I recommend different tables to visualize different kinds of trace links.

Types of trace links

In SysML, trace relations are all stereotypes of dependency. *Table 5.2* shows the common relations in SysML:

Relation	Source type	Target type	Description
«trace»	Any	Any	A general relation and can be used in all circumstances where a navigable relation is needed. A common use is to relate requirements in different contexts, such as system requirements (source) and stakeholder requirements (target).
«copy»	Requirement	Requirement	Establishes that a requirement used in a context is a replica of one from a different context.
«deriveReqt»	Requirement	Requirement	Use when the source requirement is derived from the target requirement; this might be used from subsystem to system requirements, for example.
«refine»	Any	Any	Represents a model transformation; in practice, it is often used to relate a requirement (target) with a behavioral description (source), such as an activity diagram.

«allocate»	Any	Any	Relates elements of different types or in different hierarchies; in practice, it is most commonly used to relate a design element (source) to a requirement (target) and is, in this usage, similar to «satisfy».
«satisfy»	Design element	Requirement	A relation from a model element (source) and the requirement that it fulfills (target).
«verify»	Test case	Requirement	Indicates that the source is used to verify the correctness of the target. The source may be any kind of model element, but it is almost always a test case. For further information, refer to the *Model-based testing* recipe, earlier in this chapter, for more information.

Table 5.2 – SysML trace relations

You may, of course, add your own relations by creating your own stereotype of dependency. I often use «represents» to trace between levels of abstraction; for example, a physical interface «represents» a logical interface.

It is reasonable to ask why there are different kinds of trace relations. From a theoretical standpoint, the different kinds of relations clarify the relations' semantic intent. In practice, different tables can be constructed for the different kinds of relations and make them easier to apply in real projects.

Traceability and Agile

Many Agilistas devalue traceability; for example, Scott Ambler says:

> *Too many projects are crushed by the overhead required to develop and maintain comprehensive documentation and traceability between it. Take an Agile approach to documentation and keep it lean and effective. The most effective documentation is just barely good enough for the job at hand. By doing this, you can focus more of your energy on building working software, and isn't that what you're really being paid to do?*

> **Note**
>
> Refer to the following link for more information:
>
> `http://www.agilemodeling.com/essays/`
> `agileRequirementsBestPractices.htm.`

However, in my books on Agile systems engineering and Agile development for real-time safety-critical software, I make a case that traceability is both necessary and required:

> *Traceability is useful for both change impact analysis and to demonstrate that a system meets the requirements or that the test suite covers all the requirements. It is also useful to demonstrate that each design element is there to meet one or more requirements, something that is required by some safety standards, such as DO-178B.*

> **Note**
>
> For further notes, refer to Bruce Douglass, Ph.D. Real-Time Agility (Addison-Wesley, 2009): `https://www.amazon.com/Real-Time-Agility-Harmony-Embedded-Development/dp/0321545494`.

In my Agile projects, I add traceability relations as the work product content stabilizes to minimize rework, usually after most of the work has been done but before the system is verified and reviewed.

Purpose

The purpose of traceability is manifold, as stated earlier in this recipe. It enables model consistency and completeness verification as well as the performance of impact analysis. Additionally, it may be required by standards a project must meet.

Inputs and preconditions

The sets of elements being related are well developed enough to justify the effort to create the trace relations.

Outputs and postconditions

Relations between related elements in different sets have been created and are captured in one or more trace matrices.

How to do it...

Figure 5.41 shows the simple workflow for this recipe. Although the steps themselves are simple, not thinking deeply about the steps may result in unsatisfactory outcomes:

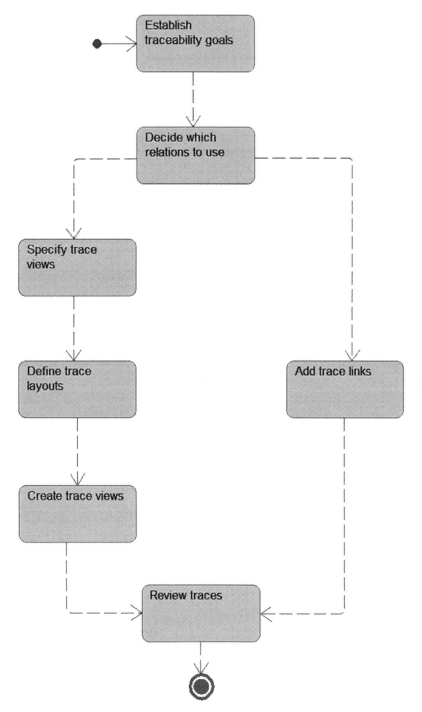

Figure 5.41 – Create traceability

Establish traceability goals

Traceability can be done for a number of specific reasons. Different stakeholders care about demonstrating that the design meets the requirements versus that the test cases adequately cover the design versus ensuring that the stakeholder requirements are properly represented in the system requirements. All of these are reasons to create traceability, but different trace views should be created for each.

Common traceability goals in MBSE include tracing between the following:

- Stakeholder needs and system requirements

- System and subsystem requirements

- Subsystem requirements and safety goals

- Facet (for example, software or electronic) requirements and system requirements

- Requirements and test cases

- Design and test cases

- Design and safety goals

- Logical schemas and corresponding physical schemas, including data schema and interfaces

- Model products and standards, such as ASPICE, DO-178, and ISO26262

- Design and implementation work products

For your project, you must decide on the objectives you want to achieve with traceability. In general, you will create a separate traceability view for each trace goal.

Decide which relations to use

SysML has a number of different kinds of stereotyped dependency relations that can be used for traceability purposes. In modern modeling tools, you can easily create your own to meet any specified needs you have. For example, I frequently create a stereotype of dependency named «represents» to specifically address trace relations across abstraction levels, such as between physical and logical schemas.

Which relation you use is of secondary importance to establishing the relations themselves, but making good choices in the context of the set of traceability goals that are important to you can make the whole process easier. *Table 5.3* shows how I commonly use the relations for traceability:

Source	Target	Relation	Purpose
Requirement	Requirement	«trace»	Relate different sets of requirements, generally from more recently developed to older, such as system (source) to stakeholder (target).
Use case	Requirement	«trace»	Show which requirements are related to a use case.
Requirement	Requirement	«deriveReqt»	Relate a more detailed requirement (source) to a more abstract one.
Design element	Requirement	«satisfy»	Identify which requirements a design element satisfies.
Design element	Requirement	«allocate»	Identify to which design elements (source) requirements (targe) are allocated.
Model element	Requirement	«refine»	Provide a detailed, often behavioral, representation of a textual requirement, such as an activity or state diagram elaborating one or more requirements.
Test case	Requirement, design element	«verify»	Relate test cases to either requirements or to the design elements .
Comment	Model element	«rationale»	Provide an explanation for the existence or representation of one or more model elements.
Model element	Model element	«represents»	Relate elements that are intended to be the "same thing" but at different levels of abstraction, such as logical versus physical data schema.

Table 5.3 – Common trace relation usage

Specify trace views

Once the element type and relations are decided, you must decide the best way to represent them. The first decision here is whether to use a matrix or a table.

A matrix is often the first choice for traceability. A matrix is a relation table between element sets, one set shown in the rows and the other in the columns. The contents of the cells in the matrix indicate the presence or absence of the desired relation. This is a great view for determining the presence or absence of relations. For example, a «satisfy» matrix between requirements and design elements is very useful to determine absence; an empty requirements row means that the requirement isn't represented in the design while an empty design element column means that the design element isn't there to meet any requirements. The downside of a matrix is that you can't see anything other than the name of the involved elements and the presence or absence of the desired relation. If you want to see other data, such as the text of the requirements or a list of the value properties of blocks, or the metadata tags, then a table is preferable.

> **Note**
>
> For practical reasons, I prefer the smaller set of elements to be shown as columns and the larger set of elements to be shown as rows. Rhapsody matrices have a **Switch Rows and Columns** feature I use for this purpose.

Tables consist of rows of data, one per primary table element, along with information owned by or about the element about which you care. Table elements that have properties – such as textual specifications, value properties, or metadata held in owned tags – can display that data in an easy-to-read summary form. In the context of traceability, one of the kinds of properties the elements can own are relations, such as «trace» or «verify», and these can be shown in tables as well. In Rhapsody, to show the elements pointed to by such relations, you must use *context patterns* to traverse the properties and relations. In general, if you want to show more than just the presence or absence of a relation but also want to show element data or metadata, then tables are preferred.

Or, you can create both tables and matrices.

Define trace layouts

Once you've decided what you want to see and how you'd like it organized, it is time to define the actual layouts. In Rhapsody, tables and matrices are defined by a layout that serves as the specification of one or more views. A layout defines the kind of elements involved and identifies the information about them you want to see. The view identifies the set of elements to view (by their location in the model) and shows information about them specified in the layout.

Create trace views

Once the layouts are defined, create views that apply the layouts on the specific set of elements.

Add trace links

You can use the trace views as a means for creating the trace views if you like, but you are not required to do so. I often create a use case diagram whose mission is to show the «trace» relation between one use case and a set of requirements, but then use a trace matrix to summarize the results for all such use case diagrams. It's perfectly reasonable to simply create an (empty) matrix and add the relations directly in the matrix. However you do it, this step adds the relations of the selected type to the appropriate elements in your model.

Review traces

Once the previous steps are complete, you can open the views and use the trace views to achieve your traceability objectives.

Example

In this example, we'll consider the relation of the system architecture to the system requirements. In the *Subsystem and component architecture* recipe of *Chapter 3, Developing System Architectures*, we created a subsystem architecture for the Pegasus system. While incomplete (it was for an early iteration after all), we created subsystems to meet those interfaces. Let's apply this recipe to develop a traceability view from the subsystems to the requirements.

Establish traceability goals

In this example, the purpose of the traceability is to show that all the requirements are allocated to the iteration and allocated to a subsystem. If there are requirements in the iteration not allocated, then we can either directly allocate the requirements or create derived requirements that are then allocated.

Decide which relations to use

We will use the «allocate» relation. In some senses, the «satisfy» relation is more, well, *satisfying*, but the «allocate» relation has some built-in tool support lacking from other relations. It's very common to use «allocate» to relate requirements to architectural elements.

Specify trace views

We will use a matrix of **Block versus Requirement** «allocate» relations for our view.

Define trace layouts

The matrix layout parameters are shown in *Figure 5.42*. Only three parameters must be specified: the *from element* (**Block**), the *to element* (**Requirement**), and the cell element type (**Allocation**):

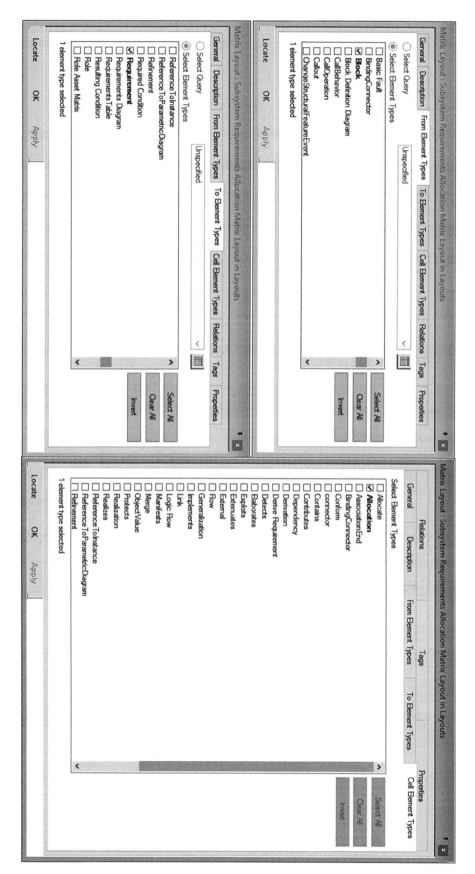

Figure 5.42 – Allocate matrix layout definition

Create trace views

The matrix view uses the layout to display the specified data. The matrix view must identify from where to get the *from* and *to* elements, and what layout to use *(Figure 5.43)*:

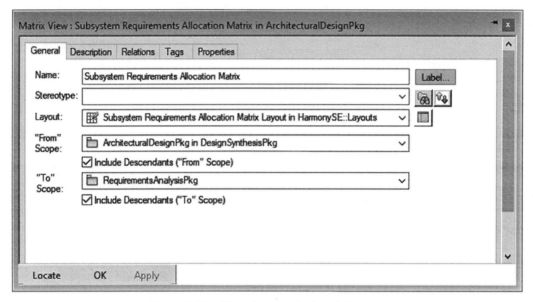

Figure 5.43 – Allocation matrix view definition

Add trace links

There are a couple of ways to populate the **«allocate»** relations from the blocks. In this case, I prefer to diagram the relations rather than work in the matrix directly. The reason is that on the diagram, I can see the text of the requirement, while in the matrix, I can only see the name of the requirement. *Figure 5.44* shows one of the requirements diagrams created to create the relations:

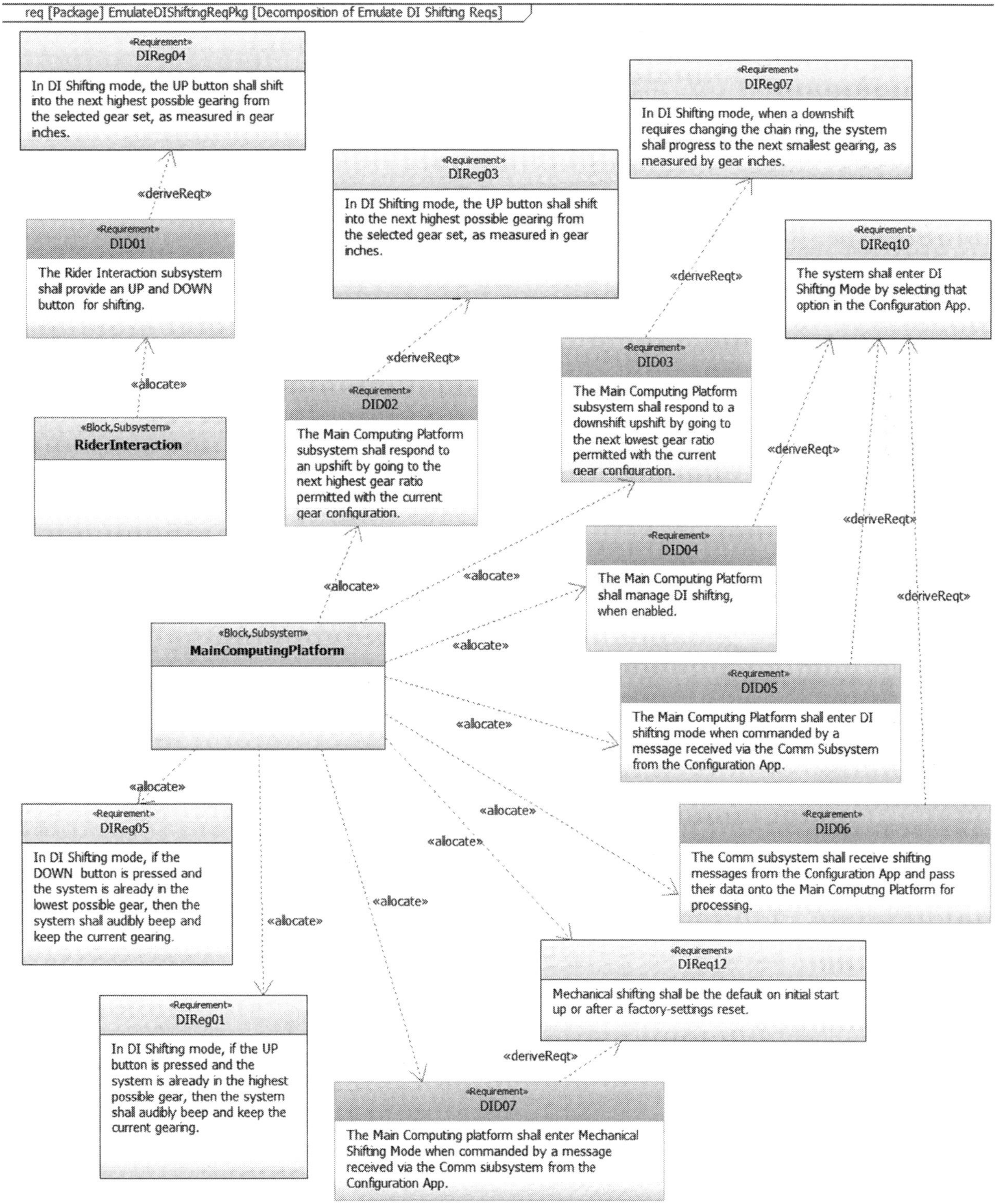

Figure 5.44 – Example requirements diagram to add allocations

Review traces

Figure 5.45 shows a portion of the resulting allocation relations from the subsystem elements to the requirements. I used the **Switch Rows and Columns** feature to show the requirements as rows:

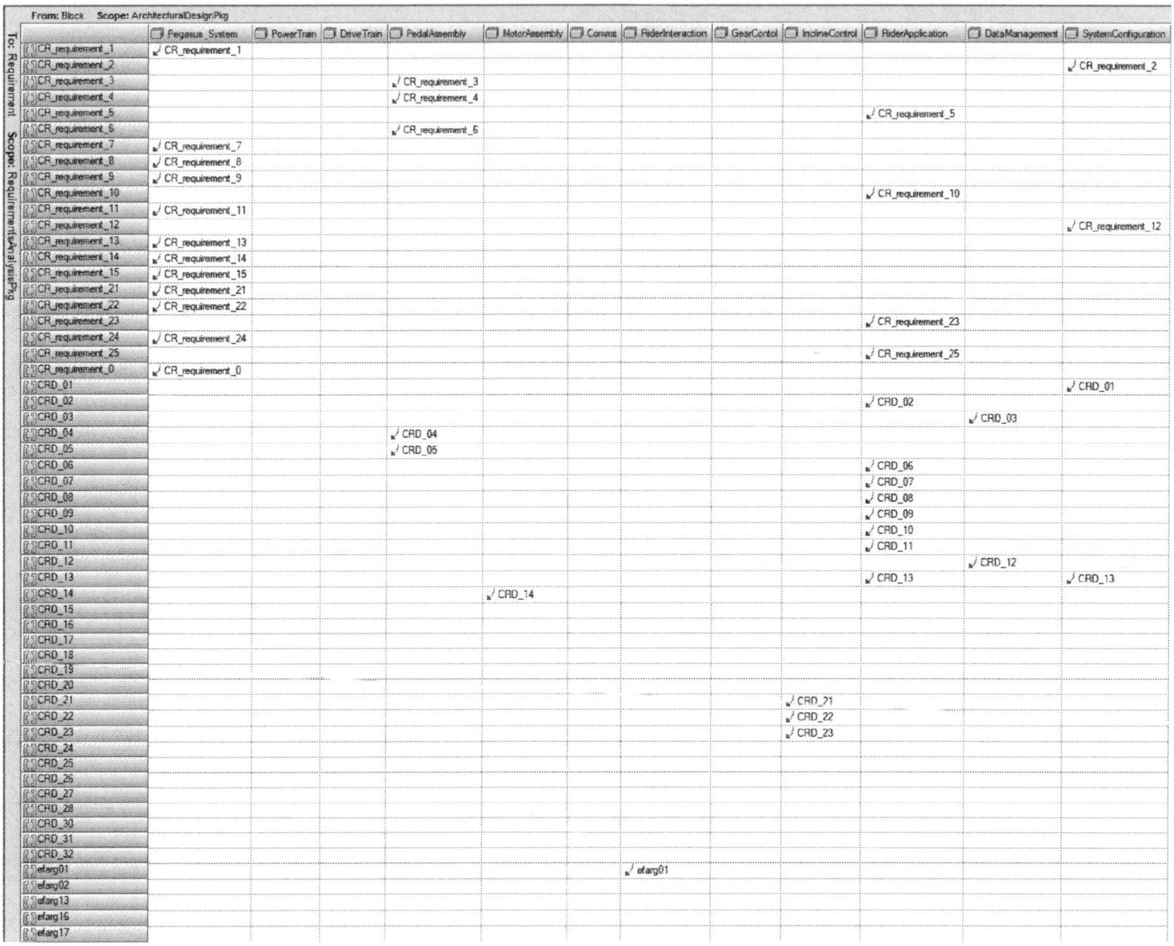

Figure 5.45 – Subsystem requirement allocation matrix

Effective reviews and walk-throughs

At the beginning of this chapter, I talked about reviews being the easiest but weakest form of model verification. This shouldn't be construed to mean that I don't believe reviews have value. Properly applied, reviews are very useful as an adjunct to other, more rigorous forms of verification. Reviews can contribute to both syntactic and syntactic verification. They are relatively easy to perform and can provide input that is otherwise difficult to obtain.

Syntactic reviews, performed by quality assurance personnel, demonstrate the compliance of the model to the project modeling guidelines, including the organization of the model, the presence of required elements and views, the structuring of those views, compliance with naming conventions, and more.

Semantic reviews are performed by **subject matter experts** (**SMEs**, for short). Some of the questions such reviews can address include the following:

- Does the model appropriately cover the necessary subjects (breadth)?
- Does the model include an appropriate level of detail (depth)?
- Are the levels of precision, accuracy, and fidelity appropriate?
- Does the model accurately represent the physics of the situation?
- Are the relevant standards properly taken into account?
- Is the technology accurately represented?
- Are all primary ("sunny day") conditions considered?
- Are exceptional and edge cases ("rainy day") cases adequately addressed?
- Is there anything of significance missed or inappropriately modeled?
- How will the correctness be verified?
- Is the information (typically the views) consumable by the stakeholders?

Reviews can be a valuable adjunct to other verification means. However, it is easy and far too common to perform them poorly in ways that are both expensive and ineffective. Reviews are very expensive because they typically have several to many people engaged for a significant number of hours. It is imperative that the meeting time is used efficiently. It is common for people to turn up unprepared, wasting other's time with questions to which they should already have answers. It is also common to "go down the rabbit hole" in exploring solutions; that is out of scope in the review. It is enough to identify the problem and move on. If a reviewer has a suggestion for a solution, they can present it to the author *after the meeting*. Further, because authors are putting their egos on the line, it is important that review comments address the product aspects and not what the author did wrong ("The product has this defect," not "you made a mistake here."). Subsequent reviews of the same product should be limited solely to the resolution of action items unless new information appears that invalidates the previous review.

The recipe described here is adapted from the notion of *Fagan inspections*, which were originally a means for source code review. I've adapted them to apply to engineering work products in general and especially to models.

> **Note**
>
> For more information, refer to `https://en.wikipedia.org/wiki/Fagan_inspection`.

Purpose

All models are abstractions but some are *useful abstractions*. A review ascertains whether they are the *right abstractions* covering the *appropriate topics* with adequate *precision, depth, and breadth,* and represent the system *correctly* in such a way that the model *fulfills its intended purpose.*

The recipe provided here is very general and can be applied to any technical work product, but our focus will be on the review of models and their content and views.

Note that this recipe describes how to conduct a review only. There are other reasons to have meetings dealing with technical work products, including the dissemination of information held within the work product.

Those may be valid and important meetings to have but they are not *reviews*. The purpose of a review is to *verify the content of a collection of project data, either syntactically, semantically, or both.*

Inputs and preconditions

A body of work is completed to the extent that the project can profitably conduct a review.

Outputs and postconditions

The primary outcomes are either a quality assurance record that the review was performed and no significant defects or issues were found *or* an action list of issues for the product authors to resolve.

How to do it...

Figure 5.46 shows the workflow for the recipe. A couple of main points in the figure should be emphasized.

First, the reviewers are expected to come to the review having reviewed the work products. This is not a meeting for *explanation*, although questions of clarification are permitted. Secondly, solutions to identified issues are not discussed; suggestions can be discussed directly with the author *after* the review. Lastly, subsequent reviews are limited to the resolution of the action items from previous reviews:

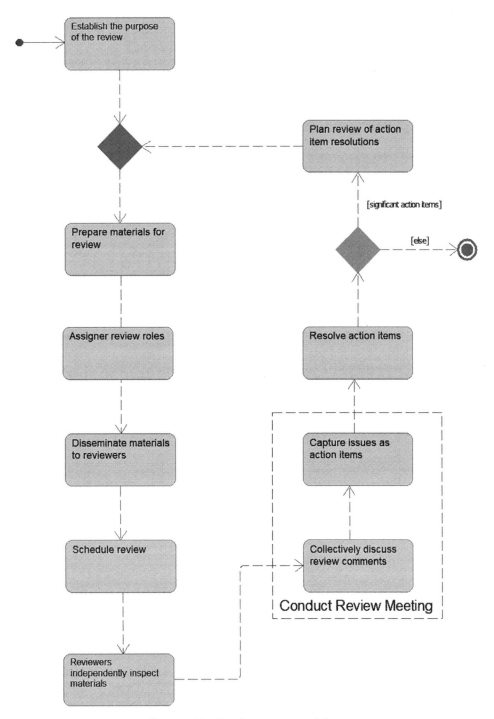

Figure 5.46 – Conduct review workflow

Establish the purpose of the review

Real models are too large to be reviewed in their entirety in a single review. Each review must have a specific purpose or intent that can be performed in a reasonable timeframe, and consider only the subset of the model relevant to that purpose. Some common review intents are to perform the following actions:

- Evaluate and understand systems engineering hand-off models.
- Evaluate the use cases and their details.
- Evaluate architectural models.
- Evaluate design models.
- Evaluate the adequacy and coverage of a test plan and its details.
- Evaluate the result of the actions taken after a previous review.

Prepare materials for review

In this step, the material is gathered together for a review. There are almost always multiple artifacts that are reviewed together. For example, a review of a use case model usually includes the following artifacts:

- Relevant use case diagrams.
- Corresponding requirement text.
- Use case sequence diagrams.
- Use case state machines and activity diagrams.
- Quality of service constraints
- Use case descriptions.
- List of actions from previous reviews (if applicable).

For the review of a design model, common artifacts include the following, for each use case in the design model:

- Block definition diagram(s) showing the collaboration of elements realizing the use case

- Internal block diagram(s) showing how the collaborating elements connect

- Original use case sequence diagram(s)

- Elaborated sequence diagrams showing the interaction of the design elements

- State machine diagrams for stateful classes

- Activity diagrams for complex algorithms

- A list of actions from previous reviews (if applicable)

Assign reviewer roles

Reviews have a number of roles that people can fulfill during the review. These need to be assigned to actual people to play those roles:

- **Review coordinator**: This role organizes and runs the meeting, ensuring compliance with the review's rules of conduct, such as "Direct comments to product not the author" and "Discuss solutions with the author after the meeting".

- **Product owner/presenter**: This is generally one of the authors of the material under review. This person is technically knowledgeable and can answer questions of clarification during the meeting.

- **SME reviewer**: This role is expected to provide a critical eye from a semantic viewpoint, whether it is about the specific technology, tool use, or engineering.

- **QA reviewer**: The QA role is there to ensure syntactic correctness and review the work product for compliance with relevant standards, including both internal standards (such as modeling guidelines and process definition) and external standards (such as industry or regulatory standards).

- **Scribe**: The scribe takes the meeting minutes and creates and updates the *action list*, the list of actions and issues to be addressed after the meeting. The action list will serve as the basis for subsequent reviews of the work product.

Disseminate materials to reviewers

The materials should be in the hands of the reviewers no less than 2 nor more than 14 days prior to the review.

Schedule review

The room for the review – along with any special equipment required (for example, a projector, whiteboards, an internet connection, a computer, modeling tool availability, and so on) – is scheduled and invitations are issued to the reviewers. This may also be done virtually.

> **Note**
>
> Both Cameo Magic Draw (via *Collaborator*) and Rhapsody (via *Model Manager*) support the online review of models, removing the need to generate work products for people who do not have access to the tools.

Reviewers independently inspect materials

The time to read the materials is *not* within the review meeting itself! The reviewers should come to the meeting with comments and issues they want to address. For complex work products, there may be value in the authors presenting the content and organization of the information to be reviewed. However, this should be a separate meeting, done prior to the review.

If the work product being reviewed is a model, then either the reviewers must have access to the relevant modeling tool, a web-based review environment (such as Rhapsody Model Manager running on the Jazz platform), or reports must be generated for the purpose of the review that show the model content in an accessible format, such as Word, PowerPoint, or PDF.

Collectively discuss reviewer comments

Each issue or comment from a review should be heard and addressed by the product owner. If it is determined to be an issue, the issue is specified on the list of actions to be resolved.

Do not discuss solutions during this meeting. If someone has a solution they want to offer, have them do it outside the meeting with the work product owner.

Capture issues as action items

The primary outcome of the review is either an approval *or* a set of action items to be resolved that will lead to approval. Some action items might require modification to the work product, while others might require exploration or a trade study.

The action item list must be captured and will be used as the agenda for any subsequent reviews of the same work product set.

Resolve action items

As a result of the list of actions identified in the review, the product owner must modify the model or in some way address each of the issues. Then, if the changes are not trivial, a follow-up meeting is planned (repeat the recipe from the first step).

Plan review of action item resolutions

Unless the action items are considered trivial and not worth following up, a subsequent meeting should be scheduled specifically to address what was done to resolve the action items, and, typically, nothing more.

This subsequent review is performed in the same fashion as the original review.

Example

Let's consider doing a review of one of the use cases from the Pegasus system, **Emulate Front and Rear Gearing** presented as an example in the **Functional Analysis with State Machines** recipe.

Establish the purpose of the view

The primary outcomes of use case analysis are the following:

- Ensure a good set of requirements.
- Define system interfaces necessary to support the related requirements.

The purpose of the review is to examine the work products created to perform that analysis and its outputs to ensure that the analysis done was adequate for the need and that the work products fulfill their purpose.

Prepare materials for review

The purpose of the review is to look at the work products around the following:

1. The use case and associated actors and their key properties (such as descriptions):

- A use case diagram showing actors and related use cases
- Traced requirements – use case diagram showing traced requirements

2. The use case sequence diagrams:

- Specification scenarios
- Animated scenarios

3.   The use case execution context:

- BDD/IBD showing the use case block and actor blocks

4.   Use case block specification:

- State and/or activity diagram for use case or use case block

- State and/or activity diagrams for the actors or actor blocks

- Value and flow properties owned

5.   Data schema:

- BDD showing information known or relevant to the use case, including value types, dimensions (quantity kind), and units.

6.   The interfaces needed to support the use case:

- BDD showing the interface blocks and their supported flow properties, operations, and event receptions

Collectively, these diagrams and views form the work product to be reviewed. They are shown in *Figure 2.32* through *Figure 2.42* in *Chapter 2, System Specification*.

Assign reviewer roles

This step identifies the various roles. The review coordinator and the scribe are singletons – there are only one of each of those in the review. There must be at least one product owner (author) to present the materials and answer questions. The QA reviewer is optional, but if present is usually a single person. There may be multiple SME reviewers, however. For the purpose of this example, let's assume two software engineers, one mechanical engineer, two electronic engineers, one systems engineer, and one marketer are invited as SMEs.

The identified personnel must be notified of their responsibilities.

Disseminate materials to reviewers

In this case, some of the SMEs may not have access to the modeling tool and may not be skilled in SysML (I'm looking at you, Marketing). For those reviewers, we can print out a report of the parts of the model relevant to their concern, such as a requirements table for the marketing SME. Other SMEs who have access and skill with the modeling tool can be granted access to the model in a shared repository or even emailed the model.

Schedule review

Scheduling the meeting is generally easy but finding a time available for all attendees can be a challenge.

Reviewers independently inspect materials

This is a place where compliance can be spotty, especially when the workflow is introduced. In my experience, it is common for people who "meant to get around to" reviewing the materials to show up unprepared and expect to be walked through the materials they should have already examined. It is better to cancel a review if most people haven't reviewed the materials and reschedule than to waste everyone's time.

Here, the reviewers are expected to examine the use case, requirements, structural and behavioral views for syntactic conformance (in the case of the QA reviewer), and semantic correctness (in the case of the engineering SMEs). The marketer here is serving as a proxy for the customer (training athlete) and should look at the appropriateness and quality of the requirements.

Collectively discuss reviewer comments

The comments often vary widely in terms of usefulness. Syntactic comments about spelling and standards conformance are useful, to be sure. Most useful are comments about semantic content. This will not only improve the product but also improve understanding and agreement among the attendees.

I believe in what are known as *ego-less* reviews, but they can seem a little awkward at first. The idea is that comments only refer to the work product and never to the author. You would never say, *You made a mistake here* to the author, but rather *This requirement seems incorrect* or *There is a missing value property here*. This is an attempt to avoid hurt feelings and focus on the technical aspects of the work product.

Here are some (hypothetical) comments and issues that might be raised by the reviewers:

- **QA reviewer**: The use case diagram doesn't have a *mission statement*, as defined by the modeling guidelines standard.

- **QA reviewer**: The requirements standard says that each use case should specify the reliability, in MTBF, of the service delivery. There is no requirement specifying reliability traced to the use case.

- **Marketer**: Requirement `efarg17` says *The default number of teeth for 12 cassette rings shall be 11, 13, 15, 17, 19, 21, 24, 28, 32, 36, 42, and 50.* I think the gearing for the cassette should be from 12 to 28 instead.

- **Marketer**: Requirement `efarg19` says that the default starting gear should be the lowest possible gear. I think that's okay for the very first ride, but subsequent rides should start up in the last gear the rider used.

- **SME 1**: The use case block has a value property `cassette` of type `int`. It isn't clear the value being held is the number of teeth of the currently selected cassette or which cassette is in use. Please either add a comment or rename the value property to make that clear.

- **SME 2**: The name of the `ChangeGearing` state for the use case block state machine is misleading. It is actually waiting for a gear change, not performing a gear change while in that state.

The product owner can respond to these comments, and a discussion of the comment ensues. Some action items may be resolved as not requiring action because of a corrected misunderstanding on the part of the reviewer, or as inconsequential. The group may decide that other issues must be acted upon, and these end up as action items.

Capture issues as action items

The scribe records the action items and may add annotation as to the urgency or criticality of the concerns. After the meetings, the action items are typically sent to all attendees so they can ensure their issues are properly recorded or understood.

Resolve action items

The product owner can then address the concerns. In this case, they can add the missing mission statement to the use case diagram, add reliability requirements, and change the name of the value property to `cassetteIndex` and the name of the state to `WaitingToChangeGear`.

Plan review of action item resolutions

Since the changes are minor, the group can decide that a subsequent review isn't needed.

Test-driven modeling

For the last recipe in the book, I'd like to present a recipe that is central to my view of the integration of modeling and Agile methods. The archetypal workflow in Agile software methods is **test-driven development** (**TDD**), in which you do the following:

```
Loop
    Write a test case
    Write a bit of code to meet that test case
    Apply test case
    If (defect) fix defect;
Until done;
```

It's an appealing story, to be sure. Each loop shouldn't take more than a few minutes. This is a key means in Agile methods to develop high-quality code; test incrementally throughout the coding process.

TDD aligns with this law of Douglass:

The best way not to have defects in your system is to not put any defects into your system.

- Law of Douglass #30

> **Note**
> The law can be found here: `https://www.bruce-douglass.com/geekosphere`

This points out that it is far easier to develop high-quality systems if you avoid entering defects rather than putting defects in and trying to identify, isolate, and correct them sometime in the future. TDD is a way to do that.

The same kind of approach is possible with respect to developing models, particularly executable models, an approach I call **test-driven modeling** (**TDM**). These models needn't be limited to design models; they can also be models of architecture, requirements, or any kind of computational model. Such models can be developed in small, incremental steps and verified as the model evolves.

When it comes to modeling, this is *not* what people typically do. Most people build huge monolithic models before deciding to verify them. I remember one consulting customer who had a state machine with 800 states. They had put it together and then attempted to "beat it with the testing stick" until it worked. They gave up after several months without ever getting it to even compile, let alone run properly. Then they called me.

The first thing I did was discard the expensive-yet-unworkable state machine and developed an equivalent using this TDM recipe. Each small iteration (known as a *nanocycle* in the *Harmony aMBSE* process) executed in anywhere from 30-60 minutes. In less than a week, the state machine was compiling, running, and working. It was then possible to uncover a number of subtle, yet important, specification defects from their source material.

> **Note**
>
> You can read about nanocycles here: Agile Systems Engineering by Bruce Douglass (Morgan Kaufmann, 2016)

As I said, TDM is not the way most people create models. Let's change that.

Purpose

The purpose of this recipe is to quickly develop a demonstrably correct model by frequently executing and running the model.

Inputs and preconditions

The input is a well-defined modeling objective that can be rendered with executable modeling constructs.

Outputs and postconditions

The output is a well-constructed, executable, and verified model.

How to do it...

Figure 5.47 shows the basic flow. I would take care to note that I don't really care whether the test case is created just prior to the *Model a bit* step or just after; they are essentially done at the same time. Classic TDD has the test case definition first, but it doesn't really matter to me. The primary point is that the test case isn't defined weeks to months after the design work is done but is done continuously as the work product is developed:

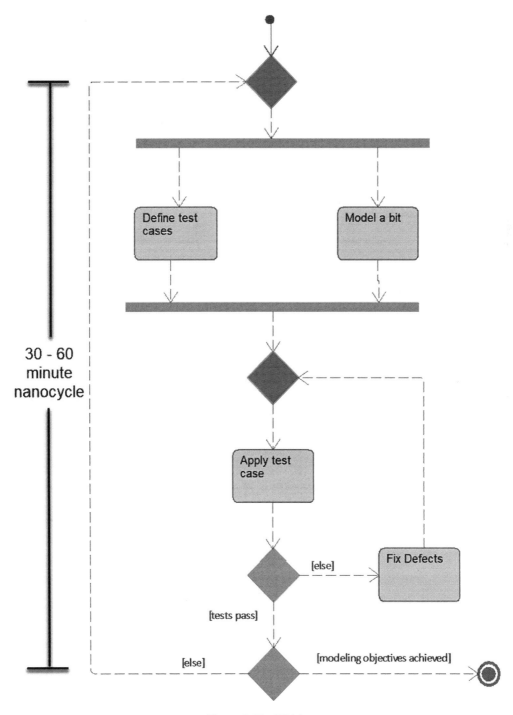

Figure 5.47 – TDM

Define test case

This step can come immediately before or after the *Model a bit* step, but logically they are done at about the same time. The test case defines a **minimal testable feature** (**MTF**, sometimes known as a **minimal verifiable feature**, or **MVF**) that is to be modeled in this particular nanocycle. The MTF in this context is a small evolution of the model from its current state, *en route* to the complete model that satisfies the initial modeling objective. The tendency is to make the nanocycles too large, so keep it short. The properties of the MTF to strive for are the following:

- The feature can be modeled in a few (<30) minutes.

- The feature is testably different from the previous model condition.

- The feature contributes to the final desired modeling objective.

For example, suppose the modeling objective is to construct an executable use case. Each nanocycle would add one or more requirements to the use case model, such that the state machine adds a few transitions, actions, or states. A state machine with 30 states and 40 transitions might be done as a series of 10-15 nanocycle iterations, each of which has a small MTF evolution.

Model a bit

In this step, the model is evolved by added a small number of features: a value property or two, perhaps a couple of transitions, a state, or a small set of other model elements.

Apply test case

At this point, you have a (small) model evolution and a (small) test case. In this step, you apply the test case to ensure that it is modeled correctly.

Fix defects

If the model fails the test, it is fixed in this step.

The nanocycles repeat until the initial modeling objective is satisfied.

Example

I want to introduce my favorite example for TDM. I've used this example in numerous courses and found it to be instructive and accessible by my students. I've even done an experiment: I told some groups to develop the model without giving them guidance (and they all tried to do it in a single step) or given explicit instruction to do it in several separate steps with a short description of the MTF increments. The results were that in the time frame allotted, 100% of the unguided groups failed and 80% of the nanocycle groups succeeded.

The problem

Consider an intersection **Traffic Light Controller** (TLC). The TLC controls traffic (via lights) on a primary road and a secondary road. The roads contain both through-lane traffic and left-turn-lane traffic. In addition, the TLC also controls pedestrian traffic along those roads as well (again, via lights). The basic control rules are listed here:

1. In the absence of both pedestrians and left-turn cars, the through lights operate entirely based on time:

- Turn lane lights remain red; pedestrian lights remain on *DON'T WALK*.

- All lights are red for *RED TIME*.

- The through lanes (both directions for a given road) go green for *GREEN TIME* while cross-traffic lights are red and cross-traffic remains stopped.

- The through lanes (again, in both directions) go yellow for *YELLOW TIME*.

- The through lanes all turn red and the cross-traffic gets to go next, using the same flow.

- Repeat forever.

- If cars are present in the left-turn lane for a given road, the behavior is slightly different.

    When a road is ready to set through-traffic green but there is a car waiting in that road's left-turn lane, the turn lanes (both directions on the same road) go first, and the through lane remains red:

    Turn lanes go green for *GREEN TIME*.

    Turn lanes go yellow for *YELLOW TIME*.

    Turn lanes go red for *RED TIME*.

    Now the through lanes can continue normally.

2. If pedestrians are present along a road (that is, they want to cross the cross-traffic road), then the behavior is modified:

- When the through light goes green, the pedestrian light displays *Walk* for *WALK TIME*.

- The pedestrian light then displays flashing *Don't Walk* for *RUN TIME*.

- The pedestrian light then displays a solid *Don't Walk* and the through light now goes yellow for *YELLOW TIME*.

- The through lane proceeds normally.

I like this example because it is easy to describe, it is conceptually simple, and it is very familiar.

Since this is a short, iterative cycle, we'll just run the cycle multiple times in the example.

Define test case: MTF 0: Episode III: The Revenge of the Through Light

Let's define the first MTF step.

Test case: A single light should go through the colors in the right sequence with the right timing: red for *RED TIME*, green for *GREEN TIME*, and yellow for *YELLOW TIME*.

Model a bit: MTF 0: Episode III: The Revenge of the Through Light

Evolution: Add a single traffic light that cycles through its colors.

This model is pretty simple. It consists of two blocks: **Traffic Light System** (which will also serve as our tester) and **Traffic Light**, with a single, directed composition from the former to the latter. We need to define the timings – I used value types in Rhapsody with a `#define` definition for the named constants. I also added an enumerated COLOR_TYPE type to define the different colors. A `setcolor(color: COLOR_TYPE)` just prints out the value of the color to standard output for the purpose of this model. This simple model is shown in *Figure 5.48*:

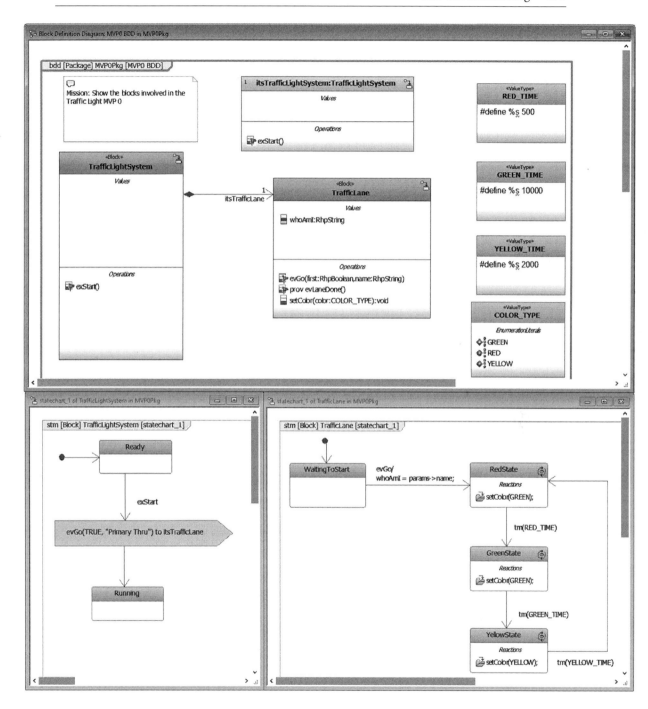

Figure 5.48 – Structure and behavior of MTF 0

Apply test case: MTF 0: Episode III: The Revenge of the Through Light

Now let's run the model. In Rhapsody, we use `Generate-Make-Run` to generate the code, make the application, and then run it. When we run, we manually insert the **exStart** event into the **Traffic Light System** to kick it off and we can view the execution outcomes in *Figure 5.49*:

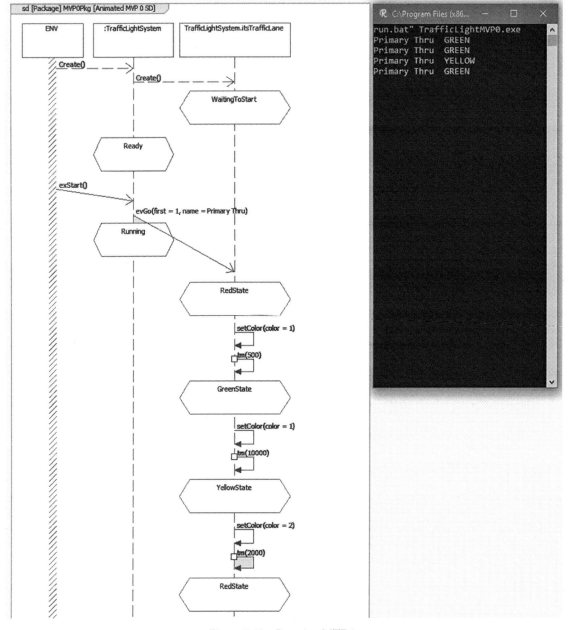

Figure 5.49 – Running MTF 0

Oops! We see that on start up the light initializes to **GREEN** when it should initialize to **RED**.

Fix Defects: MTF 0: Episode III: The Revenge of the Through Light

The fix for this defect is pretty simple: change the entry action on the **RedState** to **setColor(RED)**. If we make that change and rerun it, we can see that the model works as expected.

We've now completed our first nanocycle. It was very short – and it didn't do much – but we quickly got it to work despite it having a defect.

Define test case: MTF 1: Episode IV: A New Hope (For the secondary through lane)

Let's define the next MTF step.

Test case: Both roads should cycle through the lights, with cross-traffic held on red while the current lane cycles through.

Model a bit: MTF 1: Episode IV: A New Hope (For the secondary through lane)

Evolution: Add a second composition to the through lane to add the secondary road; the system now contains two traffic light instances. Modify the state machine of the traffic light so that the two instances of **Traffic Light** can properly coordinate. In this case, we add proxy ports **pOutThru** and **pInThru**, both typed by the interface block **ibLane**.

One of these ports is conjugated to it and can send and receive the same event, though via different ports. See *Figure 5.50*:

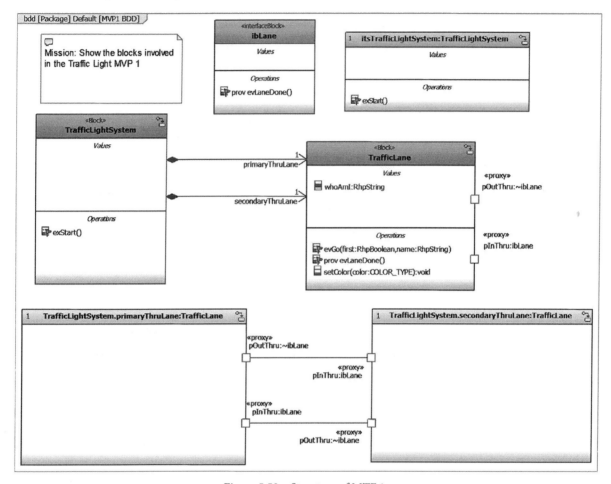

Figure 5.50 – Structure of MTF 1

In the figure, we take advantage of Rhapsody's ability to put instances on a block definition diagram. In Cameo Magic Draw, this would require a separate internal block diagram.

The state machine for the **Traffic Light System** is exactly the same except that it now sends the **evGo** event to both instances. This event carries two arguments. The first (Boolean) value tells the instance whether it should go first or wait. The second gives the instance its identity for the **whoAmI** value property. *Figure 5.51* shows the two state machines; the state machine for **Traffic Light System** is on the left while the state machine for the **Traffic Light** lane is on the right:

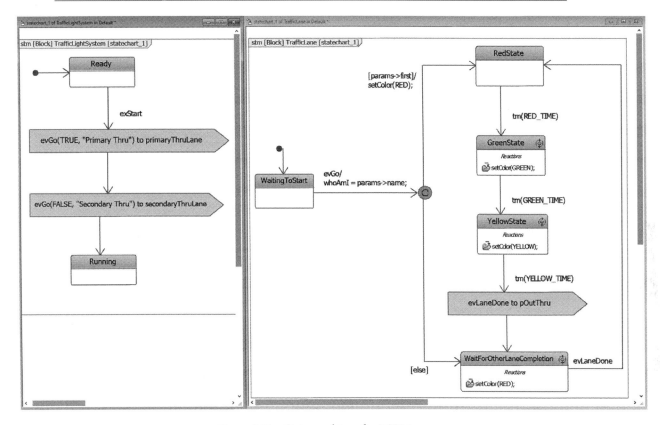

Figure 5.51 – State machines for MTF 1

Apply test case: MTF 1: Episode IV: A New Hope (For the secondary through lane)

Now the model is getting interesting. Is it right? Let's run the test case and see.

Figure 5.52 shows the outcomes, both in the animated sequence diagram and the output window. The scenario is a bit small to read but you can see in the output window it operates as expected:

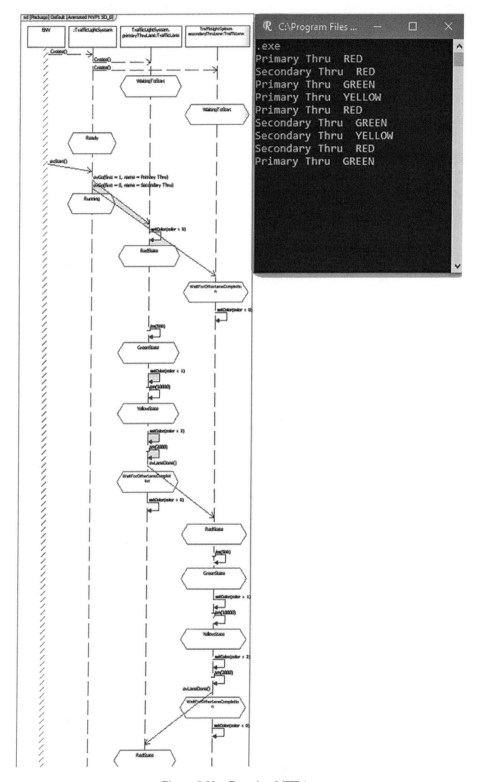

Figure 5.52 – Running MTF 1

Fix Defects: MTF 1: Episode IV: A New Hope (For the secondary through lane)

There are no defects to fix in this nanocycle.

Define test case: MTF 2: Episode V: The Turn Lane Strikes Back

Test case: When a car arrives on a road *regardless of when in the cycle that occurs*, the system properly allows turn lanes to cycle through, followed by the through light on the same road.

Test case: In subsequent cycles, the system "forgets" the turn lane was previously activated.

Model a bit: MTF 2: Episode V: The Turn Lane Strikes Back

Evolution: Add turn lanes and update state machines to manage them.

We must add two more lights to the system to support the left-turn lanes, and make them composite parts of the **Traffic Light System**. In this case, the through lights and the turn lights are actually different types because while the through lights must coordinate with the cross-traffic through-light, the turn lane coordinates in a different way with its corresponding road through-light. We'll make the **Thru Lane** and **Turn Lane** lights different subclasses of **Traffic Lane**, and remove the state behavior from **Traffic Lane** altogether. The structural model is shown in *Figure 5.53*:

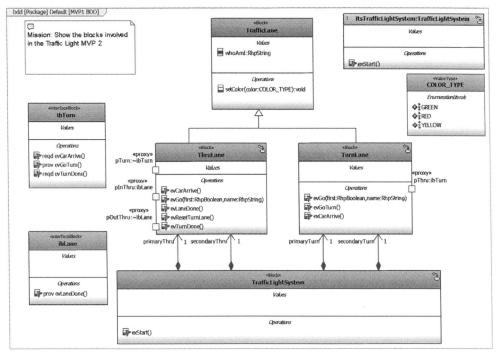

Figure 5.53 – Structure for MTF 2

The **Traffic Light System** internal block diagram (*Figure 5.54*) shows the expected connections among the instances:

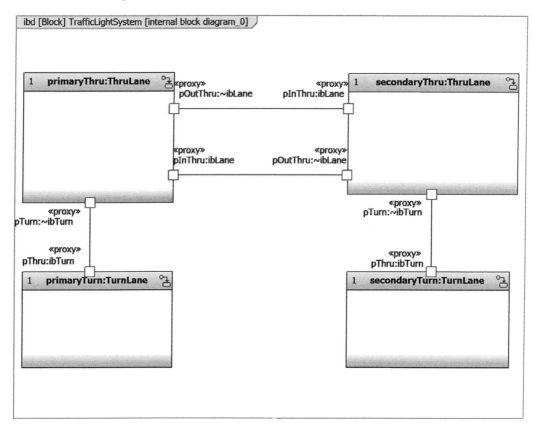

Figure 5.54 – MTF 2 IBD

The state machine for **Traffic Light System** is modified so that it starts the turn-lane lights in addition to the through-lane lights. See *Figure 5.55*:

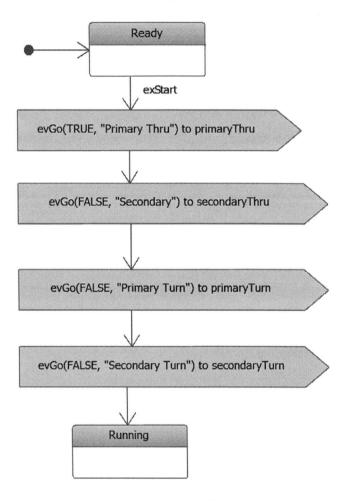

Figure 5.55 – State machine for Traffic Light System MTF 2

More interesting are the modifications to the **Thru Lane** and **Turn Lane** lights. The state machine on the left side of *Figure 5.56* is for the **Thru Lane** and the one on the right is for the **Turn Lane**. The send actions on the state machines show the coordination of the through lanes as well as between the through lane and its connected turn lane:

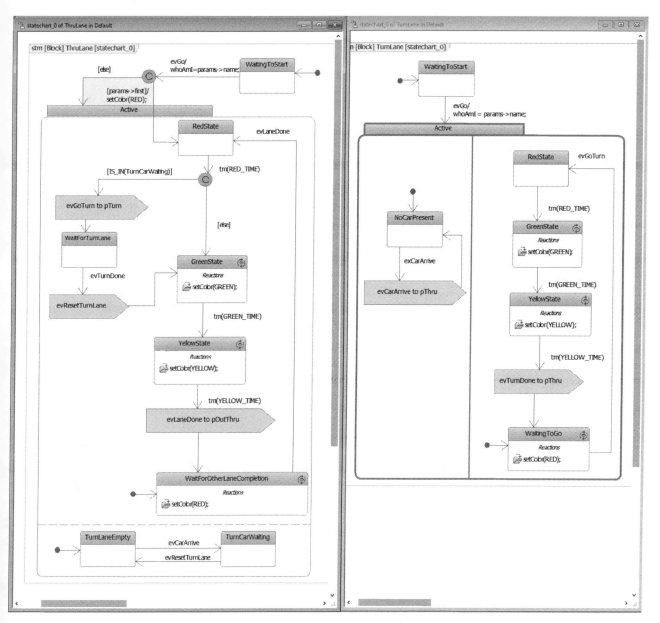

Figure 5.56 – Through and turn light state machines for MTF 2

Apply test case: MTF 2: Episode V: The Turn Lane Strikes Back

Running the test case results in long sequence diagrams. Looking at the output window still works, but at this point, we can create a panel diagram (*Figure 5.57*) to allow us to view and set values and see the states of the various instances. The colored LEDs indicate the current states of the lights and the buttons allow us to insert events into the running system. We can see in the output window that the case we ran (a car arrives in the turn lane immediately after the system starts up with the primary through-lane on green) is handled properly:

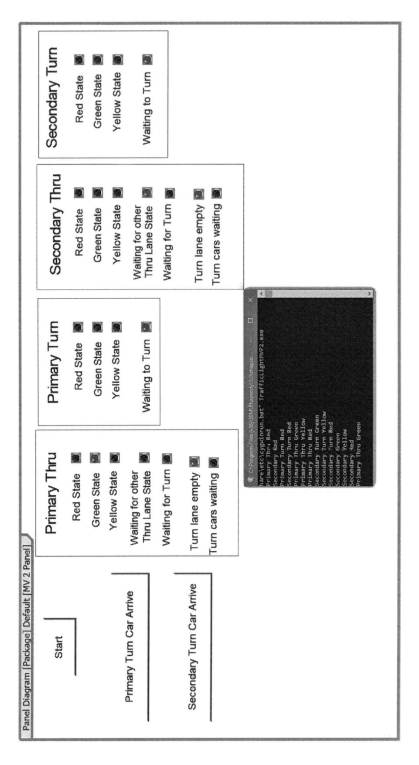

Figure 5.57 – MTF 2 panel diagram and output window

Fix Defects: MTF 2: Episode V: The Turn Lane Strikes Back

No defects to fix.

Define test case: MTF 3: Episode VI: Return of the Pedestrian

Test case: when a pedestrian arrives on the secondary road and the primary through-light is green, the pedestrian gets the walk light at the same time that the secondary through-lane gets a green light.

Test case: when a pedestrian arrives on the primary road and the primary through-light is currently green, the pedestrian gets a walk light the next time the primary through-lane gets a green light.

Model a bit MTF 3: Episode VI: Return of the Pedestrian

Evolutions: Add pedestrians and update state behavior to manage them.

This last nanocycle adds the pedestrians as another subclass of **Traffic Lane** and updates the behavior of the **Traffic Light System** and the through lanes to properly interact with them. The BDD shows the evolving structure (*Figure 5.58*):

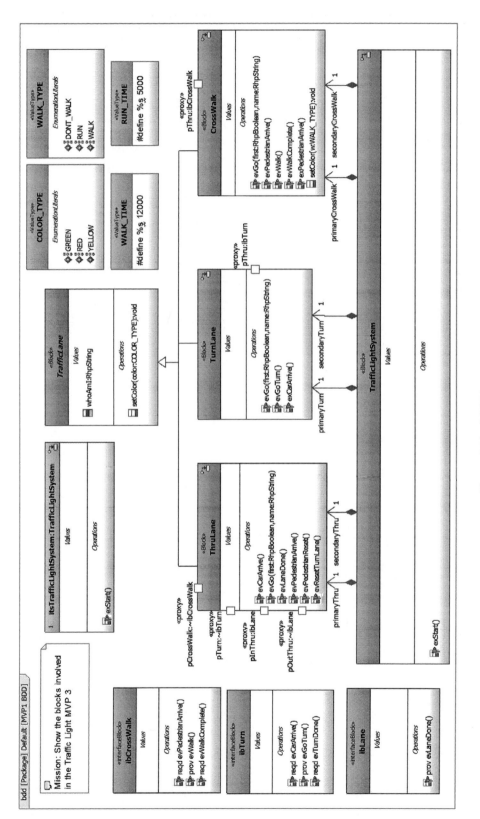

Figure 5.58 – MTF 3 structure

The Traffic Light System IBD is shown in the connected design in *Figure 5.59:*

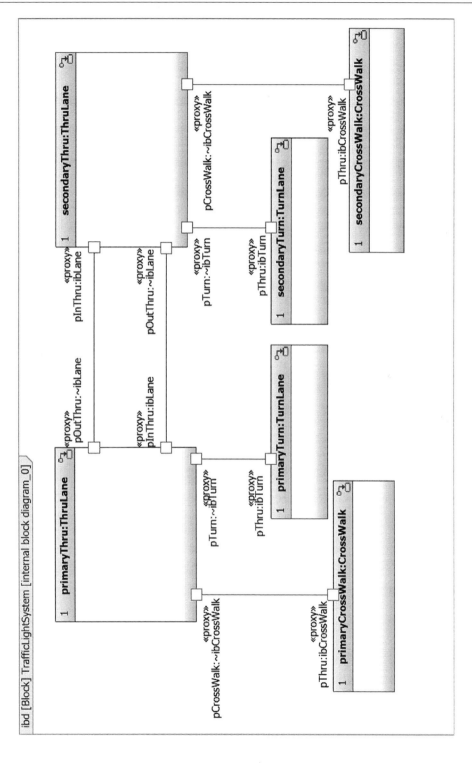

Figure 5.59 – Traffic Light System IBD for MTF 3

The **Traffic Light System** has a minor change to its state machine to initialize and start the **Cross Walk** instances (*Figure 5.60*):

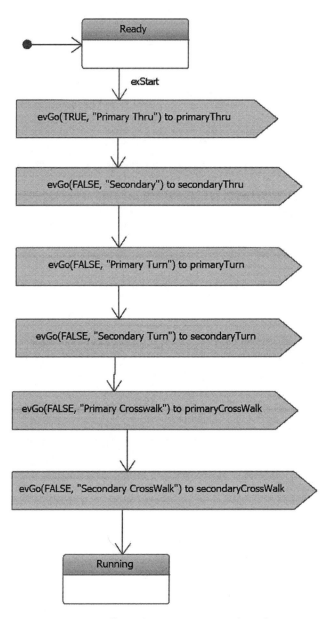

Figure 5.60 – Traffic Light System state machine for MV3

The state machine for the **through** lanes adds an **AND-state** for keeping track of whether pedestrians are waiting and a few states to handle the behavior when a pedestrian is crossing (*Figure 5.61*). If you compare this state machine with the **Thru Lane** state machine from MTF 2 (*Figure 5.56*), you can see that the updated state machine is a fairly simple evolution of its previous condition:

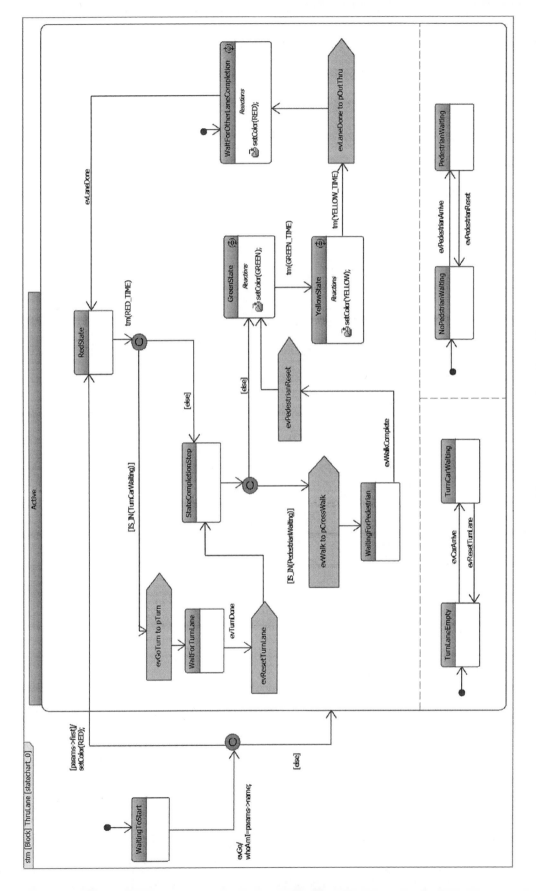

Figure 5.61 – Thru Lane state machine for MTF 3

Lastly, the state machine for the **Cross Walk** is straightforward, as can be seen in *Figure 5.62*:

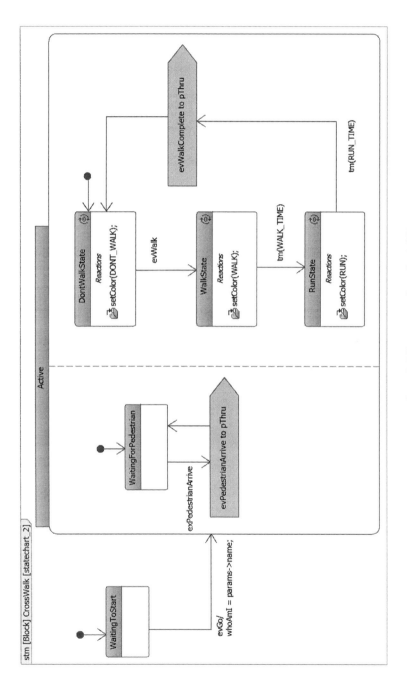

Figure 5.62 – Cross Walk state machine for MTF 3

Apply test case MTF 3: Episode VI: Return of the Pedestrian

The model is getting a bit complex to rely solely on the animated sequence diagrams for testing, so we elaborate the panel diagram to add controls related to the pedestrian traffic. This MTF has two test cases: the output window in *Figure 5.63* shows the outcome for test case 2:

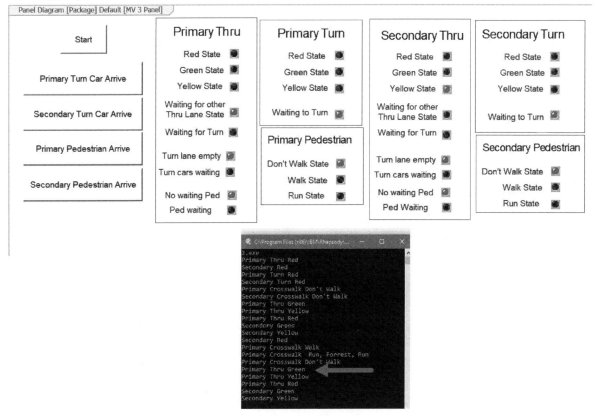

Figure 5.63 – Output from MTF 3 test case 2 run

What's this? It looks like when the pedestrian walks, the primary through-lane light is still red, and it turns green only *after* the cross-walk cycle completes. That's not what we want; the pedestrian and through traffic are supposed to go together and then the through-lane light is supposed to turn yellow.

Fix Defects MTF 3: Episode VI: Return of the Pedestrian

This defect is easy to fix. The modified states are highlighted in *Figure 5.64*:

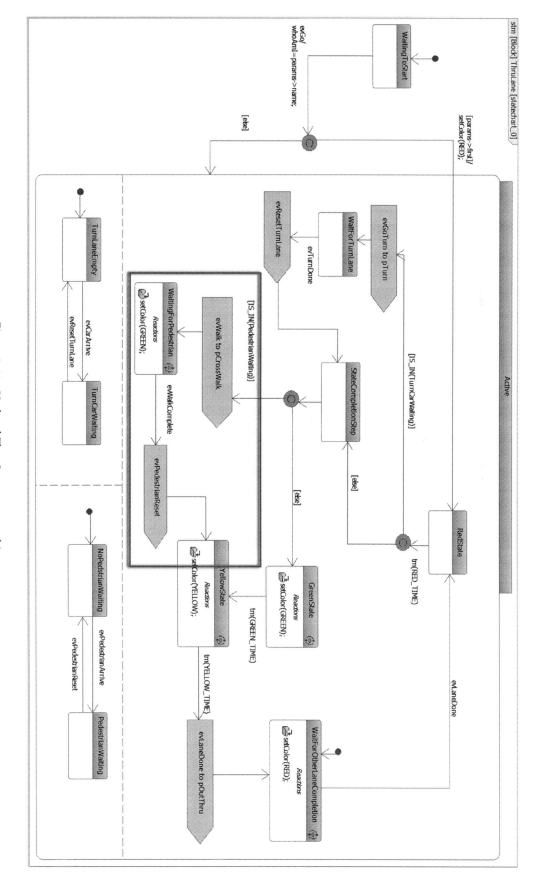

Figure 5.64 – Updated Thru Lane state machine

The output of the corrected model is shown in *Figure 5.65*. In it, we see the primary through-lane light goes green while the primary pedestrian walk light cycles through its states, then the primary through-lane light goes yellow, as it should:

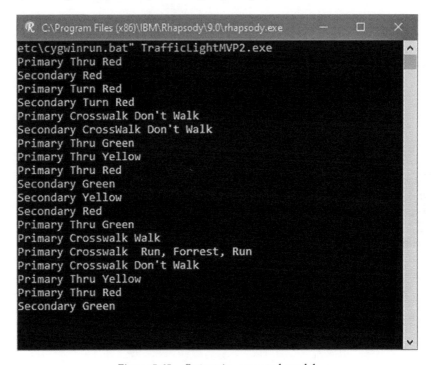

Figure 5.65 – Output in corrected model

This example illustrates that it was pretty simple to construct a (somewhat complex) model easily by developing it in small iterations and verifying its correctness *so far* before moving on.

Now *that's* pod racing! Er, I mean test-driven modeling.

Appendix A – The Pegasus Bike Trainer

The Pegasus is an indoor cycle training system to support both casual and professional athletes in their cycle training. It has a large set of features to make indoor training effective and enjoyable. It simulates the feel of the road, including automated control of power-on-pedal requirements and bike incline. It is expected that the bike will not be used in isolation, but will be used with an iOS, Android, or Windows device that receives, displays, records, and analyzes data from exercise sessions. Support is provided through standard **Bluetooth Low Energy** (**BLE**), ANT+, and ANT FEC interfaces:

Figure A.1 – Pegasus indoor training bike

Pegasus high-level features

This section describes a number of the key features and benefits of the Pegasus Bike Trainer.

Highly customizable bike fit

The Pegasus fits users from 5' to 6'4" tall, with a maximum rider weight of 300 lbs. It has an adjustable crank length from 160 mm to 180 mm. Refer to the following diagram:

Figure A.2 – Customizing the bike fit

Monitoring exercise metrics

Metrics monitored include speed, distance, power, cadence, time, and grade (incline). Data will be uploaded to connected devices at a rate of at least 5 Hz.

Export/upload exercise metrics

The system monitors, stores, and reports metrics over the BLE, ANT+, and ANT FEC interfaces. It is assumed that the user will provide their own heart rate strap for capturing and reporting heart rate data to their iOS, Android, or Windows devices.

Variable power output

Output can be set from 0 W to 2,000 W with a heavy flywheel to provide power smoothing over changing effort with an accuracy of 1%. Resistance may be manually set by the user or externally controlled via the BLE or ANT FEC interfaces. Resistance is provided by electromagnetic resistance.

Gearing emulation

The system simulates standard bicycle gearing including the ability of the user to change gears in the same way they would on a road bike. The user can select the kind of gearing to be emulated, including standard mechanical index shifting as well as DI-2 electronic shifting. The system can emulate 1-3 front-chainrings with 30 to 60 teeth. The rear cassette emulation ability supports 9-12 rings ranging from 10 to 40 teeth.

Controllable power level

The power level can be controlled from 0-2,000 W and provides a similar user feel for the current cadence and power output as the user would experience on a road with similar gearing. Operational modes are provided for both the user-set output level (*level mode* or *resistance mode*) and the externally-set output level (*ERG mode*).

Incline control

The incline angle of the bike may be set manually by the user using the provided pair of buttons, or via an external system over the BLE or ANT FEC interfaces. The range of incline may be set in the range of -15 to + 20 degrees. This can be automatically changed by an external device to emulate a journey over changing terrain as the user rides over virtual bike courses.

User interface

A simple user interface is provided for viewing and changing the selected gears on both the front chainring and rear cassette. It comprises the following settings:

- **Gearing**: User buttons on the brake hoods of the handlebars provide buttons for increasing or decreasing the selected gear. An LED display on the system frame shows the current selected front and rear chainrings.

- **Incline**: Up and down buttons on the frame allows the user to select the bike incline. A small LED display shows the current incline.

- **Set up**: Separate (provided) iOS, Android, and Windows apps provide configuration and setup assistance.

- **Ride**: There is no interface provided for the exercise or performance metrics. It is assumed that the user will provide a third-party app running on an iOS, Android, or Windows device for this purpose.

Online training system compatibility

Almost all users will use third-party training systems that support the required interfaces to monitor and control the workout. These systems provide a range of capabilities ranging from running downloadable workouts and fitness assessment protocols to social gaming environments for virtual riding and racing. The most popular systems include Strava™, Trainer Road™, Zwift™, and Sufferfest™.

These applications run on third-party iOS, Android, or Windows devices and support the ANT FEC, ANT+ and/or BLE communications protocols. The system is open with published interfaces so that additional third-party device vendors can support the Pegasus.

Configuration and Over-the-Air (OTA) firmware updates

The Pegasus configuration app allows the user to register their product, search for and download firmware upgrades, set their rider profile (height, weight, age, and gender), and the selected crank arm length. The app also provides the means for the initial calibration of the settings via a guided protocol. This app is provided to the user and runs on iOS, Android, and Windows devices.

The Wahoo Kickr Bike

This system is loosely based on the Wahoo Kickr Bike (`https://www.wahoofitness.com/devices/smart-bike/kickr-bike`). I own and train on this bike for ironman triathlons and ultra-marathon bike events. If you're looking for an indoor bike training option, I cannot recommend this system highly enough.

Packt›

Other Books You May Enjoy

If you enjoyed this book, you may be interested in these other books by Packt:

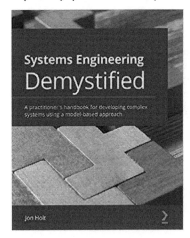

Systems Engineering Demystified

Jon Holt

ISBN: 978-1-83898-580-6

- Understand the three evils of systems engineering - complexity, ambiguous communication, and lack of understanding
- Realize successful systems using model-based systems engineering
- Understand the concept of life cycles and how they control the evolution of a system
- Explore processes and related concepts such as activities, stakeholders, and resources
- Discover how needs fit into the systems life cycle and which processes are relevant and how to comply with them
- Find out how design, verification, and validation fit into the life cycle and processes

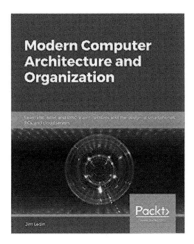

Modern Computer Architecture and Organization

Jim Ledin

ISBN: 978-1-83898-439-7

- Get to grips with transistor technology and digital circuit principles
- Discover the functional elements of computer processors
- Understand pipelining and superscalar execution
- Work with floating-point data formats
- Understand the purpose and operation of the supervisor mode
- Implement a complete RISC-V processor in a low-cost FPGA
- Explore the techniques used in virtual machine implementation
- Write a quantum computing program and run it on a quantum computer

Packt is searching for authors like you

If you're interested in becoming an author for Packt, please visit `authors.packtpub.com` and apply today. We have worked with thousands of developers and tech professionals, just like you, to help them share their insight with the global tech community. You can make a general application, apply for a specific hot topic that we are recruiting an author for, or submit your own idea.

Leave a review - let other readers know what you think

Please share your thoughts on this book with others by leaving a review on the site that you bought it from. If you purchased the book from Amazon, please leave us an honest review on this book's Amazon page. This is vital so that other potential readers can see and use your unbiased opinion to make purchasing decisions, we can understand what our customers think about our products, and our authors can see your feedback on the title that they have worked with Packt to create. It will only take a few minutes of your time, but is valuable to other potential customers, our authors, and Packt. Thank you!

Index

N

O